P O W E R Learning
Strategies for Success in College and Life

2004 Edition

Robert S. Feldman
University of Massachusetts–Amherst

DeVry University

McGraw Hill Custom Publishing

Boston   Burr Ridge, IL   Dubuque, IA   Madison, WI   New York   San Francisco   St. Louis
Bangkok   Bogotá   Caracas   Lisbon   London   Madrid
Mexico City   Milan   New Delhi   Seoul   Singapore   Sydney   Taipei   Toronto

POWER Learning: Strategies for Success in College and Life, 2004 Edition

This book is a McGraw-Hill Custom Publishing textbook and contains select material from *POWER Learning; Strategies for Success in College and Life,* 2004 Edition by Robert S. Feldman. Copyright © 2004, 2003, 2000 by The McGraw-Hill Companies, Inc. Reprinted with permission of the publisher. Many custom published texts are modified versions or adaptations of our best-selling textbooks. Some adaptations are printed in black and white to keep prices at a minimum, while others are in color.

1 2 3 4 5 6 7 8 9 0 QSR QSR 0 9 8 7 6 5 4

ISBN 0-07-310398-5

Editor: Shawn Allen
Production Editor: Nicole Baumgartner
Printer/Binder: Quebecor World

Professional Development Course Guide: Putting It All Together

By

Lawrence Eisenberg and Corey S. Vigdor

Table of Contents

Introduction

Philosophy of PROF101

PROF-101 is intended for first-term DeVry University students and assumes that you have no previous education regarding the strategies of professional development. The course will introduce you to the skills, attitudes, and behaviors necessary to be a successful student and professional. Operating in a collaborative and open environment, you will measure and reflect upon you prior education, beliefs, attitudes, behaviors, current skill sets and occupational goals in an effort to identify directions strengths and opportunities for personal improvement. Following the identification process, you will be introduced to a variety of college success strategies and concepts surrounding professionalism, which will help you maximize your learning experiences at DeVry and growth in you career. Concurrently you will develop ownership over your growth as a student and professional as well as accept personal responsibility for it. Finally you will produce deliverables, which will demonstrate a synthesis of the material into a refined direction and motivation to succeed.

Official Course Description

This course will assist students in the identification of, reflections on, and articulation of the skills necessary to be a successful student and professional. Through coursework students will confront their own attitudes, motivations, beliefs, learning skills and behaviors as they relate to their own educational and professional development. Upon successful completion of the course, students will have a firm understanding of themselves as learners and their roles and responsibilities within the learning process.

PROF101 and General Education Objectives

As a required course for all new entering students PROF101 prepares students for their academic challenges at DeVry University. Through self-reflection, students gain a deeper understanding of themselves as students and future professionals. The course is designed to give students the knowledge and skills they need to maximize their success at DeVry and, subsequently, in a technological workplace and society. The approach of this course is consistent with the "Philosophy of General Education for DeVry" statements and objectives. It will directly satisfy the following competencies:
- Communicate clearly with particular audiences for particular purposes.
- Work collaboratively to help achieve individual and group goals.
- Apply critical thinking skills in learning, conducting applied research, and defining and solving problems.
- Develop tolerance of ambiguity and mature judgment in exploring intellectual issues.

- Build on intellectual curiosity with fundamental concepts and methods of inquiry from the sciences, social sciences, and humanities to support life-long learning.
- Use study and direct experience of the humanities and social sciences to develop a clear perspective on the breadth and diversity, as well as the commonality, of human experience.
- Connect general education to the ethical dimensions of issues and to responsible, thoughtful citizenship in a democratic society.

Terminal Course Objectives

1. Given new status as a college student, develop reflective abilities about one's skills, behaviors, and attitudes as it relates to their education, professional and occupational development.

2. Given a hypothesis that every student knows people who have made successful critical life decisions at various points in their life, study those people to identify their critical decisions.

3. Given that students can identify their own productive student, work, and commitment behaviors create a plan that maximizes their own strengths and abilities

4. Given new status as a college student, develop an appreciation of the necessary skills to increase the likelihood of success. These skills include: decision-making, critical reading, note taking, effective listening, teamwork and time management.

5. Given new status as a college student, develop an appreciation for the role of higher education and its importance in their development as professionals.

6. Given new status as a college student, develop an understanding of the important roles that family and friends play in the educational process.

7. Given new status as a college student, develop an appreciation for the financial implications that going to school assumes both in the short and long terms

8. Given the necessity to be able to appreciate growth and achievements, develop a portfolio that is reflective and well documented

Course Components

Similar to other courses you take at DeVry, PROF101 utilizes a variety of tools and techniques to meet the course objectives. The following is a list of components contained in PROF101 with a brief explanation.

Assessments

In this course there are three standardized assessments utilized and each one has a specific purpose.

Noel-Levitz: College Student Inventory (CSI)
The CSI is a 100 question assessment that measures your motivation as well as helps you identify strengths and potential barriers to their success in college. Three main areas are studied with customized reports and recommendations provided based on your responses; these areas include: Academic Motivation, General Coping and Receptivity to Support Services.

Learning and Study Skills Inventory (LASSI)
The LASSI is an 80 question assessment that measures your awareness of learning skills. Research suggests that study behaviors, thoughts, and attitudes all affect success. By measuring these items, you will get an idea on your learning strategies, attitudes towards college, self discipline, the lengths you are willing to go to succeed, time management, and other items compared to other college students. By understanding and discussing the results you will be able to more effectively prioritize how and what you study.

Strong Inventory-Personal Styles
The Strong is an occupational inventory assessment. Taken online, the Strong shows your preferences for and comfort with styles of living and working. The results can help you learn more about how you like to work, learn, play, or live. The results can show you how to organize your current job to better match your interests or they can give you insights into how you might structure your life overall. You could also discover that your preferred style is at odds with your current job. You might stay in the same career field, yet move into a different role or area that is a better fit. Either way it is an exciting piece of knowledge.

Seven Habits of Highly Effective College Students

The Seven Habits of Highly Effective College Students by FranklinCovey will be an integral part of the learning process in helping all of you become more effective the varied aspects of your life. The habits include:

1. Be Proactive
2. Begin with the End in Mind
3. Put First Things First
4. Think Win-Win
5. Seek First to Understand, Then be Understood
6. Synergize
7. Sharpen the Saw

Course Project

The course project is an opportunity for you to spend a significant amount of time thinking about yourself in a reflective and purposeful manner. Reflective in that you will think back to how you got to where you are now as well as the values and characteristics you possess and purposeful in looking ahead towards solutions and goals. In the end, you will construct a document all about you that examine every facet of your past, present and future. You will heavily utilize the course assessment, memories, inputs from people who know you, professor observations and anything else that you might need to complete this picture of where you have been, who you are now and where you are going.

Readings

The course utilizes the following three textbooks:

- P.O.W.E.R. Learning by Robert Feldman
- Seven Habits of Highly Effective College Students by FranklinCovey
- Portfolio Solutions for DeVry University Students

Midterm Grades

PROF101 will constantly encourage you to examine your progress in your courses throughout the term. Nearing the midpoint of the term, however, you will be asked to solicit direct feedback from your other professors in an effort to give you solid information on exactly how you are doing. This information will become a critical aspect of the course project. It is important to you take your professor's formal or informal feedback seriously and acknowledge their praises or recommendations to ensure success.

Portfolios

Electronic Portfolios will be introduced in this course. You will learn how to appreciate the work you do on a daily basis through a self-assessment process. Additionally, the value of saving work for future promotional use will be discussed and strongly encouraged through the uploading of the PROF101 Course Project. Finally, the discussions surrounding Electronic Portfolios will help you gain a deep understanding of your major, goals and overall life direction.

Success

Success is a funny thing. Most of us think of it in terms of financial success and while that is an important kind of success, it is not the one that makes people the happiest. In a study of people who were million dollar lottery winners, a researcher discovered that the first thing most of them bought was a new car. Usually, winners purchased large cars such as Cadillacs and Buicks. One millionaire bought a Cadillac even when he found he could not park the car near his home because the street was too narrow. Despite the expense of these vehicles, many lottery winners were unhappy. They were particularly upset about the low mileage they got. Others had cars that developed serious engine problems. In this first use of their winnings, the money did not bring most winners happiness. (Kaplan, H. Roy, *Lottery Winners: How They Won and How Winning Changed Their Lives*, Harper & Row)

Often grades, good jobs, or a mate don't bring happiness either. What kind of success does bring satisfaction? That's part of what we want to find out.

<u>Roadmap to Professional Development</u>
Through the readings, course project component and activities you will define success for yourself and recognize that you have already achieved it to some degree.

Readings:	Feldman: Chapter 1
	FranklinCovey: Foundational Principles
	As assigned by your Professor
Activities:	Who do you know?
	Storyboard Activity
Course Project:	Past: Background Essay

Discovering Yourself

Discovering yourself and what you are capable of can be motivating in itself. The first time you rode a bike, drove a car, or read a book by yourself were high points in your life. The discovery that you had absorbed these skills and made it your own pushed you to practice it and do it more often. It is often hard to separate newly licensed drivers from their cars simply because it is exciting. DeVry provides you with opportunity to discover a great deal about yourself – what kind of a person you are and what you are capable of. Reflecting on your academic and successes and failures provides you the chance to identify what to appreciate and what to wrestle with. Step one is opening your eyes to discovering yourself.

Roadmap to Professional Development
Through the readings, course project component and activities you will become aware of the positive results you will achieve by discovering yourself and the wonderful opportunities this presents.

Readings: Feldman: Chapter 3
FranklinCovey: Habit #1
As assigned by your Professor

Activity: Paying for College

Course Project: Present Analysis: Noel Levitz, CSI

Setting Goals

Habit Two is to *Begin with the End in Mind.* Setting goals is crucial to this period of your life. There are so many tasks, so many responsibilities, and so many things to study that it's hard to know what to do if you don't know where you are going. Covey points out the first step to establishing a goal is to viualize it. Graduating DeVry is an obvious goal and we examine it in this chapter. Being the person you want to be to significant others in your life is another goal. We're going to look at that as well.

<u>Roadmap to Professional Development</u>
Through the readings, course project component and activities you will become aware of the positive results you will achieve as you set goals based on understandings of who you are and the values and interests you possess.

Readings: Feldman: Chapter 9
                                  Covey: Habit #2
                                  As assigned by your Professor

Activities: Values Clarification Activity
                                  Core Competency Activity

Course Project: Present Analysis-Strong Interest Inventory, Personal Style Scales

Learning

Your Psych 110 text will define learning as a permanent change in behavior due to experience. Seems simple enough; but sometimes not so simple. We all have preferred styles in learning; we all have special ways of taking in information; and we all have different levels of skills in learning. This week in Prof we will take a look at the LASSI results and try to both appreciate what are your special skills are and which skills you need to develop.

<u>Roadmap to Professional Development</u>
Through the readings, course project component and activities you will become aware of the positive results you will achieve as you develop an understanding of yourself and the skills you possess as a learner.

Readings:	Feldman, Chapter 4, 5 and 6
	Covey: Habit #3
	As assigned by your Professor
Activities:	Lightbulb Activity
Course Project:	Present Analysis-LASSI

Making Decisions

Making important decisions seems to get harder the more you learn. All the new information you learn lets you see different possibilities; different paths. It doesn't have to get harder – the more you know who you are, what you are about, and what your values are, decisions get easier and easier. Part of this course is finding out those things and letting decisions flow easily. It isn't as hard as you think.

Roadmap to Professional Development
Through the readings, course project component and activities you will become aware of the positive results you will achieve as you make decisions based on understanding who you are and what is important to you.

Readings: Feldman, Chapters 11 and 13
                     As assigned by your Professor

Activity: Grade Point Average Activity

Course Project: Present Analysis-Midterm Grades

Getting Along with Others

Much of our successes in life are defined by our relationships at work, home and in all of our activities therefore working well with others is an important part of life that cannot be overlooked or taken for granted. If we do not give them proper attention and put forth the right attitudes and communication skills, we will never be able to achieve a higher level of accomplishments and self-realization.

This is a very difficult lesson for college students to learn for this environment is perhaps the first time when students are confronted with the immediate need to work with and get along with strangers. In addition to the interactions that happen continuously in the college environment between a variety of different people with diverse backgrounds and roles, teams will be formed in classes that require the need to work well together and produce things such as papers, presentations and projects. As a member of the college community, you will need to examine your attitudes and skills as they relate to working with others in order to get the most out of your learning experiences as well as establish healthy relationships.

Roadmap to Professional Development
Through the readings, course project component and activities you will gain an understanding of the importance of relationships and working well with others. You will understand the need to embrace the differences of others, display the proper attitudes and put forth positive communication skills to enable goals to become realities.

Readings: Feldman, Chapter 12
Covey Habits 4, 5 and 6
As assigned by your Professor

Taking Care of Yourself

In order to get the most out of your efforts in your busy life full of all sorts of obligations and responsibilities, you need to pay attention to yourself. Although it is tempting for you to put yourself last as you work hard at work, school and home, you need to realize that in doing so you might become less effective in all arenas. Through taking care of yourself and paying attention to your needs you will maintain positive relationships, have terrific mental health, a strong physical well being and a healthy attitude which will help you achieve your goals. It takes a good deal of positive energy to be successful in your multi-tasking, demanding life and the first step towards making this happen is acknowledging that you have needs and then acting.

Roadmap to Professional Development
Through the readings, course project component and activities you will become aware of the positive results you will achieve as you take care of yourself in all aspects of your life.

Readings: Feldman, Chapter 14
                              Covey Habit #7
                              As assigned by your Professor

Activities: Activity Analysis

Moving Forward

You have spent a good deal of time in this course examining your past and your present but always with an eye on the future. Through readings, discussions, activities and assessments, you learned a great deal about your successes, challenges and skills. You have analyzed your behaviors along the way and have made some very important decisions. It is now time for you to appreciate your growth during the course as well as look forward. Crystallizing your newly discovered understandings and planning for the subsequent terms and years to follow is the last important task to accomplish. Taking the time to draw a blueprint that will allow you to achieve future successes, meet goals and continue to grow as a person is an important step in your professional development.

<u>Roadmap to Professional Development</u>
Through the readings, course project component and activities you will become aware of the positive results you will achieve as you take time to plan for the future based on an understanding of who you are as well as the values and interests you possess.

Readings:	Covey: Habit #2, pages 20-21
	As assigned by your Professor
Activities:	Portfolio Activation and Course Project Upload
	Final Thoughts on PROF101 Worksheet
Course Project:	Future Visions-Mission Statement
	Future Visions-Noel Levitz CSI Revisited
	Future Visions-Conclusions and Recommendations

Course Project-Assignment

Self Analysis Paper

The course project is titled, "Self-Analysis Paper". Throughout this paper, you will take the position of a counselor who is working with you in an effort to examine all aspects of your life. You will only refer to yourself in the 3rd person meaning calling yourself by name and using words such as him/her or he/she; you will never use the word "I". There will be a series of tasks, detailed throughout the subsequent pages, for you to complete followed by at least two pages of response detailed by your counselor (yourself).

The following is how the paper is structured:
- Past: Background Essay
- Present
    - Noel Levitz: CSI Analysis
    - LASSI Analysis
    - Midterm Grades Analysis
    - Strong Occupational Analysis
- Future
    - Mission Statement
    - Noel Levitz: CSI Revisited
    - Conclusion and Recommendations
- Upload the paper to the Electronic Portfolio

How to interpret the Noel-Levitz: College Student Inventory

The College Student Inventory measures how much you believe in your abilities – particularly your verbal and mathematical abilities. Your test results are going to measure your level of confidence in your math and verbal skills. Why is this important to know? In part because you have to believe you can do something before you can actually do it. In Psychology class, you'll learn more about this belief. It is called *self-efficacy*. Self-efficacy has nothing to do with actual skill; it's more about the creativity and belief you bring to different tasks. What does it mean if your math confidence level is high? It might mean that your faith in your abilities gives you an edge and enthusiasm for mathematical studies.

But what if your verbal confidence is a lower percentile rank? What if the CSI indicates you rank lower than many of your contemporaries in your belief about these abilities? That can be pretty sobering. Does it mean you can't do the work? Not at all – it means you that you don't believe you can read and write with assurance. Could be true – it might be false. The test only measures your confidence. A low percentile ranking suggests that you need to work on your confidence.

How do you do that? It's not like there's a gym or exercise routine for confidence. You gain belief by giving yourself reason to gain belief. You ask your professors for extra feedback on your work during their office hours. If your writing grades are not as high as you like, you make appointments at the Academic Support Center to go over your work. You can rewrite assignments and showing them to your professor or a confident student even if it doesn't improve your grade. If your confidence is low or your skills are not as developed as you like, your grades are not that important; certainly not as important as raising your confidence and strengthening your skills.

One of the authors spent a lifetime struggling with math, disliking math, and believing he had little mathematical ability. Upon taking the CSI at the ripe old age of 51, he discovered a low percentile rating for mathematical confidence. At first he laughed at himself; thank God the test was accurate; he was about to administer it to hundreds of students. But then he stopped and reflected. What was the low confidence about? He had passed math courses in high school, in college, and in graduate school and did well in all of them. Maybe he did have mathematical ability; maybe what he did not have was confidence. It was if someone had turned on the light. A belief he held for over forty years was discovered to be incorrect. The recognition changed his life.

Dealing with your confidence levels involves being genuine – true to yourself. How are the confidence scores going to affect how you conduct your education? Will you reflect on the meaning of the scores and search for the truth? Or will you just conclude the test is incorrect and uncomfortable fact? Will you be proactive?

Your response to every test is an opportunity to reflect and develop potential. Someone who doesn't score as well as they might like have a responsibility to interact with the test again and again until they get the results they like. Someone who does well has the potential to see how they arrived at the point of confidence or success. If the CSI says you have high academic confidence, how did that happen? Can you help build your confidence even more? Can you believe?

> *For a long time it had seemed to me that life was about to begin – real life. But there was always some obstacle in the way. Something to be got through first, some unfinished business, time still to be served, a debt to be paid. Then life would begin. At last it dawned on me that these obstacles were my life.*
>
> Father Alfred D'Souza

The CSI report on your perceived level of family support can be difficult to look at. It doesn't take much to realize that family support is often critical to success in life – especially at the beginning of new enterprises like college. The percentile rank next to level of family support on your CSI scoring report places the amount of family support you perceive in the context of students who took this survey at about 500 colleges. The score is solely in relationship to the other students. If you score a percentile rank of 50, it means that fifty percent of students perceive more family support than you and fifty percent receive less. If you score a percentile rank of 40, then sixty percent of students perceive more family support than you; thirty nine percent perceive less.

Our families are complicated. In some ways, they're everything we want them to be. In other ways, they fall short. It's just the nature of family. Raising our awareness of exactly what the relationship is can be a little surprising. In fact, recognizing that we don't perceive the level of support we would prefer might be a little discouraging. Should it be? In some cases the answer is yes.

In your family the answer may be no. Your family may not be aware of how much work, effort, and money, college actually requires. At most DeVry's only a small minority of students have family members who attended college. They may see you absenting yourself from family functions and take it personally. In other cases family members see their student tired and less able to take care of family responsibilities. All of this while being very proud you are in college.

So what can you do about a perceived lack of support? Remember, this is about your perception. Give other dynamics a chance to work. You can open the topic to discussion. Ask family (and friends), parents, siblings, and children what they feel about you going to college. Inquire if they feel it is a burden on them. See if they have questions. Perhaps they'd like to take a ride over to campus just to see where you spend so much time. A famous politician once observed that people liked to be asked – for help, for their opinion, and for their thoughts. Bringing the subject up may begin a dialog and greater appreciation. On both sides.

Father D'Souza talks about different viewpoints on life's obstacles. Are they something to wade through, just to get past or are they valuable experiences that should be appreciated for themselves? Many students and families look at school as something to get through. That's certainly an option. Another is to pause and reflect on the experience of college. You probably have not had an experience like this before and you may not again. You and your family may want to appreciate your ability to do something new and different. Reality is created by people. Your perceptions of family support may be the wellspring of a new way of looking at things; a new reality. Most of us spend much effort on warding off unpleasant truths. Welcoming these feelings as full partners is an action with a great deal of potential.

How to interpret the LASSI: Learning and Study Skills Inventory

How do we learn? There is no one answer. We all have different styles and different ways of understanding new material. Understanding where our strengths are permits us to focus on the things we do best. Like the CSI, The LASSI aids you in looking at yourself in comparison to other college students. For instance, do you worry about school performance more than other students or less? Do you demonstrate characteristics associated with strong motivation in line with other students? How do you manage your time relative to others?

Students most often agree with LASSI results; they tend to confirm what we know about ourselves. Your follow up to this test is what is important. The LASSI measures your skills and attitudes on ten scales:

- o Anxiety
- o Attitude
- o Concentration
- o Information Processing
- o Motivation and/or self discipline
- o The degree you prepare for class
- o The strength of your ability to sift out important information
- o How well you utilize support
- o Time Management Abilities
- o Test Preparation Strategies

What do your scores mean? If you score in the 75th percentile of higher in any scale, it is an indication of strength. While we can always improve our strong areas, this type of score indicates that you can probably appreciate where you are on this characteristic and not devote that much time on it. On the other hand, a percentile ranking below the 50th percentile indicates a sphere where you need to improve skills. These lower percentile rankings should not be discouraging. Most of us are not going to score above the 50th percentile on every scale. We all face challenges.

Scores under the fiftieth percentile do present a challenge. Improving these items should be very important. It is likely that these scores represent skills and strategies that might prevent you from doing well in college. It is essential to success that you develop an active strategy to gain skills in these areas. Your class will help everyone develop those strategies this week. Figuring out how to implement them is a critical task to your success.

The LASSI results give you a head start to creating a plan. Talking and writing honestly about them is the first step in developing the commitment necessary to succeed. The assessment is pretty good at describing who you are right now. Who you become depends more on the choices and commitments you make. By making commitments to yourself to change the way you do some things, you are making a commitment to graduation and success. Being proactive means you get to decide which challenges to take up and which to avoid. The responsibility is yours. So is the outcome.

How to Interpret the Strong Inventory-Personal Styles

By comparing your interests to the interests of people who enjoy specific jobs, the Strong Inventory makes recommendations to you about what careers you might find interesting. The report is based on the concept that if they like their jobs, and you share the same interests, you'll likely find similar work enjoyable. This is not a skills assessment; it does not tell you if you have the background for any career or if you will be successful. It will show you where you could start your search or focus your efforts. Many people find the Strong confirms what they've felt all along. The Strong can also help you eliminate choices or see patterns in your interests.

Course Project: Background Essay

Directions

Step 1:
Create a Title page with the following information:

Self

Analysis of _____

_____ *Fall* _____ Term

PROF 101, Section *Friday*

You will use this title page throughout the entire project

Step 2:
In an essay format and in the third person voice, describe the following:

o Your Demographic Information – *Where you Live*
o Your Family Information – *Siblings, wife/Husband, Kids, -Background*
o Your Educational Experiences – *Schools, Achievements, What you've Learned*
o Your Life Experiences –

Available Sources

o Storyboard Activity
o Insights and Reflections from self and others

Specifications

o Minimum 2 pages double-spaced, 12 point font, 1 inch margins
o The Background Essay should have the title of "Background" at the top.
o The essays should begin "_____ was born on _____ in _____."
o The essay will end with why your arrival at DeVry and why.

Course Project: Present Analysis-Noel Levitz, CSI

Directions

Complete the first Noel-Levitz College Student Inventory and in the third person voice, describe and discuss the following:

o Your top concern in the Academic Motivation Category and recommendations for behaviors that gets you dealing with those concerns over the next three months
o Your top concern in the General Coping Category and recommendations for behaviors that gets you dealing with those concerns over the next three months
o Your top concern in the Receptivity to Support Services Category and recommendations for behaviors that gets you dealing with those concerns over the next three months
o Discussion of Specific Recommendations and recommendations for behaviors that gets you dealing with those concerns over the next three months

Available Sources

o Insights and reflections others
o Noel-Levitz College Student Results

Specifications

o Minimum 2 pages double-spaced, 12 point font, 1 inch margins
o The Present Analysis should have the title of "Present Analysis" at the top with a subsection noting that this is Noel-Levitz: College Student Inventory
o The section should begin with the following: "_____ was asked to take the Noel-Levitz College Student Inventory."

Course Project: Present Analysis-LASSI

Directions

Complete the Learning and Study Skills Inventory (LASSI) and in the third person voice, describe and discuss the following:

o Your analysis of the score presented on the Attitude Scale and proactive steps you could take in this area that would lead to improvements.
o Your analysis of the score presented on the Motivation Scale and proactive steps you could take in this area that would lead to improvements.
o Your analysis of the score presented on the Anxiety Scale and proactive steps you could take in this area that would lead to improvements.
o Identify two of the remaining areas that are of a concern to you and identify proactive steps you could take in this area that would lead to improvements.

Available Sources

o Insights and reflections from others
o LASSI Results

Specifications

o Minimum 2 pages double-spaced, 12 point font, 1 inch margins
o The Present Analysis should have the title of "Present Analysis" at the top with a subsection noting that this is LASSI
o The section should begin with the following: "_____ was asked to take the Learning and Study Skills Inventory."

Course Project: Present Analysis-Midterm Grades

Directions

Obtain feedback from at least three of your current Professors on your performance utilizing the Midterm Grades Analysis Form located on the next three pages. In an essay format and in the third person voice, describe and discuss the following:

Your analysis of the instructor feedback presented to you from your course instructors with proper problem identification and solutions through the Seven of Highly Effective College Students.

Available Sources

o   Noel Levitz Analysis
o   LASSI Analysis
o   7 Habits of Highly Effective College Students
o   Insights and Reflections from others

Specifications:

o   Minimum 2 pages double-spaced, 12 point font, 1 inch margins
o   The Present Analysis should have the title of "Present Analysis" at the top with a subsection noting that this is the Midterm Grades Analysis
o   Start the section with the following statement, " _____ received some preliminary feedback in courses he/she is taking this current term."

Academic Progress Report

Course _____ Section _____

Student's Name _____ Date _____

Observation of Performance. Please check all that apply.

Demonstrates a good attitude _____   Missing homework _____
Enhances the class _____   Not prepared for class _____
Active participation _____   Lack of attention _____
Hands work in on time _____   Lack of participation _____
Good writing skills _____   Missing labs _____
Works well with peers _____   Poor attendance _____
Demonstrates leadership qualities_____

Recommendations:

_____ Responsible approach to studies needed
_____ Seek extra help
_____ Attend class regularly
_____ Speak with instructor
_____ Keep up the good work

Overall Status:

Satisfactory _____
Unsatisfactory _____

Comments (Optional):

_____
_____
_____
_____

Instructor Signature_____

Academic Progress Report

Course _____ Section _____

Student's Name _____ Date _____

Observation of Performance. Please check all that apply.

Demonstrates a good attitude   _____   Missing homework   _____
Enhances the class   _____   Not prepared for class   _____
Active participation   _____   Lack of attention   _____
Hands work in on time   _____   Lack of participation   _____
Good writing skills   _____   Missing labs   _____
Works well with peers   _____   Poor attendance   _____
Demonstrates leadership qualities _____

Recommendations:
_____ Responsible approach to studies needed
_____ Seek extra help
_____ Attend class regularly
_____ Speak with instructor
_____ Keep up the good work

Overall Status:

Satisfactory   _____
Unsatisfactory   _____

Comments (Optional):

_____

_____

_____

_____

Instructor Signature_____

Academic Progress Report

Course _____ Section _____

Student's Name _____   Date _____

Observation of Performance. Please check all that apply.

Demonstrates a good attitude   _____   Missing homework   _____
Enhances the class   _____   Not prepared for class _____
Active participation   _____   Lack of attention   _____
Hands work in on time   _____   Lack of participation   _____
Good writing skills   _____   Missing labs   _____
Works well with peers   _____   Poor attendance   _____
Demonstrates leadership qualities _____

Recommendations:
_____ Responsible approach to studies needed
_____ Seek extra help
_____ Attend class regularly
_____ Speak with instructor
_____ Keep up the good work

Overall Status:

Satisfactory   _____
Unsatisfactory   _____

Comments (Optional):

_____
_____
_____
_____

Instructor Signature_____

Course Project: Present Analysis-Strong Inventory, Personal Style Scales

Directions

Complete the Strong and in the third person voice, describe and discuss the following:

o   Your analysis of the results presented in the Work Style Scale
o   Your analysis of the results presented in the Learning Environment Scale
o   Your analysis of the results presented in the Leadership Scale
o   Your analysis of the results presented in the Risk Taking/Adventure Scale
o   Discussion of how the results in these scales are consistent/inconsistent with your chosen academic career with DeVry

Available Sources

Feel free to use the following sources:
o   Strong Printouts Campbell Interest and Skills Inventory
o   Insights and reflections from others

Specifications

o   Minimum 2 pages double-spaced, 12 point font, 1 inch margins
o   The Present Analysis should have the title of "Present Analysis" at the top with a subsection noting that this is the Strong Analysis
o   Start the section with the following statement, "_____ was asked to take the Strong Interest Inventory, Personal Styles Scales."

Course Project: Future Visions-Mission Statement

Directions

Create your own personal Mission Statement.

Available Sources

o Insights and Reflections from self and others
o Material found in "Seven Habits of Highly Effective College Students"
o Values Clarification Activity
o Completed Reflections

Specifications

o No size restrictions or limitations
o The Future Visions should have the title of "Future Visions" at the top with a subsection noting that this is the Mission Statement
o The section should begin with the following: "As an assignment, _____ was asked to create a personal mission statement. Below is what was submitted:"

Course Project: Future Visions-Noel Levitz CSI Revisited

Directions

Complete the second Noel-Levitz College Student Inventory and in the third person voice, describe and discuss the following:

o Was there any change in your top concern in the Academic Motivation Category from the first College Student Inventory? How do you explain the change or lack of change? Where do you go from here?
o Was there any change in your top concern in the General Coping Category from the first College Student Inventory? How do you explain the change or lack of change? Where do you go from here?
o Was there any change in your top concern in the Receptivity to Support Services Category from the first College Student Inventory? How do you explain the change or lack of change? Where do you go from here?

Available Sources

o Insights and Reflections from self and others
o First Noel-Levitz College Student Inventory Analysis
o Completed Reflections

Specifications

o Minimum 2 pages double-spaced, 12 point font, 1 inch margins
o The Future Visions should have the title of "Future Visions" at the top with a subsection noting that this is Noel-Levitz: College Student Inventory Revisited
o The section should begin with the following: "_____ was asked to take the Noel-Levitz College Student Inventory for the second time."

Course Project: Future Visions-Conclusions

Directions

In the third person voice, express the following:
o What the self-analysis has meant to you
o What lessons you have learned about yourself that you are happy with
o What lessons you have learned about yourself that needs improvement
o Have you experienced any sort of change during the self-analysis period
o Will your approach towards education be any different? If yes, how? If no, why not?

Available Sources

o Insights and Reflections from self and others
o Mission Statement
o Analysis completed from the following sources:
   o Background Analysis
   o Noel Levitz Analysis
   o LASSI Analysis
   o Midterm Grades Analysis
   o Campbell Analysis
o Completed course activities
o Completed Reflections

Specifications

o No size restrictions or limitations
o The Future Visions should have the title of "Future Visions" at the top with a subsection noting that this is "Conclusions"
o The section should begin with the following: "We are now at the end of our analysis and the following are observations/conclusions as well as future recommendations for _____."
o This section should be submitted with the previous sections of the Course Project as a completed Self-Analysis Document
o Attach proof of upload to E-Folio with the completed Self-Analysis document

Activities

The suggested activities correspond to the main sections of this book. These activities are meant to serve as additional resources to the fine ones found in all of your texts for the course. They have been utilized in previous PROF101 courses and found to enhance learning.

Success

Who Do You Know Activity

We all know people who are successful. They may not necessarily be the richest, smartest or best looking but they have certain qualities that help them standout in your eyes as being a success. It is important to recognize those things that make them so important for they serve as examples for you to strive towards in your own life.

Directions
Think of someone you know who is a success and answer the following questions:
- Who is this person?
- What characteristics make them a success?
- How did they get to be successful?
- In small groups, discuss your answers to the above questions.

Note: This activity can be used to help you prepare for your Mission Statement in the Course Project.

Storyboard Activity

It is important to recognize that your life has been a journey full of successes and critical points that serve to make up who you are today.

Directions:
In a word processing application, create a table with three rows and four columns. With a pencil, draw pictures that represent your life. Start off with birth in the first box and enrollment in DeVry in the last box. The rest is up to you but make sure you donate at least three boxes to your past education.

Note: This activity can be used to help you prepare for the Background Essay in the Course Project.

Discovering Yourself

Paying for College Activity/Web quest

Do you think it wise to depend on the Financial Aid Office to answer all your financial aid questions? Should you be doing your own investigations? Where would you begin to look? The aim of this Web quest is to develop a strategy to improve your college financial situation.

Step 1: The Process – What Do You Need?
It's hard to know what College might cost. You've already encountered unexpected expenses. Let's try and figure out what your situation is by completing the following worksheet:

Projected Income:

Available Savings	
Family Contribution	
Work	
Work-Study	
Scholarships	
State Grants	
Stafford Loans	
Other Loans	
Private Loans	
Total Available Money	

Estimated Expenses You Are Responsible For:

Annual Tuition	
Fees	
Books	
Rent	
Phone	
Food	
Clothing	
Laundry	
Transportation	
Medical	
Family Contribution	
Misc. Personal	
Credit Cards	

Insurance	
Social Life	
Other	
Total Annual Expenses	

Reality Formula
TOTAL ANNUAL INCOME – TOTAL ANNUAL EXPENSES = GAP _____

If you have a gap, it's time to be proactive. After all, this is your education. Time to talk to your advisor, financial aid, family, friends, and anyone else you can think of to come up with a strategy for shrinking the GAP. Almost everyone has a GAP and almost everyone has to solve it. When you think you've got a strategy, run it by a few trusted people and get their reaction. Your strategy can be an important part of your Mission Statement in the Course Project. Make some useful notes here:

_____

_____

_____

_____

_____

_____

Step 2: Understanding the Options
The goal of this step is for you to understand key terms and locate simple resources that will provide you with basic understandings of the wide variety of different ways college can be paid for.

Directions
Using internet search engines develop a list of options related to paying for college and search for them. List those options with clear definitions. A visit to the college library can assist you in this search. Utilize the space below for notes.

_____

_____

_____

_____

Step 3: Understanding Financial Aid

The Federal Student Aid office has a variety of programs to help you pay for your college education. Find out more about available grants, campus-based aid, and a variety of loans at:

http://studentaid.ed.gov/PORTALSWebApp/students/english/funding.jsp?tab=funding

Answer the following questions:
- What is the difference between the different forms of aid?
- What are the payback rules?
- Based upon the amount you are currently borrowing, how much will you have to payback and when?

Step 4: Understanding Scholarships

Locate the websites for three of the seven scholarships listed below and answer the following questions:
- What's the eligibility?
- How do you apply?
- How is a winner determined?

1. The Dale E Fridell Scholarship
2. TextbookX.com Scholarship
3. Blacknews.com Scholarship
4. Hispanic Issues.com Scholarship
5. Students Helping Other Students: I can make a Difference Scholarship
6. Writers of the Future
7. Reuben Trane Scholarship

Describe two of the five websites, locate one applicable scholarship in each and answer the following questions:
- What's the eligibility?
- How do you apply?
- How is a winner determined?

1. www.FastWeb.Com
2. www.srnexpress.com
3. www.uiowa.edu/~upr/research/sources/nfagen.htm
4. www.echoices.com   Username: 1003454, Password: EAST101
5. www.collegeboard.com

Setting Goals

Values Clarification Activity

Values in large part define who we are. Every person has a unique set of values which in turn directs how we spend our time and dictates our behaviors and actions. Additionally, they an indication to others of what matters most to us. Finally, values are directly connected with life goals.

For the reasons stated above, it is important for everyone to not only identify what their values are but to prioritize them. Once values are clearly identified and articulated, goal planning can meaningfully occur.

- What are your top five values now? What were your top five values this time last year? What were your top five values five years ago?
- Did your values change with time and circumstance or are they static?
- Do you currently act in manners that contradict your values?
- Do your goals coincide with what matters most to you?
- Can you achieve your goals and hold onto your values at the same time?

Core Competency Activity

In order to be successful in college, the goal needs to be clear as to what you are working towards. Understanding your major and related core competencies is a critical step in this process. Take some time to list out your major objectives as well as those for General Education and then through reading the catalogue course descriptions list which course you believe will satisfy those core competencies. Finally attribute the skills you believe you will be obtaining as a result of achieving the core competencies.

Program Objective (Core Competency)	Course(s)	Projected Skill(s) to be Learned
1.		
2.		
3.		
4.		
5.		
6.		
7.		
8.		
9.		
10.		
11.		
12.		
13.		
14.		
15.		

Learning

Lightbulb Activity

Similar to cartoons, sometimes when learning happens we imagine a lightbulb going on in our heads. It is a moment that lets you realize that you understand something new about yourself or the world that forever changes you.

Describe an event when the light bulb went on for you.

_____

_____

_____

How did you feel?

_____

_____

_____

How did it change you?

_____

_____

_____

Could you go back to the way you were before learning occurred? Why or why not?

_____

_____

_____

Making Decisions

Grade Point Average Activity

Usually based on a four point scale, the Grade Point Average (GPA) is often used as a measuring stick of success in college. It is therefore important for you to understand how the courses you are taking, the credits they are worth and the grades you earn compute to form the GPA so you can make sound decisions regarding your time and effort.

Directions
- Go to http://www.okc.cc.ok.us/orientation/Computing_Your_GPA.htm and print the image for "The Formula"
- Plug in your schedule information and project, based on where you stand right now in your courses, what your potential Grade Point Average would be right now assuming the courses were to end today.
- Answer the following questions:
  - o Are you satisfied with what you see?
  - o What do you owe your successes and shortcomings to?
  - o What decisions do you need to make?
  - o What will happen if you do not make any necessary adjustments?

Note: *This activity can be used to help you prepare for the Grades Analysis portion in the Course Project.*

Taking Care of Yourself

Activity Analysis

It is important for you to occasionally pause and analyze where you are spending our time. If you are like the majority of students out there, you are so busy juggling a wide range of responsibilities that you often lose sight of what is most important-taking care of yourself. This activity is meant to force you to take that pause and look deeply at how you spend your time.

Directions
Pick four consecutive days this week and keep an hourly diary which details how you spent your time from the time you woke up to the time you went to sleep. Create a detailed account of your time and discuss the following:

- o Is this a typical schedule for you?
- o Did you spend any time during these days on yourself? If so, how much time and what were the activities? If not, why not?
- o How could you make time to for yourself? Is it important?

Note: This activity can be used to help you prepare for your Conclusions and Recommendations section in the Course Project.

Expectations of PROF101

1. What are your impressions of the philosophies behind PROF101?

----

2. What aspects of this course do you anticipate will be most beneficial to you?

----

3. What do you perceive to be your strengths to be that will ensure your chances of success in college?

----

4. What do you perceive to be your opportunities for improvement that need to be addressed to ensure your success in college?

Final Thoughts on PROF101

1. Did PROF101 meet, exceed or fall short of your expectations?

----

2. What aspects of the course were most beneficial to you?

----

3. What strengths things did you learn about yourself in PROF101 that will enhance your chances for success in college?

----

4. What opportunities for improvement still exist that need to be addressed to ensure your success in college?

Weekly Timetable

	Mon	Tues	Wed	Thurs	Fri	Sat	Sun
6–7 AM							
7–8 AM							
8–9 AM							
9–10 AM							
10–11 AM							
11–12 AM							
12 (noon)–1 PM							
1–2 PM							
2–3 PM							
3–4 PM							
4–5 PM							
5–6 PM							
6–7 PM							
7–8 PM							
8–9 PM							
9–10 PM							
10–11 PM							
11 PM–12 (midnight)							

POWER
Learning

Second Edition

Strategies
for
Success
in College
and Life

Robert S. Feldman

University of Massachusetts—Amherst

McGraw Hill

Boston   Burr Ridge, IL   Dubuque, IA   Madison, WI   New York   San Francisco   St. Louis
Bangkok   Bogotá   Caracas   Kuala Lumpur   Lisbon   London   Madrid   Mexico City
Milan   Montreal   New Delhi   Santiago   Seoul   Singapore   Sydney   Taipei   Toronto

McGraw-Hill Higher Education

*A Division of The **McGraw-Hill** Companies*

P.O.W.E.R. LEARNING: STRATEGIES FOR SUCCESS IN COLLEGE AND LIFE
Copyright by McGraw-Hill, a business unit of The McGraw-Hill Companies, Inc., 1221 Avenue of the Americas, New York, NY, 10020. Copyright © 2003, 2000 by The McGraw-Hill Companies, Inc. All rights reserved. No part of this publication may be reproduced or distributed in any form or by any means, or stored in a database or retrieval system, without the prior written consent of The McGraw-Hill Companies, Inc., including, but not limited to, in any network or other electronic storage or transmission, or broadcast for distance learning.
Some ancillaries, including electronic and print components, may not be available to customers outside the United States.

This book is printed on acid-free paper.

4 5 6 7 8 9 0 QPD/QPD 0 9 8 7 6 5 4 3
2 3 4 5 6 7 8 9 0 QPD/QPD 0 9 8 7 6 5 4 3

ISBN 0-07-248070-X (Student Edition)
ISBN 0-07-248072-6 (Annotated Instructor's Edition)

Editorial director: *Phillip A. Butcher*
Executive editor: *Sarah Touborg*
Senior sponsoring editor: *Leslie Oberhuber*
Senior developmental editor: *Alexis Walker*
Senior marketing manager: *David Patterson*
Lead project manager: *Mary Conzachi*
Senior production supervisor: *Michael R. McCormick*
Senior designer: *Jennifer McQueen*
Cover images: *© Photodisc, Inc. All rights reserved.*
Supplement producer: *Matthew Perry*
Photo research coordinator: *David A. Tietz*
Photo researcher: *Elyse Rieder*
Typeface: *10.5/13 Palatino*
Compositor: *ElectraGraphics, Inc.*
Printer: *Quebecor World Dubuque Inc.*

Library of Congress Cataloging-in-Publi1cation Data

Feldman, Robert S. (Robert Stephen), 1947–
     P.O.W.E.R. learning: strategies for success in college and life/Robert S. Feldman.—
  2nd ed.
       p. cm.
     Includes index.
   ISBN 0-07-248070-X (alk. paper)
   1. College student orientation. 2. Study skills. 3. Life skills. 4. Success   I. Title:
POWER learning. II Title
LB2343.3 .F44 2003
378.1'98—dc21   2002020222

www.mhhe.com

To my students, who make teaching a joy.

Brief Contents

Contents

Part One
Getting Started

1 P.O.W.E.R. Learning: Becoming an Expert Student   1

2 Making the Most of Your Time   27

3   Recognizing How You Learn, Who You Are, and What You Value   55

Part Two
Using P.O.W.E.R.
for Academic Success

4 Taking Notes   87

5 Taking Tests   117

6 Building Your Reading Skills 145

Part Three
P.O.W.E.R.
Foundations of Success

7 Writing and Speaking 169

8 Memory 201

9   Choosing Your Courses and Major   223

Part Four
Life Beyond the Classroom

10 Making the Most of Technology 249

11 Making Decisions That Are Right for You 283

12 Getting along with Others 309

13 Money Matters 335

14 Stress, Health, and Wellness 363

Preface

In the first edition of *P.O.W.E.R. Learning,* I wrote about Mark Johnson, a student I encountered early in my teaching career. Smart, articulate, and likable, he certainly wanted to succeed in college, and he seemed every bit as capable as students who were doing quite well. Yet Mark was a marginal student, someone who allowed multiple opportunities to succeed to pass him by. Although he clearly had the ability to do well in college—and ultimately in life—he lacked the skills needed to take full advantage of his talent.

Over the years, I encountered other students like Mark. I began to wonder: Was there a way to teach *every* student how to succeed, both academically and beyond the classroom? *P.O.W.E.R. Learning* is my answer.

Based on the conviction that *good students are made, not born,* the central message of *P.O.W.E.R. Learning* is that students can be successful in college if they follow the basic principles and strategies presented in this book. Once mastered, these principles and strategies can help students to maximize their potential, both in and out of the classroom.

This text is designed to be used by students in first-year experience courses. For many students, the first-year experience course is a literal lifeline. It provides the means to learn what it takes to achieve academic success and to make a positive social adjustment to the campus community. If students learn how to do well in their first term of college, they have built a foundation that will last a lifetime.

I wrote *P.O.W.E.R. Learning* because no existing text provides a systematic framework that helps students develop learning and problem-solving strategies that work effectively both in and out of the classroom. The book is an outgrowth of my experience as a college instructor, most of it involving first-year students, combined with my research as a psychologist on the factors that influence learning.

Judging from the response to the first edition—now in use at hundreds of colleges and universities in North America and beyond—the approach embodied in the book resonates with the philosophy and experience of many educators. *P.O.W.E.R. Learning* provides a framework that students can begin to use immediately to become more effective students. That framework is designed to be

- easy-to-grasp, logical, and compelling, so that students can readily see its merits;

- effective for a variety of student learning styles—as well as a variety of teaching styles;

- workable within a variety of course formats and for supplemental instruction;

- valuable for use in learning communities;

- transferable to settings ranging from the classroom to the dorm room to the boardroom;

effective in addressing both the mind *and* the spirit. P.O.W.E.R. explains useful cognitive strategies and skills to students, while at the same time engaging the natural enthusiasm, motivation, and inclination to succeed that students carry within them.

Based in part on comprehensive, detailed feedback obtained from both instructors and students, *P.O.W.E.R. Learning* meets these aims. The book will help students confront and master the numerous challenges of the college experience through use of the P.O.W.E.R. learning approach, embodied in the five steps of the acronym *P.O.W.E.R.* (*P*repare, *O*rganize, *W*ork, *E*valuate, and *R*ethink). Using simple—yet effective—principles, *P.O.W.E.R. Learning* teaches the skills needed to succeed in college and on the job.

Changes that Make a Difference: P.O.W.E.R. Learning, 2/E

Consistent with the extensive class-testing and reviewing that shaped the first edition, each chapter in this second edition has been reviewed by a large group of seasoned first-year experience instructors. Their responses, in addition to classroom testing and feedback from the many students and instructors who used the first edition, have resulted in some significant enhancements to the text:

Personal Styles Assessments: Every chapter now includes a new *Personal Styles* Try It. These self-diagnostic questionnaires help students measure their learning style or other personal style. Examples include "Find Your Time Style" (Chapter 2); "Measure Your Test-Taking Style" (Chapter 5); and "Find Your Problem-Solving Style" (Chapter 11).

Civic Engagement, Civility, and Classroom Etiquette: Increasingly important in and out of the classroom, the topic of appropriate respect and concern for others is now directly addressed in several chapters, including Chapters 1, 5, 10, and 12.

Chapter 10: Making the Most of Technology. From distance learning to using e-mail effectively, this new chapter includes coverage of word-processing, working and studying online, presentation and spreadsheet programs, and locating and evaluating information, both in libraries and on the Web.

Speaking of Success Interviews: These informative and inspiring profiles have been refreshed with several new faces, including Kenisha Creary (University of Hartford) in Chapter 3; Catalina Angeles (California State University at San Marcos) in Chapter 9; Naison Nayamatutu (Carthage College) in chapter 10; Ben Carson (Yale University) in Chapter 11; Sandra Marotta (Metropolitan State University, St. Paul, MN) in Chapter 12; Jerry Yang (Stanford University, co-founder and director of Yahoo) in Chapter 13; and Justin McCarthy (Washington College) in Chapter 14. (Additional *Speaking of Success* interviews, along with all of those from the first edition of the book, are available on the *P.O.W.E.R. Learning* website.)

Reorganized Table of Contents: Many instructors, especially those using customized versions of the text, requested that the most important (and most often assigned) chapters be moved to the beginning of the book. That has been done. Additionally, material on listening has been incorporated into the note-taking chapter, better suiting the approach of most instructors.

An overall streamlining and tightening of textual material. Every sentence has been reassessed with the goal of making the text even more readable and the vocabulary precisely appropriate for first-year students.

Addition of new design features. The overall graphic design, which was the source of considerable enthusiasm from instructors in the first edition, has been slightly modified to reflect new material and improve readability.

The Goals of P.O.W.E.R. Learning

Although *P.O.W.E.R. Learning* has been thoroughly revised, the goals of the book remain the same in this new edition:

- **To provide a systematic framework for organizing the strategies that lead to success.** First and foremost, the book provides a systematic, balanced presentation of the skills required to achieve student success. Using the *P.O.W.E.R.* framework and relying on proven strategies, *P.O.W.E.R. Learning* provides specific, hands-on techniques for achieving success as a student.

- **To offer a wide range of skill-building opportunities.** *Students learn by doing.* *P.O.W.E.R. Learning* provides a wealth of interactive exercises, diagnostic questionnaires, case studies, and journal writing activities designed to help students try out and eventually *master* the skills and techniques they need to become effective learners and problem-solvers.

- **To demonstrate the connection between academic success and success beyond the classroom.** Stressing the importance of *self-reliance* and *self-accountability*, the book demonstrates that the skills required to be a successful student are tied to career and personal success.

- **To develop critical thinking skills:** Whether to evaluate the quality of information found on the Internet or to judge the merits of a position taken by a friend, the ability to think critically is more important than ever in this age of information. Through carefully crafted questionnaires, exercises, journal activities, and guided group work, *P.O.W.E.R. Learning* helps students to develop their capacity to think critically.

- **To provide an engaging, accessible, and meaningful presentation.** The fifth goal of this book underlies the first four: to write a student-friendly book that is relevant to the needs and interests of its readers and that will promote enthusiasm and interest in the process of becoming a successful student. Learning the strategies needed to become a more effective student should be a stimulating and fulfilling experience, and *P.O.W.E.R. Learning* makes that experience possible. In short, *P.O.W.E.R. Learning: Strategies for Success in College and Life* is designed to give students a sense of mastery and success as they work through the book. It is meant to engage and nurture students' minds and spirits, stimulating their intellectual curiosity about the world and planting a seed that will grow throughout their lifetime.

Achieving the Goals of P.O.W.E.R. Learning

The goals of **P.O.W.E.R. Learning: Strategies for Success in College and Life** are achieved through a consistent, carefully devised set of features common to every chapter. They include the following:

Chapter-opening scenarios

Each chapter begins with a short vignette, describing an ordinary individual grappling with a situation that is relevant to the subject matter of the chapter. Different chapters feature students running behind schedule (Chapter 2), figuring out a way to keep up with reading assignments (Chapter 7), or facing a long list of French vocabulary words to memorize (Chapter 9).

Looking Ahead sections

These sections provide a bridge between the opening vignettes and the remainder of the chapter and include questions that allow students to articulate the chapter's objectives.

Try It! activities

These sections, interspersed throughout the chapter, include written exercises of all types. There are at least five *Try It!* activities in every chapter, and at least one of these is designated as an in-class, group exercise. Examples of *Try It!* exercises include "Assessing Your Analytical and Relational Learning Style" (Chapter 3), "Take a Test-Taking Test" (Chapter 5), "What's Your Level of Self-Consciousness?" (Chapter 7), and "Work the Web" (Chapter 10).

Journal Reflections

This feature provides students with journal prompts that ask students to reflect on and think critically about the chapter content and about related prior experiences. For example, the "Journal Reflections" in Chapter 8, "Writing and Speaking," asks students to reflect on their feelings about the writing process, and the one in Chapter 13, "Money Matters" asks students to evaluate their financial savvy after performing a few simple but eye-opening exercises (e.g., "How much money do you now have in your pockets and wallet? [Guess first, and then look.] How close did you come?").

Speaking of Success

Every chapter includes interviews with people who exemplify academic success. Some of these individuals are well-known figures, such as Bill Cosby, Rebecca Lobo, and John Irving; others are current students or recent graduates. Many of these individuals have struggled to overcome difficulties in their personal lives or in school before achieving academic or career success.

Career Connections

This feature links the material in the chapter to the world of work, offering practical demonstrations of how the strategies discussed in the chapter are related to career choices and success. Topics addressed in these sections include narrowing career choices, applying for jobs, and developing workplace listening skills.

Running Glossary

Key terms appear in boldface in the text and are defined in the margins. In addition, they are listed in a "Key Terms and Concepts" section at the end of the chapter, with accompanying page references. Glossary terms are highlighted in color in the index.

End-of-chapter material

Each chapter ends with a "Looking Back" summary that restates the chapter's objectives, a list of key terms and concepts, and an annotated list of student resources. These resources include campus offices, relevant supplemental readings, and "Taking It to the Net" exercises, which provide students with practice in using the World Wide Web.

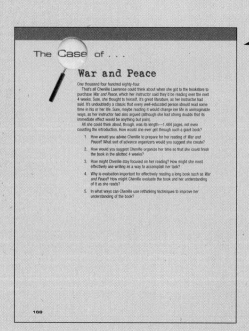

Case Study

Each chapter ends with "The Case of . . . ," a case study that invites students to apply that chapter's principles in solving a unique problem. Case studies are based on situations that students might themselves encounter. For instance, the case study in Chapter Four, "Taking Notes," describes the difficulties experienced by a student who writes down the instructor's every word ("The Case of . . . The Human Dictation Machine"); the case study in Chapter 11, "Making Decisions That Are Right for You," describes an all-too-typical problem involving an apartment lease and roommates. Each case provides a series of questions that encourage students to use what they've learned in responding to these dilemmas.

P.O.W.E.R. Tools for Instructors and Students

The same philosophy and goals that guided the writing of *P.O.W.E.R. Learning: Strategies for Success in College and Life* have informed the development of a comprehensive, first-rate set of teaching aids. Through a series of focus groups, questionnaires, and surveys, we asked instructors what they needed to optimize their courses. We also reviewed what other publishers provided in the way of teaching aids to make sure that the ancillary materials accompanying *P.O.W.E.R. Learning* would meet and exceed the level of support to which instructors are accustomed. We are confident that whether you are an instructor with long experience or one who is new to the course, this book's instructional package will provide practical guidance that will enhance instruction inside the classroom and maximize your time outside of the classroom.

Print Resources

Annotated Instructor's Edition (AIE) (0-07-248072-6): The AIE, prepared by Joni Webb Petschauer and Cindy Wallace of Appalachian State University, contains the full text of the student edition of the book with the addition of marginal notes that provide a rich variety of teaching strategies, discussion prompts, and helpful cross-references to the Instructor's Resource Manual.

Instructor's Resource Manual and Testbank (0-07-248071-8): Written by Joni Webb Petschauer and Cindy Wallace of Appalachian State University with additional contributions from experienced instructors across the country, this manual provides specific suggestions for teaching each topic, tips on implementing a first-year experience program, handouts to generate creative classroom activities, transparency masters, audiovisual resources, sample syllabi, tips on incorporating the Internet into the course, and a bank of chapter quizzes.

Customize Your Text: *P.O.W.E.R. Learning, 2/e* can be customized to suit your needs. The text can be abbreviated for shorter courses and can be expanded to include semester schedules, campus maps, additional essays, activities, or exercises, along with other materials specific to your curriculum or situation.

Distance Learning Faculty Guide: *Designing and Teaching a Distance Learning Course with P.O.W.E.R. Learning, 2/e,* written by Christopher Poirier and Robert S. Feldman, will provide instructors with an overview of distance learning, an introduction to the most popular distance learning platforms, and detailed instructions on how to design and teach a distance learning course with *P.O.W.E.R. Learning.*

Human Resources

Workshops with Author and Author Team: Are you faced with the challenge of launching a first-year experience course on your campus? Would you like to invigorate your college success program, incorporating the most recent pedagogical and technological innovations? Is faculty recruitment an obstacle to the success of your program? Are you interested in learning more about the P.O.W.E.R. system?

Workshops are available on these and many other subjects for anyone conducting or even just considering a first-year experience program. Led by author Robert Feldman, *P.O.W.E.R. Learning* Instructor's Manual authors Joni Webb Petschauer and Cindy Wallace, or one of the McGraw-Hill *P.O.W.E.R. Learning* consultants, each workshop is tailored to the needs of individual campuses or programs. For more information, contact your local representative, or drop us a line at fye@mcgraw-hill.com.

Digital Resources

P.O.W.E.R. Learning Student CD-ROM (0-07-248073-4): This CD-ROM (available in Windows and in Mac) provides students with a rich multimedia extension of the text's content. Each module of the CD-ROM is tied to a chapter of the text, featuring interactive self-assessments, simulations, video and audio clips, crossword puzzles, Web links, journal activities, and an Internet primer. The CD-ROM is available free when packaged with new copies of the text.

P.O.W.E.R. Learning Website (www.mhhe.com/power): Instructors and students will find downloadable resources, demonstrations of all of our software programs, opportunities for online discussion, e-mail access to the author and project contributors, Web exercises, and a rich bank of links for college success.

PageOut, WebCT, Blackboard, and more: The online content of *P.O.W.E.R. Learning* is supported by WebCT, eCollege.com, and Blackboard. Additionally, our PageOut service, free to qualified adopters, is available to get you and your course up and running online in a matter of hours! To find out more contact your local McGraw-Hill representative or visit http://www.pageout.net.

PowerPoint Slides: These slides, drawn from the book's graphics and other sources, offer a variety of electronic options to enhance instructor and student presentations.

Study Smart: *Study Skills for Students*, 2.0 (Online at www.mhhe.com/studysmart2 or on CD-ROM (0-07-245515-2): Developed by Andrea Bonner and Mieke Schipper of Sir Sanford Fleming College, this innovative study skills tutorial teaches students essential note-taking methods, test-taking strategies, and time management secrets. *Study Smart* is free when packaged with new copies of *P.O.W.E.R. Learning.*

Video Resource (0-07-236710-5): *Real People Talk About Real Success:* Filmed expressly for **P.O.W.E.R. Learning** on various campus locations and "real world" settings, this documentary-style video features a variety of inspiring people, both professionals and students, describing life challenges and how the elements of the P.O.W.E.R. system help them achieve success. Designed for use during the early part of the semester, this video is ideal for helping break the ice and stimulating discussion. Ask your McGraw-Hill representative for details.

Start Right Video Series: Produced in conjunction with the National Orientation Directors Association, this program consists of six videos (approximately 20 minutes each) on diversity, residential life, academic success, wellness, alcohol, and money. The series is supported by an instructor's guide by Nancy Hunter Denny, offering discussion questions, handouts and worksheets, and student exercises. An additional hour-long program, *The Facilitator's Training Video,* illustrates effective methods and strategies for peer discussion leaders. Ask your McGraw-Hill representative for details.

Additional Value-Added Packaging Options

Random House Webster's College Dictionary (0-07-366069-8): Updated for the 21st century, this dictionary is available for a nominal cost when packaged with the text.

Spanish/English Glossary English as a Second Language Guide: Created for students who learned English as a second language, this guide provides a glossary of key concepts, useful vocabulary terms and explanations of each chapter of *P.O.W.E.R. Learning.*

Dear Student:

Do you find that there's not enough time to accomplish all the things you want to do? Do you put off studying for tests until the last minute? Do you sometimes have trouble making decisions?

If so, you're not alone. Every first-year college student encounters challenges such as these, and many others. That's where *P.O.W.E.R. Learning: Strategies for Success in College and Life* comes in. It is designed to help you master the challenges you'll face in college and in your everyday life. The P.O.W.E.R. Learning system—which is based on five key steps embodied in the word *P.O.W.E.R.* (*Prepare, Organize, Work, Evaluate,* and *Rethink*)—teaches strategies that will help you become a more successful student and that will give you an edge in attaining what you want to accomplish in life.

But it's up to you to make use of the book. By familiarizing yourself with its features and using the built-in learning aids, you'll maximize its usefulness and be more likely to get the most out of it.

Familiarize yourself with the scope of P.O.W.E.R. Learning. Begin by skimming the Table of Contents, which provides an overview of the book. By reading the chapter titles, you'll get a sense of the topics that are covered and the logic of the sequence of chapters.

Take some time to flip through the book. Choose a chapter that sounds interesting to you, skim a few pages, and see for yourself the kinds of practical information the book provides. Note that every chapter has the same diamond-shaped pattern:

Opening Prologue
Looking Ahead
The Main Body of the Chapter
Looking Back/Resources
Case Study

Use the built-in learning aids

Now that you have a broad overview of *P.O.W.E.R. Learning,* you're ready to consider the book's different components.

Opening Prologue. This is a brief account of a student confronting a typical challenge that is relevant to the chapter topic.

Looking Ahead. This opening section orients you to the topics covered in each chapter, providing a link between the opening situation and the rest of the chapter. It also includes a list of key questions that are addressed—and answered—in the chapter.

Journal Reflections. This feature poses questions related to chapter content; the idea here is for you to think about them and keep your responses in a journal that will serve as a record of your progress through the course.

Try It! Every chapter offers at least five opportunities for you to gain hands-on experience with the material covered in the chapter. These activities include questionnaires, self-assessments, and group exercises that you can do with your classmates. The name says it all: Try It!

Speaking of Success. Every chapter includes an in-depth interview with someone who has achieved academic success. Some of these people are well-known individuals, whereas others are current students or recent graduates who have overcome academic difficulties to achieve success.

Career Connections. *Career Connection* boxes illustrate how the strategies and skills discussed in the chapter can help you on the job—in addition to helping you find a job in the first place.

Running Glossary. Key terms appear in boldface in the text and are defined in the margins. In addition, they are listed in a "Key Terms and Concepts" section at the end of the chapter. (All these terms are also identified in the index in color.)

Looking Back. *Looking Back* is a summary that lists the key points discussed in the chapter.

Key Terms and Concepts. This list of important terms is alphabetized, and the page numbers refer back to the point in the chapter where the term was introduced.

Resources. Every chapter includes a list of the three types of resources that can help you find information relevant to the chapter: a list of on-campus resources; books; and websites. There are also exercises in using the web, called *Taking It to the Net.*

Case Study. Every chapter ends with a case study ("The Case of . . .") and accompanying questions. These cases are designed to provide you with an opportunity to apply what you've learned in the chapter.

Every chapter contains these features, which will serve as familiar guideposts as you make your way through the book. The structure will help you in organizing the book's content, and in learning and remembering the material.

Get in touch

I welcome your comments and suggestions about *P.O.W.E.R. Learning,* as well as the website and CD-ROM that accompany the book. You can send letters to me at the Department of Psychology at the University of Massachusetts, Amherst, Massachusetts 01003 or send me an e-mail message at feldman@psych.umass.edu. I *will* write back!

A final word: *P.O.W.E.R. Learning* presents the tools that can maximize your chances for academic and life success. But remember that they're only tools, and their effectiveness depends on the way in which they are used. Ultimately, you are the one who is in charge of your future.

The start of college offers a wonderful point of departure. Make the journey a rewarding, exciting, and enlightening one!

Robert S. Feldman

Acknowledgments

I am indebted to the many reviewers of *P.O.W.E.R. Learning* who provided input at every step of development of the book. These dedicated instructors and administrators provided thoughtful, detailed advice, and I am very grateful for their help and insight. They include the following:

Saiful Abdul-Ahad, U. of Central Florida; Veronica Allen, Texas Southern University; Val Becker, U. of North Dakota; Dee F. Bostick, Midlands Technical College; Kathleen A. Bottaro, Manchester CC; Elizabeth F. Boucher, Tennessee Tech. U.; Phyllis Bunnell, Our Lady of the Lake University; Sue G. Byrd, U. of Tennessee at Martin; Linda Beall Caplin, Austin CC; Caroline Chiccarelli, Worcester State College; Leslie Chilton, Arizona State U.; Rachel Cohen, Cañada College; Carol Cooper, Miami-Dade CC, North Campus; Anne Marie Coyne, Montgomery County CC; John DeLeon, Southwest Texas State University; Corley F. Dennison, Marshall U.; Robin A. Diana, Rochester Institute of Technology; Katherine Erdman, South Dakota State U.; Cherry Gooden, Texas Southern University; Carol J. Ham, Garden City CC; Thomas Hollins, Florida State University; Randy Jedele, Des Moines Area CC; Laura Kauffman, Indian River CC; William H. Kellar; Liz Kennedy, Florida Atlantic U.; Ron Klinger, Texas A&M U. at Galveston; Joan L. Krabbe, Miami U.; Ann Marie Ladner, Vincennes U.; Sue V. Lape, Columbus State CC; Valerie Lazzara, Palm Beach CC—Lake Worth; Jodi H. Levine, Temple U.; Linda Long, University of Wisconsin—Whitewater; Tracy Jarrell Lopez, U. of Texas at San Antonio; Jonathan A. Maisonpierre, U. of North Carolina, Pembroke; Felicia McGinty, Montclair State University; Eldon McMurray, Utah Valley State College; Elisabeth Morgan, Eastern Michigan U.; Mary Nakano, Leeward CC; Barbara Nicholls, Ashland CC; Bill Osher, Georgia Tech; Sue Palmer, Brevard CC—Cocoa; Lois Pasapane, Palm Beach CC—Lake Worth; Joanne Pedersen, California State U., San Marcos; Madeline Haug Penna, Nova Southeastern U.; Sheryl Peterson, St. Petersburg Jr. College; Virginia Rinella, Southern Illinois University; Louise C. Rosenberg, U. of Hartford; Arleen Cedeño Schreiner, York College CUNY; Patty Scott, Southwestern Oregon CC; Kathy Seyler, Palm Beach CC—Palm Beach Gardens; Rita Sheldon, Palm Beach CC—Lake Worth; Anna E. Shiplee, U. of West Florida; Karla K. Thompson, New Mexico State U.—Carlsbad; Russ Tiberii, U. of Central Florida; Joan Vintle, Lorain County CC; Tom G. Walter, Gainesville College; Peggy Walton, Howard CC; Arthur Webb, Oklahoma State U.; Margaret Felder Wilson, South Carolina State U.; and Fran Zaniello, Northern Kentucky U.

The students in my own first-year experience course (shown at the right) in the fall of 2001 provided thoughtful and wise advice as they were class-testing the manuscript that was to become *P.O.W.E.R. Learning, 2/e.* I thank them for their enthusiasm and willingness to participate in the development process.

Professors Cindy Wallace and Joni Webb Petschauer of Appalachian State University wrote the Instructor's Resource Manual and provided marginal notes and tips for the Annotated Instructor's Edition. I thank both of them for their enthusiasm, good ideas, creativity, and dedication.

Edward Murphy, an educational testing expert, helped develop the exercises in the book, and editor Leslie Carr made many creative contributions and stylistic improvements to the text. I'm grateful to both of them for their superb work.

John Graiff participated in every aspect of putting this book together. He was a great help on every level, and I thank him for his willingness to go the extra mile. I could not have written this book without his unflagging support.

I am proud to be part of an extraordinary McGraw-Hill editorial team. Leslie Oberhuber, Senior Sponsoring Editor and chief P.O.W.E.R.-meister, has brought enthusiasm, intelligence, and a wealth of ideas to the project. Sarah Touborg, Executive Editor, provided the inspiration for the book, and I am grateful for her unwavering support and good ideas. Alexis Walker and Rhona Robbin, Senior Developmental Editors, gave unstintingly of their expertise and support. It was also terrific to be back in Editorial Director Phil Butcher's fold, at least for a bit, and I thank him for his support not only on this book, but also on other projects throughout the years. Vice President and Editor-in-Chief Thalia Dorwick gave generously of her time and good ideas, albeit making me feel like a time management slacker in the process. I value her above-and-beyond-the-call-of-duty contributions immensely. Finally, Steve Debow, President of Social Sciences and Humanities, gave strong and imaginative support to this project, and I am grateful for his input. Without a doubt, there is no better editorial group in the business, and I count myself extremely lucky not only to have found myself a part of this world-class team, but to count each of them as friends.

Burrston House, personified by Glenn and Meg Turner, provided editorial and marketing advice at an extraordinary level. I thank them for their good ideas, creativity, constant prodding, and careful calculation of grade point averages. I am also grateful to photo researcher Elyse Rieder and text permissions editor Elsa Peterson. Finally, I am indebted to David Patterson, marketing manager *par excellence,* in whose capable hands *P.O.W.E.R. Learning* thrived.

I am also deeply appreciative of the efforts of the fine production team who worked on the book. Project manager Mary Conzachi overcame obstacles with grace and good cheer. Designer Jennifer McQueen created the beautiful design for the book, under the direction of Art Director Keith McPherson. These professionals worked under the stewardship of Merrily Mazza, Vice President of Editing, Design, and Production, who has been gracious and helpful from the very start of the project.

In the end, I am eternally indebted to my family, both extended and immediate. Sarah, Josh, and Jon, and of course Kathy, thank you for everything.

About the Author

Robert S. Feldman still remembers those moments of being overwhelmed when he started college at Wesleyan University. "I wondered whether I was up to the challenges that faced me," he recalls, "and—although I never would have admitted it at the time—I really had no idea what it took to be successful at college."

That experience, along with his encounters with many students during his own teaching career, led to a life-long interest in helping students navigate the critical transition that they face at the start of their own college careers. Professor Feldman, who went on to receive a doctorate in psychology from the University of Wisconsin—Madison, is now Professor of Psychology at the University of Massachusetts at Amherst, where he is Director of Undergraduate Studies. As Director of Undergraduate Studies, he initiated the Minority Mentoring Program, and he teaches the first-year experience course and a course in the Talent Advancement Program for new students.

Professor Feldman's proudest professional accomplishment is winning the College Outstanding Teaching Award at UMass. He also has been named a Hewlett Teaching Fellow and is a Senior Online Instruction Fellow. He has taught courses at Mount Holyoke College, Wesleyan University, and Virginia Commonwealth University.

Professor Feldman is a Fellow of both the American Psychological Association and the American Psychological Society. He is a winner of a Fulbright Senior Research Scholar and Lecturer award and has written some 100 scientific articles, book chapters, and books. His books, some of which have been translated into Spanish, French, Portuguese, and Chinese, include *Fundamentals of Nonverbal Behavior, Development of Nonverbal Behavior in Children, Understanding Psychology, 6/e,* and *Development Across the Life Span, 3/e.* His research interests encompass the study of honesty and truthfulness in everyday life, development of nonverbal behavior in children, and the social psychology of education. His research has been supported by grants from the National Institute of Mental Health and the National Institute on Disabilities and Rehabilitation Research.

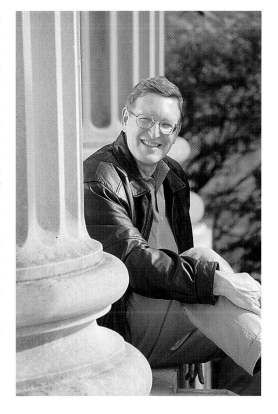

With the last of his three children starting college last fall—and facing the proverbial empty nest—Professor Feldman occupies his spare time with serious cooking and earnest, but admittedly unpolished, piano playing. He also loves to travel with his wife, who is also a college professor. He lives with her in a home that looks out on the Holyoke mountain range in Amherst, Massachusetts.

P.O.W.E.R. Learning: Becoming an Expert Student

1

The day has started off with a bang. Literally. As Jessie Trevant struggles sleepily to turn off her clock radio's continual buzzing at 7:30 A.M., she knocks it off the desk next to her bed. The loud bang it makes not only wakes her fully but also rouses her roommate, who grumbles resentfully.

Struggling out of bed, Jessie reflects on the day ahead. It's one of her most intense class days—four different classes, scattered across the campus. She also must put in several hours of work in the college bookstore, where she has a 15-hour-a-week job, and she knows she better get started on her history paper, due next week. And then there's that biology test that she must take this morning.

After a quick shower, Jessie joins the flood of students making their way to classes. She glances at her biology textbook and feels a wave of anxiety flood over her: Will I do well enough? How will I manage to hold down a job and have enough time to study? Will I make friends here? Will it ever feel like home? Will I make my family proud? . . . And underlying them all is a single challenge: *Will I be successful in college?*

Looking Ahead

Whether academic pursuits are a struggle or come easily to you, whether you live on campus or commute, whether you are fresh out of high school or are returning to school many years after high school graduation, college is a challenge. Every one of us has concerns about our capabilities and motivation, and new situations—like starting college—make us wonder how well we'll succeed.

That's where this book comes in. It is designed to help you learn the most effective ways to approach the challenges you encounter not just in college but outside the classroom, too. It will teach you practical strategies, hints, and tips that can lead you to success, all centered around an approach to achieving college success: P.O.W.E.R. Learning.

This book is designed to be useful in a way that is different from other college texts. It presents information in a hands-on format. It's meant to be used—not just read. Write on it, underline words and sentences, use a highlighter, circle key points, and complete the questionnaires right in the book. The more exercises you do, the more you'll get from the book. Remember, this is a book to help you with your course work throughout college. It's a good idea to invest your time here and now. If the learning techniques you master here become second nature, the payoff will be enormous.

This first chapter lays out the basics of P.O.W.E.R. Learning. By the time you finish this chapter, you'll be able to answer these questions:

- **What are the benefits of a college education?**

- **What are the basic principles of P.O.W.E.R. Learning?**

- **How do expert students use P.O.W.E.R. Learning?**

Why Go to College?

Congratulations. You're in college.

But *why*? Although it seems as if it should be easy to answer why you're continuing your education, for most students it's not so simple. The reasons that people go to college vary from the practical ("I want to get a good job"), to the lofty ("I want to learn about people and the world"), to the unreflective ("Why not?—I don't have anything better to do"). Consider your own reasons for attending college, as you complete Try It 1 on page 4.

Surveys of first-year college students show that almost three-quarters say they want to get training for a specific career, land a better job, and make more money (see Figure 1.1).[1] And, in fact, it's not wrong to expect that a college education helps people find better jobs. The average person with a college degree earns about 50 percent more each year than the average person with a

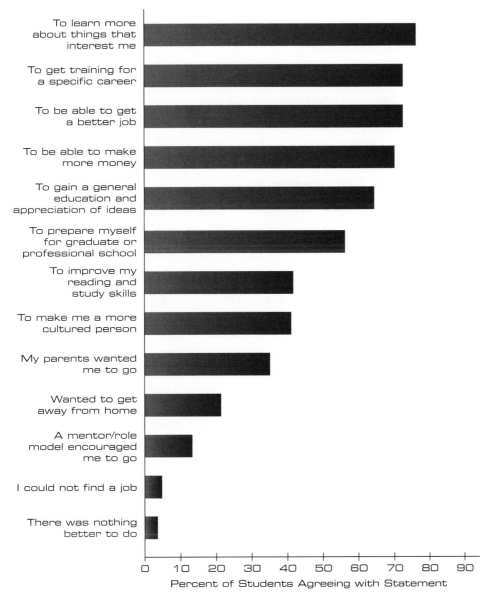

Percent of Students Agreeing with Statement

Figure 1.1

Choosing College

These are the most frequently-cited reasons that first-year college students gave for why they enrolled in college when asked in a national survey.[2]

Try It! 1

Why Am I Going to College?

Place a 1, 2, and 3 by the three most important reasons that you have for attending college:

_____ I want to get a good job when I graduate.

_____ My parents want me to go.

_____ I couldn't find a job.

_____ I want to get away from home.

_____ I want to get a better job.

_____ I want to gain a general education and appreciation of ideas.

_____ I want to improve my reading and study skills.

_____ I want to become a more cultured person.

_____ I want to make more money.

_____ I want to learn more about things that interest me.

_____ A mentor or role model encouraged me to go.

_____ I want to prove to others that I can succeed.

Now consider the following:

- What do your answers tell you about yourself?

- Did you think about these reasons when you were applying to college?

- How do you think your reasons compare with those of other first-year students who are starting college with you?

To Try It online, go to **www.mhhe.com/power**.

high school education only. Furthermore, as jobs become increasingly complex and technologically sophisticated, college will become more and more of a necessity.

But the value of college extends far beyond dollars and cents. Consider these added reasons for pursuing a college education:

- **You'll learn to think and communicate better.** Here's what one student said about his college experience after he graduated: "It's not about what you major in or which classes you take. . . . It's really about learning to think and to communicate. Wherever you end up, you'll need to be able to analyze and solve problems—to figure out what needs to be done and do it."[3]

  Education improves your ability to understand the world as it is now and prepares you to understand it as it will be.

- **You'll be able to better deal with advances in knowledge and technology that are changing the world.** Genetic engineering . . . drugs to reduce forgetfulness . . . computers that respond to our voices. No one knows what the future will hold, but you can prepare for it through a college education. Education can provide you with the intellectual tools that you can apply regardless of the specific situation in which you find yourself.

- **You'll learn to adapt to new situations.** College is a different world from high school. It presents new experiences and new challenges. Your adjustment to the college culture will prepare you for future encounters with new situations.

- **You'll be better prepared to live in a world of diversity.** The racial and ethnic composition of the United States is changing rapidly. Whatever your ethnicity, chances are you'll be working and living with people whose backgrounds, lifestyles, and ways of thinking may be entirely different from your own.

  You won't be prepared for the future unless you understand others and their cultural backgrounds—as well as how your own cultural background affects you.

Civic engagement
Broadly, making contributions to the society and community in which you live

- **You'll learn to lead a life of civic engagement.** In its broadest sense, **civic engagement** involves making contributions to the society and community in which you live. College provides you with the opportunity to become involved in community service activities, doing your part to better the world. On a more personal level, college also allows you to develop the skills involved in acting toward others with **civility**—respectful, courteous behavior.

> "Civilization is the making of civil persons."
>
> John Ruskin, *The Crown of Wild Olive*, 1866

Civility
respectful, courteous behavior

- **You'll make learning a lifelong habit.** Higher education isn't the end of your education. Education will build upon your natural curiosity about the world, and it will make you aware that learning is a rewarding and never-ending journey.

- **You'll understand the meaning of your own contributions to the world.** No matter who you are, you are poised to make your own contributions to society and the world. Higher education provides you with a window to the past, present, and future, and it allows you to understand the significance of your own contributions. Your college education provides you with a compass to discover who you are, where you've been, and where you're going.

Now it's time to introduce you to a process that will help you achieve your goal of attaining a college education, as well as succeeding in life beyond college: P.O.W.E.R. Learning.

P.O.W.E.R. Learning: The Five Key Steps to Achieving Success

P.O.W.E.R. Learning itself is merely an acronym—a word formed from the first letters of a series of steps (see the P.O.W.E.R. Plan below)—that will help you take in, process, and make use of the information you'll acquire in college. It will help you to achieve your goals, both while you are in college and later after you graduate.

Prepare, **O**rganize, **W**ork, **E**valuate, and **R**ethink. That's it. It's a simple framework, but an effective one. Using the systematic framework that P.O.W.E.R. Learning provides will increase your chances of success at any task, from writing a college paper to purchasing the weekly groceries.

Keep this in mind: P.O.W.E.R. Learning isn't a product that you can simply pull down off the bookshelf and use without thinking. P.O.W.E.R. Learning is a process, and you are the only one who can make it succeed. Without your personal investment in the process, P.O.W.E.R. Learning consists of just words on paper.

Relax, though. You already know each of the elements of P.O.W.E.R. Learning. You've graduated from high school and been accepted into college. You've also probably held down a job, had a first date, and registered to vote. Each of these accomplishments required that you use strategies of P.O.W.E.R. Learning. What you'll be doing throughout this book is becoming more aware of these strategies and how they can be used to help you in situations you will encounter in college and beyond.

P repare

Chinese philosopher Lao Tzu said that travelers taking a long journey must begin with a single step.

But before they even take that first step, travelers need to know several things: what their destination is, how they're going to get there, how they'll know when they reach the destination, and what they'll do if they have trouble along the way. In the same way, you need to know where you're headed as you embark on the intellectual journeys involved in college. Whether it be a major, long-term task, such as college attendance, or a more limited activity, such as getting ready to complete a paper due in the near future, you'll need to prepare for the journey. To see this for yourself, complete Try It 2, "How I Enrolled in College."

"Goal setting, as far as I can see it, is simply a state of mind, a way of thinking about things. A goal setter makes sure he accomplishes what he needs to accomplish."

Greg Gottesman, Stanford University[4]

Setting Goals Before we seek to accomplish any task, all of us do some form of planning. The trouble is that most of the time such planning is done without conscious thinking, as if we are on autopilot. The key to success, however, is to make sure that planning is systematic.

The best way to plan systematically is to use goal-setting strategies. In many cases, goals are clear and direct. It's obvious that our goal in washing

Try It! 2

How I Enrolled in College

Academic journeys are similar to other major trips you may have taken, and they require the same sort of preparation. Consider, for instance, the steps you needed to take to enroll in the college you're now attending. Think back to how you proceeded, and write in the first column below as many of the preparatory steps as you can think of, in the order you did them:

Actual Order of Steps I Took to Enroll in College   **Ideal Order**

Now go back and use the second column to number the steps in the most ideal, logical order.

- How closely does this numbering match the order in which you actually accomplished them?

- If you actually did some of the steps in a less-than-ideal order, how did it hinder or help your attainment of the goal of enrolling in college?

To Try It online, go to **www.mhhe.com/power**.

---

dishes is to have the dishes end up clean. We know that our goal at the gas station is to fill the car's tank with gas. We go to the post office to buy stamps and mail letters.

Other goals are not so clear-cut. In fact, often the more important the task, the less obvious are our goals.

Let's consider taking a college course, for example. You probably have several goals for each course you are taking this term. Completing Try It 3 will give you a chance to evaluate them.

What's the best way to set appropriate goals? Here are some guidelines:

- **Set both long-term and short-term goals. Long-term goals** are aims relating to major accomplishments that take some time to achieve. **Short-term goals** are relatively limited steps you would take on the road to accomplishing your long-term goals. For example, one of the primary

Long-term goals
Aims relating to major accomplishments that take some time to achieve

Short-term goals
Relatively limited steps toward the accomplishment of long-term goals

Try It! 3

Course Goals

Think about one of the classes that you are taking this term. List as many goals as you can think of for taking the class in the first column below:

Goals for Class   **Goals in Order of Importance**

_____   _____

_____   _____

_____   _____

_____   _____

_____   _____

_____   _____

The goals you've listed most likely range from the specific ("passing the class with a good grade") to the more general and vague ("becoming educated in the subject matter of the class").

Now, rank order them to determine which are the most important to you. Note that some of these goals may be short-term goals ("get a decent grade") and some represent longer-term goals ("complete all college requirements"). In addition, your goals may be specific ("get an A in the course") or relatively vague ("do well in the class").

Now consider the following:

- What is the difference between those goals that are most important to you and least important to you?

- Are your goals mostly short-term or long-term?

- How specific are your goals?

- What implications might your different goals have for your future success in the course?

 Working in a Group: Compare your goals for the course with those of other students and consider the similarities and differences.

To Try It online, go to **www.mhhe.com/power**.

reasons you're in college is to achieve the long-term goal of getting a degree. But to reach that goal, you have to accomplish a series of short-term goals, such as completing a set of required courses, taking a series of elective courses, and choosing a major. Even these short-term goals can be broken down into shorter-term goals. To complete a required course, for instance, you have to accomplish short-term goals, such as completing a paper, taking several tests, and so on.

- **Recognize that who you are determines your goals.** Goal setting starts with knowing yourself. As you'll see when we focus on understanding yourself in Chapter 3, it is self-knowledge that tells you what is and is not important to you, and this knowledge will help you keep your goals in focus and your motivation up when things get tough.

- **Make goals realistic and attainable.** Someone once said, "A goal without a plan is but a dream." We'd all like to win gold medals at the Olympics or star in rock videos or write best-selling novels. Few of us are likely to achieve such goals.

    Be honest with yourself. There is nothing wrong with having big dreams. But it is important to be realistically aware of all that it takes to achieve them. If our long-term goals are unrealistic and we don't achieve them, the big danger is that we may wrongly reason that we are inept and lack ability and use this as an excuse for giving up. If goals are realistic we can develop a plan to attain them, spurring us on to attain more.

- **State goals in terms of behavior that can be measured against current accomplishments.** Goals should represent some measurable change from a current set of circumstances. We want our behavior to change in some way that can usually be expressed in terms of numbers—to show an increase ("raise my grade point average 10 percent") or a decrease ("reduce wasted time by two hours each week"); or to be maintained ("keep in touch with my out-of-town friends by writing four e-mail messages each month"), developed ("participate in one workshop on critical thinking"), or restricted ("reduce my phone expenses 10 percent by speaking less on the telephone").

- **Be sure goals involve behavior over which you have control.** We all want world peace and an end to poverty. Few of us have the resources or capabilities to bring either about. On the other hand, it is realistic to want to work in small ways to help others, such as by becoming a Big Brother or Big Sister or by volunteering at a local food bank.

- **Take ownership of your goals.** Make sure that the goals you choose are your goals, and not the goals of your parents, teachers, brothers and

Journal Reflections

My School Experiences

Throughout this book, you will be given opportunities to write down your thoughts. These opportunities—called Journal Reflections—can be thought of as journal entries in which you record your reactions to what you have read, your ideas, notes, questions, and concerns. But above all, be honest. If you save these entries and return to them later, you may be surprised at the changes they record over the course of the term.

1. Think of one of the successful experiences you've had so far in your years in school. What was it?

2. What made the experience successful? What did you learn from your success?

3. Think of an unsuccessful experience or failure you had in school. Why did it occur?

4. How could you have prevented it? What did you learn from it?

sisters, or friends. If you're attending college only because others have told you to, and you have no commitment of your own, you'll find it hard to maintain the enthusiasm—not to mention the hard work—required to succeed.

- **Identify how your short-term goals fit with your long-term goals.** Your goals should not be independent of one another. Instead, they should fit together into a larger dream of who you want to be. Every once in a while step back and consider how what you're doing today relates to the kind of person that you would ultimately like to be.

O rganize

By determining where you want to go and expressing your goals in terms that can be measured, you have already made a lot of progress. You might think you're now ready to head out and begin the intellectual trip to student success. But there's another step you must take before you get going.

The second step in P.O.W.E.R. Learning is to organize the tools you'll need to accomplish your goals. Building upon the goal-setting work you've undertaken in the preparation stage, you must now determine the best way to accomplish the goals you've identified.

How do you do this? Suppose you've decided to build a set of bookshelves for one room in your house. Let's say that you've already determined the kind of bookshelves you like and figured out the basic characteristics of the ones you will build (the preparation step in P.O.W.E.R. Learning). The next stage in-

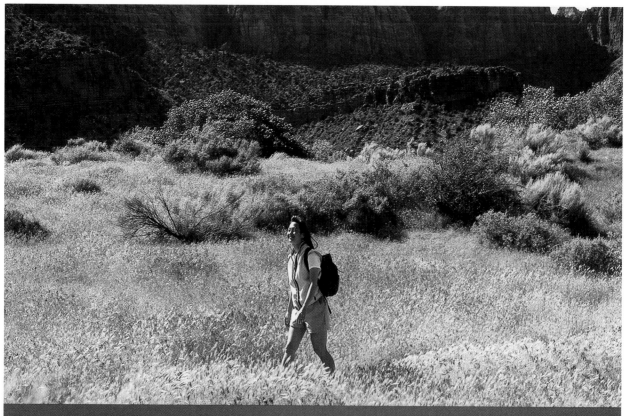

College is not an endpoint, but part of a lifelong educational journey.

volves gathering the necessary tools, buying the wood and other building materials, sorting the construction supplies, and preparing the room for the shelving project—all aspects of organizing for the task.

Similarly, your academic success will hinge to a large degree on the thoroughness of your organization for each academic task that you face. In fact, one of the biggest mistakes that students make in college is plunging into an academic project—studying for a test, writing a paper, completing an in-class assignment—without being organized.

There Are Several Kinds of Organization   On a basic level is organization involving the *physical aspects* of task completion. For instance, you need to ask yourself if you have the appropriate tools, such as pens, paper, and a calculator. If you're using a computer, do you have access to a printer? Is the printer working? Do you have disks to back up your files? Do you have the books and other materials you'll need to complete the assignment? Will the campus bookstore be open if you need anything else? Will the library be open when you need it?

Intellectual organization is even more critical. Intellectual organization is accomplished by considering and reviewing the academic skills that you'll need to successfully complete the task at hand. You are an academic general in command of considerable forces; you will need to make sure your forces—the basic skills you have at your command—are at their peak of readiness.

For example, if you're working on a math assignment, you'll want to consider the basic math skills that you'll need and brush up on them. Just actively thinking about this will help you organize intellectually. Similarly, you'd want to mentally review your understanding of the causes of the American Civil War before beginning an assignment on the Reconstruction period that followed the war.

Why does creating an intellectual organization matter? The answer is that it provides a context for when you actually begin to work. Organizing paves the way for better subsequent learning of new material.

Too often students are in a hurry to meet a deadline and figure they better just dive in and get it done. Organizing can actually save you time, because you're less likely to end up losing your way as you work to complete your task.

Much of this book is devoted to strategies for determining— *before* you begin work on a task—how to develop the intellectual tools for completing an assignment. However, as you'll see, all of these strategies share a common theme: success comes not from a trial-and-error approach but from following a systematic plan for achievement. Of course, this does not mean that there will be no surprises along the way, nor that sheer luck is never a factor in great accomplishments. But it does mean that we often can make our own luck through careful preparation and organization.

 ork

You're ready. The preliminaries are out of the way. You've prepared and you've organized. Now it's time to get started actually doing the work.

In some ways work is the easy part, because—if you conscientiously carried out the preparation and organization stages—you should know exactly where you're headed and what you need to do to get there.

It's not quite so easy, of course. How effectively you'll get down to the business at hand depends on many factors. Some may be out of your control. There may be a power outage that closes down the library or a massive traffic jam that delays your getting to campus. But most factors are—or should be—under your control. Instead of getting down to work, you may find yourself thinking up "useful" things to do—like finally hanging that poster that's been rolled up in a corner for three months—or simply sitting captive in front of the TV. This kind of obstacle to work relates to motivation.

Finding the Motivation to Work
"If only I could get more motivated, I'd do so much better with my _____" (insert *schoolwork, diet, exercising,* or the like).

All of us have said something like this at one time or another. We use the concept of **motivation**—or its lack—to explain why we just don't work hard at a task. But when we do that, we're fooling ourselves. We all have some motivation, that inner power and psychological energy that directs and fuels our behavior. Without any motivation, we'd never get out of bed in the morning.

We've all seen evidence of how strong our motivation can be. Perhaps you're an avid runner and you love to jog in the morning and compete in weekend races. Or maybe your love of music helped you learn to play the guitar, making practicing for hours a pleasure rather than a chore. Or perhaps you're a single mother, juggling work, school, and family, and you get up early every morning to make breakfast for your kids before they go off to school.

All of us are motivated. The key to success in and out of the classroom is to tap into, harness, and direct that motivation.

If we assume that we already have all the motivation we need, P.O.W.E.R. Learning becomes a matter of turning the skills we already possess into a habit. It becomes a matter of redirecting our psychological energies toward the work we wish to accomplish.

In a sense, everything you'll encounter in this book will help you to improve your use of the motivation that you already have. But there's a key concept that underlies the control of motivation—viewing success as a result of effort:

Effort is the cause of success.

Suppose, for example, you've gotten a good grade on your midterm. The instructor beams at you as she hands back your test. How do you feel?

You will undoubtedly be pleased, of course. But at the same time you might think to yourself, "Better not get a swollen head about it. It was just luck. If she'd asked other questions I would have been in trouble." Or perhaps you explain your success by thinking, "Pretty easy test."

If you often think this way—and you can find out if you do by completing Try It 4—you're cheating yourself. Using this kind of reasoning when you succeed, instead of patting yourself on the back and thinking with satisfaction, "All my hard work really paid off," is sure to undermine your future success.

Motivation
The inner power and psychological energy that directs and fuels behavior

Try It! 4

🏂 Personal Styles
Who's in Charge?

To get a sense of your ideas of why things happen to you, check the statement from each of the pairs below that best describes your views:[5]

_____ 1a. In the long run, people get the respect they deserve in this world.

_____ 1b. Unfortunately, an individual's worth often passes unrecognized no matter how hard he or she tries.

_____ 2a. The idea that teachers are unfair to students is nonsense.

_____ 2b. Most students don't realize the extent to which their exam results are influenced by accidental happenings.

_____ 3a. I have often found that what is going to happen will happen.

_____ 3b. Trusting fate has never turned out as well for me as making a decision to take a definite course of action.

_____ 4a. In the case of the well-prepared student, there is rarely if ever such a thing as an unfair exam.

_____ 4b. Many times exam questions tend to be so unrelated to course work that studying is really useless.

_____ 5a. Becoming a success is a matter of hard work; luck has little or nothing to do with it.

_____ 5b. Getting a good job depends mainly on being in the right place at the right time.

_____ 6a. It is not always wise to plan too far ahead because many things turn out to be a matter of good or bad fortune anyhow.

_____ 6b. When I make plans, I am almost certain that I can make them work.

_____ 7a. In my case, getting what I want has little or nothing to do with luck.

_____ 7b. Many times I might just as well decide what to do by flipping a coin.

_____ 8a. Many times I feel that I have little influence over the things that happen to me.

_____ 8b. It is impossible for me to believe that chance or luck plays an important role in my life.

_____ 9a. What happens to me is my own doing.

_____ 9b. Sometimes I feel that I don't have enough control over the direction my life is taking.

_____ 10a. Sometimes I can't understand how teachers arrive at the marks they give.

_____ 10b. There is a direct connection between how hard a person studies and the grades he or she gets.

Scoring: Give yourself one point for each of the following answers and then add up your score:

1. a. 2. a. 3. b. 4. a. 5. a. 6. b. 7. a. 8. b. 9. a. 10. b.

Your total score can range from 0 to 10. The higher your score, the more you believe that you have a strong influence over what happens to you and are in control of your life and your own behavior.

The lower your score, the more you believe that your life is outside of your control and what happens to you is caused by luck or fate.

If you score below 5 on this questionnaire, consider how rethinking your views of the causes of behavior might lead to greater success. To Try It online, go to **www.mhhe.com/power**.

A great deal of psychological research has shown that thinking you have no control over what happens to you sends a powerful and damaging message to your self-esteem—that you are powerless to change things. Just think of how different it feels to say to yourself, "Wow, I worked at it and did it," as compared with "I lucked out" or "It was so easy that anybody could have done well."

In the same way, we can delude ourselves when we try to explain our failures. People who see themselves as the victims of circumstance may tell themselves, "I'm just not smart enough" when they don't do well on an academic task. Or they might say, "Those other students don't have to work five hours a day."

> "The function of the university is not simply to teach bread-winning, or to furnish teachers for the public schools or to be a center of polite society; it is, above all, to be the organ of that fine adjustment between real life and the growing knowledge of life, an adjustment which forms the secret of civilization."
>
> W.E.B. DuBois, *The Souls of Black Folk* (1903), 5

The way in which we view the cause of success and failure is, in fact, directly related to our success. Students who generally see effort and hard work as the reason behind their performance usually do better in college. It's not hard to see why: When they are working on an assignment, they feel that the greater the effort they put forth, the greater their chances of success. So they work harder. They believe that they have control over their success, and if they fail, they believe they can do better in the future.

Here are some tips for keeping your motivation alive, so you can work with your full energy behind you:

- **Take responsibility for your failures—and successes.** When you do poorly on a test, don't blame the teacher, the textbook, or a job that kept you from studying. Analyze the situation, and see how you could have changed what you did to be more successful in the future. At the same time, when you're successful, think of the things you did to bring about that success.

- **Think positively.** Assume that the strengths that you have will allow you to succeed and that, if you have difficulty, you can figure out what to do.

- **Accept that you can't control everything.** Seek to understand which things can be changed and which cannot. You might be able to get an extension on a paper due date, but you are probably not going to be excused from a collegewide requirement.

To further explore the causes of academic success, consider the questions in Try It 5, discussing them with your classmates.

 valuate

"Great, I'm done with the work. Now I can move on."

It's natural to feel relief when you've finished the work necessary to fulfill the basic requirements of an assignment. After all, if you've written the five double-spaced pages required for an assignment, why shouldn't you heave a sigh of relief and just hand your paper in to the instructor?

Try It! 5

Working in a Group
Examining the Causes of Success and Failure

Complete this Try It! while working in a group. First, consider the following situations:

1. Although he studied for a few hours the night before the test, Jack gets a D on a midterm. When he finds out his grade, he is disgusted and says to himself, "I'll probably never do any better in this course. I'd better just blow it off for the rest of the term and put my energies into my other classes."

2. Anne gets an A– on her history exam. She is happy, but when her instructor tells the class that they did well as a group and that the average grade was B+, she decides that she did well only because the test was so easy.

3. Chen gets a C on his first math quiz. Because he didn't do as well as he expected, he vows to perform better the next time. He doubles the amount of time he studies for the next quiz, but still his grade is only slightly higher. Distressed, he considers dropping the class because he thinks that he'll never be successful in math.

Now consider the following questions about each of the situations:

1. What did each student conclude was the main cause of his or her performance?

2. What effect does this conclusion seem to have on the student?

3. Taking an outsider's point of view, what would *you* think was probably the main cause of the student's performance?

4. What advice would you give each student?

Now consider these broader questions:

1. What are the most important reasons why some students are more academically successful in college than others?

2. How much does ability determine success? How much does luck determine success? How much do circumstances determine success?

3. If someone performs poorly on an exam, what are the possible reasons for his or her performance? If someone performs well on an exam, what are the possible reasons for his or her performance? Is it harder to find reasons for good compared with poor performance? Why?

To Try It online, go to **www.mhhe.com/power**.

The answer is that if you stop at this point, you'll almost be guaranteed a mediocre grade. Did Shakespeare dash off the first draft of *Hamlet* and, without another glance, send it off to the Globe Theater for production? Do professional athletes just put in the bare minimum of practice to get ready for a big game? Think of one of your favorite songs. Do you think the composer wrote it in one sitting and then performed it in a concert?

In every case, the answer is no. Even the greatest work does not spring forth as the embodiment of perfection, immediately meeting all the goals of its producer. Consequently, the fourth step in the P.O.W.E.R. process is *evaluation,* which consists of determining how well the work we have produced matches our goals for it. Let's consider some steps to follow in evaluating what you've accomplished:

- **Take a moment to congratulate yourself and feel some satisfaction.** Whether studying for a test, writing a paper, preparing a review sheet, or reading an assignment, you've done something important. You've moved to a spot that's closer to your goal. Maybe you've reached the midpoint of your journey; maybe you're just about where you want to be. Whatever the specific spot you've reached, the fact that you've already prepared, organized, and done the work means that you've successfully navigated through many difficulties.

- **Compare what you've accomplished with the goals you're seeking to achieve.** Think back to the goals, both short-term and long-term, that you're seeking to achieve. How closely does what you've done match what you're aiming to do? Zero in on your short-term goal for the task, and see how close you've come. For instance, if your short-term goal is to complete a statistics problem set with no errors, you'll need to check over the paper carefully to make sure you've made no mistakes.

- **Have an out-of-body experience: Evaluate your accomplishments as if you were a respected teacher from your past.** If you've written a paper, reread it from the perspective of that teacher. If you've completed a worksheet, think about what comments you'd write across the top if you were that teacher.

- **Evaluate what you've done as if you were your current instructor.** Now exchange bodies and minds again. This time, consider what you're doing from the perspective of the instructor who gave you the assignment. How would he or she react to what you've done? Have you followed the assignment to the letter? Is there anything you've missed?

- **Be fair to yourself.** The guidelines for evaluation will help you to determine just how much further work is necessary and, even more important, what work is necessary. But don't go too far: It's as counterproductive to be too hard on yourself as it is to be too easy. Stick to a middle ground, always keeping your final goal in mind.

- **Based on your evaluation, revise your work.** If you're honest with yourself, it's unlikely that your first work will satisfy you. So go back to *Work* and revise what you've done. But don't think of it as a step back: Revisions you make as a consequence of your evaluation bring you closer to your final goal. This is a case where going back moves you forward.

They thought they had it perfect. But they were wrong.

In fact, it was a 1.5 billion dollar mistake—a blunder on a grand scale. The finely ground mirror of the Hubble space telescope, designed to provide an unprecedented glimpse into the vast reaches of the universe, was not so finely ground after all.

Despite an elaborate system of evaluation designed to catch any flaws, there was a tiny blemish in the mirror that was not detected until the telescope had been launched into space and started to send back blurry photographs. By then, it seemed too late to fix the mirror.

Or was it? NASA engineers rethought the problem for months, devising and discarding one potential fix after another. Finally, after bringing a fresh eye to the situation, they formulated a daring solution that involved sending a team of astronauts into space. Once there, a space-walking Mr. Goodwrench would install several new mirrors in the telescope, which could refocus the light and compensate for the original flawed mirror.

Although the engineers could not be certain that the $629 million plan would work, it seemed like a good solution, at least on paper. It was not until the first photos were beamed back to earth, though, that NASA knew their solution was A-OK. These photos were spectacular.

The daring mission to repair the Hubble space telescope was the culmination of months of rethinking how to fix the flaw in the telescope. It worked: A new time-lapse movie of images taken by the telescope showed the seasonal changes on Uranus, as well as other celestial wonders.

It took months of reconsideration before NASA scientists could figure out what went wrong and devise a solution to the problem they faced. Their approach exemplifies—on a grand scale—the final step in P.O.W.E.R. Learning: rethinking.

To *rethink* what you've accomplished earlier means to bring a fresh eye to what you've done. It involves using **critical thinking,** thinking that involves reanalyzing, questioning, and challenging our underlying assumptions. While evaluation means considering how well what we have done matches our initial goals, rethinking means reconsidering not just the outcome of our efforts, but the ideas and the process we've used to get there.

We'll be considering critical thinking throughout this book, examining specific strategies in every chapter. For the moment, the following steps provide a general framework for using critical thinking to rethink what you've accomplished:

Critical thinking
A process involving reanalysis, questioning, and challenge of underlying assumptions

- **Reanalyze, reviewing how you've accomplished the task.** Consider the approach and strategies you've used. What seemed to work best? Do they suggest any alternatives that might work better the next time?

- **Question the outcome.** Take a big-picture look at what you have accomplished. Are you pleased and satisfied? Is there something you've somehow missed?

- **Identify your underlying assumptions; then challenge them.** Consider the assumptions you made in initially approaching the task. Are these underlying assumptions reasonable? If you had used different assumptions, would the result have been similar or different?

Career Connections

P.O.W.E.R.
Learning Meets
the World of
Work

Although the focus of the P.O.W.E.R. Learning system is on developing school success, its applications extend well beyond the classroom. In particular, the principles of P.O.W.E.R. Learning are useful in the world of work, and your ability to use them will provide you with keys to success in the workplace.

Skeptical? In Career Connections boxes in future chapters we'll explore how the principles we're discussing can help you choose an appropriate career and excel in the workplace. For now, though, take a look at the following "help wanted" advertisements, which illustrate the importance of the components of P.O.W.E.R. Learning in the workplace.

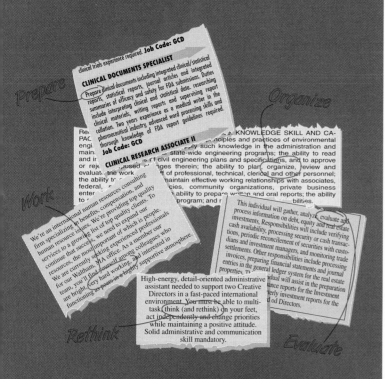

Consider alternatives rejected earlier. You've likely discarded possible strategies and approaches prior to completing your task. Now's the time to think about those approaches once more and determine whether they might have been more appropriate than the road you've followed. It's still not too late to change course.

Completing the Process The rethinking step of P.O.W.E.R. Learning is meant to help you understand your process of work and to improve the final product if necessary. But mostly it is meant to help you grow, to become better at whatever it is you've been doing. Like a painter looking at his or her finished work, you may see a spot here or there to touch up, but don't destroy the canvas. Perfectionism can be as paralyzing as laziness. Keep in mind these key points:

- **Know that there's always another day.** Your future success does not depend on any single assignment, paper, or test. Don't fall victim to self-defeating thoughts such as "If I don't do well, I'll never graduate" or "Everything is riding on this one assignment." Nonsense. There is almost always an opportunity to recover from a failure.

- **Realize that deciding when to stop work is often as hard as getting started.** Knowing when you have put in enough time studying for a test, have revised a paper sufficiently, or have reviewed your answers adequately on a worksheet is as much a key to success as properly preparing. If you've carefully evaluated what you've done and seen that there's a close fit between your goals and your work, it's time to stop work and move on.

Are You Ready for College Success?

Maybe you're asking yourself why you should bother with P.O.W.E.R. Learning and the techniques that will be described in this book. You may believe that because you did OK in high school, you'll be just fine in college without changing the way you did things there.

But college isn't high school.[6]

In high school, you were probably told what you needed to learn from assignments; in college, it will be up to you to read and understand assignments on your own. You'll be tested on material in college that the professor may never once have mentioned in class.

High school teachers monitored your class attendance and graded all homework; in college, professors may not take attendance and may not look at every bit of homework—although they expect you to be in class and do all homework. And while you may be used to frequent tests in high school, in college you may have only a few exams, covering large chunks of material.

In high school, your time was mostly structured by others; in college, you have to manage it yourself. In a broader sense, in high school, you were told what your responsibilities were, while in college you're viewed as an adult who needs to figure out on your own what your responsibilities are. (To think more about the differences between college and high school, complete Try It 6 on page 20.)

Becoming an accomplished student depends on your willingness to accept wholeheartedly the possibility of change in yourself and to embrace success. The techniques for doing this are in this book, but only you can implement them. The road to success may not be simple or direct (see the Speaking of Success interview with Normaris Gonzalez for a glimpse of one student's journey), but there are few goals that are more important in life than attaining a college education.

Try It!
6

What's Different about College?

Read each statement and decide whether it would make most sense coming from a typical high school student or typical college student.[7] Place a check in the appropriate column.

	High School	College
1. My parents or teachers will remind me of my assignments and other responsibilities.	___	___
2. I have to manage my own time instead of "following the crowd" to classes and other places.	___	___
3. I have a lot of choices to make and the freedom to make mistakes.	___	___
4. At least they can't just throw me out if I do poorly.	___	___
5. I don't really need to be that careful about my spending—there's nothing to spend money on anyway.	___	___
6. I have to make sure that I take enough courses and fulfill all my requirements to graduate.	___	___
7. I have a lot of "down time" each day and free time during the week and it's up to me to use it well.	___	___
8. Most of my academic work takes place in class, not outside class on homework, the computer, or the library.	___	___
9. If I forget a homework assignment, the teacher will remind me that it's due.	___	___
10. My teachers are more like experts or scientists giving lectures; they are less focused on reaching me personally.	___	___
11. Teachers help to identify the important material by writing key words or ideas on the board.	___	___
12. If there's a textbook, the teacher may not follow it closely, but I'll still be expected to keep up with the reading on my own.	___	___
13. The teaching is less about facts than concepts.	___	___
14. The teacher will go over in class what I was assigned to read for homework.	___	___
15. Teachers take account of school events and other teachers' assignments when they assign papers or schedule tests.	___	___
16. On tests, students are expected to apply what they've learned to new situations or problems, not just repeat what they've learned.	___	___

Note: The statements that are more accurate for high school are 1, 4, 5, 8, 9, 11, 14, and 15. The others (2, 3, 6, 7, 10, 12, 13, and 16) are more accurate for college. Carefully consider the items that you miscategorized to determine the kind of misconceptions that you might hold, and consider how that might affect your college success.

To Try It online, go to **www.mhhe.com/power**.

Speaking of Success

Name: *Normaris Gonzalez*

Education: *University of Massachusetts at Amherst, BA in psychology; State University of New York at Albany, currently enrolled in counseling psychology doctoral program*

Home: *Albany, New York*

For Normaris Gonzalez, college success did not come easily. The first member of her family to attend college, she faced the typical challenges confronting college students. In addition, her English language skills were not good at first. But through hard work and strong self-motivation, she was able to develop techniques that helped propel her through college and, ultimately, into a doctoral program, where she is studying to become a psychologist.

"It was hard," Gonzalez says about her start in college. "Initially, I had no clue what my instructors were speaking about," she says. "I found myself writing down so many words that I didn't know. It made me anxious not knowing what was going on."

To train herself to understand the unfamiliar words, Gonzalez made constant use of a dictionary, and she also sought out other students to help her along.

"I would meet with my friends and ask not only about the meanings of words, but also about what went on in their classes and what was being taught. I found this sort of buddy

system to be very helpful," she explains.

In addition, Gonzalez would frequently visit her instructors outside of class. Not only did this permit them to get to know her, but it helped her understand what they were presenting in class.

"In some classes I would go to the professor at least once a week and talk about what was going on in the

course," Gonzalez explains. "I always made it clear that I was personally having difficulty, but that I didn't want to be treated differently. It helped open up contact and also made myself noticeable to them."

Being the first of her family to go to college and now to pursue a doctorate is her prime motivation to continue to excel in her studies.

"If there was anyone who motivated me, it was me," she says. "I've always looked within myself to get motivated. I think self-motivation is the rule in college, where you are on your own and have to make many decisions for yourself.

"No one in my family ever went to college. I'm the first to graduate and go to graduate school. I'm also motivated to be a role model. I want to give something to my culture, and allow younger kids to look up to me and say, 'She's Hispanic and she's doing it, so I can too.'"

What are the benefits of a college education?

- The reason first-year college students most often cite for attending college is to get a better job, and college graduates do earn more on average than nongraduates.

- College also provides many other benefits. These include becoming well-educated, understanding the interconnections between different areas of knowledge and our place in history and the world, practicing civic engagement, and understanding diversity.

What are the basic principles of P.O.W.E.R. Learning?

- P.O.W.E.R. Learning is a systematic approach people can easily learn, using abilities they already possess, to acquire successful habits for learning and achieving personal goals.

- P.O.W.E.R. Learning involves preparation, organization, work, evaluation, and rethinking.

How do expert students use P.O.W.E.R. Learning?

- To *prepare,* learners set both long-term and short-term goals, making sure that their goals are realistic, measurable, and under their control—and will lead to their final destination.

- They *organize* the tools they will need to accomplish those goals.

- They get down to *work* on the task at hand. Using their goals as motivation, expert learners also understand that success depends on effort.

- They *evaluate* the work they've done, considering what they have accomplished in comparison with the goals they set for themselves during the preparation stage.

- Finally, they *rethink,* reflecting on the process they've used and taking a fresh look at what they have done.

Key Terms and Concepts

Civic engagement (p. 5)
Civility (p. 5)
Critical thinking (p. 17)
Long-term goals (p. 7)

Motivation (p. 12)
P.O.W.E.R. Learning (p. 6)
Short-term goals (p. 7)

Resources

On Campus

If you are commuting to school, your first "official" encounters on campus are likely to be with representatives of the college's Student Affairs Office or its equivalent. The Student Affairs Office has the goal of maintaining the quality of student life, helping to ensure that students receive the help they need.

If you are living on campus, your first encounter will more likely be with representatives of the residence halls, often called the Residential Life Office. Their job is to help you settle in and orient you to campus. Your residence hall also probably has student residential advisors living on every floor; they can give you an insider's view of college life.

Whomever you encounter during your first days of college, remember that they're there to help you. Don't feel shy about asking questions about what you may expect, how to find things, and what you should be doing. Be sure to seek them out if you are experiencing any difficulties.

In Print

In *The Art of Academic Finesse: How Ordinary Students Achieve Extraordinary Grades* (Nova Press, 1998), Eric Evans provides a first-person account of his journey through college, beginning his career with little promise and ending as an honors graduate.

Melanie and Joseph Sponholz offer a wealth of information on college life from a student's vantage point in *College Companion: Real Students, True Stories, Good Advice* (Random House, 1996).

Finally, to learn more about who your first-year classmates are, take a look at Alexander Astin and colleagues' *The American Freshman: National Norms for Fall 2001* (Higher Education Research Institute, 2000). The book provides a comprehensive look at the attitudes and opinions of first-year college students, based on the results of a national survey.

On the Web

The following sites on the World Wide Web provide the opportunity to extend your learning about the material in this chapter. (Although the Web addresses were accurate at the time the book was printed, check the P.O.W.E.R. Learning website [**www.mhhe.com/power**] for any changes that may have occurred.)

- The Indiana Career and Postsecondary Advancement Center's Info-Series (**icpac.indiana.edu/publicationsinfoseries/biglist.html**) provides information on a variety of useful topics regarding adjustment to college life, including comments by students on their experiences. It covers such topics as where to live, how to select classes, how to study and learn, and much more.

- Columbia University's Teacher's College has posted the U.S. Department of Education's *Preparing Your Child For College: A Resource Guide for Parents* (**eric-web.tc.columbia.edu/families/preparing/general. html**). Though geared toward parents' concerns, the publication offers answers to a host of valuable questions such as "Why attend college?" and "What kinds of jobs are available to college graduates?"

- About College (**www.aboutcollege.com/**) is a commercial site that bills itself as a "complete guide to everything you ever wanted to know about college but didn't know who to ask."

Taking It to the Net

1 Find out what percentage of the population of the United States has received an undergraduate degree. Use the two strategies below. (If you've never used the Internet at all, see Chapter 10 for suggestions that will get you started.)

- Go to Yahoo! (**www.yahoo.com**) and click on the category "Reference." From there, click on "statistics" and then again on "education@." From there, click on "Education census" and then again on "Educational attainment." (This procedure will lead you to **www.census.gov/population/www/socdemo/educ-attn.html**, a page on the site of the U.S. Census Bureau.)

- Searching with keywords will also give you the answer to the question. For example, a search on **www.google.com** will lead you to sites that include data that are derived from the Census Bureau website.

The Census Bureau site provides information about the level of education achieved by people over 25 years of age. Click on "Preliminary data" and examine the chart. How many men have received a bachelor's degree? How many women?

2 Consider the reasons for going to college. The U.S. Department of Education's "Think College" site (**www.ed.gov/offices/OPE/thinkcollege/**) offers various rationales for continuing your education beyond high school. Were you aware of them prior to your enrollment in college?

The Case of . . .

Clueless in Seattle

It was during the second week of classes that the questioning started. Until then, Roger hadn't thought much about his decision to attend a large state college in a Seattle suburb. It had seemed like a good idea, and he was excited when he was accepted, but he couldn't really pinpoint why he was there.

And that was becoming a problem. As he was walking to class, he began to think about all that had happened to him in the last few weeks. First-year orientation . . . meeting his roommate, and trying to deal with his odd neatness . . . enrolling for classes . . . finding his way around campus . . . meeting an overwhelming number of new people, and trying to figure out where he fit in. Everyone else seemed to know what they were doing. Why didn't he?

It was overwhelming. He wanted to run that minute and call his parents and tell them to come pick him up. He needed to sit on the porch where it was familiar and comfortable and not overwhelming and try to figure out what he should do. Nothing seemed to make sense. He began to question his decision to attend college. What was he going to do with his life? The question made him feel even more overwhelmed. Did he really need a college degree? With his computer skills, he could probably get a job right away. Hadn't his father's friend told him that he had a job waiting for him whenever he wanted it? At least then he'd be making money.

Why bother, he thought to himself. What an expense, and what a hassle. For what? He realized, to his surprise, he had no real clue as to why he was in college.

1. What arguments could you provide Roger as to the value of a college education?

2. Do you think that Roger's doubts are common? Do people often attend college without thinking about it very much?

3. What might you suggest that Roger do to help deal with his doubts about the value of college?

4. Why might a student's doubts about the value of college be especially strong during the beginning weeks of college?

5. Do you share any of Roger's concerns about the value of a college education? Do you have additional ones? Did you think carefully about the reasons for attending college before you enrolled?

Making the Most of Your Time

2

As Meadow Baresi stands in the long line at the Dining Commons, she mentally goes over the things she needs to get done during the day: *Review notes for the 8:30 A.M. management quiz . . . work on philosophy paper . . . computer sci class at 11:15 A.M . . . pick up ticket receipts from last night's game . . . work at student affairs office from 1:00 to 4:00 . . . go to library to research philosophy paper.* She has the nagging feeling that there's something else she needs to do, but she can't put her finger on it. She finally gets to the head of the line to pay for her bagel, which she's already half-devoured. Glancing at a clock as she leaves the Commons, she gives up the thought of getting in some last-minute studying for her management quiz. It will be a minor miracle if she even makes it to class on time.

She's been up less than an hour, and already Meadow is running behind schedule.

Looking Ahead

Are your days like Meadow's? Are you constantly trying to cram more activities into less time? Do you feel as if you never have enough time?

You're not alone: Most of us wish we had more time to accomplish the things we need to do. However, some people are a lot better at juggling their time than others. What's their secret?

There is no secret. No one has more than 168 hours a week. The key to success lies in figuring out our priorities and using our time better.

Time management is like juggling a bunch of tennis balls: for most of us, juggling doesn't come naturally, but it is a skill that can be learned. Not all of us will end up perfect jugglers (whether we are juggling tennis balls or time), but, with practice, we can become a lot better at it.

This chapter will give you strategies for improving your time management skills. After first helping you learn to account for the ways you currently use—and misuse—time, it gives you strategies for planning your time, including some ways to deal with the inevitable interruptions and counterproductive personal habits that can sabotage your best intentions.

We also consider techniques for dealing with competing goals. There are special challenges involved in juggling the priorities of college work with other aspects of life, such as child rearing or holding a job.

After reading this chapter, you'll be able to answer these questions:

- **How can I manage my time most effectively?**
- **How can I deal better with surprises and distractions?**
- **How can I balance competing priorities?**

Time for Success

Without looking up from the page, answer this question: What time is it?

Most people are pretty accurate in their answer. And if you don't know for sure, it's very likely that you can find out. There may be a watch on your wrist; there may be a clock on the wall, desk, or computer screen; or maybe you're riding in a car that has a clock in the dashboard.

Even if you don't have a timepiece of some sort nearby, your body keeps its own beat. Humans have an internal clock that regulates the beating of our heart, the pace of our breathing, the discharge of chemicals within our bloodstream, and myriad other bodily functions.

Time is something from which we can't escape. Even if we ignore it, it's still going by, ticking away, second by second, minute by minute, hour by hour. So the main issue in using your time well is, "Who's in charge?" We can allow time to slip by and let it be our enemy. Or we can take control of it and make it our ally.

By taking control of how you spend your time, you'll increase your chances of becoming a more successful student. Perhaps more importantly, the better you are at managing the time you devote to your studies, the more time you will have to spend on your outside interests. (You can get a sense of your own personal "time style" by completing Try It 1.)

The goal of time management is not to schedule every moment so we become pawns of a timetable that governs every waking moment of the day. Instead, the goal is to permit us to make informed choices as to how we use our time. Rather than letting the day slip by, largely without our awareness, the time management procedures we'll discuss can make us better able to harness time for our own ends.

> **"Time ripens all things. No man's born wise."**
>
> Cervantes, *Don Quixote*, 2.4.33, tr. John Ozell

P repare: Learning Where Time Is Going

Before you get somewhere, you need to know where you're starting from and where you want to go. So the first step in improving your time management skills is to figure out how you're managing your time now.

Create a Time Log   "Where did the day go?" If you've ever asked yourself this, one way to figure out where you've spent your time is to create a time log. A **time log** is the most essential tool for improving your use of time.

A time log is simply a record of how you actually have spent your time—including interruptions. It doesn't have to be a second-by-second record of every waking moment, but it should account for blocks of time in increments as short as 15 minutes.

Look at the blank time log in Try It 2 on page 32. As you fill out the log, be specific, indicating not only what you were doing at a given time (for example, "reading history assignment") but also the interruptions that occurred (such as "answered phone twice" or "switched to Internet for 10 minutes").

By looking at how much time you spend doing various activities, you now know where your time goes. How does it match with your perceptions of how you spend your time? Be prepared to be surprised, because most people find

Time log
A record of how one spends one's time

Try It!
1

🏃 Personal Styles
Find Your Time Style

Rate how well each of the statements below describes you. Use this rating scale:

1 = Doesn't describe me at all

2 = Describes me only slightly

3 = Describes me fairly well

4 = Describes me very well

	1	2	3	4
1. I often wake up later than I should.				
2. I am usually late for classes and appointments.				
3. I am always in a rush getting places.				
4. I put off big tasks and assignments till the last minute.				
5. My friends often comment on my lateness.				
6. I am easily interrupted, putting aside what I'm doing for something new.				
7. When I look at a clock, I'm often surprised at how late it is.				
8. I often forget appointments and have to reschedule them.				
9. When faced with a big task, I feel overwhelmed and turn my mind away from it until later.				
10. At the end of the day, I have no idea where the time went.				

Rate yourself by adding up the points you assigned. Use this scale to assess your time style:

10–15 = Very efficient time user

16–20 = Efficient time user

21–30 = Time use needs work

31–40 = Victim of time

To Try It online, go to **www.mhhe.com/power**.

that they're spending time on a lot of activities that just don't matter very much.

Identify the "Black Holes" That Eat Up Your Time
Do you feel like your time often is sucked into a black hole, disappearing without a trace?

We all waste time, spending it on unimportant activities that keep us from doing the things that we should be doing or really want to do. For example, suppose when you're studying you get a phone call from a friend, and you end up speaking with her for an hour. You could have (a) let the phone ring and not answered it; (b) answered, but told your friend you were studying and promised to call her back; or (c) spoken to her, but only for a short while. If you had done any of these things, you would have taken control of the interruption and kept time from sinking into a black hole.

To get a sense of how your time is sucked into black holes, complete Try It 3 on page 34.

Set Your Priorities By this point you should have a good idea of what's taking up your time. But you may not know what you should be doing instead.

To figure out the best use of your time, you need to determine your priorities. **Priorities** are the tasks and activities you need and want to do, rank-ordered from most important to least important. There are no right or wrong priorities; you have to decide for yourself what you wish to accomplish. Maybe spending time on your studies is most important to you, or maybe your top priority is spending time with your family. Only you can decide. Furthermore, what's important to you at this moment may be less of a priority to you next month, next year, or five years from now.

For the purpose of effective time management in college, the best procedure is to start off by identifying priorities for an entire term. What do you need to accomplish? Don't just choose obvious, general goals, such as "passing all my classes." Instead, think about your priorities in terms of specific, measurable activities, such as "studying 10 hours before each chemistry exam." (Look at the example of a priority list in Figure 2.1.)

Write your priorities on the chart in Try It 4 on page 36. After you've filled out the chart, organize it by giving each priority a priority index number from 1 to 3. A "1"

Journal Reflections

Where Does My Time Go?

1. On the typical weekday morning, what time do you wake up? When would you prefer to wake up if you had the choice?

2. Would you characterize yourself as a "morning person," who accomplishes the most in the early morning, or do you see yourself more as a "night person," who is most comfortable doing work in the evenings? What implications does this have for your scheduling of classes and when you do the most work?

3. If a day suddenly contained more than 24 hours, how would it change your life? What would you do with the extra time? Do you think you would accomplish more?

4. Generally speaking, how would you characterize your time management skills? What would be the benefit to you personally if you could manage time more effectively?

"Hello and welcome to the game that'll be put off until tomorrow, but should've been played today."

Try It! 2

Create a Time Log

Keep track of the way you spend your time across seven days on time logs. Insert the amount of time you spend on each activity during each one-hour period for a single day. Do the same thing for every day of the week on separate time logs. (Be sure to make copies of this log before you fill it in for the first day.)

Day of the week and date: _____

	personal care	food	classes	studies	work	recreation	other personal	sleep	other
12:00 A.M. (MIDNIGHT) to 1:00 A.M.									
1:00 A.M. to 2:00 A.M.									
2:00 A.M. to 3:00 A.M.									
3:00 A.M. to 4:00 A.M.									
4:00 A.M. to 5:00 A.M.									
5:00 A.M. to 6:00 A.M.									
6:00 A.M. to 7:00 A.M.									
7:00 A.M. to 8:00 A.M.									
8:00 A.M. to 9:00 A.M.									
9:00 A.M. to 10:00 A.M.									
10:00 A.M. to 11:00 A.M.									
11:00 A.M. to 12:00 P.M. (NOON)									
12:00 P.M. (NOON) to 1:00 P.M.									
1:00 P.M. to 2:00 P.M.									
2:00 P.M. to 3:00 P.M.									
3:00 P.M. to 4:00 P.M.									
4:00 P.M. to 5:00 P.M.									
5:00 P.M. to 6:00 P.M.									
6:00 P.M. to 7:00 P.M.									
7:00 P.M. to 8:00 P.M.									
8:00 P.M. to 9:00 P.M.									
9:00 P.M. to 10:00 P.M.									
10:00 P.M. to 11:00 P.M.									
11:00 P.M. to 12:00 A.M. (MIDNIGHT)									
Total Hours									

Analyze your Log: After you complete your log for a week, analyze how you spend your time according to the major categories on the log. Add up the amount of time you spend on each category. You can also create other broad categories that eat up significant amounts of time.

Now consider the following: (1) What do you spend most of your time on? (2) Are you satisfied with the way that you are using your time? Are there any areas that seem to use up excessive amounts of time? (3) Do you see some simple fix that will allow you to use time more effectively?

 Working in a Group: Compare your use of time during an average week with those of your classmates. What are the major differences and similarities in the use of time?

To Try It online, go to **www.mhhe.com/power**.

represents a priority that absolutely must be done; without it you'll suffer a major setback. For instance, a paper with a fixed due date should receive a "1" for a priority ranking; carving out time to take those guitar lessons you always wanted to take might be ranked a "3" in terms of priority. The important point is to rank order your priorities to reveal what is and is not important to accomplish during the term.

Setting priorities will help you to determine how to make the best use of your time. No one has enough time to complete everything; prioritizing will help you make informed decisions about what you can do to maximize your success.

Identify Your Prime Time   Take a look inward. Do you enthusiastically bound out of bed in the morning, ready to start the day and take on the world? Or is the alarm clock a hated and unwelcomed sound that jars you out of pleasant slumber? Are you the kind of person who is zombielike by 10 at night, or a person who is just beginning to rev up at midnight?

Each of us has our own style based on some inborn body clock. Some of us are at our best in the morning, while others do considerably better at night. Being aware of the time or times of day when you can accomplish your best work will help you plan and schedule your time most effectively. If you're at your worst in the morning, try to schedule easier, less-involving activities for those earlier hours. On the other hand, if morning is the best time for you, schedule activities that require the greatest concentration at that time.

"Time moves slowly, but passes quickly."

Alice Walker, *The Color Purple*

But don't be a slave to your internal time clock. Even night people can function effectively in the morning, just as morning people can accomplish quite a bit in the evening. Don't let your concerns become a self-fulfilling prophecy.

Priorities

The tasks and activities that one needs and wants to do, rank-ordered from most important to least important

Figure 2.1

List of Priorities

Priority	Priority Index
Study for each class at least 30 minutes/day	1
Start each major paper 1 week in advance of due date	2
Hand in each paper on time	1
Review for test starting a week before test date	2
Be on time for job	2
Check in with Mom once a week	3
Work out 3 x/week	3

Try It! 3

Working in a Group
Identify the Black Holes of Time Management

The first 19 items on this list are common problems that prevent us from getting things done.[1] Check off the ones that are problems for you, and indicate whether you have control over them (controllable problems) or they are out of your control (uncontrollable problems).

	Big Problem for Me	Often a Problem	Seldom a Problem	Controllable (C) or Uncontrollable (U)?
1. Telephone interruptions				
2. Drop-in visitors				
3. E-mail interruptions				
4. Hobbies				
5. Mistakes				
6. Inability to say no				
7. Socializing				
8. Snacking				
9. Errands and shopping				
10. Meals				
11. Children's interruptions				
12. Perfectionism				
13. Family appointments				
14. Looking for lost items				
15. Redoing mistakes				
16. Jumping from task to task				
17. Surfing the World Wide Web				
18. Reading newspapers, magazines, recreational books				
19. Car trouble				
20. Other				
21. Other				
22. Other				
23. Other				
24. Other				
25. Other				

Working in a Group: Examine the problems that affect each group member and then discuss these questions: Do time management problems fall into any patterns? Are there problems that at first seem uncontrollable that can actually be controlled? What strategies for dealing with such problems have you used in the past?

To Try It online, go to **www.mhhe.com/power**.

Organize: Mastering the Moment

You now know where you've lost time in the past, and your priority list is telling you where you need to head in the future.

Now for the present. You've reached the point where you can organize yourself to take control of your time. Here's what you'll need:

- **A master calendar.** The **master calendar** shows all the weeks of the term on one page. You don't need to buy one; you can make it easily enough yourself. It need not be great art; a rough version will do. The important point is that it must include every week of the term and seven days per week. (See the example of a master calendar on page 37.)

- **A weekly timetable.** The **weekly timetable** is a master grid with the days of the week across the top and the hours, from 6:00 A.M. to midnight, along the side. This will permit you to write in all your regularly scheduled activities, as well as one-time appointments when they arise. (A blank weekly timetable is provided opposite the inside front cover of this book.)

- **A daily to-do list.** The **daily to-do list** can be written on a small, portable calendar that includes a separate page for each day of the week. Or it can simply be a small notebook, with a separate sheet of paper for every day of the week. Whatever form your daily to-do list takes, make sure it's portable, because you'll need to keep it with you all the time.

The basic organizational task you face is filling in these three schedules. You'll need at least an hour to do this, so set the time aside. In addition, there will be some repetition across the three schedules, and the task may seem a bit tedious. *But every minute you invest now in organizing your time will pay off in hours that you will save in the future.*

Follow these steps in completing your schedule:

- **Start with the master calendar, which shows all the weeks of the term on one page.** In most classes, you'll receive a syllabus, a course outline that explains what the course is all about. Traditionally, a syllabus includes course assignments and their due dates, and the schedule for tests that will be given during the term. Write on the master calendar every assignment you have, noting it on the date that it is due. If the instructor hasn't included due dates, ask; he or she probably already knows, or at least has a general idea, of the week that various assignments will be due. Pencil in tentative assignments on the appropriate date.

Master calendar
A schedule showing the weeks of a longer time period, such as a college term, with all assignments and important activities noted on it

Weekly timetable
A schedule showing all regular, prescheduled activities due to occur in the week, together with one-time events and commitments

Daily to-do list
A schedule showing the tasks, activities, and appointments due to occur during the day

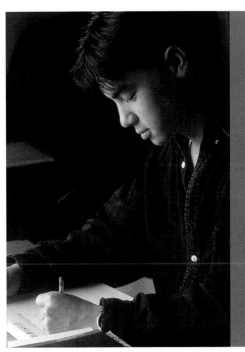

Each of us has an internal body clock that helps govern when we feel most alert. Becoming aware of your own body clock can help you to schedule study sessions at times when you're able to work at peak efficiency.

Try It!

4

Set Priorities

Set your priorities for the term. They may include getting to class on time, finishing papers and assignments by their due dates, finding a part-time job that fits your schedule, and reading every assignment before the class for which it is due. To get started, list priorities in any order. Be sure to consider priorities relating to your school work, other work, family, social obligations, and health. After you list them, assign a number to each one indicating its level—giving a "1" to the highest priority items, a "2" to medium priority items, and a "3" to the items with the lowest priority.

List of Priorities

Priority	Priority Index

Now redo your list, putting your number 1s first, followed by as many of your number 2s and 3s to which you feel you can reasonably commit.

Final List of Priorities

Priority
1.
2.
3.
4.
5.
6.
7.
8.
9.
10.
11.
12.

Now consider the following:

- What does this list tell you about your greatest priorities? Are they centered around school, friends and family, jobs, or some other aspect of your life?

- Do you have so many "1" priorities that they will be difficult or impossible to accomplish successfully? How could you go back to your list and trim it down even more?

- What does this listing of priorities suggest about how successful you'll be during the upcoming term?

To Try It online, go to **www.mhhe.com/power**.

M	T	W	TH	F	SA	S
Sept. 7	8	9 Classes Start	10	11	12 Camping →	13
14	Add/drop 15 ends	16	English 17 short paper due	18	19	20
21	22	23	English 24 short paper due	Russian 25 quiz	26	27
28	29 Psych exam	30	OCT 1 Music quiz English short paper due	1st Psych 2 paper due	3	4
5	Music 6 paper due	7	English 8 short paper due	Russian 9 quiz	10	11
12	13	14	Music quiz 15 English short paper due	16	17	18
First-yr 19 seminar journal due	20	21 Psych exam	English 22 short paper due Dad's bd—call	Theater 23 Midterm	24 Bartending job	25
Russian 26 midterm exam	English 27 midterm exam	28	Eng-short 29 paper due Music quiz	30	31	NOV 1
2	3	4	English 5 short paper due	Russian 6 short paper due	7	8 Darcey's Wedding!
9	10	Holiday— 11 Veteran's Day	Eng-short 12 paper due Music quiz	Russian 13 quiz Psych exam	14	15
First-yr 16 seminar group project due	17	18 Preregistration for next semester	English 19 short paper due	20	21	22
23	24	25	26 Thanksgiving	27 No Classes!	28	29
30	DEC 1 Music paper due	2	English 3 short paper due	Russian 4 quiz	5	6
First-yr 7 seminar final journal due	8	9	Music 10 quiz	Theater 11 project due! Psych exam Last day of class!!	12	13
English 14 final exam	Theater 15 final exam Russian final exam	16	Psych 17 final exam	Music exam 18 MY birthday!	19	20
21	22	23	24	25 Xmas	26	27

Don't put only assignments on the master calendar. Also include important activities from your personal life, drawn from your list of priorities. For instance, if you're involved in a club that is bringing a guest speaker to campus, mark down the date of the event. Finally, schedule some free time—time when you promise yourself you will do something that is just plain fun. Consider these days to be written in stone—promise yourself that you won't use them for anything else except for something enjoyable.

You now have a good idea of what the term has in store for you. In most cases, the first few weeks have few assignments or tests. But as the term rolls on—particularly around the middle and end of the term—things will get more demanding. The message you should take from this: *Use the off-peak periods to get a head start on future assignments.*

Completing a master schedule also may help you head off disaster before it occurs. Suppose, for instance, you find that six weeks in the future you have two papers due and three tests—all in the same week!

After cursing your bad luck, it's time to take action. Begin to think of strategies for managing the situation, such as working on the papers or studying in advance. You might also try to change some due dates. Instructors are far more receptive to requests for extensions on papers if the requests are made well in advance. Similarly, it might be possible to take a test later—or earlier—if you make prior arrangements.

- **Now move to the weekly timetable provided in Figure 2.2.** Fill in the times of all your fixed, prescheduled activities—the times that your classes meet, when you have to be at work, the times you have to pick up your child at day care, and any other recurring appointments.

Once you've filled in the weekly timetable, as in the sample shown in Figure 2.3, you get a bare-bones picture of the average week. You will still need to take into account the specific activities that are required to complete the assignments on the master calendar.

To move from your "average" week to specific weeks, make photocopies of the weekly timetable that now contains your fixed appointments. Make enough copies for every week of the term. On each copy write the week number of the term and the specific dates it covers.

Using your master calendar, add assignment due dates, tests, and any other activities on the appropriate days of the week. Then pencil in blocks of time necessary to prepare for those events.

How much time should you allocate for schoolwork? One very rough rule of thumb holds that every one hour that you spend in class requires, on average, two hours of study outside of class to earn a B and three hours of study outside of class to earn an A. Do the arithmetic: If you are taking 15 credits (with each credit equivalent to an hour of class per week), you'll need to plan for 30 hours of studying each week to earn a B average—an intimidating amount of time. Of course, the amount of time you must allocate to a specific class will vary from week to week, depending on what is happening in the class.

For example, if you estimate that you'll need five hours of study for a midterm exam in a certain class, pencil in those hours. Don't set up a single block of five hours. People remember best when their studying is spread out over shorter periods rather than attempted in one long block of time. Besides, it will probably be hard to find a block of five straight hours on your weekly calendar.

Similarly, if you need to write a paper that's due on a certain date, you can block out the different stages of the writing process that we'll describe in Chapter 7. You'll need to estimate how much time each stage will take, but you probably have a pretty good idea from previous papers you've written.

Weekly Timetable

Week of: _____   **Week #** _____

	Mon	Tues	Wed	Thurs	Fri	Sat	Sun
6–7 AM							
7–8 AM							
8–9 AM							
9–10 AM							
10–11 AM							
11–12 (noon)							
12 (noon)–1 PM							
1–2 PM							
2–3 PM							
3–4 PM							
4–5 PM							
5–6 PM							
6–7 PM							
7–8 PM							
8–9 PM							
9–10 PM							
10–11 PM							
11 PM–12 (midnight)							

Figure 2.2

A Weekly Timetable
Make a single copy of this blank timetable or the timetable that is printed on the inside front cover of the book. (You can also use similar timetables that are found in online sites such as **www.calendar.yahoo.com.**) Then fill in your regular, predictable time commitments.

Next, make as many copies as you need to cover each week of the term. Then, for each week, fill in the date on the left and the number of the week in the term on the right, and add in your irregular commitments.

Some classes may need only a few hours of study in a given week. With good luck, heavy weeks in one class will be compensated for by lighter weeks in others.

Keep in mind that estimates are just that: estimates. Don't think of them as set in stone. Mark them on your weekly calendar in pencil, not pen, so you can adjust them if necessary.

But remember: It's also crucial not to overschedule yourself. You'll still need time to eat, to talk with your friends, to spend time with your family, and to enjoy yourself in general. If you find that your life is completely filled with things that you feel you must do to survive and that there is no room for fun, then take a step back and cut out something to

Figure 2.3

A Sample Completed
Weekly Timetable

Weekly Timetable

Week of: ___9/28___

Week # ___3___

	Mon	Tues	Wed	Thurs	Fri	Sat	Sun
6–7 AM							
7–8 AM							
8–9 AM							
9–10 AM	9...05 Psych	9...05 Music	9...05 Psych	9...05 Music	9...05 Psych		
10–11 AM							
11–12 AM		11...15 English		11...15 English			
12 (noon)– 1 PM	12...20 Theater		12...20 Theater		12...20 Theater		
1–2 PM							
2–3 PM							
3–4 PM	3:00 Russian		3:00 Russian		3:00 Russian		
4–5 PM	First-year seminar	Work		Work			
5–6 PM							
6–7 PM							
7–8 PM							
8–9 PM							
9–10 PM							
10–11 PM							
11 PM– 12 (midnight)							

make some time for yourself in your daily schedule. Finding time for yourself is as important as carving out time for what others want you to do. Besides, if you are overworked, you're likely to "find" the time by guiltily goofing off without really setting aside the time and enjoying it.

- **If you've taken each of the previous steps, you're now in a position to work on the final step of organization for successful time management: completing your daily to-do list.**

  Unlike the master calendar and weekly timetable—both of which you develop at the beginning of the term—complete your daily to-do list just one day ahead of time, preferably at the end of the day.

List all the things that you intend to do during the next day, and their priority. Start with the things you know you *must* do and which have fixed times, such as classes, work schedules, and appointments. These are your first priority items. Then add in the other things that you *should* accomplish, such as an hour of study for an upcoming test, working on research for an upcoming paper, or finishing up a lab report. Finally, list things that are lower priority but enjoyable, setting aside time for a run or a walk, for example.

Don't schedule every single minute of the day. That would be counterproductive, and you'd end up feeling like you'd failed if you deviated from your schedule. Instead, think of your daily to-do list as a path through a forest. If you were hiking, you would allow yourself to deviate from the path, occasionally venturing onto side tracks when they looked interesting. But you'd also be keeping tabs on your direction so you end up where you need to be at the end and not miles away from your car or home.

Like the sample daily to-do list that follows, include a column to check or cross off after you've completed an activity. There's something very satisfying in acknowledging what you have accomplished.

W ork: Controlling Time

You're in luck: There is no work to time management—or at least not much more than you've already done. The work of time management is to follow the schedules that you've prepared and organized. But that doesn't mean it will be easy. Our lives are filled with surprises: Things take longer than we've

To-Do List for _____ (date)		
Item	**Priority** 1 = highest 2 = medium 3 = lowest	**✓**
Call Chris to get English notes	1	✓
Meet with Prof. Hernandez	1	✓
Review Russian	1	✓
Work on outline for psych paper	2	✓
Return books to library	2	
Call Nettie	2	✓
Set up meeting with music group	2	
Meet Deena	2	
Do laundry	3	

planned. A friend we haven't spoken to in a while calls to chat, and it seems rude to say that we don't have time to talk. A crisis occurs; buses are late; computers break down; kids get sick.

The difference between effective time management and time management that doesn't work lies in how well you deal with the inevitable surprises.

There are several ways to take control of your days and permit yourself to follow your intended schedule:

- **Just say no.** You don't have to agree to every request and every favor that others ask of you. You're not a bad person if you refuse to do something that will eat up your time and prevent you from accomplishing your goals.

  Suppose, for example, a friend sees you in the library and asks to borrow the notes from a class that she missed yesterday and that you attended. It's not an unreasonable request. Here's the problem, though: You don't have your notebook with you, and you'd have to stop by your house to pick it up.

  Think through what the request entails. *It may be only 10 minutes to your house, but it's another 10 minutes back. That's 20 minutes. And then there's the time that you'll spend meeting her to give her the notes. And then the time it takes to meet her again, once she's copied the notes. Or suppose you decide to wait while she copies them. Overall, you may end up losing an hour.*

  The solution? You should probably say no to the immediate request. It's not unreasonable to tell your friend that you don't have the time today to get your notebook. You don't have to refuse her completely. She could stop by your house in the evening to pick up the notes, or you could bring them with you the next day. In short, there are ways to accomplish the goal of helping out your friend without wasting time and sabotaging your schedule.

- **Get away from it all.** Go to the library. Lock yourself into your bedroom. Find an out-of-the-way unused classroom.

  Any of these places can serve to isolate you from everyday distractions and thereby permit you to work on the tasks that you wish to complete. Try to adopt a particular spot as your own, such as a corner desk in a secluded nook in the library. If you use it enough, your body and mind will automatically get into study mode as soon as you seat yourself at it.

- **Enjoy the sounds of silence.** Although many students insist they accomplish most while a television, radio, or CD is playing, scientific studies suggest otherwise: We are able to concentrate most when our environment is silent. So even if you're sure you work best with a soundtrack playing, experiment and work in silence for a few days. You may find that you get more done in less time than you would in a more distracting environment.

- **Take control of your communications.** The telephone, e-mail, regular mail. Who doesn't love to receive messages from others?

We may not control when communications arrive, but we can make the message wait until we are ready to receive it. Telephone calls can be stored on answering machines or voice-mail systems; e-mail can be saved on a computer; and regular mail can sit in a mailbox.

- **Let your fingers do the walking.** As an old telephone company advertisement for the yellow pages says, Let your fingers do the walking. Many things can be done over the phone—or via e-mail or voice mail—rather than in person.

- **Expect the unexpected.** Interruptions and crises, minor and major, can't be eliminated. However, they can be prepared for.

  How is it possible to plan for surprises? Though it may still be too early in the term to get a clear picture of what sorts of unanticipated events you'll encounter, you should keep an eye out for patterns. Perhaps one instructor routinely makes surprise assignments that aren't listed on the syllabus. Maybe you're asked to work extra hours on the weekends because someone doesn't show up and you have to work overtime.

  You'll never be able to escape from unexpected interruptions and surprises that require your attention. But by trying to anticipate them in advance, and thinking about how you'll react to them, you'll be positioning yourself to react more effectively when they do occur.

- **Combat procrastination.** Procrastination is like a microscopic parasite on your day, invisible to the naked eye, but eating up your time nonetheless.

  It's 10:30 A.M. You've just come out of your German class. You know that there's going to be a test next week, and you've planned to go over the flash cards you made up last night. It's right there in your schedule: "10:30 A.M.—study German vocabulary." But you're thirsty after sitting in class, so you decide to go and buy yourself something to drink.

  As you head into the snack bar, you pass by the campus store, and you think about how you need to buy a couple of pens. After finding the kind of pen you like, you go to the checkout line. You pass by a rack of magazines, and, after leafing through a few, decide to purchase one. You can read it while you have your drink. You make your way to the snack bar, buy your soda, and sip it as you read the magazine.

  Suddenly, nearly a half-hour has gone by. Because so much time has passed, you decide that it won't be worth it to start studying your German vocabulary. So you spend a little more time reading the magazine and then head off to your next class, which is at 11:00 A.M.

  You can't control interruptions and crises that are foisted upon you by others. But even when no one else is throwing interruptions at us, we make up our own. **Procrastination,** the habit of putting off and delaying tasks that are to be accomplished, is a problem that many of us face. To identify whether you are a procrastinator, find your "Procrastination Quotient" (see Try It 5, page 44).

One antidote to procrastination is working in a study group. You'll be motivated by the presence of others who face the same challenges and assignments that you do.

Procrastination
The habit of putting off and delaying tasks that are to be accomplished

Try It!
5

Find Your Procrastination Quotient

Do you procrastinate?[2] To find out, circle the number that best applies for each question using the following scale:

Strongly agree   4   3   2   1   **Strongly disagree**

1. I invent reasons and look for excuses for not acting on a problem.

Strongly agree   4   3   2   1   **Strongly disagree**

2. It takes pressure to get me to work on difficult assignments.

Strongly agree   4   3   2   1   **Strongly disagree**

3. I take half measures which will avoid or delay unpleasant or difficult tasks.

Strongly agree   4   3   2   1   **Strongly disagree**

4. I face too many interruptions and crises that interfere with accomplishing my major goals.

Strongly agree   4   3   2   1   **Strongly disagree**

5. I sometimes neglect to carry out important tasks.

Strongly agree   4   3   2   1   **Strongly disagree**

6. I schedule big assignments too late to get them done as well as I know I could.

Strongly agree   4   3   2   1   **Strongly disagree**

7. I'm sometimes too tired to do the work I need to do.

Strongly agree   4   3   2   1   **Strongly disagree**

8. I start new tasks before I finish old ones.

Strongly agree   4   3   2   1   **Strongly disagree**

9. When I work in groups, I try to get other people to finish what I don't.

Strongly agree   4   3   2   1   **Strongly disagree**

10. I put off tasks that I really don't want to do but know that I must do.

Strongly agree   4   3   2   1   **Strongly disagree**

Scoring: Total the numbers you have circled. If the score is below 20, you are not a chronic procrastinator and you probably have only an occasional problem. If your score is 21–30, you have a minor problem with procrastination. If your score is above 30, you procrastinate quite often and should work on breaking the habit.

Now, consider the following:

- If you do procrastinate often, why do you think you do it?

- Are there particular subjects or classes or kinds of assignments that you are more likely to procrastinate on?

 Working in a Group: Think about the last time you procrastinated. Describe it as completely as you can. What was the task? What did you do rather than doing what needed to be done? What could you have done to avoid procrastinating in this situation? Ask others what strategy they might suggest for avoiding procrastinating.

To Try It online, go to **www.mhhe.com/power**.

If you find yourself procrastinating, several steps can help you:

Break large tasks into small ones. People often procrastinate because a task they're seeking to accomplish appears overwhelming. If writing a 15-page paper seems nearly impossible, think about writing a series of five 3-page papers. If reading a 750-page book seems impossible, think of it as reading several 250-page books.

Start with the easiest and simplest part of a task, and then do the harder parts. Succeeding initially on the easy parts can make the harder parts of a task less daunting—and make you less apt to procrastinate in completing the task.

Work with others. Just being in the same physical location with others can motivate you sufficiently to accomplish tasks that you consider unpleasant and on which you might be tempted to procrastinate. For instance, studying vocabulary words can be made easier if you plan a study session with several of your classmates. Beware, though—if you spend too much time socializing, you lower the likelihood of success.

Keep the costs of procrastination in mind. Procrastination doesn't just result in delay; it may also make the task harder than it would have been if you hadn't procrastinated. Not only will you ultimately have less time to complete the task, but you may also have to do it so quickly that its quality may be diminished. In the worst scenario, you won't even be able to finish it at all.

> "I had a friend who was concentrating in pre-med. He put off studying for his chem midterm until 10 P.M. the night before, spending his time instead at the movies and the campus hang-out. After bombing the exam, he told us he did not have enough time to study. Basically, he gave himself an excuse to fail."
>
> Thom McDade, Pomona College[3]

- **Balancing school and family demands.** If you are a full-time student and full-time caregiver for children, time management is especially challenging. Not only do children demand—and deserve—substantial quantities of time, but juggling school and family obligations can prove to be more than a full-time job. There are some specific strategies that can help, however:

    Provide activities for your children. Kids enjoy doing things on their own for part of the day. Plan activities that will keep them happily occupied while you're doing schoolwork.

    Make spending time with your children a priority. Carve out "free play" time for your kids. Even 20 minutes of good time devoted to your children will give all of you—you and them—a lift. No matter how busy you are, you owe it to your children—and yourself—to spend time as a family.

    Enlist your children's help. Children love to play adult so, if they're old enough, ask them to help you study. Maybe they can help you clear a space to study. Perhaps you can give them "assignments" that they can work on while you're working on your assignments.

Encourage your children to invite friends over to play. Some children can remain occupied for hours if they have a playmate.

Use television appropriately. Television viewing is not all bad, and some shows and videos can be not just engaging but also educational. The trick is to pick and choose what your children watch. *The Magic Schoolbus, Sesame Street,* and videos of children's classics, for example, can, for an hour or so, be a worthwhile way for children to spend their time while you study.

Find the best child care or baby sitters that you can. The better the care your children are getting, the better you'll be able to concentrate on your schoolwork. You may still feel guilty that you're not with your children as much as you'd like, but accept that guilt. Remember, your attendance in college builds a better future for your children.

Accept that studying will be harder with kids around. It may take you longer to study, and your concentration may suffer from the noise that kids make. But remind yourself what that noise represents: the growth and development of someone that you love. One day your children will be grown, and without a doubt there will be times that you'll miss their high level of energy and activity.

- **Balancing school and work demands.** Juggling school and a job can be exhausting. Not only must you manage your time to complete your schoolwork, but in many cases you'll also face time management demands while you are on the job. Here are some tips to help you keep everything in balance:

Make to-do lists for work, just as you would for your schoolwork. In fact, all the time management strategies that we've discussed can be applied to on-the-job tasks.

If you have slack time on the job, get some studying done. Of course, you should never do schoolwork without your employer's permission. If you don't get permission, you may jeopardize your job.

Ask your employer about flextime. If your job allows it, you may be able to set your own hours, within reason, as long as the work gets done. If this is an option for you, use it. Although it may create more time management challenges for you than would a job with set hours, it also provides you with more flexibility.

Accept new responsibilities carefully. If you've barely been keeping up with the demands of work and school, don't automatically accept new job responsibilities without carefully evaluating how they fit with your long-term priorities. If your job is temporary and you're not planning to stay, you might want to respectfully decline substantial new duties or an increase in the number of hours you work. On the other hand, if you plan to continue in the job once you're done with school, then accepting new responsibilities may be more reasonable.

PREPARE

Learn where time is going

ORGANIZE

Use a master calendar, weekly timetable, and daily to-do list

WORK

Follow the schedules you've put together

EVALUATE

Keep track of your short-term and long-term accomplishments

RETHINK

Reflect on your personal style of time management

P.O.W.E.R. Plan

Always keep in mind why you're working. If you're working because it's your sole means of support, you're in a very different position from someone who is working to earn a bit of extra money for luxuries. Remember what your priorities are. In some cases, school should always come first; in others, your job may have to come first, at least some of the time. Whatever you decide, make sure it's a thoughtful decision, based on an evaluation of your long-term priorities.

E valuate: Checking Your Time

Evaluating how you use your time is pretty straightforward: You either accomplished what you intended to do in a given period, or you didn't. Did you check off all the items on your daily to-do list? If you go over your list at the end of every day, not only will you know how successful your time management efforts have been, but you will also be able to incorporate any activities you missed into the next day's to-do list.

> "Our costliest expenditure is time."
>
> Theophrastus, quoted in Diogenes Laertius' *Lives and Opinions of Eminent Philosophers,* tr. R.D. Hicks

The check-off is important because it provides an objective record of what you have accomplished on a given day. Just as important, it provides you with concrete reinforcement for completing the task. As we have noted, there are few things more satisfying than gazing at a to-do list with a significant number of check marks.

Of course, you won't always accomplish every item on your to-do list. That's not surprising, nor even particularly bad, especially if you've included some second- and third-level priorities that you don't absolutely have to accomplish and that you may not really have expected you'd have time for anyway.

R ethink: Reflecting on Your Personal Style of Time Management

At the end of the day, after you've evaluated how well you've followed your time management plan and how much you've accomplished, it's time to rethink where you are. Maybe you've accomplished everything you set out to do, and every task for the day is completed, and every item on your to-do list has a check mark next to it.

Or maybe you have the opposite result. Your day has been a shambles, and you feel as if nothing has been accomplished. Because of a constant series of interruptions and chance events, you've been unable to make headway on your list.

Or—most likely—you find yourself somewhere between these two extremes. Some tasks got done, while others are still hanging over you. Now is the time to rethink in a broad sense how you manage your time by doing the following:

Reconsider Your Personal Style of Time Management We've outlined one method of time management (summarized in the P.O.W.E.R. Plan at the left). Although it works well for most people, it isn't

Career Connections

Taking a Long-Term View of Time

In considering different careers, it is important to consider the length of time it takes to prepare for them. Every profession has a different set of educational and other preparatory requirements, and in order to have informed career goals, it is necessary to determine the kind of things you need to do to prepare.

One of the most effective ways of comparing careers is to construct a career timeline that lists the steps you'll need to take to prepare for a particular career. Start off by considering what (if anything) you'll need to do in the first year of college. Take into account the preparatory steps for each career you wish to compare, including the kind of courses you'll need to take, the educational and professional requirements that you'll need to fulfill, and any internships or residencies you will need. Different careers may have very different timelines.

Obviously your plan will change as your interests become more firm. The idea is not to identify a rigid path for yourself but to begin the process of understanding what it takes to enter various professions. The more knowledge you have, the greater your ability to make wise choices.

for everyone. Some people just can't bring themselves to be so structured and scheduled. They feel hemmed in by to-do lists.

If you're one of those people, fine. You don't need to follow the suggestions presented in this chapter exactly. In fact, if you go to your college bookstore, you'll find lots of other aids to time management. Many publishing companies produce elaborate planners, such as Day-Timer, and software companies produce computerized time management software, such as Microsoft's Outlook (see the Resources section at the end of this chapter). Some people use high-tech devices such as Palm Pilots or online websites like **www. calendar.yahoo.com**.

However you choose to manage your time, the important thing is to do so consistently. And remember that whatever approach to time management you take, it will work best if it is compatible with your own personal values and strengths. Keep experimenting until you find an approach that works for you.

Consider Doing Less If you keep falling behind, do less. There are only 24 hours in the day, and we need to sleep for about a third of the time. In the remaining hours, it is simply impossible to carry a full load of classes and work full-time and care for a child and still have some time left to have a normal life.

Consequently, if you consistently fall behind in your work, it may be that you are just doing too much. Reassess your goals and your priorities, and make choices. Determine what is most important to you. It's better to accomplish less, if it is accomplished well, than to accomplish more, but poorly.

Do More Although it is a problem that many of us would envy, some people have too much time on their hands. Their classes may not be too demanding, or work demands may suddenly slacken off. If this happens to you, take advantage of your time. For example, you might use the extra time to simply relax and enjoy your more unhurried existence. There is a good bit to be said for having time to let your thoughts wander. We need to take time out to enjoy our friends, admire the flowers in the park, exercise, consider the spiritual side of our lives, and the like.

On the other hand, if you consistently have more time than you know what to do with, reflect on what you want to accomplish and add some activities

Speaking of Success

Name: Kenisha Creary
Education: University of Hartford
Home: Hartford, Connecticut

In spite of having to drop out of college due to financial difficulties and the responsibilities of single parenthood, Kenisha Creary never lost her vision of completing college and eventually studying law.

After a few years, she was able to get back on track toward her goals. "I definitely knew I wanted to go back to school," she said. "It's where my heart is. I'm living my dream," she said.

Time is of the essence for Creary, who not only takes care of her young daughter, but is also fully involved with studies, tutoring, school activities, and work. She has even done a stint as an intern in the office of the Secretary of State.

"My school schedule is from 8:30 A.M. to 5 P.M., and from 5:30 to 10 P.M. I go to work," Creary said. "My studying is basically done from 11:00 at night to about 2:00 and sometimes

3:00 in the morning. But my schedule varies according to my classes and what is required."

Because of her tight schedule, Creary says that she prioritizes her work based on what needs to be done and takes advantage of every spare minute.

"If I have a paper due, the research and writing come before everything else. Reading assignments will come last," she said. "One thing I always do is to review my notes on a daily basis since I have so little time to study. If my class ends at 11:30 and the next one is at 11:45, I take the 15 minutes between classes to study. Whether I'm eating, at school, or even at the doctor's office, I always have my books with me.

"I'm a pretty good note taker," Creary explained. "In addition, I always take advantage of faculty office hours. They have helped me educationally, personally, and professionally."

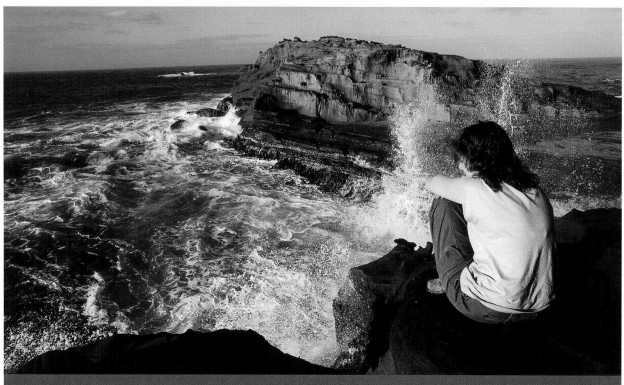
Managing your time effectively will allow you to spend more of it doing the things that are important to you.

that help you reach your goals. For example, consider becoming involved in an extracurricular activity. Engage in community service, volunteering your time to the community. Consider taking an extra course during the next term.

But whatever you decide to do, make it a decision. Don't let the time slip away. Once it's gone, it's gone forever.

Looking *Back*

How can I manage my time most effectively?

- Decide to take control of your time.
- Become aware of the way you use your time now.
- Set clear priorities.
- Use such time management tools as a master calendar, weekly timetable, and a daily to-do list.

How can I deal better with surprises and distractions?

- Deal with surprises by saying no, getting away from it all, working in silence, taking control of communications, using the telephone to conduct transactions, and leaving slack in the schedule to accommodate the unexpected.

- Avoid procrastination by breaking large tasks into smaller ones, starting with the easiest parts of a task first; working with other people; and calculating the true costs of procrastination.

How can I balance competing priorities?

- You *can* balance competing priorities if you begin to see how they coexist. Manage work time carefully, use slack time on the job to perform school assignments, use flextime, accept new responsibilities thoughtfully, and assign the proper priority to work.

Key Terms and Concepts

Daily to-do list (p. 35)
Master calendar (p. 35)
Priorities (p. 33)

Procrastination (p. 43)
Time log (p. 29)
Weekly timetable (p. 35)

Resources

On Campus

The college official that schedules classes on campus is known as the *registrar.* If you are having difficulty in scheduling your classes, the registrar's office may be helpful. In addition, your academic advisor can help you work out problems in enrolling in the classes you want.

In Print

Stephen Covey's *The Seven Habits of Highly Successful People* (Fireside, 1990) and Alan Axelrod and James Holtje's *201 Ways to Manage Your Time Better* (McGraw-Hill, 1997) offer practical, hands-on guides to time management.

How to Do Everything with Microsoft Outlook (Osborne-McGraw-Hill, 2000), by Julia Kelly and Megg Bonar, provides a quick, hands-on introduction to Microsoft's Outlook software, a popular time management program that accompanies the word processing program Word. (You can also find guides to other time management software programs.)

Veronique Vienne and Erica Lennard's *The Art of Doing Nothing: Simple Ways to Make Time for Yourself* (Clarkson Potter, 1998) is an antidote to the impulse to schedule every minute of our days. The book celebrates taking time out and devoting it to oneself, providing a practical guide to rest and relaxation.

On the Web

The following sites on the World Wide Web provide the opportunity to extend your learning about time management. (Although the Web addresses were accurate at the time the book was printed, check the P.O.W.E.R. Learning website [**www.mhhe.com/power**] for any changes that may have occurred.)

- For effective hints on how to plan study time, ideas about when to study, as well as tips on how to study, visit **www.coun.uvic.ca/learn/program/hndouts/plan_ho.html**.

- For a handy self-management checklist that allows visitors to better achieve their goals with the time that they have, go to **www.coun.uvic.0ca/learn/program/hndouts/slfman.html**. It also provides effective techniques for avoiding procrastination and digression, two major obstacles to effective time management.

- Mind Tools Book Store sponsors a site (**www.mindtools.com/page5.html**) with useful information on how to get the most out of one's time. Topics covered include analyzing what time is really worth, prioritizing goals, and planning effective use of the time that one actually has.

Taking It to the Net

1 Create a weekly organizer. Find a site on the Web that offers shareware or freeware featuring a weekly planner (e.g., **www.in-focus.com/store/qc.htm**). Create a weekly schedule sheet for yourself based on this design. Be sure to write in all of your classes and any other regular obligations that you have. Be sure to set specific times in your daily schedule to study and do homework. (If you already use Outlook or another kind of communications software, use its calendar function to do the same thing.)

2 Make a master calendar for the term, using the same software you used for the exercise above. If your calendar does not provide this information automatically, you can go to Yahoo! (**www.yahoo.com**), click on "Reference," then again on "Calendars." Here you'll find many links to different calendar-related information such as when holidays occur. Be sure to indicate dates when important assignments are due and when exams occur.

The Case of . . .

The Time of His Life

Will Linz couldn't believe it. On the same day he had completed his term paper and handed it in, his instructor announced a test for the following week. When the class protested that the test hadn't been listed in the syllabus, the instructor murmured that she'd made a mistake and was sorry about the short notice.

Will panicked when he remembered that next week he also had to complete two lab reports he had put off because he had been working on his term paper. Even worse, next weekend was lost. He had promised—promised!—his girlfriend, who was working full-time, that he would go with her to her annual company picnic. Although he dreaded the thought of being with a bunch of people he barely knew, he'd finally agreed to go just last week.

As he was driving home thinking about all this, his car started to sputter and then stalled. He was unable to get it started. That was it. He sat there on the side of the road, feeling like his life had completely fallen apart and wondering how he'd ever get it back together again.

1. What might you tell Will that could help solve his predicament?

2. Is there anything Will could have done to prevent the situation he now faces from occurring in the first place?

3. What specific time-management techniques might Will have employed in the past to avoid these problems?

4. What strategies might Will use now to take control over his limited time during the coming week?

5. What advice could you give Will to try and prevent problems in time management for his next term?

Recognizing How You Learn, Who You Are, and What You Value

3

he transformation began when Shaniqua Turner got her first paper back from her English literature instructor. It wasn't the grade—which was good—that mattered so much, but what her instructor uttered, almost as an afterthought, as she handed the paper back to Shaniqua: "Nice job. Your insights were good, and you have great potential as a writer."

Shaniqua was thrilled. She had always thought of herself as having only modest talent in English and, although at one point she had harbored the fantasy of being a newspaper reporter, she had never felt she was good enough to make it.

But now something clicked: Maybe she did have the ability to succeed in a career involving writing.

Looking *Ahead*

Through the experiences we have in life, we build up a sense of our strengths and weaknesses, what we like and dislike about ourselves. In the process, the sense of who we are also affects the choices we make and the things that we do.

In this chapter you will be asked to consider various aspects of yourself. First you'll look at the ways in which you learn and how you can use your personal learning style to study more effectively.

You'll then explore who you are more broadly, considering the various aspects of your personality. You'll see how your self-esteem—the way you perceive your strengths and weaknesses—can lead to success or failure.

Finally, the chapter helps you investigate where you are headed. By creating your own personal mission statement, you'll begin to solidify the knowledge of who you are and where you would be happiest and most productive in the future.

After reading this chapter, you'll be able to answer these questions:

- **What are my learning styles, and how have they affected my academic success?**

- **What is self-concept and how does it affect me?**

- **How does my level of self-esteem affect my behavior?**

- **How can I make wise personal decisions throughout life?**

Discovering Your Learning Styles

Consider what it would be like to be a member of the Trukese people, a small group of islanders in the South Pacific.

Trukese sailors often sail hundreds of miles on the open sea. They manage this feat with none of the navigational equipment used by Western sailors. No compass. No chronometer. No sextant. They don't even sail in a straight line. Instead, they zigzag back and forth, at the mercy of the winds and tides. Yet they make few mistakes. Almost always they are able to reach their destination with precision. How do they do it?

They can't really explain it. They say it has to do with following the rising and setting of the stars at night. During the day, they take in the appearance, sound, and feel of the waves against the side of the boat. But they don't really have any idea of where they are at any given moment, nor do they care. They just know that ultimately they'll reach their final destination.

It would be foolhardy to suggest that the Trukese don't have what it takes to be successful sailors. The fact that they don't use traditional Western navigational equipment when they're sailing does not mean that they are any less able than Western navigators.

What about academic success? Isn't it reasonable to assume that there are different ways to reach academic goals? Wouldn't it be surprising if everyone learned in exactly the same way?

Each of us has preferred ways of learning, approaches that work best for us. And our success is not just dependent on how well we learn, but on how we learn.

Learning styles reflect our preferred manner of acquiring, using, and thinking about knowledge. We don't have just one learning style, but a profile of styles. Even though our ability may be identical to someone else's, our learning styles might be quite different.

You probably already know quite a lot about your learning styles. Maybe you do particularly well in your biology classes while struggling with English literature. Or it may be the other way around. Because biology tends to be about natural processes, teachers present the subject as a series of related facts. English literature, however, requires you to think more abstractly, analyzing and synthesizing ideas.

Though we may have general preferences for fact-based learning or learning that requires more abstract thinking, we all use a variety of learning styles. Some involve our preferences regarding the way information is presented to us, some relate to how we think and learn most readily, and some relate to how our personality traits affect our performance. We'll start by considering the preferences we have for how we initially perceive information.

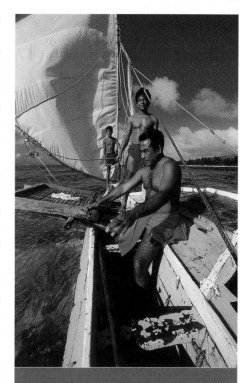

Trukese sailors, who live on a small group of islands in the South Pacific, are able to navigate with considerable accuracy across great expanses of open seas, and they do so without the use of any of the standard navigation tools used by sailors in Western cultures. The navigational achievements of the Trukese sailors illustrate that there are multiple ways to attain our goals and that there is no single route to success.

Learning style
One's preferred manner of acquiring, using, and thinking about knowledge

Are You a Primarily Visual, Auditory, or Tactile Learner?

Receptive learning style
The way in which we initially receive information

Visual/verbal learning style
A style that involves a preference for written material, favoring reading over hearing and touching

Visual/nonverbal learning style
A style that favors material presented visually in a diagram or picture

One of the most basic aspects of learning styles concerns the way in which we initially receive information from our sense organs—our **receptive learning style.** People have different strengths in terms of how they most effectively process information. Specifically, there are four different types of receptive learning styles:

- **Visual/verbal learning style.** If you have a **visual/verbal learning style,** you prefer information that is presented visually in a written format. You feel most comfortable reading, and you may recall the spelling of a word by thinking of how the word looks. You probably learn best when you have the opportunity to read about a concept rather than listening to a teacher explain it.

- **Visual/nonverbal learning style.** Students with a **visual/nonverbal learning style** learn most effectively when material is presented visually in a diagram or picture. You might recall the structure of a chemical compound by reviewing a picture in your mind, and you benefit from instructors who make frequent use of visual aids such as videos, maps, and models. Students with visual learning styles find it easier to see things in their mind's eye—to visualize a task or concept—than to be lectured about them.

Learning styles reflect our preferred manner of acquiring, using, and thinking about knowledge. Tactile learners prefer hands-on learning that comes about through touching, manipulating, and doing things.

"To be fond of learning is to be near to knowledge."

Tze-Sze

Auditory/verbal learning style
A style that favors listening as the best approach to learning

Tactile/kinesthetic learning style
A style that involves learning by touching, manipulating objects, and doing things

- **Auditory/verbal learning style.** Have you ever asked a friend to help you put something together by having her read the directions to you while you worked? If you did, you may have an auditory/verbal learning style. People with **auditory/verbal learning styles** prefer listening to explanations rather than reading them. They love class lectures and discussions, because they can easily take in the information that is being talked about.

- **Tactile/kinesthetic learning style.** Students with a **tactile/kinesthetic learning style** prefer to learn by doing—touching, manipulating objects, and doing things. For instance, some people enjoy the act of writing because of the feel of a pencil or a computer keyboard—the tactile equivalent of thinking out loud. Or they may find that it helps them to make a three-dimensional model to understand a new idea.

To get a sense of your own receptive learning style, complete Try It 1 on the next page. But remember, having a particular receptive learning style simply means that it will be easier to learn material that is presented in that style. It does not mean you cannot learn any other way!

Receptive learning styles have implications for effective studying:

If you have a visual/verbal style, consider writing out summaries of information, highlighting and underlining written material, and using flashcards. Transform diagrams and math formulas into words.

If you have a visual/nonverbal style, devise diagrams and charts. Translate words into symbols and figures.

If you have an auditory/verbal style, recite material out loud when studying. Work with others in a group, talking through the material, and consider tape recording lectures.

If you have a tactile/kinesthetic style, incorporate movement into your study. Trace diagrams, build models, arrange flash cards and move them around. Keep yourself active during class, taking notes, drawing charts, and jotting down key concepts.

Handling Information: Do You Focus on Pieces or the Whole?

When you are putting a jigsaw puzzle together, do you focus more on the individual pieces and how each one fits together with the one next to it, or is your strategy to concentrate on the whole picture, keeping the finished product in mind?

The way you approach a jigsaw puzzle provides a clue to the process by which you fit together bits of information. Specifically, the strategy you use suggests which of the following two learning styles you are more comfortable with:

- People with **analytic learning styles** learn most easily if first exposed to the individual components and principles behind a phenomenon or situation. Once they have identified the underlying components involved, they find it easier to figure out and grasp the broad picture and determine whether particular cases exemplify the principle.

Journal Reflections

How I Learn

1. Would you rather read a newspaper, listen to the news on the radio, or watch it on TV? Why do you think you have this preference?

2. When you get a new piece of software or a new tool, do you like to read the instructions or just "play with it" until you get the hang of it?

3. Suppose a friend is teaching you a new and complex procedure (such as a new game or the way to use a piece of computer software). Do you prefer to get the big picture first, or the details?

4. When you're in class, what do you do during lectures? Do you try to write down the instructor's exact words, draw diagrams and make tables, or jot down a few big ideas?

5. What do you think your answers to the previous questions reveal about the way you prefer to learn new information?

Analytic learning style

A style that starts with small pieces of information and uses them to build the big picture

Try It! 1

Personal Styles: What's Your Receptive Learning Style?

Read each of the following statements and rank them in terms of their usefulness to you as learning approaches. Base your ratings on your personal experiences and preferences, using the following scale:

1 = Not at all useful

2 = Not very useful

3 = Neutral

4 = Somewhat useful

5 = Very useful

	1	2	3	4	5
1. Studying alone					
2. Studying pictures and diagrams to understand complex ideas					
3. Listening to class lectures					
4. Performing a process myself rather than reading or hearing about it					
5. Learning a complex procedure by reading written directions					
6. Watching and listening to film, computer, or video presentations					
7. Listening to a book or lecture on tape					
8. Doing lab work					
9. Studying teachers' hand-outs and lecture notes					
10. Studying in a quiet room					
11. Taking part in group discussions					
12. Taking part in hands-on classroom demonstrations					
13. Taking notes and studying them later					
14. Creating flash cards and using them as a study and review tool					

(continued)

Relational learning style

A style that starts with the big picture and breaks it down into its individual components

- Those with **relational learning styles** learn most readily if exposed to the full range of material that they are aiming to learn. Rather than focusing on the individual components of a problem, as those with analytic styles prefer to do, people with relational learning styles do best when they are first given the full picture. They can then take this broad view and break it down into its individual components.

For example, consider trying to understand the way that food is converted to energy in a cell. A more analytic learner would approach the task by learning each individual step in the process, first to last. In contrast, a more relational learner would consider the big picture, focusing on the general, overall process and its purpose.

	1	2	3	4	5
15. Memorizing and recalling how words are spelled by spelling them "out loud" in my head					
16. Writing key facts and important points down as a tool for remembering them					
17. Recalling how to spell a word by seeing it in my head					
18. Underlining or highlighting important facts or passages in my reading					
19. Saying things out loud when I'm studying					
20. Recalling how to spell a word by "writing" it invisibly in the air or on a surface					
21. Learning new information by reading about it in a textbook					
22. Using a map to find an unknown place					
23. Working in a study group					
24. Finding a place I've been to once by just going there without directions					

Scoring: The statements cycle through the four receptive learning styles in this order: (1) visual/verbal; (2) visual/nonverbal; (3) auditory/verbal; and (4) tactile/kinesthetic.

To find your primary learning style, disregard your 1, 2, and 3 ratings. Add up your 4 and 5 ratings for each learning style (i.e., a "4" equals 4 points and a "5" equals 5 points). Use the following chart to link the statements to the learning styles and to write down your summed ratings:

Learning Style	Statements	Total (Sum) of Rating Points
Visual/verbal	1, 5, 9, 13, 17, and 21	
Visual/nonverbal	2, 6, 10, 14, 18, and 22	
Auditory/verbal	3, 7, 11, 15, 19, and 23	
Tactile/kinesthetic	4, 8, 12, 16, 20, and 24	

The total of your rating points for any given style will range from a low of 0 to a high of 30. The highest total indicates your main receptive learning style. Don't be surprised if you have a mixed style, in which two or more styles receive similar ratings.

To Try It online, go to **www.mhhe.com/power**.

Students who use an analytic style study most effectively by focusing on facts and specific principles, for they excel at organizing information. They often work best on their own, and science and math may come particularly easy to them. On the other hand, students with a relational style perceive concepts globally, thinking in terms of the big picture. They may be drawn to subject areas that demand the ability to forge a broad overview of material, such as English and history. You probably already have a good idea of whether you have an analytic or relational learning style, but Try It 2 on page 62, "Assessing Your Analytical and Relational Learning Styles," will help you understand your learning style further.

Try It! 2

Assessing Your Analytical and Relational Learning Styles

Consider the following pairs of statements. Place a check next to the statement in each pair that more closely describes your style.

_____1a.   Before tackling a complex task that I'm unfamiliar with, I prefer to have detailed instructions on how to do it.

_____1b.   I prefer to dive into a new task, trying things out to see what happens and finding my way as I go.

_____2a.   I like watching movies a second time because then I know where they're going.

_____2b.   I generally don't like watching movies a second time because I know their plots already.

_____3a.   I prefer to solve math or science problems using formulas and directions.

_____3b.   I prefer to figure out why formulas work.

_____4a.   When I read mystery stories, I usually let the author tell the story and reveal the mystery.

_____4b.   When I read mystery stories, I like to try figuring out the mystery before the author reveals it.

_____5a.   I usually read the instruction booklet before trying out a new piece of software.

_____5b.   I never read the instruction booklet before trying out a new piece of software.

_____6a.   I prefer to have someone who knows about a subject explain it to me before I try my hand at it.

_____6b.   I'm impatient when others try to explain things to me, preferring to get involved in them myself without much explanation.

_____7a.   Whenever I see a really amazing special effect in a movie, I like to sit back and enjoy it.

_____7b.   Whenever I see a really amazing special effect in a movie, I try to figure out how they did it.

If you tended to prefer the "a" statements in most pairs, you probably have a relational style. If you preferred the "b" statements, you probably have a more analytic style. Remember that no one is purely analytical or purely relational.

To Try It online, go to **www.mhhe.com/power**.

Personality Styles

Our learning styles are also influenced by our personality. Are you likely to try out for school productions? Or is the idea of getting on a stage totally lacking in appeal (if not completely terrifying)? Do you relate to the world around you primarily through careful planning or by spontaneously reacting?

According to the rationale of the *Myers-Briggs Type Indicator,* a questionnaire frequently used in business and organizational settings to place people in one of 16 categories, personality type plays a key role in determining how we react to different situations. Specifically, we work best in situations in which others—both students and instructors—share our preferences and in which our personality is most suited to the particular task on which we are working.

Four major personality dimensions are critical. Although we'll describe the extremes of each dimension, keep in mind that most of us fall somewhere between the end-points of each dimension.

- **Introverts versus extroverts.** A key difference between introverts and extroverts is whether they enjoy working with others. Independence is a key characteristic of introverted learners. They enjoy working alone and they are less affected by how others think and behave. In contrast, extroverts are outgoing and more affected by the behavior and thinking of others. They enjoy working with others, and they are energized by having other people around.

- **Intuitors versus sensors.** Intuitors enjoy solving problems and being creative. They get impatient with details, preferring to make leaps of judgment, and they enjoy the challenge of solving problems and taking a big-picture approach. People categorized as sensors, on the other hand, prefer a concrete, logical approach in which they can carefully analyze the facts of the situation. Although they are good with details, they sometimes miss the big picture.

- **Thinkers versus feelers.** Thinkers prefer logic over emotion. They reach decisions and solve problems by systematically analyzing a situation. In contrast, feeling types rely more on their emotional responses. They are aware of others and their feelings, and they are influenced by their personal values and attachments to others.

- **Perceivers and judgers.** Before drawing a conclusion, perceivers attempt to gather as much information as they can. Because they are open to multiple perspectives and appreciate all sides of an issue, they sometimes have difficulty completing a task. Judgers, in comparison, are quick and decisive. They like to set goals, accomplish them, and then move on to the next task.

The Origins of Our Learning Styles

For many of us, our learning style preferences result from the kind of processing our brain "specializes" in. **Left-brain processing** concentrates more on tasks requiring verbal competence, such as speaking, reading, thinking, and reasoning. Information is processed sequentially, one bit at a time. For instance, people who are naturally inclined to use left-brain processing might be more likely to prefer analytic learning styles, because they first like to look at individual bits of information and then put them together.

On the other hand, **right-brain processing** tends to concentrate more on the processing of information in nonverbal domains, such as the understanding of spatial relationships, recognition of patterns and drawings, music, and emotional expression. Furthermore, the right hemisphere tends to process information globally, considering it as a whole. Consequently, people who naturally tend toward right-brain processing might prefer relational learning styles.

Left-brain processing
Information processing primarily performed by the left hemisphere of the brain, focusing on tasks requiring verbal competence, such as speaking, reading, thinking, and reasoning; information is processed sequentially, one bit at a time

Right-brain processing
Information processing primarily performed by the right hemisphere of the brain, focusing on information in nonverbal domains, such as the understanding of spatial relationships, recognition of patterns and drawings, music, and emotional expression

Here are some key facts to remember about learning, personality, and processing styles:

- **You have a variety of styles.** As you can see in the summary of different categories of styles in Table 3.1, there are several types of styles. For any given task or challenge, some types of styles may be more relevant than others. Furthermore, success is possible even when there is a mismatch between what you need to accomplish and your own pattern of preferred styles. It may take more work, but learning to deal with situations that require you to use less-preferred styles is important practice for life after college.

- **Your style reflects your preferences regarding which abilities you like to use—not the abilities themselves.** Styles are related to our preferences and the mental approaches we like to use. You may prefer to learn

Table 3.1

Learning, Personality, and Processing Styles

All of us have particular learning, personality, and processing styles that we tend to rely on. At the same time, we also have capabilities in less-preferred styles. So, for example, although you may be primarily a visual/verbal learner, you have the capacity to use auditory/verbal and tactile/kinesthetic approaches. Note in particular that the four categories of personality styles are considered independent of each other. For instance, you may be an extrovert and at the same time a sensor, a feeler, and a judger. Furthermore, although the "Using the Style" column suggests ways that students with a particular style can make the most of that style, you should also try out strategies that work for styles different from your own.

Category	Type	Description	Using the Style[1]
Receptive Learning Styles	Visual/verbal	A style that involves a preference for material in a written format, favoring reading over hearing and touching.	Read and rewrite material; take notes and rewrite them; organize material in charts and tables; transform diagrams and math formulas into words.
	Visual/nonverbal	A style that favors material presented visually in a diagram or picture.	Use figures and drawings; replay classes and discussions in your mind's eye; visualize material; translate words into symbols and figures.
	Auditory/verbal	A style in which the learner favors listening as the best approach.	Recite material out loud when studying; consider how words sound; study different languages; tape record lectures; work with others, talking through the material.
	Tactile/kinesthetic	A style that involves learning by touching, manipulating objects, and doing things.	Incorporate movement into studying; trace figures and drawings with your finger; create models; make flash cards and move them around; keep active during class, taking notes, drawing charts, jotting down key concepts.
Information Processing Styles	Analytic	A style in which the learner starts with small pieces of information and uses them to build the big picture.	Consider the sequence of material; organize information into logical patterns.
	Relational	A style in which the learner starts with the big picture and breaks it down into its individual components.	Build models and break them down; split written material into its components.

tactilely, but that in itself doesn't guarantee that the products that you create tactilely will be good—you still have to work!

- **Your style will change over the course of your life.** You can learn new styles and expand the range of learning experiences in which you feel perfectly comfortable. In fact, you can conceive of this book as one long lesson in learning styles because it provides you with strategies for learning more effectively in a variety of ways.

- **You should work on improving your less-preferred styles.** Although it may be tempting, don't always make choices that increase your exposure to preferred styles and decrease your practice with less-preferred styles. The more you use approaches for which you have less of a preference, the better you'll be at developing the skills associated with those styles.

Category	Type	Description	Using the Style
Personality Styles	Introvert versus extrovert	Independence is a key characteristic of introverted learners, who enjoy working alone and are less affected by how others think and behave. In contrast, extroverts are outgoing and more affected by the behavior and thinking of others. They enjoy working with others.	Experiment with studying in groups compared with working alone; consider your performance in class discussions compared with working on your own.
	Intuitors versus sensors	Intuitive people enjoy solving problems and being creative, often taking a big-picture approach. Sensors, on the other hand, prefer a concrete, logical approach in which they can carefully analyze the facts of the situation.	For intuitors, reflect on the personal meaning of material and seek out tasks that involve creativity. For sensors, seek out concrete tasks that involve the application of logical principles.
	Thinker versus feeler	Thinkers prefer logic over emotion, reaching decisions through rational analysis. In contrast, feelers rely more on their emotions and are influenced by their personal values and attachments to others.	Thinkers should seek to systematically analyze situations, attempting to identify patterns. For feelers, use emotional responses to reflect on material.
	Perceiver versus judger	Before drawing a conclusion, perceivers attempt to gather as much information as they can and are open to multiple perspectives. Judgers, in comparison, are quick and decisive, enjoying setting goals and accomplishing them.	Perceivers organize material sequentially and into component parts; for judgers, using goal-setting preferences facilitates learning.
Brain Processing Styles	Left-brain processing	Information processing that focuses on tasks requiring verbal competence, such as speaking, reading, thinking, and reasoning; information is processed sequentially, one bit at a time.	Organize material logically; identify patterns; make tables of key information; break material into component parts.
	Right-brain processing	Information processing focusing on information in nonverbal domains, such as the understanding of spatial relationships, recognition of patterns and drawings, music, and emotional expression.	Identify patterns; use graphs and drawings; read aloud; create models.

Try It!
3

🏂 Working in a Group:
Instructor Styles

Working as a group with your classmates, try to determine your course instructor's learning style by answering the following questions:

1. What clues does the language your instructor uses give you about his or her learning style? _____
   _____
   _____
   _____

2. What assignments has the instructor scheduled, and what do they tell you about the instructor's learning style? _____
   _____
   _____

3. Are there constraints (such as class size, scheduling factors, school traditions) that also influence the instructor's teaching style, apart from his or her underlying learning style?
   _____
   _____
   _____

To Try It online, go to **www.mhhe.com/power**.

- **Work cooperatively with others who have different styles.** If your instructor asks you to work cooperatively in groups, seek out classmates who have styles that are different from yours. Not only will your classmates' differing styles help you to achieve collective success, but you can also learn from observing others' approaches to tackling the assignment.

Using Your Instructors' Teaching Styles

In the same way that each of us has preferred learning styles, instructors have their own styles of teaching. They may not even be aware of them, but their learning styles have an important impact on the way they teach—and that, in turn, will help determine how well you do in their classes.

Instructors who make frequent requests to "list," "label," "diagram," "outline," or "define," may favor a more analytic learning style. In contrast, if their tendency is to ask you to "compare," "analyze," "discuss," "criticize," or "evaluate," they may be more in tune with relational learning.

Similarly, instructors who assign frequent projects that involve oral presentations and demonstrations might be indicating that their learning style is somewhat auditory. On the other hand, instructors whose assignments consist of frequent written work may have a more visual style. Work on "Instructor Styles" (Try It 3) to get a sense of your instructor's learning style.

What if your learning styles are mismatched with those of your instructor? Several approaches might improve the situation:

- **Consider the instructor's learning styles when studying.** If your natural tendency is to stick to the facts, and your instructor appears to prefer broad, conceptual views of the material, then be sure to consider the material from the instructor's broader view. In contrast, if your instructor's learning preferences lean toward factual views of material, pay special attention to the details that your instructor will likely be more interested in. For example, an instructor who focuses on the broad view is not likely to ask you to repeat a detailed series of dates of particular events during the French Revolution. Yet this may be exactly what another instructor, more focused on the details, is interested in.

- **Seek out alternative assignments.** A second approach to a mismatch between your learning styles and those of your instructor is to seek out alternative assignments. Occasionally instructors are willing to provide substitute assignments that tap into your preferences and strengths.

  However, instructors have many students, and it would be nearly impossible to come up with independent assignments for each one. Furthermore, many instructors feel that it is part of their job to maximize student exposure to various learning approaches—which leads to the final point about mismatches between student and instructor styles:

- **Accept discomfort as a necessary evil.** Real learning is often difficult and uncomfortable. To become an accomplished student, you'll have to use a variety of strategies and approaches.

"Know Thyself."

Learning styles are just one example of how your personal characteristics affect your academic success. We now turn to a broader consideration of who you are as we examine how your understanding of yourself influences your success in college.

Self-Concept: "Who Am I?"

Of course you know who you are. You know your first and last name. You know where and when you were born, and you have no trouble identifying your ethnic background. You can probably recite your social security number with ease.

But if this is all that comes to mind when you think about who you are, you're missing a lot of the picture. There's a lot more to you than name, rank, and serial number. What makes you unique and special are your thoughts, your beliefs, your dreams. You have a unique past history, and this set of experiences together with your genetic makeup—the combination of genes you inherited from your parents—is unlike anyone else's.

"When I discover who I am, I'll be free."

Ralph Ellison

Our view of ourselves—our **self-concept**—has three parts:

1. Our physical self is both who we are physically—the color of our eyes or the curliness of our hair—and how we feel about our physical form. We all have our blemishes, protruding stomachs, long noses, or other physical quirks, but we don't all feel the same way about them.

2. Our social self is made up of the roles we play in our social interactions with others. As you're reading these words, you're not only a student but you're also a son or daughter, a friend, a citizen, and possibly an employee, a spouse, a lover, and/or a parent. Each of these roles plays an important part in defining your self-concept. Each also helps to determine how you behave while acting in that particular role.

3. Finally, our self-concept also contains a personal self—our inner core, which is that private part of ourselves that no one knows about except us. It consists of the innermost thoughts and experiences that we may or may not choose to share with others.

Self-Concept and Self-Fulfilling Prophecies

The way we view ourselves determines how we interact with others, what challenges we feel ready to take on, and our expectations for future success. If you see yourself as a successful student, you are likely to expect that you'll continue to be a successful student. On the other hand, if you see yourself as an incapable, inept student, your chances for future success are diminished.

In short, our self-concept can act as a self-fulfilling prophecy. A **self-fulfilling prophecy** occurs when we hold a belief or expectation that affects our behavior, thereby increasing the likelihood that our beliefs or expectations *will* come true. For instance, a person who views herself as a poor student may find herself thinking: "Why bother working hard? I'm no good as a student; that's just the way I am." It's easy to see how such a view could lead to a self-fulfilling prophecy: By not working hard, the student guarantees that the prophecy of poor performance comes true.

On the other hand, self-fulfilling prophecies can have positive effects. A person who sees herself as a good student will probably be motivated to study and complete assignments enthusiastically. Her view of herself can therefore bring about the expected behavior—in this case, success.

To get a clearer picture of your own self-concept:

- **Examine the roles you play.** To understand who we are, we need to understand the different roles that we play in life. Consider which of these roles are central to who you are—and who you want to be. Consider how an outsider might look at your actions, beliefs, and interests. How would that person characterize you?

- **Identify your strengths and weaknesses.** Look at yourself with a clear and objective eye, and consider what you do particularly well and what you don't do particularly well. If you're honest, you'll come up with several areas in which you need work—and many other areas in which you're already quite strong. (Use Table 3.2 to help you organize your thoughts and build an initial inventory of your strengths and weaknesses.)

Table 3.2

Inventory Your Strengths and Weaknesses

Complete an honest inventory of your strengths and weaknesses. To help you organize your thoughts, use the following table.

Aspects of Self	Strengths	Weaknesses
Physical self		
Health and fitness		
Sports		
Nutrition and diet		
Appearance		
Other		
Social self		
Friend		
Son/daughter		
Lover/spouse		
Citizen/community member		
Employee		
Student		
Roommate		
Classmate		
Team or group member (e.g., sports, band, club)		
Other		
Personal self		
Personal experiences		
Unique traits		
Personality		
Spiritual self		
Habits		
Attitudes/opinions		
Ideas/thoughts		
Other		

As you consider your strengths and weaknesses, don't place a value on them. The fact that you procrastinate and put off tasks doesn't make you a bad person, just as the fact that you're a good student doesn't necessarily make you a good person. The point in seeking to identify who you are is to determine your self-concept with accuracy, not to determine how good (or bad) a human being you are.

Furthermore, be sure you construct your own definition of who you are. Don't let what you believe others think about you determine what *you* think you're good at and bad at. See yourself through your own eyes, not someone else's.

- **Pull your selves together.** Try to form a coherent view of your self-concept. Seek to understand how the various parts of your self-concept—physical, social, and personal—fit together.

- **Accept your entire self-concept.** If you're being honest with yourself, you'll find that there are parts of yourself that you like more than others. That's OK. Don't disown the parts you don't like; they're also part of who you are. Instead, accept that some parts of yourself need work, while others are the source of justifiable pride.

Make Sure Your Self-Concept Is Yours

Our own perceptions are not the only source of self-fulfilling prophecies. We sometimes permit others' views of who we are and their expectations about us to determine our behavior.

For example, if we think an instructor views us as a particularly hard worker, we may not want to disappoint him by slacking off. If we believe that our boss admires our persistence, we may be motivated to show her persistence when we're working on a difficult problem on the job.

> "Respect yourself if you would have others respect you."
>
> Baltasar Gracián

Responding to others' positive perceptions can be fine, for the results are good. But what happens if someone holds a negative view of who we are? What if we're constantly told that we're not working hard enough . . . or that we're not as smart as our older brother . . . or that we are the hard worker, but not the creative one?

The results can be devastating. If we consistently hear such messages about who we are, we can come to believe them. Even worse, our behavior can begin to reflect the negative messages. If we're constantly told that we don't work hard enough, we may in fact not work very hard. If we're told we're not as smart as someone else, we may begin to think of ourselves as not very bright. Or if someone tells us we're not creative, we may not try very hard to be creative.

In short, the negative messages that we hear from others can come to act as a prison, placing us in bondage to others' negative beliefs about who we are and what our capabilities are. It's crucial, then, not to buy into others' negative views of who we are. Our biggest help, and sometimes handicap, in this effort is self-esteem.

Self-Esteem: Building a Positive View of Yourself

When you think about yourself as a student, you probably don't stop there. Instead, you likely see yourself as a "good" student, a "bad" student, or maybe a "just OK" student. Similarly, when you consider yourself in the role of friend, you may view yourself as a "loyal-to-the-end" friend or maybe, in the opposite case, a "fair-weather" friend. In short, when we look inward at who we are, we don't just stop with a characterization of the different roles that we play in the world. Instead, we place a value on them. We see the various facets of our self-concept not in neutral terms, but as either positive or negative.

Self-esteem is the overall evaluation we give ourselves as individuals. It reflects the degree to which we see ourselves as individuals of worth and determines our general acceptance of ourselves. If we have high self-esteem, we generally feel respect for and acceptance of ourselves. On the other hand, if we have low self-esteem, we generally lack respect for ourselves, reject parts of who we are, and judge ourselves negatively.

To get a sense of your own general level of self-esteem, complete the self-assessment in Try It 4.

Self-esteem
The overall evaluation we give ourselves as individuals

Why Self-Esteem Matters

People with high self-esteem are generally happier and better able to cope with adversity. High self-esteem provides a sense of security, because people with high self-esteem feel they are able to deal with problems that may arise. They also have a sense of **self-efficacy,** the expectation that they are capable of achieving their goals in many different kinds of situations. High self-esteem can also give people a sense of purpose and the belief that they are productive members of society.

In contrast, individuals lacking in self-esteem are more insecure, and their belief in their ability to reach their goals is weak. They feel less tied to others, and their sense of purpose is not firm. And when others are successful, people with low self-esteem may feel jealousy and envy.

Low self-esteem can produce a cycle of failure in which low self-esteem leads to low expectations, reduced effort, elevated anxiety, poor performance,

Self-efficacy
The expectation that one is capable of achieving one's goals in many different kinds of situations

Calvin and Hobbes   by Bill Watterson

Try It! 4

Measuring Your Self-Esteem

To get an informal estimate of your self-esteem, complete the following scale.[2]

Statement	Strongly Agree	Agree	Disagree	Strongly Disagree
1. On the whole, I am satisfied with myself.				
2. At times I think I am no good at all.				
3. I feel that I have a number of good qualities.				
4. I am able to do things as well as most other people.				
5. I feel I do not have much to be proud of.				
6. I certainly feel useless at times.				
7. I feel that I am a person of worth, at least the equal of others.				
8. I wish I could have more respect for myself.				
9. All in all, I am inclined to feel that I am a failure.				
10. I take a positive attitude toward myself.				

Scoring: For statements 1, 3, 4, 7 and 10, score as follows:

Strongly agree	= 4 points
Agree	= 3 points
Disagree	= 2 points
Strongly disagree	= 1 point

For statements 2, 5, 6, 8, and 9, score as follows:

Strongly agree	= 1 point
Agree	= 2 points
Disagree	= 3 points
Strongly disagree	= 4 points

Add your points together, and interpret the total as follows:

The highest possible score (i.e., an apparently very high level of self-esteem) is 40 points, and the minimum score (i.e., an apparently very low level of self-esteem) is 10. Most people score in the 30- to 40-point range. A much smaller number of people score in the 20s. A score of 10 to 20 is often found in people who suffer from severe depression. Keep in mind that this is a very rough gauge of self-esteem and that scores will vary depending on a number of factors, including your mood when you complete the questionnaire.

Now consider the following

- Do the results of the questionnaire match your own gut feelings about yourself?

- Do you think your self-esteem has changed? Do you have any ideas as to why?

To Try It online, go to **www.mhhe.com/power**.

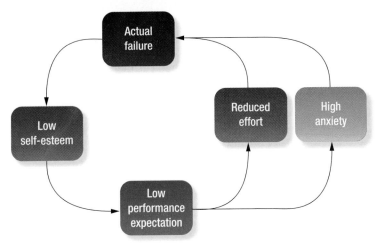

Figure 3.1

The Cycle of Failure

Low self-esteem can lead to low performance expectations. In turn, low performance expectations can produce reduced effort and high anxiety, both of which can lead to failure—and ultimately reinforce the low self-esteem that started the cycle.

and, finally, an affirmation of the low self-esteem that began the cycle in the first place. Such a cycle can be difficult to break (see Figure 3.1).

If a student with low self-esteem begins studying for a test believing that he is likely to do badly, he may put forth relatively little effort. Moreover, because he is virtually sure he is going to do poorly on the test, he may experience extremes of anxiety, feeling that (another) failure is lurking just ahead.

Ultimately, the combination of lack of effort and anxiety produced by his low self-esteem does him in, and he actually does do poorly on the test. But the cycle of failure is not yet complete: Rather than telling himself that low effort and elevated anxiety caused his poor test performance, he views it as an affirmation of his inferior ability. In turn, this misperception serves to reinforce his low self-esteem.

Breaking the Self-Esteem Cycle of Failure "OK," you may be saying to yourself, "I understand that self-esteem is important. But how am I supposed to ignore a lifetime of learning and improve my self-esteem? Especially when I have low self-esteem to begin with!"

It's not a simple matter to shed a less-than-ideal view of ourselves and adopt a more positive one. And you certainly won't be able to change your basic conception of yourself in the course of a few days.

But there are steps you can take to bring yourself closer to an ideal level of self-esteem. They include the following:

- **Accept yourself, warts and all.** No one is perfect, and becoming a perfect person should not be your goal in life. If it were, you'd be doomed to failure, because you'd never measure up.

  Accept the fact that there are certain aspects of yourself and your life that you're not pleased with. In fact, embrace your awareness of your displeasure: If you didn't realize that there were some things about yourself that needed improvement, you'd be out of touch with who you are.

- **Understand that everyone has value and self-worth.** Every individual has value and self-worth, some unique

Stephen Hawking, a world-renowned physicist, suffers from Lou Gehrig's disease, a disorder that eliminates voluntary muscle control. However, despite significant physical limitations, Hawking continues to make important contributions to society.

spark that sets him or her apart from everyone else. Examine yourself and your life, and get a picture of the particulars that make you you.

Low self-esteem can lead to low performance expectations. In turn, low performance can produce reduced effort and high anxiety, both of which can lead to failure—and ultimately reinforce the low self-esteem that started the cycle.

- **Distinguish the different parts of who you are.** No one is all bad, just as no one is all good. Maybe a person who never reached the level of success she wanted to in school turns out to be an excellent employee, the person who always seems to be asked to solve problems or take on challenges no one else can deal with. Another person may not be the kind of husband he wants to be, but turns out to be a terrific parent.

  Understanding that you have failings in one arena of life doesn't mean that you can't be successful in others. It makes no sense to base your self-esteem on what you do worst in life, so don't make the mistake of focusing solely on your failings and minimizing your successes.

- **Don't just rely on—or wait for—others' praise.** Your self-esteem should not be solely dependent on the praise you get from others. Use your own judgment to evaluate the level of success you've achieved on a given task.

  For instance, you know when you've done your best in writing a paper. If you feel proud of it, celebrate your accomplishment and take pride in it. Instead of waiting for your instructor's feedback, permit yourself to feel good about what you've done. Your self-esteem should be based on your own assessment of your accomplishments, not only on others' assessments.

- **Understand that building self-esteem is a lifelong undertaking.** It's taken a lifetime to develop whatever level of self-esteem you currently have. Your self-esteem is not going to change overnight.

  Rebuilding self-esteem isn't easy. It's particularly hard to do at a time when you face a major life transition, such as the beginning of your college experience; your oldest friends and family may not be nearby, and the level of academic work you encounter presents new challenges. In fact, starting college presents a special opportunity to grow and develop. It's a new environment, giving you the opportunity to unlearn old patterns of behavior that have held you back and master new ones that will permit you to have a more positive view of yourself. Don't let low self-esteem keep you from becoming what you can be.

Preparing a Personal Mission Statement

The life that is unexamined is not worth living.

Twenty-five hundred years later, Plato's words are still true. If you never consider what you want out of life, what your dreams and aspirations are, and where you're heading, you're in danger of missing out on the most fundamental and meaningful parts of life. The day-to-day details of life will use up all your time, and you won't know exactly where it has gone.

One way to get a clearer picture of our life is to create a formal statement of what we actually hope to achieve during our lifetime. The P.O.W.E.R. framework provides a systematic series of steps that can help us look inward and determine the way we wish to carry out our lives.

P repare: Identifying Your Values

The first step toward understanding ourselves is to assess our underlying values systematically. To do this, work through the following steps:

1. Choose the five values that you hold most dear. Here are some examples, but don't necessarily restrict yourself to these: a comfortable life, an exciting life, a sense of accomplishment, world peace, beauty, equality, security, freedom, happiness, inner harmony, love, national security, pleasure, religion, self-respect, fame, friendship, wisdom, work, financial security, risk taking, being challenged.

2. For each value, answer each of these questions: why is it important to you, who taught it to you, how has it affected your behavior in the past, and in what ways can you affirm it through your future behavior?

   Value #1 _____

   Why is it important:

   Who taught it to you:

   How has it affected your past behavior:

   In what ways can you affirm it through future behavior:

   Value #2 _____

   Why is it important:

   Who taught it to you:

   How has it affected your past behavior:

   In what ways can you affirm it through future behavior:

   Value #3 _____

   Why is it important:

   Who taught it to you:

   How has it affected your past behavior:

   In what ways can you affirm it through future behavior:

   Value #4 _____

   Why is it important:

   Who taught it to you:

   How has it affected your past behavior:

   In what ways can you affirm it through future behavior:

   Value #5 _____

   Why is it important:

   Who taught it to you:

   How has it affected your past behavior:

   In what ways can you affirm it through future behavior:

Organize: Placing Order on What Motivates You

Abraham Lincoln. Albert Einstein. Eleanor Roosevelt.

What is the common link among these three people? According to psychologist Abraham Maslow, each of them achieved **self-actualization,** a state of self-fulfillment in which people realize their highest potential in their own unique way.[3]

According to Maslow, self-actualization is the highest of the various needs that motivate our behavior. As you can see in the illustration in Figure 3.2, our underlying needs form a pyramid. At the bottom of the pyramid are our most basic needs, such as the biological needs that drive our behavior, including food, water, sleep, and sex. The basic needs are not much different from those that drive the behavior of nonhuman animals. The needs on the next higher level of the pyramid are safety needs; we need a safe, secure environment to function effectively.

Self-actualization
A state of self-fulfillment in which people realize their highest potential in their own unique way

> "Authentic values are those by which a life can be lived."
>
> Allan Bloom

But as humans are able to meet their more-basic survival needs, they have a chance to become acquainted with levels of need that relate to more-advanced qualities, such as the need for love. As the pyramid indicates, our love and belongingness needs come next: our need to form relationships with others and to look outside ourselves. We seek to give affection and to be contributing members of groups within society.

After these needs are fulfilled, we strive for the esteem of others. Esteem relates to the desire to develop a sense of self-worth. We want others to be aware of our competence and worth and to acknowledge our value in the world.

Only after we meet these physiological, safety, love and belongingness, and esteem needs can we strive for self-actualization. Although early views of self-actualization restricted this quality to a few well-known individuals, self-

Figure 3.2

Pyramid of Motivational Needs

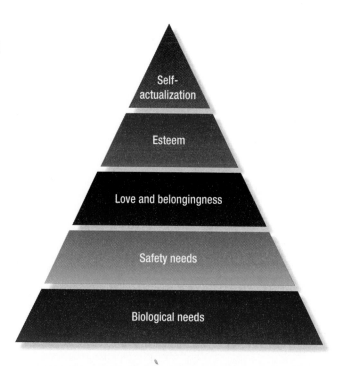

actualization is now generally regarded as a concept that can apply to any of us.

For instance, a parent with excellent nurturing skills who raises a family, a teacher who year after year creates an environment that maximizes students' opportunities for success, and an artist who realizes her creative potential might all be self-actualized individuals. The crucial characteristic of self-actualization is that we feel at ease with ourselves and satisfied that we are using our talents to the fullest.

W ork: Creating a Personal Mission Statement

- *To make, distribute and sell the finest quality all natural ice cream and related products in a wide variety of innovative flavors made from Vermont dairy products.*

- *To operate the Company on a sound financial basis of profitable growth, increasing value for our shareholders, and creating career opportunities and financial rewards for our employees.*

- *To operate the company in a way that actively recognizes the central role that business plays in the structure of society by initiating innovative ways to improve the quality of life of a broad community—local, national, and international.*[4]

You may have already guessed the name of the company that would make the statements reproduced above: Ben & Jerry's Ice Cream Corporation. Like almost every other major organization, Ben & Jerry's has a mission statement, a series of statements about what the organization does and the principles that guide its corporate life.

What's good for Ben & Jerry's is good for you. Each of us should set out a personal mission statement, a description encompassing our own personal objectives, long-term goals, and guiding philosophy. It's a kind of personal constitution that sets out broad principles of how we wish to conduct our lives. It is a guideline that allows us to adapt our behavior to changes in our lives without straying from our overall direction and purpose.

A personal mission statement also helps us to move from our abstract values and motivational needs to something concrete by providing the foundation for developing specific goals to guide our behavior. By making our values explicit, we are better able to formulate short- and long-term goals that reflect what is important to us.

For example, consider the following mission statement created by one student:

My mission is to use my personal abilities fully to become an engineer who will work on projects that will help others improve the quality of their lives. In addition, I hope to form meaningful relationships with others and to marry and raise children who will make their own contributions to society. Finally, I wish to participate in bettering the world by volunteering in organizations that will enhance the quality of my own community.

This mission statement reflects several underlying values and needs: the desire to use work to improve others' lives, the wish to form relationships with others, and the desire to make the world a better place. In some respects it is fairly specific (such as the desire to become an engineer and to marry and have children), while in others it is fairly vague (such as the wish to partici-pate in organizations that can improve community life). The key point is that it provides a general framework, a way of evaluating whether any particular choice fits into this individual's overall personal mission.

To create your own personal mission statement, follow these three prelimi-nary steps:

- **Summarize your most important values and motivational needs.** You've already assessed your values and motivational needs. Try to dis-till them into several key principles that will guide your life.

- **Consider what you want your major product to be.** Ben & Jerry's makes ice cream. What do you want to be known and remembered for? Your work? Your family? Your good deeds? Your relationships with others? Something you've created—art, photos, writings?

- **Reflect on the kind of person you want to be.** Do you wish to be kind, friendly, helpful, assertive, powerful, wealthy, altruistic?

Once you've completed these three steps, you're in a position to create your own mission statement. Write it in Try It 5.

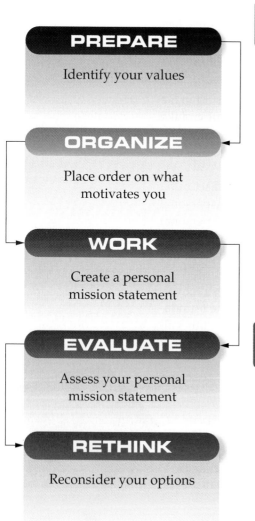

PREPARE

Identify your values

ORGANIZE

Place order on what motivates you

WORK

Create a personal mission statement

EVALUATE

Assess your personal mission statement

RETHINK

Reconsider your options

P.O.W.E.R. Plan

E valuate: Assessing Your Personal Mission Statement

After you've written a personal mission statement, consider whether it accurately captures what you are looking for out of life. Would a friend who knows you well see it as a valid reflection of who you are? Does the mission statement take a long-term view, reflecting not just where you are now, but where you wish to be in the future? Is it general enough to fit the many different circumstances in which you will find yourself?

Only you can determine the ability of your personal mis-sion statement to capture what is important to you. If you feel it doesn't, rewrite it. Eventually you'll come up with a statement that illustrates what you feel makes you special.

R ethink: Reconsidering Your Options

Personal mission statements are not set in stone like the Ten Commandments. Instead, they should be considered living documents that you can change as you become clearer about what you want for yourself.

That's why it's important to periodically revisit your per-sonal mission statement, the final step in the P.O.W.E.R. Plan for creating a personal mission statement (summarized at the right). When you do rethink your statement, ask yourself if it's still representative of your values and moti-vational needs. Consider whether it should be amended to reflect changes that have occurred in your life.

Write a Mission Statement

1. What are your most important values (e.g., comfort, environmental awareness, kindness to others, inner harmony, challenge, etc.)?

2. What are your motivational needs (e.g., love and belonging, esteem, self-actualization)?

3. In what general area or career do you wish to work?

4. What will be your most important "product," for which you want to be known and remembered (e.g., good deeds, wealth, power, prestige, artistic creations, business acumen, etc.)?

5. What kind of person do you want to be (helpful, kind, solitary, powerful, wealthy, etc.)?

6. In what sort of community do you want to live (large city, small city, small town, suburbs, country, woods, farm, etc.)?

7. With whom do you want to live (e.g., spouse, friends, children, etc.)?

8. What words describe your ideal life style (e.g., sophisticated, woodsy, agricultural, down-home, laid back, ambitious, etc.)?

Now write your mission statement. You might, for example, state how you plan to achieve your motivational needs and realize your values through your chosen career. Next you might describe the sort of person you want to be and the "product" you plan to contribute to the world. Finally, you might describe your intended lifestyle, including the type of community you would like to live in and the nature of your ideal family.

To Try It online, go to **www.mhhe.com/power**.

Personal Mission Statement

Prepared by: _____

Date: _____

Career Connections

Identifying Your Interests

Creating a personal mission statement can help you think more productively about one the most important decisions of your college career: identifying your profession. One way to jump-start this process is to systematically identify your current interests, a critical step in determining what kind of work will be most fulfilling and satisfying for you.

Few of us, however, are fully aware of the complete range of our interests, primarily because we don't take the time to systematically inventory them. Consequently, career advisor Richard Bolles[5] suggests answering the following questions to identify the scope of your interests:

- What are your favorite subjects and hobbies?
- What do you like to talk about most?
- When you go to a newsstand, what are the subjects of magazines that you are attracted to?
- When you read a newspaper, what section do you read first?
- If you're wandering around a bookstore, what kinds of books do you spend the most time looking at?
- When you surf the World Wide Web, what sites do you find yourself returning to regularly?

- When you watch TV game shows, what categories would you choose?
- If you were to write a book, what would you write about?
- When you get so engrossed in thought that you lose track of time, what is it you are thinking about?

Once you've got a better grip on your interests after answering each of these questions, the next step is to prioritize them, rank ordering them from most interesting to least interesting. You can then use this rank-ordered list to investigate careers, seeking out work involving interests similar to your own. For example, if you have strong interests in the visual arts, you might explore careers involving graphic design, computer-assisted graphics, or architecture. If you avidly keep up with the news of the day, you might consider journalism or television news production. The critical point is to try to match what you like to do (as well as your learning and personality style strengths) with what you'll be doing when you're on the job. The closer the match, the happier and more successful you'll be.

Even if you don't modify it, periodically reading your personal mission statement is important. It will remind you of who you are and what you are trying to get out of the one life you have.

To Thine Own Self Be True: No One Is Responsible for Your Life But You

"Don't take many English courses; they won't help you get a decent job." "How about pre-med? You'd make a great doctor." "Sign up for management classes so you'll be ready to join the family business when you graduate."

Sound familiar? Many of us have heard suggestions like these proposed by parents or others close to us. Such comments often sound quite reasonable.

Why, then, should suggestions like these be taken with great caution? The reason is they relate to decisions that you, and only you, should make. You are the one who must live with their consequences. You are the one who must live with yourself.

One of the worst reasons to follow a particular path in life is that other people want you to. Decisions that affect your life should be your decisions—decisions you make after you've considered various alternatives and chosen the path that suits you best.

Making your own decisions does not mean that you should ignore the suggestions of others. For instance, your parents do have their own unique experiences that may make their advice helpful, and having participated in a great deal of your personal history, they may have a clear view of your strengths and weaknesses. Still, their views are not necessarily accurate. They may still see you as a child, in need of care and protection. Or they may see only your strengths. Or, in some unfortunate cases, they may focus only on your flaws and shortcomings.

People will always be giving you advice. Ultimately, though, you have to make your own judgments about what's right for you, following your head—and your heart.

Speaking of Success

Name: *Bill Cosby*

Education: *Undergraduate, Temple University; PhD, University of Massachusetts*

Home: *Shelburne Falls, Massachusetts*

When comedian Bill Cosby received his Doctor of Education degree at the age of 40, he recounts that his mother was the happiest person at the graduation ceremony. According to Cosby, "She said to me, 'You finally got something that you can fall back on.' "[5]

Whether or not Cosby's mother actually believed what she said, it is clear that Cosby thinks that educational success has been a key part of his life. "I feel that school, achieving education and going higher, is something that I wanted to do for myself," he says.

He didn't start out in life as an educational success story. Attending school in the Philadelphia ghetto with friends Fat Albert, Old Weird Harold, Dumb Donald, and others who were later immortalized in his comedy routines, Cosby performed so poorly in the classroom that he was forced to repeat the 10th grade. He dropped out of high school and joined the Navy. Eventually, he finished high school through a correspondence course, realizing that he had to "use the intelligence I was born with."[6]

Cosby became determined to further his education. After completing his stint in the Navy, he enrolled at Temple University, supported by a football scholarship. His goal was to become a physical education teacher.

At Temple, Cosby's schedule was hectic; he was a member of several sports teams, and he also had a number of part-time jobs. His most serious commitment, however, was to academics, and he maintained a B average. He commented, "If I didn't make good at Temple, I knew what waited for me was a lifetime as a busboy or factory hand. I was so afraid that I made myself do well. On an evening when all I wanted was to go out with the boys, the specter of what might happen to me reared up,

and boom, I was right back in my room studying."[7]

Cosby's life took another turn when, while in college, he began to work as a part-time bartender. Customers found him hilarious, and they encouraged him to take his brand of comedy on the road. The rest is legend: After graduating from Temple, he became one of the most successful comedians of our era.

Cosby has remained committed to education even after achieving fame and riches as an entertainer. Years after completing his undergraduate degree, he enrolled in a graduate program at the University of Massachusetts, where he received both a master's and a doctoral degree in education.

Cosby has supported various educational institutions with huge gifts, including $20 million to Spelman College in Atlanta. He sees education as a noble enterprise, saying, "Things are not all that hard as long as someone is there to explain it to you, and we should not be afraid of those things."

Looking Back

What are my learning styles, and how have they affected my academic success?

- People have patterns of diverse learning styles—characteristic ways of acquiring and using knowledge.

- Learning styles include visual/verbal, visual/nonverbal, auditory/verbal, and tactile/kinesthetic styles (the receptive learning styles), and analytic and relational styles (information-processing styles).

- Personality styles that influence learning are classified along dimensions of introversion/extroversion, intuition/sensing, thinking/feeling, and perceiving/judging.

What is self-concept and how does it affect me?

- Self-concept is the understanding of the self that a person forms over time. Its major components are the physical, social, and personal self.

- Self-concept is important because of the effects it has on people's attitudes and behavior. Self-concept can act as a self-fulfilling prophecy, in that people act in accordance with their self-concepts.

How does my level of self-esteem affect my behavior?

- Self-esteem is the overall evaluation we give ourselves as individuals.

- High self-esteem can lead to greater happiness, an enhanced ability to cope with adversity, a sense of security and confidence, and a sense of self-efficacy.

- Low self-esteem can lead to insecurity, low self-efficacy, and a cycle of failure.

How can I make wise personal decisions throughout life?

- A personal mission statement can be used to determine important values and to state the principles by which we intend to lead our lives.

- People's needs can be organized into a hierarchy in which the most-basic and fundamental needs form the base of a pyramid and higher orders of needs sit atop the basic needs.

- Although we should consider the ideas and opinions of others, we need to make our own decisions and choose our own path.

Key Terms and Concepts

Analytic learning style (p. 59)
Auditory/verbal learning style (p. 58)
Learning style (p. 57)
Left-brain processing (p. 63)
Receptive learning style (p. 58)
Relational learning style (p. 60)
Right-brain processing (p. 63)
Self-actualization (p. 76)

Self-concept (p. 68)
Self-efficacy (p. 71)
Self-esteem (p. 71)
Self-fulfilling prophecy (p. 68)
Tactile/kinesthetic learning style (p. 58)
Visual/nonverbal learning style (p. 58)
Visual/verbal learning style (p. 58)

Resources

On Campus

If you are interested in learning more about your pattern of learning styles, visit your campus counseling center or career center, where you may be able to take special assessment tests that can pinpoint your learning preferences and offer study strategies based on those preferences.

When dealing with the uncertainties of life and establishing your own sense of direction, it may help to speak to someone who has perspective and experience with college students. Here, too, a good place to start on campus is either a general counseling center or one that is designed to help students choose career paths. Mental health offices can also be helpful in putting you in touch with a therapist with whom you can explore issues revolving around your self-concept and self-esteem. Don't hesitate to get help. You are doing it for yourself.

In Print

Gail Wood's book *How to Study: Use Your Personal Learning Style to Help You Succeed When It Counts* (Learning Express Press, 2000) provides an introduction to learning styles, offering tips and suggestions for making use of the way that you learn.

Don't Sweat the Small Stuff . . . and It's All Small Stuff (Hyperion, 1997), written by Richard Carlson, is a down-to-earth guide that is meant to help you sort out what is—and is not—important in your life.

On the Web

Many sites on the World Wide Web provide the opportunity to extend your learning about the material in this chapter. (Although the Web addresses were accurate at the time the book was printed, check the P.O.W.E.R. Learning website [**www.mhhe.com/power**] for any changes that may have occurred.)

- Greg Kearsley, an instructional designer and online course developer at Walden Institute, has developed a useful site called "Explorations in

Learning & Instruction: The Theory Into Practice Database" (**tip. psychology.org/index.html**). This database contains short summaries of 50 major theories of learning and instruction.

- Bulls Eye Consultancy (a human resources firm) provides a basic self-assessment process (**www.bulls-eye.nl/self_1.php**) to help you clarify your values or beliefs. Use this to help you write a personal mission statement.

- The Barksdale Foundation, a nonprofit organization offering "self-esteem and stress control materials and programs," hosts a detailed, online self-esteem evaluation (**barksdale.org/Evaluation/eval69.html**). Simply click which response best describes how you feel about each statement. When you're done, click the submit button and your score will be automatically calculated.

Taking It to the Net

1 This exercise can help you write your own mission statement. Mental Help Net (an online guide to mental health, psychology, and psychiatry) offers a website entitled "Writing Your Own Philosophy of Life" (**www. mentalhelp.net/psyhelp/chap3/chap3k.htm**), in which a list of goals is grouped in three categories. Use your responses to help you create a mission statement.

2 Building self-esteem. Go to the University of South Florida's Counseling Center website entitled "Changing Your Self-Concept and Building Self-Esteem" (**www.usf.edu/counsel/self-hlp/self-est.htm**). Write down the six strategies listed there for enhancing your self-esteem. How do these suggestions compare to the suggestions offered in this book? Now use a search engine to locate other sources of information about raising self-esteem. (Possible search term: the phrase "raising self-esteem," in quotes.) Did you locate any other suggestions for raising self-esteem? How do they compare to the suggestions in this book?

The Case of . . .

The Instructor Who Spoke Too Much

Lana Carlson, a 26-year-old woman living in Carlsbad, Missouri, was at her wits' end. The instructor in her introductory psychology class spent each 50-minute lecture talking nonstop. He barely paused to acknowledge students' questions, and his only goal seemed to be to present as much material as possible. He even gave assignments in the same fast, nasal tone that he used throughout class.

If it weren't for her friend Darren Rubbell, who was in the same class, Lana would never have managed to figure out how to complete the assignments, which the professor never bothered to write down. The strange thing was that Darren didn't seem to have much trouble with the professor's endless talking. In fact, he claimed to enjoy the class a lot. He had no trouble following the lectures and understanding the assignments, seeming to absorb like a sponge the information the instructor was spouting.

1. Based on what you know about learning styles, what might be the source of Lana's difficulties?

2. What learning style does the instructor apparently assume all students have? Do you think this is one of Lana's learning styles? Why or why not?

3. How might the instructor change his presentation to accommodate diverse learning styles?

4. Why does Lana's friend Darren have so little trouble with the instructor's lectures?

5. Why do you think Lana has less trouble understanding Darren after class than she has understanding her instructor?

6. If you were Lana, what might you do to improve your situation?

Taking Notes

4

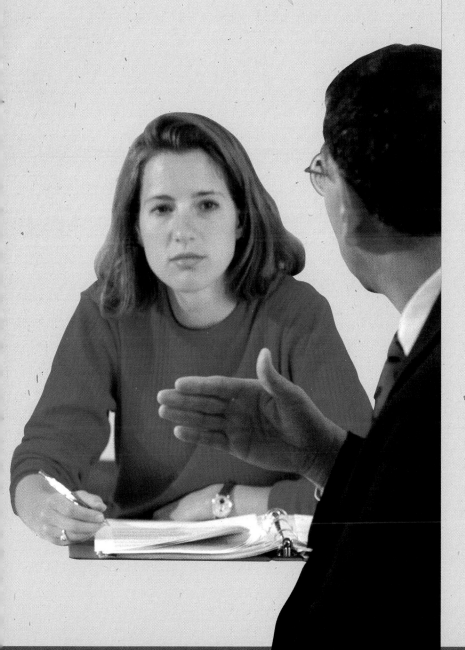

When he sat himself down in the front row of his biology class at the start of his second semester in college, Hill Taylor realized that something fundamental had changed.

In the past, Hill would have sat as far back in the classroom as he could. That's what he had done all through high school and the beginning of his first semester.

But then he received Cs on three midterms.

In a notetaking workshop Hill enrolled in afterward, he learned the importance of active listening and taking good notes in class. He also learned that one way to become more engaged in class is to sit close to the instructor.

Trying out the strategies he was taught in the workshop, Hill found—a bit to his surprise—that they helped. By the end of the semester, he'd pulled his grades way up.

Looking
Ahead

Hill Taylor's move from the back to the front of the classroom was both a source and a symbol of his academic success. Hill's ability to take good notes was also likely to pay future dividends, because notetaking skills not only help produce academic success in college but also contribute to career success.

In this chapter we discuss effective strategies for taking notes during class lectures, during other kinds of oral presentations, and from written sources such as textbooks. There's a lot more to good notetaking than you probably think—and a lot less if you view notetaking as essentially "getting everything down on paper." As we explore the ins and outs of notetaking, we'll pause along the way to discuss the tools of the notetaking trade, how to be an active learner, how to think your way to good notes, and how to deal with disorganized instructors.

After reading this chapter, you'll be able to answer these questions:

- **What is effective notetaking?**
- **How can I take good notes in class?**
- **What techniques apply to taking notes from written materials?**

Taking Notes in Class

You know the type: the student who desperately tries to write down everything the instructor says—no spoken word goes unwritten. And you know what you think to yourself: "If only I took such painstaking notes—I'd do *much* better in my classes."

Contrary to what many students think, good notetaking does *not* mean writing down every word that an instructor utters. With notetaking, less is often more. We'll see why as we consider the basic steps in P.O.W.E.R. notetaking.

P repare: Considering Your Goals

As with other academic activities, preparation is a critical component of notetaking. The following steps will prepare you for action:

- **Identify the instructor's—and your—goals for the course.** On the first day of class, most instructors talk about their objectives, what they hope you'll get out of the class, and what you'll know when it's over. Most restate the information on the class syllabus, the written document that explains the assignments for the semester. For example, they may say that they want you to "develop an appreciation for the ways that statistics are used in everyday life."

  The information you get during that first session and through the syllabus is critical. If the instructor's goals aren't stated explicitly, you should attempt to figure them out. In addition to those "external" goals, you should have your own goals. What is it you want to learn from the course? How will the information from the course help you to enhance your knowledge, achieve your dreams, improve yourself as a person?

- **Complete assignments before coming to class.** Your instructor enthusiastically describes the structure of the neuron, recounting excitedly how neurons don't physically touch one another and how electrons flow across neurons, changing their electrical charge. One problem: You have only the vaguest idea what a neuron is. And the reason you don't know is that you haven't read the assignment.

  Chances are you have found yourself in this situation at least a few times, so you know firsthand that sinking feeling as you become more and more confused. Because you can't follow the discussion, you can't get interested either, so the class seems boring, and you end up thinking about what you'll have for lunch or the movie you saw last night.

  The moral: Always go to class prepared. Do all of your assignments

PREPARE

Consider your goals

ORGANIZE

Get the tools of notetaking together

WORK

Process—don't copy— information

EVALUATE

Think critically about your notes

RETHINK

Review your notes shortly after class to activate your memory

P.O.W.E.R. Plan

An engaging lecturer can make even the most complex material come alive in the classroom, whereas an instructor who is unorganized or dull can make coming to class sheer drudgery. No matter what the lecturer's style, however, you need to be prepared to take effective notes.

beforehand. Instructors assume that their students have done what they've assigned, and their lectures are based upon that assumption. It's virtually impossible to catch on to the gist of a lecture if you haven't completed the assignments.

- **Accept the instructor, warts and all.** Not every instructor is a brilliant lecturer. Accept the fact that, just as there are differences in skills among students, some instructors are more adept at lecturing than others.

  Don't let a miserable lecture style—or the fact that the instructor has a bad haircut or a mouth that droops to one side or wrinkled clothing—get in the way of your education. You're going to notice these things, but don't let them interfere with your goals. Good notetaking requires being prepared to listen to the material.

- **Perform a pre-class warm-up.** No, this doesn't mean doing jumping jacks just before each class. As you head to class or settle into your seat, skim your notes from the previous lecture, looking over what the instructor said and where that lecture left off. You should also briefly review the main headings or summary section of any reading you've been assigned.

  The warm-up doesn't have to be long. The goal is simply to refresh yourself, to get yourself into the right frame of mind for the class.

- **Choose a seat that will promote good notetaking.** You should certainly choose a seat that permits you to see and hear clearly, but there's more to your choice than that. Picking the right seat in a classroom can make a big difference.

"The highest result of education is tolerance."

Helen Keller

Where is the best place to sit? Usually it's front and center. Instructors make more eye contact with the people near them, and they sometimes believe that the best, most-engaged students sit closest.

Furthermore, sitting in the back of the class may make you feel disengaged and out of touch with what is happening at the front of the room. In turn, this may make it easier for your mind to wander.

Organize: Getting the Tools of Notetaking Together

Do you have a favorite pen? A preferred type of notebook?

By the time we reach college, most of us have developed distinct tastes when it comes to the materials we use in class. Although taking your favorite kind of notebook and pen to class will not make you a better notetaker, not having them certainly will interfere with your getting the most out of class.

There are several things to consider as you prepare for class:

- **Choose the appropriate writing utensil and paper.** Generally, using a pen is better than using a pencil. Ink is less likely to smudge, and what you produce with ink is usually brighter and clearer—and therefore easier to use when studying. On the other hand, for math and science classes, where you may be copying down or even working through formulas in class, a pencil might be better, because it's easier to erase if you make a mistake when copying detailed, complex information.

  Sometimes you may want to use a combination of pen and pencil. And in some cases you might use several different colors. One color—such as red—might signify important information that the instructor mentions will be on the test. Another color might be reserved for definitions or material that is copied from the board. And a third might be used for general notes on the lecture.

- **Choose a notebook that assists in notetaking.** Loose-leaf notebooks are particularly good for taking notes because they permit you to go back later and change the order of the pages or add additional material in the appropriate spot. But whatever kind of notebook you use, *use only one side of the page for writing; keep one side free of notes.* There may be times when you're studying that you'll want to spread out your notes in front of you, and it's much easier if no material is written on the back of the pages.

You should configure notebook pages spatially to optimize later review. According to educator Walter Pauk,[1] the best way to do this is to draw a line down the left side of your notebook page, about 2½ inches from the left-hand margin (illustrated in Figure 4.1). Keep the notes you write in class to the right of the line. Indent major supporting details beneath each main idea, trying to use no more than one line for each item, and leave space between topics to add information. When it comes time to review your notes later, you'll be able to jot down a keyword, catch phrase, or major idea on the left side of the page.

Journal Reflections

How Do I Take Notes?

1. Describe your typical notetaking techniques in a few sentences. Do you try to write down as much of what the instructor says as possible? Do you tend to take only a few notes? Do you often find you need more time to get things down?

2. Overall, how effective would you say your notetaking techniques are?

3. In which classes do your techniques work best? Worst? Why?

4. Do your notes ever have "holes" in them—due to lapses of attention or times when you couldn't get down everything you wanted to? When do you usually discover them? What do you do about them?

- **Decide whether you should take your textbook to class.** You may or may not need to take your textbook to class. Sometimes instructors will refer to information contained in it, and sometimes it's useful to have it handy to clarify information that is being discussed. You can also use it to look up key terms that may momentarily escape you. But don't, under any circumstances, use class time as an opportunity to read the textbook!

Figure 4.1

In this example of a student's notes on a lecture about memory, she has written the material in the larger right-hand column during class. Later, when reviewing her notes, she wrote down key pieces of information in the left-hand column.

	3 ways to store information
	sensory memory—everything sensed
aka working memory (like Computer RAM)	short term memory—15-25 sec.
	Stored as meaning
	5-9 chunks
(like hard disk)	long-term memory—unlimited
Rehearsal: STM to LTM	rehearsal
	visualization
Chunking	Organize information into chunks:
	birds, instruments, body parts, etc.
	Mnemonics
Roy G. Biv	acronyms
Every good boy deserves fun	acrostics
30 days hath September	rhyming
Unfinished Symphony	jingles
pato, caballo	keyword technique
room and furniture	loci technique
sun, zoo, me, store . . .	peg method
	Using senses
	moving
	draw, diagram
	visualize
	Overlearning

- **Consider taking a laptop computer to class.** If you're comfortable with computers and have a laptop, consider using it to take notes. There are several advantages: Legibility problems are avoided, and it's easy to go back and revise or add material after you've taken the notes.

  There are also potential pitfalls. If you do intend to use a laptop for taking notes, remember these guidelines:

  1. Make sure your computer battery is fully charged.

  2. Use only computers that have a quiet keyboard so you don't annoy your follow students, and make sure the speaker in the computer is turned off.

  3. Although you may be tempted to type in virtually everything an instructor says because it is relatively effortless, don't. As we'll discuss next, it's important to be selective in notetaking.

  4. Have an alternative means of notetaking available. Sometimes instructors present graphical material or formulas that are hard to input into a computer. And sometimes your computer may fail.

W ork: Processing—Not Copying—Information

With pen poised, you're ready to begin the work of notetaking. The instructor begins to speak, and you start to write as quickly as you can, taking down as many of the instructor's words as possible.

Stop! You've made your first mistake. The central act in taking notes is not writing; listening and thinking are far more important. The key to effective notetaking is to write down the right amount of information—not too much and not too little.

Successful notetaking involves not just *hearing* what the instructor says, but *listening actively.* **Hearing** is the involuntary act of sensing sounds. The annoying drip of a faucet or the grating sound of a roommate's voice speaking on the phone in the next room are two examples of how hearing is both involuntary and often meaningless. In contrast, **active listening** is the voluntary act of focusing on what is being said, making sense of it, and thinking about it in a way that per-

Hearing
The involuntary act of sensing sounds

> "I had tons of notes—I copied every word the professor said. Actually, I was so busy writing that I didn't understand a thing."
>
> Junior, Saint Joseph's University[2]

Active listening
The voluntary act of focusing on what is being said, making sense of it, and thinking about it in a way that permits it to be recalled accurately

mits it to be recalled accurately. Listening involves concentration. And it requires shutting out competing thoughts, such as what we need to pick up at the grocery store or why our date last night was so terrific. (To get a sense of your own listening skills, complete Try It 1 on the next page.)

Keeping the importance of active listening in mind, consider the following recommendations for taking notes:

- **Listen for the key ideas.** Not every sentence in a lecture is equally important, and one of the most useful skills you can develop is separating the key ideas from supporting information. Good lecturers strive to make just a few main points. The rest of what they say consists of explanation, examples, and other supportive material that expands upon the key ideas.

Try It! 1

🎧 **Personal Styles:** Determine Your Listening Style

Consider the following pairs of statements. Place a check next to the statement in each pair that more closely describes your style.

_____ 1a. When I'm listening in class, I lean back and get as comfortable as possible.
_____ 1b. When I'm listening in class, I sit upright and even lean forward a little.

_____ 2a. I let the instructor's words wash over me, generally going with the flow of the lecture.
_____ 2b. I try to guess in advance what the instructor is going to say and what direction the lecture is taking.

_____ 3a. I regard each lecture as a separate event, not necessarily related to what the instructor has said before or will say the next time.
_____ 3b. As I listen, I regularly ask myself how this relates to what was said in previous classes.

_____ 4a. When I take notes, I try to reproduce the instructor's words as closely as possible.
_____ 4b. When I take notes, I try to interpret and summarize the ideas behind the instructor's words.

_____ 5a. I don't usually question the importance of what the instructor is saying or why it's the topic of a lecture or discussion.
_____ 5b. I often ask why the content of the lecture is important enough for the instructor to be speaking about it.

_____ 6a. I rarely question the accuracy or logic of a presentation, assuming that the instructor knows the topic better than I do.
_____ 6b. I often ask myself how the instructor knows something and find myself wondering how it could be proved.

_____ 7a. I just about never make eye contact with the instructor.
_____ 7b. I often make eye contact with the instructor.

If you tended to prefer the "a" statements in most pairs, you have a more passive listening style. If you preferred the "b" statements, you have a more active listening style. Based on your responses, consider ways that you can become a more active listener.
To Try It online, go to **www.mhhe.com/power**.

Meta-message
The underlying main ideas that a speaker is seeking to convey; the meaning behind the overt message

Your job, then, is to distinguish the key ideas from their support. To do this, you need to be alert and always searching for the **meta-message** of your instructor's words—that is, the underlying main ideas that a speaker is seeking to convey, or the meaning behind the overt message you hear.

How can you discern the meta-message? One way is to *listen for key-words*. Instructors know what's important in their lecture; your job is to figure it out, not just from what they say but from how they say it.

For instance, listen for clues about the importance of material. Phrases like "don't forget . . . ," "be sure to remember that . . . ," "you need to know . . . ," "the most important thing that must be considered . . . ," "there are four problems with this approach . . . ," and—a big one—"this will be on the test . . . " should cause you to sit up and take notice. Another good sign of importance is repetition. If an instructor says the same thing in several ways, it's a clear sign that the material being discussed is important.

Be on the lookout for nonverbal signals too. Does an instructor get excited about a particular topic? Does the speaker seem unenthusiastic when talking about something? Use nonverbal cues to gauge the importance of a particular part of a message relative to other things being said. Finally, listen for what is *not* being said. Sometimes silence is not just golden, but informative as well. By noting what topics are not being covered in class, or are presented only minimally, you can gauge the relative importance of ideas in comparison with one another.

This is where preliminary preparation and organization come in. The only way to know what's left out of a lecture is to have done the assigned readings in advance.

- **Use short, abbreviated phrases—not full sentences—when taking notes.** Forget everything you've ever heard about always writing in full sentences. If you try to write notes in complete sentences, you'll soon become bogged down, paying more attention to your notes than to your instructor. In fact, if you use full sentences, you'll be tempted to try transcribing every word the instructor utters, which, as you now know, is not a good idea at all.

  Instead, write in phrases, using only key words or terms. Save full sentences for definitions or quotes that your instructor clearly wants you to know word for word. For example, consider the following excerpt from a lecture:

  > There are two kinds of job analyses: job- or task-oriented analyses and worker- or employee-oriented analyses. Job analyses just describe the tasks that need to be accomplished by a worker. Employee-oriented job descriptions need to describe knowledge, skills, and abilities the employee must have to get the job done. Most job analyses include elements of both job-oriented and employee-oriented types.

Using a laptop computer to take class notes ensures that they will be legible, and that it will be easy to revise them after class. On the other hand, it's difficult to input graphical material, such as complex formulas, and there's also a danger that you'll be tempted to take too many notes.

If you were taking notes, you might produce the following:

2 kinds job analyses:
(1) job-oriented (= task-oriented): what worker must do to get job done
(2) worker-oriented (= employee-oriented): describe knowledge, skills, abilities
needed most analyses include both

Note how the lecturer used 67 words, while the notes used only 29 words—fewer than half.

- **Use abbreviations.** One way to speed up the notetaking process is through the use of abbreviations. Among the most common:

and *& or +*	with *w/*	without *w/o*
care of *c/o*	leads to; resulting in *→*	as a result of *←*
percent *%*	change *Δ*	number *#*
that is *i.e.*	for example *e.g.*	and so forth *etc.*
no good *n.g.*	question *?*	compared with *c/w*
page *p.*	important! *!!*	less than *‹*
more than *›*	equals, same as *=*	versus *vs.*

- **Take notes in outline form.** It's often useful to take notes in the form of an outline. An outline summarizes ideas in short phrases and indicates the relationship among concepts through the use of indentations.

    When outlining, it's best to be formal about it, using roman numerals, regular numbers, and capital and small letters (see the example in Figure 4.2 below). Or, if you prefer, you can also simply use outlining indentations without assigning numbers and letters.

Figure 4.2

A Sample Outline

I.   Difficulties faced by college students seeking affordable housing
   A. Students are subjected to high rents for housing close to campus
      1. Forced to share apartments
      2. Sometimes must live far from campus
   B. Made to sign leases with strict provisions
II. Possible solutions
   A. College offers subsidized housing
      1. Advantage is that housing costs can be lowered
      2. Potential problems
         a. College becomes students' landlord
         b. College uses funds for housing that could be otherwise invested in education
   B. Rent control
      1. Advantage: Rent control can provide fixed, reasonably priced rents
      2. Disadvantages
         a. Creates a permanent, expensive rent-control bureaucracy
         b. Landlords may neglect rent-control property
         c. The present shortage of apartments would worsen, because little incentive for owners to increase the number of rental units
         d. Competition for rent-fixed units would dramatically increase
III. Summary
   A. There are advantages and disadvantages to both solutions
   B. May need new, creative solutions

Outlining serves a number of functions. It forces you to try to determine the structure of the lecture. Organizing the key points and noting the connections among them helps you remember the material better because you have processed it more. The effort involved in outlining also keeps your mind from drifting away from the lecture.

Use Try It 2, "Outline a Lecture," to practice your outlining skills.

- **Copy information written on the board or projected from overheads.** If your instructor takes the time to write something out to be displayed in class, you should take the time to copy it. This goes for definitions, quotations, phrases, and formulas—if you see them in writing, they're quite likely important enough to include in your notes. In fact, material displayed prominently has "test item" written all over it. You might want to highlight such material in some way in your notes.

- **Use different notetaking techniques for class discussions.** Not every course is structured as a lecture. Classes that are based less on lectures and more on class discussion pose greater challenges for notetaking.

  For example, a discussion of the use of tax support of private schools in a sociology class may raise a variety of issues. As students in the class offer their ideas, how much—and what—should you place in your notes?

  In such situations, the best approach is to take your cue from the course instructor. Often the instructor will pose some questions to get the discussion rolling. Note those questions—they're an important indicator of what the instructor is interested in. The instructor's reaction to particular comments is another clue. Listen to his or her responses. If he or she responds enthusiastically to a particular point, you'll want to highlight it in your notes. (To practice taking notes during a discussion, go to Try It 3 on page 100.)

- **Pay particular attention to the points raised by instructors at the end of discussion and lecture classes.** Instructors often provide a summary of the discussion, which is worthy of inclusion in your notes.

- **Ask questions.** One of the most important things you can do during a class is to ask questions. Raising questions will help you evaluate, clarify, and ultimately better understand what your instructor is saying. Even beyond these critical goals, questions serve several other purposes.

  For one thing, raising questions will help you to personalize the material being covered, permitting you to draw it more closely into your own framework and perspective. Furthermore, when you ask a question and it is answered, you become personally engaged in what the instructor is saying. In very large classes, asking questions may be the only way that an instructor can get a sense of you as an individual.

  Questioning also increases your involvement in the class as a whole. If you sit back and never raise questions in class, you are much less likely to feel a real part of the class. Becoming an active questioner will rightly make you feel like you have contributed something to the class.

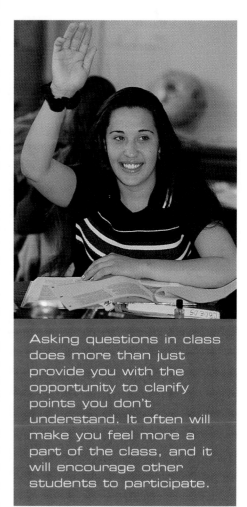

Asking questions in class does more than just provide you with the opportunity to clarify points you don't understand. It often will make you feel more a part of the class, and it will encourage other students to participate.

Try It! 2

Working in a Group: Outline a Lecture

Working with others in a group, take turns slowly reading sections of the following lecture to each other.[3] As the paragraph is being read, outline the main arguments in the space that follows the passage.

> Today most of us think that the Civil War was about slavery. We think: The Southern states seceded because they wanted to preserve the system of slavery, and the Northern states entered the war bound and determined to free the slaves. This is at best an oversimplification. In fact, only the fairly extremist Abolitionist wing of Lincoln's Republican Party ever saw the war this clearly and simply.
>
> Not even Abe Lincoln, the Great Emancipator himself, ever saw the war as solely about slavery. And the Emancipation Proclamation, which he did eventually sign in late 1862, was never a simple matter of clear conscience and moral decision. Lincoln saw slavery as one of many ills that afflicted and divided the nation, and the decision to issue the Emancipation Proclamation was to him a deeply political one.
>
> Personally, Lincoln's feelings about slavery were complex. At times he spoke of slavery as "the greatest wrong inflicted on any people" and condemned it on essentially moral grounds. At other times, he observed that emancipation of the slaves should be seen as a *means* to victory, not as an *end* in itself. The slaves, once freed, would be available to serve the needs of the Union Army—not necessarily as soldiers, but as laborers, cooks, hospital attendants, helpers. At still other times, Lincoln mirrored the prevailing prejudice of the time, advocating emigration and colonization of freed slaves in Central America, rather than their integration into U.S. culture. (Indeed, the U.S. government, under Lincoln, actually tried this, settling 453 black colonists on an island near Haiti in 1863. When smallpox and starvation caused the colony to fail, the 368 survivors were returned to the United States on a naval vessel in 1864.)
>
> Lincoln's attitude toward the Emancipation Proclamation was also complex. In July 1862, he expressed the view that emancipation was "a military necessity." "The slaves," he said, "were undeniably an element of strength to those who had their service, and we must decide whether that element should be with us or against us." At the same time, in a highly political viewpoint, he made it clear that emancipation should apply only to the rebellious states of the deep South, not to the border states, which—though slave states—had remained in the Union. This is why the proclamation, when it was ultimately issued, freed only the slaves in states that had not returned to the Union by January 1, 1963; it did not apply to the slaves in the Unionist border states (who were freed later by other means).

Remember, if you are unclear about some point, it is likely that others share your lack of clarity.

Finally, by asking questions in class, you serve as a role model for other students. Your questions may help break the ice in a class, making it easier for others to raise issues that they have about the material. And ultimately the answers that the instructor provides to others' questions may help you to better understand and/or evaluate your understanding of the material.

Breaking the Ice: Tips for Getting Over Stage Fright and Asking Questions in Class
Raising your hand in class can be intimidating. You may be afraid that you'll say something

Write your outline here.

 After you have outlined the passage, compare your outline with that of others who took notes on the same passage.

- Did you all agree on the main ideas of each passage?

- How do your notes differ from others', and what are the similarities?

- How might you improve your notes to better capture the main points?

- Would a different topic produce greater or fewer difficulties?

Collectively, produce what you believe is the ideal outline, and compare it to that produced by other groups.

To Try It online, go to **www.mhhe.com/power**.

---

dumb, making it clear to the whole class just how out of it you are; or that everyone will be staring at you; or that your instructor and fellow classmates will resent your wasting valuable class time with your own trivial questions.

Although it may not be possible to fully banish such self-defeating thoughts, there are several strategies that you can follow to make it easier to raise the questions you have.

1. **Sit in the front of the room.** Sitting close to the instructor will make it easier to ask questions. Moreover, if you sit in the back of the room and ask a question, the students in front of you will likely swivel around and look at you. In that case, if you already feel intimidated, your feelings of anxiety may soar off the charts.

Take Notes during Discussions

Take notes on the following class discussion about the growth of English as a global language. Use cues from the instructor about the importance and accuracy of each point, and record in your notes only the key points that shed light on the topic.

Instructor: OK, so why is English so important globally, not just in English-speaking countries?

Alicia: Um, well, English is spoken by a lot of people. When I was in Denmark last summer, everyone spoke it. It just seems to be everywhere.

Instructor: OK. It's certainly a very widely used language. But we're trying to figure out why. We're looking for causes, not just symptoms, right? Anyone else? Bart?

Bart: Yeah, English is becoming, like, everyone's second language simply because it has established a good base. Not only did the *English* English people—you know, the British—spread the language all over through colonizing the world—you know, the sun never sets on the British Empire and all—but now America is everywhere, too. I mean, we're cool—our culture is cool and very influencing.

Instructor: Good, good. Yes, you've given two good reasons why English is widespread. The British Empire spread the language through parts of Asia, Africa, and the Caribbean in the 18th and 19th centuries, and modern U.S. culture is highly influential, which causes many people worldwide to welcome English. What else?

Catherine: Well, the way in which the American culture is spreading is very much language-centered. It's American movies and music that are everywhere, and these involve the language, not just the style. I mean, people know a lot more than how to say Coca-Cola and Nike, don't they? They listen to American CDs and movies, and they even produce songs and movies in English. So it's not just culture we're spreading, it's our language too.

Instructor: Exactly! The language is perhaps the most important aspect of the culture that we're distributing. Damon?

Damon: Yeah, I was just going to say, another thing that's caused the language to spread is global communications, which are just about always in English. Look at the language of aviation—pilots talk to each other in English, don't they? And the Internet. The universal language of the Internet is English. So if you want to communicate globally, and now everyone does because for the first time everyone *can,* you've got to pick up some English.

Rosario: Right. It's the universal second language. And it will only get more universal as American culture spreads further and other cultures develop to the point of being able to join the party—communicating, and buying stuff and listening to our music and so on. I mean, it's the biggest game in town, and it's spoken by the people with the biggest wallets. Money talks, you know. And now it talks American English.

Instructor: You've really hit it now. Language has always gone where the resources are. If someone has what you want, you'd better speak their language. Money speaks American English. Very well put, Rosario! Excellent discussion, folks.

2. **Write down your question.** If you anticipate that you'll stumble or forget what you want to say, write down your question before raising your hand. The idea is not to read it word for word, or even refer to it at all when you actually ask your question. But writing it will help you quickly organize your thoughts, and provide a safety net in case you freeze momentarily.

Write your notes here:

Were you able to identify the information that was most important? How would actually seeing the instructor's nonverbal reactions to the students' comments be helpful? **Working in a Group:** Compare your notes on the discussion with those of your classmates. As a group, try to create an optimal set of notes, reflecting the most important points.

To Try It online, go to **www.mhhe.com/power**.

3. **Be one of the first students to ask a question.** One reason people sometimes give for not having asked questions is that others have already asked so many questions that there's no time. Or that others have already addressed the issue. Or that others' questions were so good that they make yours look silly.

To avoid these stumbling blocks, be among the first to ask questions. Don't wait for others to break the ice; go for it.

Use Special Techniques for "Problem Instructors"

He talks too fast . . . she mumbles . . . he puts down people when they ask a question . . . she rambles and goes off on boring tangents . . . she explains things in a way that doesn't make much sense.

In the real world of the college classroom, not every instructor comes to class with a clear, compelling lecture and then presents it beautifully. All of us have suffered through lectures that are deficient in one or more ways. What should you do when you find yourself in such a situation?

1. *Remember that this too shall pass.* First, keep in mind that this is a temporary condition; your experience usually won't last more than one term. Most instructors are conscientious and well prepared, and unless you have enormously bad luck, the unpleasant experience you're having now will not be routine.

2. *Ask questions about the material.* Even if you have no idea what is going on in class—or especially if you have no idea—ask questions. You are not the only one struggling with the instructor's shortcomings. You will be doing everyone in the class a favor if you admit you're not following what an instructor is saying and ask for clarification.

3. *Ask—privately—for the instructor to change his or her behavior.* It is not bad classroom etiquette to ask an instructor to speak a little slower. Instructors sometimes get carried away with enthusiasm and begin speaking faster and faster without even being aware of it. Very often a reality check from a student will be welcome. But don't couch your comment in a way that makes the instructor feel inept ("Could you slow down; you're going too fast and losing me"). Instead, keep the comment neutral, without placing blame. For instance, you might simply say, "I'm having trouble keeping up with you; would it be possible for you to speak a little more slowly?"

4. *Pool your resources.* Get together with other students in the class and work out a strategy for dealing with the situation. If an instructor speaks too fast and you just can't keep up with the flow of information, meet with your fellow students and compare what you've gleaned from the class. They may have understood or noted material that you missed, and vice versa. Together, you may

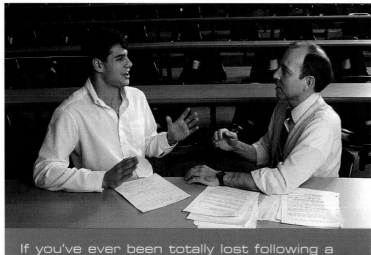

If you've ever been totally lost following a lecture, you may have discovered that speaking with your instructor immediately after class was helpful. Most instructors are very happy to go over and clarify key points that they've covered during class. They also appreciate your initiative and interest.

be able to put the pieces of the puzzle together and get a fuller understanding of the material.

5. *Listen to the lecture again.* You might bring a tape recorder to class (but request the instructor's permission first!). Then, after class, you can play back the tape at your leisure.

   There's another option: Many instructors teach multiple sections of the same course. If this is the case, you might, schedule permitting, sit in on an additional section of the course. The second time around the information may become much clearer.

6. *Talk with the instructor after class.* If you feel totally lost after a lecture, or even if you've missed only a few points, speak with the instructor after class. Ask for clarification and get him or her to reexplain points that you missed. Such a dialogue will help you to understand the material better. But it will also do something more: help build your relationship with your instructor.

Keep a Balance Between Too Many Notes and Too Few Notes The key to effective notetaking is to keep a balance between too many and too few notes.

The best way to achieve this balance is by paying close attention in class. By being alert, engaged, and involved in class, you'll be able to make the most of the techniques we've discussed. The result: notes that capture the most important points raised in class and that will optimize your recall and mastery of the course subject matter (see a sample of two students' notes in Figure 4.3).

E valuate: Thinking Critically about Your Notes

Toward the end of class, look over your notes. Now's the time—before the class has ended—to evaluate what you've written.

After being sure you can answer "yes" to the most basic question—can I read what I've written?—ask yourself these questions:

- Do my notes do a good job of representing what was covered in class?

- Do they reflect the emphases of the instructor?

- Are there any key points that are not entirely clear?

- Do I need help clarifying any of the points my instructor made?

Evaluating your notes is a critical part of the notetaking process. You can get a sense of how effective your notetaking has been while you still have a chance to ask your instructor to clarify anything that is still not clear.

Perhaps, for example, you've left out a keyword in a definition. Maybe you don't understand a concept fully, even though you've written about it in your notes. Possibly you've left out the third step in a list of six steps necessary to accomplish something.

If you look over your notes while you're still in class, you have time to ask

Figure 4.3

Notes on a Lecture

Here is an instructor's introductory lecture on Toni Morrison's *Beloved*. At the bottom of the page are two students' notes. Which student—A or B—did a better job of capturing the important points in the lecture?

Instructor: In today's class, we'll discuss Toni Morrison's *Beloved*. As I'm sure you all know, Morrison is both a popular and an acclaimed author—and it's not easy to be both. Born Chloe Anthony Wofford in 1931, Morrison has written some of the most affecting and intelligent works on the African-American experience ever written by anyone, and yet to call her an "African-American writer" doesn't seem to do her justice. In many ways, she is simply an American writer—and certainly one of our best.

Beloved is a truly remarkable work. It was nominated for nearly every major literary prize, including the National Book Award and the National Book Critics

Taking notes helps prevent daydreaming during class, because it gives you something to do besides listening passively to an instructor.

Circle Award, and it in fact won the Pulitzer Prize for fiction in 1988. Morrison herself is distinguished for having won the Nobel Prize for literature in 1993.

What makes *Beloved* unique is the skillful, sure way in which Morrison blends intensely personal storytelling and American history, racial themes and gender themes, the experience of Blacks with the experience of all people everywhere, the gritty down-to-earth reality of slavery with a sense of mystical spirituality.

We will be paying special attention to these themes as we discuss this work. I am particularly interested in your views on the relative importance of race and gender in this book. Is it more important that Sethe, the main character, is black or that she's a woman? Which contributes more to her being? How does Morrison use both race and gender to drive her plot? What does she tell us about both?

Student A Notes

Tony Morrison's Beloved

— Morrison popular and acclaimed author, not easy to be both
○ — Cloe Anthony?
— effective and intelligent African American writer
— Beloved won National Book Award, Pulitzer 1988, Nobel Prize 1993
— gritty reality of spirituality and slavery
— Seth a black woman—what does this tell us?

Student B Notes

Toni Morrison's Beloved

– M.. both popular and respected; many awards
– more than "Afr. Amer. writer"—a great Amer. writer
– Beloved:
   blend of personal and historical,
   race and gender themes,
   Black experience and universal experience,
   reality and spirituality
– Is it more imp. that Sethe is Black or female? (race/gender?)
– How race & gender move plot?

Evaluate Your Class Notes

Take a set of notes you made recently during one of your classes and evaluate it on the following criteria.

Statement	Not Even Slightly	Slightly	Moderately	Pretty Well	Very Well
1. I can read my notes (i.e., they are legible).					
2. Someone else can read my notes.					
3. My notes are complete; I missed nothing important.					
4. My notes represent the key points that were covered in class.					
5. My notes reflect the instructor's emphases.					
6. The instructor's key points are clear and understandable.					
7. The notes contain only important points, with no extraneous material.					
8. I understand not only the notes but also the class content they reflect.					
9. Using only the notes, I will be able to reconstruct the essential content of the class in 3 months.					

What do your answers tell you about the effectiveness of your notetaking skills? What might you do differently the next time you take notes? **Working in a Group:** Evaluate and compare the notes you took during the previous 20 minutes of the class you are in now. How do your notes compare with those of the other members of your group?

To Try It online, go to **www.mhhe.com/power**.

your instructor for clarification. Or you can wait till the end of class and raise your question privately. Most instructors will be happy to answer questions from students who have obviously been actively listening. Just make sure that you add what they tell you to your notes so you'll be able to refer to them later. (To practice evaluating your notes, complete Try It 4.)

Rethink: Activating Your Memory

The lecture has ended and class is over. You put the top on your pen, close your notebook, stash everything in your backpack, and head out for a cup of coffee before your next class.

Wait! Before you close up your notebook, finish the P.O.W.E.R. process. Rethink what you've heard. Spending 5 or 10 minutes reconsidering what you've written right now can save you *hours* of work later. The reason: Rethinking promotes the transfer of information into long-term memory (something discussed more in Chapter 8). As you link the new information you've taken down to what you already know and then integrate it, you essentially plug this information into your memory in a much more meaningful way, which means you can remember it better and more easily.

> "I'd think to myself I don't need to write that down, I'll remember it. A few days later, it was like, '*What* did he say . . . ?' "
>
> Junior, Duke University[4]

If you looked over your notes to clarify and evaluate the information in them in class, you've already begun the process. But once class is over, you need to review the material more formally. Here's how to do it:

- **Rethink as soon as possible.** Time is of the essence! The rethinking phase of notetaking doesn't have to take long; 5 to 10 minutes are usually sufficient. The more critical issue is *when* you do it. The longer you wait before reviewing your notes, the less effective the process will be.

  There's no doubt that the best approach is to review the material just after the class has ended. As everyone else is leaving, just stay seated and go over your notes. This works fine for classes late in the day, when no other class is scheduled in the room. But what if you must vacate the room immediately after class? The next best thing is to find a quiet space somewhere nearby and do your rethinking there.

  In any case, don't let the day end without examining your notes. In fact, reconsidering material just before you go to sleep can be particularly effective.

- **Make rethinking an active process.** Some people feel the notes they take in class are akin to historical documents in a museum, with Do Not Touch! signs hanging on them. On the contrary, think of your notes as a construction project and yourself as the person in charge of the project.

  When you review your notes, do so with an eye to improving them. If any information is not entirely clear, change the wording in your notes, adding to or amending what's there. If certain words are hard to read, fix them; it won't be any easier to read them the night before a test—in fact, chances are you'll have even more trouble.

  If, on rethinking the material, you just don't understand something, ask your instructor or a friend to clarify it. And when you receive an explanation, add it to your notes so you won't forget it. (You might want to use a different-colored pen for additions to your notes, so you'll know they came later.)

- **Take the broad view.** When you rethink your notes, don't think of them only in terms of a single lecture or a single class. Instead, take a longer view. Ask yourself how they fit into the broader themes of the class and the goals that you and the instructor have for the semester. How will the information be useful to you? Why did the instructor emphasize a particular point?

If you've configured your notes by leaving a 2½-inch column on the left-hand side of the page, now is the time to make use of that blank column. Write down keywords, significant points, major concepts, controversies, and questions. The process of adding this information will not only help you to rethink the material now, it will also provide guideposts when you study before a test.

- **Create concept maps. Concept mapping** is a method of structuring written material by graphically grouping and connecting key ideas and themes. In contrast to an outline, a concept map visually illustrates how related ideas fit together. The pictorial summary gives you another handle to store the information in memory, and it focuses your thinking on the key ideas from the lecture.

In a concept map, each key idea is placed in a different part of the map, and related ideas are placed near it—above, below, or beside it. What emerges does not have the rigid structure of an outline. Instead, a "finished" concept map looks something like a map of the solar system, with the largest and most central idea in the center (the "sun" position), and related ideas surrounding it at various distances. It has also been compared to a large tree, with numerous branches and sub-branches radiating out from a central trunk. (Figure 4.4 presents a sample concept map.)

Building a concept map has several advantages. It forces you to rethink the material in your notes in a new style—particularly important if you used traditional outlining while taking the notes. In addition, it helps you to tie together the material for a given class session. Finally, it will help you to build a master concept map later, when you're studying the material for a final exam. (To practice in the techniques we've been discussing, see Try It 5, "Practice Your Notetaking Skills" on page 109.)

Concept mapping
A method of structuring written material by graphically grouping and connecting key ideas and themes

Taking Notes As You Study

Weighing as much as five pounds, bulky and awkward, and filled with more information than you think anyone could ever need to know, it's the meat-and-potatoes of college life: your course textbook. You might feel intimidated by its size; you might be annoyed at its cost; you might think you'll never be able to read it, let alone understand, learn, and recall the material in it. How will you manage?

The answer involves taking **study notes,** notes taken for the purpose of reviewing material. They are the kind of notes that you take now to study from later. (We'll consider research notes, notes that you take to write a paper or prepare a report, in Chapter 7 when we discuss writing papers.)

Several strategies are useful for taking study notes from written material such as magazines, books, journals, and websites. Which approach works best depends on whether you're able to write on the material you wish to take notes on.

Study notes
Notes taken for the purpose of reviewing material

Figure 4.4

A Concept Map of Toni Morrison's *Beloved*

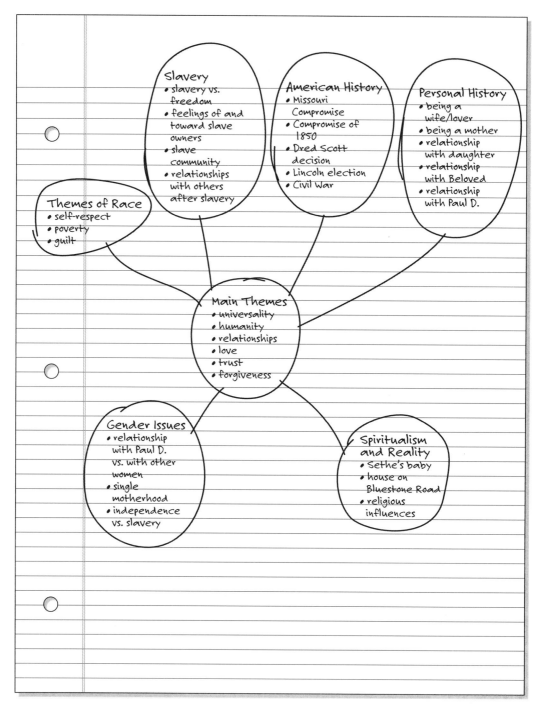

Slavery
- slavery vs. freedom
- feelings of and toward slave owners
- slave community
- relationships with others after slavery

American History
- Missouri Compromise
- Compromise of 1850
- Dred Scott decision
- Lincoln election
- Civil War

Personal History
- being a wife/lover
- being a mother
- relationship with daughter
- relationship with Beloved
- relationship with Paul D.

Themes of Race
- self-respect
- poverty
- guilt

Main Themes
- universality
- humanity
- relationships
- love
- trust
- forgiveness

Gender Issues
- relationship with Paul D. vs. with other women
- single motherhood
- independence vs. slavery

Spiritualism and Reality
- Sethe's baby
- house on Bluestone Road
- religious influences

Taking Notes on Material You Can Write On

Here are some suggestions for creating study notes for material you own, on which you're free to annotate the text directly by underlining, highlighting, or writing in the margins:

- **Integrate your text notes into your study notes.** Start by annotating the pages, using the techniques that work best for you: highlighting, under-

Practice Your Notetaking Skills

Practice your notetaking skills, using any techniques you find helpful, in one of the classes in which you are enrolled this term. Use these notes to answer these questions:

1. Which specific techniques did I use in taking notes?

2. Which of the notetaking techniques detailed in this chapter was I unable to use, and why?

3. Could I take the notes I made in class and re-do them, using one of the techniques in this chapter, such as creating a concept map?

After you have taken notes, use the techniques discussed in this chapter to evaluate and rethink them. Creating a concept map on a separate sheet of paper may be particularly helpful.
To Try It online, go to **www.mhhe.com/power**.

lining, circling, making marginal notes. (These techniques are discussed in detail in Chapter 7; you may want to look ahead to that discussion.) Keep in mind that writing on the text, by itself, is not sufficient to promote learning—it's what you do next that counts.

Specifically, after you've finished reading and annotating the material, create study notes. The study notes should provide a summary of the key points, in outline form or in the form of concept maps. Either form of summary should supplement the annotations you've made on the printed page.

Furthermore, any notes you take should stand on their own. For instance, they should include enough information to be useful whether or not you have the book or article on hand.

- **Use flash cards.** If you feel confident that the annotations you've written in the book are sufficiently comprehensive, you might consider taking notes on flash cards. **Flash cards** are simply index cards that contain key

Flash cards
Note cards that contain key pieces of information to be remembered

Career Connections

Taking Notes on the Job: Meetings of the Minds

For many people, meetings take up a good part of their professional workdays and being able to take effective notes can provide a significant career advantage.

Meetings are similar to class discussions. During a meeting you will want to look for key topics and make note of the ideas that receive the most emphasis or enthusiastic response. Note these areas and keep them in mind as likely priorities.

During meetings, tasks are often assigned. Not only do you want to clearly note what you are to do and when you are supposed to do it, but keeping track of what others are doing will also be helpful, because you may need to get information from them or otherwise coordinate efforts. For instance, if you are assigned the task of managing the development of your company's website, you'll want to clarify in your notes who has agreed to do what portion of the task.

Taking notes when others are speaking also shows that you are paying attention to what the speaker is saying. It's a kind of compliment that suggests you find what the speaker is saying to be so important that you will want to refer to it later.

Finally, notetaking plays another role: It can make seemingly interminable meetings appear to proceed faster by providing something for you to do that's more active than simply listening. In short, not only can notetaking provide you with a clear record of what occurred in a meeting, but it can also keep you engaged in what is going on.

pieces of information that you need to remember.

Flash cards are particularly useful in subjects that present many small bits of information to remember, such as foreign language vocabulary words or scientific formulas. When you need to learn a list of foreign words, for instance, you can write a foreign word on one side of a card and its English meaning on the other side.

One of the greatest virtues of flash cards is their portability. Because they are small, they can fit into your pocket or handbag, and you can look at them at odd times when you have a spare moment.

Taking Study Notes on Material You Can't Write On

Taking notes on material that can't be written on is a different story. Library books, magazines, journal articles, and materials on library reserve that are shared with others require a different approach.

- **Approach the written material as you would a class lecture.** The techniques we discussed earlier for taking notes in class can all be adapted for taking notes from written material. In fact, the task is often easier, because, as is not the case with the spoken word, you'll be able to refer back to what was said earlier—it's in black and white in front of you.

- **Laptop computers can be especially helpful in creating study notes.** If you're a good typist, it's often easier and quicker to take notes using a word-processing program. On the other hand, don't be lured into typing too much. You need to be just as selective in what you input into your computer as you would be in taking notes during a class lecture.

Speaking of Success

Name: Rebecca Lobo

Education: BA from University of Connecticut

Home: Hartford, Connecticut

When basketball star Rebecca Lobo enrolled in an 8:00 A.M. English literature class during college, she was a bit concerned about the wisdom of her choice. But her enthusiasm overcame her doubts. "That class was so enjoyable," says Lobo. "It showed me how easy something can be if you like it, even at that hour."[5]

Lobo, an All-American who was voted Female Athlete of the Year and is a star player on the New York Liberty women's basketball team, attended the University of Connecticut as an undergraduate. Academics and sports were both a central part of her first-year college experience.

"Like any freshman, I was nervous when I first entered college. I didn't know what to expect from basketball, from classes, or anything else,"[6] she says.

However, her participation on the basketball team gave her something that lowered her anxiety level. "It was

my first time away from home, but I was better off than most because I had teammates who looked out for me and who took care of me,"[7] she says.

Because practice and games reduced the time left for studying

during basketball season, Lobo developed strategies for making the most of the off-season.

"During the summers I usually took classes and lived at school so I could get ahead of my courses and take fewer credit hours during the basketball season," she says. "Since there were not many people on

campus then, I headed over to Gampel [arena] in the morning to shoot hoops. The emptiness of the court on these mornings provided me with a comfort zone I have not been able to find anywhere else in my life."[8]

During the school year there was always the need to juggle basketball and studies, but hard work and planning allowed Lobo to succeed in both endeavors.

"Come exam time, I stressed out and studied as much as I could. I was the sort who read every book on the syllabus and attended every class," she recalled. "I was known among the other athletes at school for being a nerd. 'Where were you last night, Lobo? *At the library?'*" She adds, "I could always be counted on to have the notes from every lecture."[9]

Her strategies must have worked: As a political science major, she was on the dean's list every semester and graduated with an A– average.

- **Use the tricks of the trade we discussed earlier for taking notes from a class lecture.** Look for key ideas, definitions, quotations, and formulas and include them in your notes. Use the headings that are included in the text, such as chapter and section titles. Bold or italic type is also a clue that an important point is being made. Graphs and charts often provide critical information.

- **Use the same form of notetaking that you use in class lectures.** If you take notes in class using the two-column method (in which you reserve a 2½-inch column on the left side of your paper for adding comments during later review of the notes), use that technique here as well. If you write your notes in outline form, create an outline based on the written material. If you often create graphics such as concept maps, create them now. The point is to produce notes that are consistent with those you take during class lectures.

Looking
Back

What is effective notetaking?

- The central feature of good notetaking is listening and distilling important information—not writing down everything that is said.

How can I take good notes in class?

- Prepare for taking notes by identifying the instructor's and your own goals for the course, completing all assignments before arriving in class, and "warming up" for class by reviewing the notes and assignments from the previous class.

- Before writing notes, listen and think, processing the information that the instructor is attempting to deliver.

- Notes should be brief phrases rather than full sentences and, if possible, in outline form to reveal the structure of the lecture. Material written on the board should usually be copied word-for-word.

- Before leaving class, evaluate your notes, verifying that they are complete and understandable while there is still time to correct them. As soon as possible after class, actively rethink your notes.

What techniques apply to taking notes from written materials?

- Taking good study notes from written materials involves many of the principles that apply to taking good notes from oral presentations, although the source material can be consulted repeatedly, making it easier to get the information down accurately.

- Concept maps and flash cards can be helpful tools for notetaking from textbooks.

Key Terms and Concepts

Active listening (p. 93)
Concept mapping (p. 107)
Flash cards (p. 109)

Hearing (p. 93)
Meta-message (p. 94)
Study notes (p. 107)

Resources

On Campus

If you are having difficulty taking class notes effectively, talk with your course instructor. Bring your notes with you soon after a class has ended, and let the instructor assess what you are doing correctly and what could stand improvement.

   If your problems persist, and you have great difficulty translating the spoken word into notes, then there's a small possibility that you suffer from an auditory learning disability. Be tested by your college learning disabilities office or counseling office to rule this out.

In Print

Bobbi DePorter and Mike Hernacki's *Quantum Notes* (Learning Forum, 2000) provides a broad overview of how to take good notes in class, as does Ron Fry's *Taking Notes* (Career Press, 1994). In addition, *Noteworthy: Listening and Notetaking Skills* (2nd ed.), by Phyllis Lim and William Smalzer (William S. Hein & Co., 1995) provides a fine overview of strategies for increasing your listening and notetaking expertise.

On the Web

Use the following sites on the World Wide Web to extend your learning about the material in this chapter. (Although the Web addresses were accurate at the time the book was printed, check the P.O.W.E.R. Learning website [**www.mhhe.com/power**] for any changes that may have occurred.)

- Brigham Young University's Career and Counseling Center offers a website (**www.byu.edu/stlife/cdc/Learning_Strategies/study_skills/note-tak.htm**) on the Cornell Notetaking System. This notetaking system can help you improve the organization of your notes, while allowing you to make use of your existing strengths as a notetaker.

- The University of Victoria's Learning Skills Program offers a tutorial in concept mapping at **www.coun.uvic.ca/learn/program/hndouts/class1.html**. (Other useful online information from this program can be found at **www.coun.uvic.ca/learn/**.)

- "Take Note: How to Take Notes for a Student With a Disability" (**www.dot.net.au/~ssands/coop/takenote/intro.htm**) is a cooperative venture headed by Macquarie University. The page on "Notetaking Techniques" (**central.dot.net.au/~ssands/coop/takenote/techniques.**

htm) offers some excellent suggestions for general notetaking as well. Among the other topics discussed are attitude and communication, using appropriate language, and guidelines for a student receiving notes.

Taking It to the Net

1 The best way to improve notetaking skills is to practice. Locate a current news story of interest on the Internet and take notes while reading it. Remember to leave the left margin large enough to add key points and summary information. One possible strategy is to go to the "Today's News" section of the Yahoo! home page (**www.yahoo.com/**). Click on one of the news categories (i.e., Sports, Politics, Business, etc.) and look for a story that sounds interesting.

2 Taking notes during lectures is an important part of classroom learning, but keeping up with a speaker for an entire hour can be difficult. You can improve your notetaking skills for lectures by taking notes while listening to recorded speeches on the Internet. For example, go to an Internet site containing audio recordings of speeches (e.g., **www.pbs.org/newshour/convention 96/realaudio/**) and take notes while listening to a speech. Afterward, go back and indicate the key points and terms in the left margin of your notes. You can check your comprehension by comparing the speech to news articles reporting on it. (You can also check the articles for bias!)

The Case of . . .

The Human Dictation Machine

Everyone wanted to borrow Lila Bauman's notes.

If they missed a class, or even if they had been in attendance but had just spaced out, other students in Lila's classes knew that they could find out what had happened in class by borrowing her notes. It was all there in black and white. The woman was virtually a human dictation machine. She spent her time in class in a whirlwind of notetaking, writing down seemingly every word her instructor uttered in a clear, meticulous script. By the end of a term, her notebooks were so lengthy that they approached the size of telephone books from a small city.

The strange thing, though, was that—despite her copious notes—Lila was only a mediocre student. Before tests she studied her notes thoroughly, but she never seemed to get grades higher than a C+. She didn't know why, especially in light of what she saw as her notetaking expertise.

1. How do you think Lila defines "good notetaking"?

2. Why does Lila's method of notetaking produce such poor results? What is she missing?

3. If you asked Lila to summarize the instructor's main ideas after a class lecture, how successful do you think she would be? Why?

4. Do you think it would be easy or hard to study for a final exam using Lila's notes? Why?

5. Do you think Lila evaluates her notes during or after class? Do you think she ever rethinks them? What questions would you ask to help her perform these steps?

6. In general, what advice would you give Lila on notetaking?

Taking Tests

5

So it all comes down to a test.

That was the thought that ran through Imani Brown's mind as he got ready to start the most important test he had ever faced. Yes, he had taken tests all through his high school career, and yes, he had suffered through the S.A.T. to get into college.

But now, on the verge of starting his career as a high school teacher, he had one more hurdle to jump over. The state legislature had

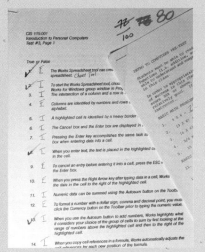

recently decided that all new graduates of teacher training programs had to pass a competency test before starting to teach. Imani had wanted to be a teacher as long as he could remember; he simply had to pass.

Although he was fairly confident—he had studied hard—he couldn't relax altogether. He told himself that he had always done well on tests in the past; he wasn't going to fail now. But still . . .

Looking Ahead

Although many tests are not as critical as Imani Brown's teacher competency exam, tests do play a significant role in everyone's academic life. Students typically experience more anxiety over tests than over anything else in their college careers.

But tests don't have to be so anxiety-producing. There are strategies and techniques you can learn to reduce your fear of test-taking. In fact, learning how to take tests is in some ways as important as learning the content that they cover. Taking tests effectively does not just involve mastering information; it also requires mastering specific test-taking skills.

One of the most important goals of this chapter is to take the mystery out of the whole process of taking tests. To do that, you'll learn about the different types of tests and strategies you can start using even before you take a test. You'll gain insight into how different kinds of tests work and how best to approach them, and

you'll also learn about the various types of test questions and strategies for responding most effectively to each type.

This chapter also explores two aspects of test-taking that may affect your performance: test anxiety and cramming. You will learn ways to deal with your anxiety and keep cramming to a minimum—but you will also learn how to make the most of cramming, if you do have to resort to it.

The chapter ends with suggestions for evaluating your performance toward the end of a test and for using what you learn to improve your performance the next time around.

After reading this chapter, you'll be able to answer these questions:

- **What kinds of tests will I encounter in college?**

- **What are the best ways to prepare for and take various kinds of tests?**

- **What are the best strategies for answering specific kinds of test questions?**

Getting Ready

Tests may be the most unpopular part of academic life. Students hate them because they produce fear, anxiety, apprehension about being evaluated, and a focus on grades instead of learning for learning's sake. Instructors often don't like them very much either, because they produce fear, anxiety, apprehension about being evaluated, and a focus on grades instead of learning for learning's sake. That's right: Students and instructors dislike tests for the very same reasons.

But tests are also valuable. A well-constructed test identifies what you know and what you still need to learn. Tests help you see how your performance compares to that of others. And knowing that you'll be tested on a body of material is certainly likely to motivate you to learn material more thoroughly.

However, there's another reason you might dislike tests: You may assume that tests have the power to define your worth as a person. If you do badly on a test, you may be tempted to believe that you've received some fundamental information about yourself from the professor and the college, information that says you're a failure in some significant way.

This is a dangerous—and wrong-headed—assumption. If you do badly on a test, it doesn't mean you're a bad person. Or stupid. Or that you'll never do better again, and that your life is ruined. If you don't do well on a test, you're the same person you were before you took the test—no better, no worse. You just did badly on a test. Period.

In short, tests are not a measure of your value as an individual—they are a measure only of how well (and how much) you studied. Tests are tools; they are indirect and imperfect measures of what we know. Someone with a great deal of knowledge can do poorly on a test; tension or going at too slow a pace can lead to unwelcome results in some cases. Another person may know considerably less and still do better on the test simply because he may have learned some test-taking skills along the way.

How we do on a test depends on a number of considerations: the kind of test it is, the subject matter involved, and, above all, how well we prepare for it. Let's turn, then, to the first step in test-taking: preparation. (The five steps are summarized in the P.O.W.E.R. Plan on the right.)

P repare: Readying Your Test-Taking Strategies

Preparation for tests requires a number of strategies. Among the most important are the following:

Remember: Everything You Do in a Course Is Preparation for a Test *All* the things you do during a course help to prepare you for a test. There is no surer way to get good grades on tests than to attend class faithfully and to complete all class assignments seriously and on time.

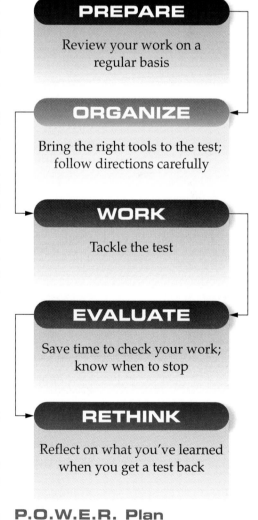

PREPARE

Review your work on a regular basis

ORGANIZE

Bring the right tools to the test; follow directions carefully

WORK

Tackle the test

EVALUATE

Save time to check your work; know when to stop

RETHINK

Reflect on what you've learned when you get a test back

P.O.W.E.R. Plan

Preparing for tests is a long-term proposition. It's not a matter of "giving your all" the night before the test. Instead, it's a matter of giving your all to every aspect of the course.

Know What You Are Preparing for Determine as much as you can about the test *before* you begin to study for it. The more you know about a test beforehand, the more efficient your studying will be.

To find out about an upcoming test, ask these questions:

> "High school is memorization and regurgitation. Here you have to think."
>
> Junior, Engineering, Notre Dame[1]

- Is the test called a "test," "exam," "quiz," or something else? As you can see in Table 5.1, the names imply different things. For simplicity's sake, we'll use the term *test* throughout this chapter, but know that these distinctions exist, and they should affect the way you prepare.

- What material will the test cover?

- How many questions will be on it?

- How much time is it expected to take? A full class period? Only part of a period?

- What kinds of questions will be on the test?

- How will it be graded?

- Will sample questions be provided?

- Are tests from previous terms available?

Match Test Preparation to Question Types Test questions come in different types (see Table 5.2), and each requires a somewhat different style of preparation.

- **Essay questions.** Essay tests focus on the big picture—ways in which the various pieces of information being tested fit together. You'll need to know not just a series of facts, but also the connections between them, and you will have to be able to discuss these ideas in an organized and logical way.

Table 5.1

Quizzes, Tests, Exams . . . What's in a Name?

Although they may vary from one instructor to another, the following definitions are most commonly used:

Quizzes. A **quiz** is a brief assessment, usually covering a relatively small amount of material. Some quizzes cover as little as one class's worth of reading. Although a single quiz usually doesn't count very much, instructors often add quiz scores together, and collectively they can become a significant part of your final course grade.

Tests. A **test** is a more extensive, more heavily weighted assessment than a quiz, covering more material. A test may come every few weeks of the term, often after each third or quarter of the term has passed, but this varies with the instructor and the course.

Exams. An **exam** is the most substantial kind of assessment. In many classes, just one exam is given—a *final exam* at the end of the term. Sometimes there are two exams, one at the midpoint of the term (called, of course, a *midterm*) and the second at the end. Exams are usually weighted quite heavily because they are meant to assess your knowledge of all the course material covered up to that point.

Essay	Requires a fairly extended, on-the-spot composition about some topic. Examples include questions that call on you to describe a person, process, or event, or those that ask you to compare or contrast two separate sets of material.
Multiple-choice	Usually contains a question or statement, followed by a number of possible answers (usually 4 or 5 of them). You are supposed to choose the best response from the choices offered.
True–False	Presents statements about a topic that are either accurate or inaccurate. You are to indicate whether each statement is accurate (true) or inaccurate (false).
Matching	Presents two lists of related information, arranged in column form. Typically, you are asked to pair up the items that go together (e.g., a scientific term and its definition, or a writer and the title of a book he wrote).
Short-answer	Requires brief responses (usually a few sentences at most) in a kind of mini-essay.
Fill-in	Requires you to add one or more missing words to a sentence or series of sentences.

Table 5.2

Types of Test Questions

The best approach to studying for an essay test involves four steps:

1. Carefully reread your class notes and any notes you've made on assigned readings that will be covered on the upcoming exam. Also go through the readings themselves, reviewing underlined or highlighted material and marginal notes.

2. Play professor: Think of likely exam questions. To do this, you can use the key words, phrases, concepts, and questions that come up in your class notes or in your text. Some instructors give out lists of possible essay topics; if yours does, focus on this list, but don't ignore other possibilities.

3. Without looking at your notes or your readings, answer each potential essay question—aloud. Don't feel embarrassed about doing this. Talking aloud is often more useful than answering the question in your head.

   You can also write down the main points that any answer should cover. (Don't write out *complete* answers to the questions unless your instructor tells you in advance exactly what is going to be on the test. Your time is probably better spent learning the material than rehearsing precisely formulated responses.)

4. After you've answered the questions, check yourself by looking at the notes and readings once again. If you feel confident that you've answered particular questions adequately, check them off. You can go back later for a quick review.

   But if there are questions that you had trouble with, review that material immediately. Then repeat the third step above, answering the questions again.

- **Multiple-choice, true–false, and matching questions.** While the focus of review for essay questions should be on major issues and controversies, studying for multiple-choice, true–false, and matching questions requires more attention to the details.

  Almost anything is fair game for multiple-choice, true–false, and matching questions, so you can't afford to overlook anything when studying. True, these kinds of questions put the material right there on the page for you to react to—Did Columbus land in 1492, or not?—rather than asking you to provide the names and dates yourself (as in the case of the essay question). Nevertheless, to do well on these tests you must put your memory into high gear and master a great many facts.

  It's a particularly good idea to write down important facts on index cards like those below. Remember the advantages of these cards: They're portable and available all the time, and the act of creating them helps drive the material into your memory. Furthermore, you can shuffle them and test yourself repeatedly until you've mastered the material.

- **Short-answer and fill-in questions.** Short-answer and fill-in questions are similar to essays in that they require you to recall key pieces of information rather than, as is the case with multiple-choice, true–false, and matching questions, finding it on the page in front of you. However, short-answer and fill-in questions—unlike essay questions—typically don't demand that you integrate or compare different types of information. Consequently, the focus of your study should be on the recall of specific, detailed information.

Political reforms of progressive age:
-direct primaries: people vote for whom they want to run; not appointed
-initiative: people propose laws on their own
-referendum: gov. proposes; people say yes or no
-recall: people can remove politicians from office before they finish term

Endoplasmic reticulum (ER):
Smooth ER—makes fats (lipids)
Rough ER—has ribosomes which make proteins
Together, they make membranes for whole cell (for plasma membrane, mitochondrion, etc.) Also make more of themselves.

Test Yourself   Once you feel you've mastered the material, test yourself on it. There are several ways to do this. One is to create a complete test for yourself, in writing, making its form as close as possible to what you expect the actual test to be. For instance, if your instructor has told you the classroom test will be primarily made up of short-answer questions, your test should be, too.

You might also construct a test and administer it to a classmate or a member of your study group. In turn, you could take a test that someone else has constructed. Constructing and taking practice tests are excellent ways of studying the material and cementing it into memory. (To be sure you're fully prepared for your next test, complete Try It 1 on page 124.)

Deal with Test Anxiety   What does the anticipation of a test do to you? Do you feel shaky? Frantic, like there's not enough time to get it all done? Do you feel as if there's a knot in your stomach? Do you grit your teeth?

Test anxiety is a temporary condition characterized by fears and concerns about test-taking. Almost everyone experiences it to some degree, although for some people it's more of a problem than for others. The real danger with test anxiety is that it can become so overwhelming that it can hurt test performance. (To assess your own test-taking style and the degree of anxiety around tests that you experience, see Try It 2 on page 125.)

You'll never eliminate test anxiety completely, nor do you want to. A little bit of nervousness can energize us, making us more attentive and vigilant. Like any competitive event, testing can motivate us to do our best. You might think of moderate test anxiety as a desire to perform at your peak—a useful quality at test time.

On the other hand, for some, anxiety can spiral into the kind of paralyzing fear that makes their mind go blank. There are several ways to keep this from happening to you:

1. *Prepare thoroughly.* The more you prepare, the less test anxiety you'll feel. Good preparation can give you a sense of control and mastery, and it will prevent test anxiety from overwhelming you.

2. *Take a realistic view of the test.* Remember that your future success does not hinge on your performance on any single exam. Think of the big picture: put the task ahead in context, and remind yourself of all the hurdles you've passed so far.

3. *Learn relaxation techniques.* You can learn to reduce or even eliminate the jittery physical symptoms of test anxiety by using relaxation techniques. These techniques are covered in Chapter 14, but the basic process is straightforward: Breathe evenly, gently inhaling and exhaling. Focus your mind on a pleasant, relaxing scene such as a beautiful forest or a peaceful farm, or on a restful sound such as that of ocean waves breaking on the beach.

4. *Visualize success.* Think of an image of your instructor handing back your test marked with a big fat "A." Or imagine your instructor congratulating you on your fine performance the day after the test. Positive visualizations that highlight your potential success can help replace images of failure that may fuel test anxiety.

Journal Reflections

How I Feel about Tests

1. How do you feel about tests in general?

2. What are your first memories of being in a testing situation? What were your feelings, and why?

3. What makes a test "good" from your perspective?

4. What makes a test "bad" from your perspective?

5. What factors contribute to your success or failure on a particular exam? Which of these factors are under your control?

Text anxiety
A temporary condition characterized by fears and concerns about test-taking

Try It!
1

Complete a Test Preparation Checklist

Before taking your next test, complete the following test preparation checklist.

Test Preparation Checklist

- ☐ I checked whether it's a quiz, test, or exam.
- ☐ I began preparation long before the test (e.g., by taking notes in class).
- ☐ I understand what material will be covered.
- ☐ I know how many questions will be on the test.
- ☐ I know how long it will take.
- ☐ I know what kinds of questions will be on the test.
- ☐ I know how it will be graded.
- ☐ I obtained sample questions and/or previous tests, if available.
- ☐ I formed or participated in a study group.
- ☐ I used different and appropriate preparation strategies for different types of questions.
- ☐ I read my class notes.
- ☐ I composed some essay questions.
- ☐ I answered essay questions aloud.
- ☐ I actively memorized facts and details.
- ☐ I made and used note cards.
- ☐ I created and used a test like the real test.

To Try It online, go to **www.mhhe.com/power**.

Special techniques for dealing with math anxiety   For many students, the greatest test anxiety comes when they're taking a math test. Math seems to bring out the worst fears in some people, perhaps because it's seen as a discipline in which answers are either totally right or totally wrong, or because they've felt they've "hit the wall" and they'll never be able to understand a concept, no matter how hard they try.

Such feelings about math can be devastating, because they can prevent you from doing well even if you know the material. If you suffer from math anxiety, keep these things in mind:

- Math is like any other subject: the greatest component of success is how hard you work, not whether you have a "math gene" that makes you naturally good at math.

ry It!
2

👤 **Personal Styles:** Measure Your Test-Taking Style

Do you feel anxious at the very thought of a test, or are you cool and calm in the face of testing situations? Get a sense of your test-taking style by checking off every statement below that applies to you.

- ☐ 1.   The closer a test date approaches, the more nervous I get.
- ☐ 2.   I am sometimes unable to sleep on the night before a test.
- ☐ 3.   I have "frozen up" during a test, finding myself unable to think or respond.
- ☐ 4.   I can feel my hands shaking as I pick up my pencil to begin a test.
- ☐ 5.   The minute I read a tough test question, all the facts I ever knew about the subject abandon me and I can't get them back no matter how hard I try.
- ☐ 6.   I have become physically ill before or during a test.
- ☐ 7.   Nervousness prevents me from studying immediately before a test.
- ☐ 8.   I often dream about an upcoming test.
- ☐ 9.   Even if I successfully answer a number of questions, my anxiety stays with me throughout the test.
- ☐ 10.   I'm reluctant to turn in my test paper for fear that I can do better if I continue to work on it.

If you checked off more than four statements, you have experienced fairly serious test anxiety. If you checked off more than six statements, your anxiety is probably interfering with your test performance. In particular, statements 3, 5, 6, 7, and 10 may indicate serious test anxiety.

If, based on your responses to this questionnaire and your previous experience, your level of test anxiety is high, follow some of the steps described in the text for dealing with it.

To Try It online, go to **www.mhhe.com/power**.

- • It's a false stereotype that women are not as good at math as men, but it's a stereotype that many women buy into. When men do badly on a math test, they're most likely to think that they haven't put in enough effort. But when women do badly on a math test, they're three times more likely than men to feel that they don't have enough ability to be successful.[2] That's an erroneous view of the world. Don't become a prisoner of stereotypes.

- • Remember that math has practical uses. Some people are afraid of math because they view it as theoretical, with no practical value. But if you want to figure out the size of a room, how to calculate a tip in a restaurant, or how much interest you'll pay on a loan, you'll need to make use of geometry, arithmetic, and algebra.

Study groups, made up of a few students who study together for a test, can help organize material, provide new perspectives, and motivate members to do their best.

Form a Study Group Study groups are small, informal groups of students who work together to learn course material and study for a test. Forming such a group can be an excellent way to prepare for any kind of test. Some study groups are formed for particular tests, while others meet consistently throughout the term.

The typical study group meets a week or two before a test and plans a strategy for studying. Members share their understanding of what will be on the test, based on what an instructor has said in class and on their review of notes and text material. Together, they develop a list of review questions to guide their individual study. The group then breaks up, and the members study on their own.

A few days before the test, members of the study group meet again. They discuss answers to the review questions, go over the material, and share any new insights they may have about the upcoming test. They may also quiz one another about the material to identify any weaknesses or gaps in their knowledge.

Study groups can be extremely powerful tools because they help accomplish several things:

- They help members organize and structure the material to approach their studying in a systematic and logical way.

- They allow students to share different perspectives on the material.

- They make it more likely that students will not overlook any potentially important information.

- They force members to rethink the course material, explaining it in words that other group members will understand. As we will discuss in Chapter 9, this helps both understanding and recall of the information when it is needed on the test.

- Finally, they help motivate members to do their best. When you're part of a study group, you're no longer working just for yourself; your studying also benefits the other study group members. Not wanting to let down your classmates in a study group may encourage you to work harder.

There are some potential drawbacks to keep in mind. Study groups don't always work well for students with learning styles that favor working independently. In addition, "problem" members—those who don't pull their weight—may cause difficulties for the group. In general, though, the advantages of study groups far outweigh their disadvantages. (To set up your own study group, see Try It 3.)

Cramming: You Shouldn't, But . . . You know, of course, that **cramming**, hurried, last-minute studying, is not the way to go. You know that you're likely to forget the material the moment the test is over because long-term retention is nearly impossible without thoughtful study. But . . .

Study groups
Small, informal groups of students whose purpose is to help members work together and study for a test

---

Cramming
Hurried, last-minute studying

🌴 **Working in a Group:** Form a Study Group

The next time you have to prepare for a test, form a study group with three to five classmates. They may have a variety of study habits and skills, but all must be willing to take the group seriously.

The first time you meet, compare notes about what is likely to be on the test and brainstorm to come up with possible test questions. If the instructor hasn't given you detailed information about the test (i.e., number and types of questions, weighting, etc.), one of you should be delegated to ask for it. Plan to meet once more closer to the test date to discuss answers to the questions you've come up with, share any new insights, and quiz each other on the material.

After you've taken the test and gotten your results, meet again. Find out if members felt the group was effective. Did the members feel more confident about the test? Do they think they did better than they would have without the group? What worked? What didn't? What could you do differently next time?

To Try It online, go to **www.mhhe.com/power**.

. . . it's been one of those weeks where everything went wrong.

. . . the instructor sprang the test on you at the last minute.

. . . you forgot about the test until the night before it was scheduled.

Whatever the reason, there may be times when you can't study properly. What do you do if you *have* to cram for an exam?

Don't spend a lot of time on what you're unable to do. Beating yourself up about your failings as a student will only hinder your efforts. Instead, admit you're human and imperfect like everyone else. Then spend a few minutes developing a plan about what you can accomplish in the limited time you've got.

The first thing to do is choose what you really need to study. You won't be able to learn everything, so you have to make choices. Figure out the main focus of the course, and concentrate on it.

Once you have a strategy, prepare a one-page summary sheet with hard-to-remember information. Just writing the material down will help you remember it, and you can refer to the summary sheet frequently over the limited time you do have to study.

Next, read through your class notes, concentrating on the material you've underlined and the key concepts and ideas that you've already noted. Forget about reading all the material in the books and articles you're being tested on. Instead, only read the passages that you've underlined and the notes you've taken on the readings. Finally, maximize your study time. Using your notes, note cards, and concept maps, go over the information. Read it. Say it aloud. Think about it and the way it relates to other information. In short, use all the

Have you ever crammed for a test? If so, you know how exhausting it can be, and how easy it is to overlook crucial material. On the other hand, time pressures sometimes make cramming your only option. When that happens, there are strategies you can use to help you make the best use of limited time.

techniques we've talked about for learning and recalling information.

Just remember: When the exam is over, material that you have crammed into your head is destined to leave your mind as quickly as it entered. If you've crammed for a midterm, don't assume that the information will still be there when you study for the final. In the end, cramming often ends up taking more time for worse results than does studying with appropriate techniques.

Organize: Facing the Day of the Test

You've studied a lot, and you're happy with your level of mastery. Or perhaps you have the nagging feeling that there's something you haven't quite gotten to. Or maybe you know you haven't had enough time to study as much as you'd like, and you're expecting a disaster.

Whatever your frame of mind, it will help to organize your plan of attack on the day of the test. What's included on the test is out of your hands, but you can control what you bring to it.

For starters, bring the right tools to the test. Have at least two pens and two pencils with you. It's usually best to write in pen because, in general, writing tends to be easier to read in pen than pencil. But you also might want to have pencils on hand. Sometimes instructors will use machine-scored tests, which require the use of pencil. Or there may be test questions that involve computations, and solving them may entail frequent reworking of calculations.

You should also be sure to bring a watch to the test, even if there will be a clock on the wall of the classroom. You will want to be able to pace yourself properly during the test. Just having your own watch will help you feel more in control of your time during the test.

Sometimes instructors permit you to use notes and books during the test. If you haven't brought them with you, they're not going to be of much help. So make sure you bring them if they're permitted. Even for closed-book tests, having such material available before the test actually starts may allow you a few minutes of review after you arrive in the classroom.

On the day of a test, avoid the temptation to compare notes with your friends about how much they've studied. Yes, you might end up feeling good because many of your fellow classmates studied less than you did. But chances are you'll find others who seem to have spent significantly *more* time studying than you, and this will do little to encourage you.

In addition, you might want to *plan on panicking*. Although it sounds like the worst possible approach, permitting yourself the option of spending a minute feeling panicky will help you to recover from your initial fears.

Finally, listen carefully to what an instructor says before the test is handed out. The instructor may tell you about a question that is optional or worth more points or inform you of a typographical error on the test. Whatever the instructor says just before the test, you can be sure it's information that you don't want to ignore.

Taking the Test

W ork: Tackling the Test

Take a deep breath—literally.

There's no better way to start work on a test than by taking a deep breath, followed by several others. The deep breaths will help you to overcome any initial panic and anxiety you may be experiencing. It's OK to give yourself over for a moment to panic and anxiety, but, to work at your best, use the relaxation techniques that we spoke about earlier to displace those initial feelings. Tell yourself, "It's OK. I am going to do my best."

Read the test instructions and then *skim through the entire exam.* Look at the kinds of questions and pay attention to the way they will be scored. If the point weighting of the various parts of the exam is not clear, ask the instructor to clarify it.

Knowing the point weighting is critical, because it will help you to allocate your time. You don't want to spend 90 percent of your time on an essay that's worth only 10 percent of the points, and you want to be sure to leave time at the end of the test to check your answers. An initial read-through will also help you verify that you have every page of the exam and that each one is readable.

If there are any lists, formulas, or other key facts that you're concerned you may forget, jot them down now on the back of a test page or on a piece of scrap paper. You may want to refer to this material later during the test.

Once this background work is out of the way, you'll be ready to proceed to actually answering the questions. These principles will help you to do your best on the test:

- **Answer the easiest questions first.** By initially getting the questions out of the way that are easiest for you, you accomplish several important things. First, you'll be leaving yourself more time to think about the tougher questions. In addition, moving through a series of questions without a struggle will build your confidence. Finally, working through a number of questions will build up a base of points that may be enough to earn you at least a minimally acceptable grade.

- **Write legibly and only on one side of the paper.** If an instructor can't read what you've written, you're not going to get credit for it, no matter how brilliant your answer. So be sure to keep your handwriting legible.

    It's also a good idea to write your answers to essay questions on only one side of a page. This will allow you to go back later and add or revise information.

- **Master machine-scored tests.** Tests will sometimes be scored, in part, by computer. In such cases, you'll usually have to indicate your answers by filling in—with a pencil—circles or squares on a computer answer sheet.

Be careful! A stray mark or smudge can cause the computer scanner to misread your answer sheet, producing errors in grading. Be sure to bring a good eraser in addition to a pencil; the biggest source of mistakes in machine grading is incomplete erasing.

It's best to write your answers not only on the answer sheet but also on the test itself (if the test is not intended for future re-use). That way you can go back and check your answers easily—a step you should take frequently.

Use Strategies Targeted to Answering Specific Types of Test Questions

Every type of question requires a particular approach. Use these strategies below:

- **Essay Questions.** Essay questions, with their emphasis on description and analysis, often present challenges because they are relatively unstructured. Unless you're careful, it's easy to wander off and begin to answer questions that were never asked. To prevent that problem, the first thing to do is read the question carefully, noting what specifically is being asked. If your essay will be lengthy, you might even want to write a short outline.

Pay attention to keywords that indicate what, specifically, the instructor is looking for in an answer. Certain action words are commonly used in essays, and you should understand them fully. For instance, knowing the distinction between "compare" and "contrast" can spell the difference between success and failure. Table 5.3 defines common action words.

Use the right language in essays. Be brief and to the point in your essay. Avoid flowery introductory language. Compare the two sentences that follow:

"In our study of world literature, it may be useful to ponder how *The Canterbury Tales* came to represent such an important milestone in the field, and it will be seen that there are several critical reasons why it did have such an impact."

"*The Canterbury Tales* were groundbreaking for several reasons."

This second sentence says the same thing much more effectively and economically.

Essays are improved when they include examples and point out differences. Your response should follow a logical sequence, moving from major points to minor ones, or following a time sequence. Above all, your answer should address every aspect of the question posed on the test. Because essays often contain several different, embedded questions, you have to be certain that you have answered every part to receive full credit. (After reviewing Table 5.3, complete Try It 4 on page 132.)

Table 5.3

Action Words for Essays

These words are commonly used in essay questions. Learning the distinctions among them will help you answer them effectively.

Analyze: Examine and break into component parts.

Clarify: Explain with significant detail.

Compare: Describe and explain similarities.

Compare and contrast: Describe and explain similarities and differences.

Contrast: Describe and explain differences.

Critique: Judge and analyze, explaining what is wrong—and right—about a concept.

Define: Provide the meaning.

Discuss: Explain, review, and consider.

Enumerate: Provide a listing of ideas, concepts, reasons, items, etc.

Evaluate: Provide pros and cons of something; provide an opinion and justify it.

Explain: Give reasons why or how; clarify, justify, and illustrate.

Illustrate: Provide examples; show instances.

Interpret: Explain the meaning of something.

Justify: Explain why a concept can be supported, typically by using examples and other types of support.

Outline: Provide an overarching framework or explanation—usually in narrative form—of a concept, idea, event, or phenomenon.

Prove: Using evidence and arguments, convince the reader of a particular point.

Relate: Show how things fit together; provide analogies.

Review: Describe or summarize, often with an evaluation.

State: Assert or explain.

Summarize: Provide a condensed, precise list or narrative.

Trace: Track or sketch out how events or circumstances have evolved; provide a history or time line.

- **Multiple-Choice Questions.** If you've ever looked at a multiple-choice question and said to yourself, "But every choice seems right," you understand what can be tricky about this type of question. However, there are some simple strategies that can help you deal with multiple-choice questions.

  First, read the instructions carefully to determine whether only one response will be correct or whether more than one of the choices may be correct. In most cases, only one choice will be right, but in some cases instructors may want you to check off more than one answer.

  Turn to the first question and read it carefully. *Before you look at the possible answers, try to answer the question in your head.* This can help you avoid confusion over inappropriate choices.

  Next, *carefully read through every possible answer.* Even if you come to one that you think is right, read them all—there may be a subsequent answer that is better.

  Look for absolutes like "every," "always," "only," "none," and "never." Choices that contain such absolute words are rarely correct. On the other

Try It!
4

Understand Action Verbs in Essay Questions

Answer the following questions about the Second Amendment to the United States Constitution by outlining your responses to them, paying attention to the different action verbs that introduce questions.

The Second Amendment states:

A well-regulated militia, being necessary to the security of a free State, the right of the people to keep and bear arms, shall not be infringed.

1. Summarize the Second Amendment to the Constitution.

2. Analyze the Second Amendment to the Constitution.

3. Discuss the Second Amendment to the Constitution.

How do your answers differ for the each of the questions? Which of the questions provoked the lengthiest response? Which of the questions could you answer best?

To Try It online, go to **www.mhhe.com/power**.

---

hand, less-absolute words, such as "generally," "usually," "often," "rarely," "seldom," and "typically" may indicate a correct response.

Be especially on guard for the word "not," which negates the sentence ("The one key concept that is not embodied in the U.S. Constitution is . . . "). It's easy to gloss over "not," and if you have the misfortune of doing so, it will be nearly impossible to answer the item correctly.

If you're having trouble understanding a question, underline key words or phrases, or try to break the question into different short sections. Sometimes it is helpful to work backwards, *Jeopardy* style, and look at the possible answers first to see if you can find one that is clearly accurate or clearly inaccurate.

*Use an **educated guessing** strategy*—which is very different from wild or random guessing. Unless you are penalized for wrong answers (a scoring rule by which wrong answers are deducted from the points you have earned on other questions, rather than merely not counting at all toward your score), it always pays to guess.

The first step in educated guessing is to eliminate any obviously false answers. The next step is to examine the remaining choices closely. Does one response choice include a qualifier that makes it unlikely ("the prob-

Educated guessing

The practice of eliminating obviously false multiple-choice answers and selecting the most likely answer from the remaining choices ability of war always increases when a U.S. president is facing political difficulties")? Does one choice include a subtle factual error ("when Columbus began his journey to the New World in 1492, he went with the support of the French monarchy")? In such cases, you may be able to figure out the correct response by eliminating the others.

- **True–False Questions.** Although most of the principles we've already discussed apply equally well to true–false questions, a few additional tricks of the trade may help you with this type of question.

  Begin a set of true–false questions by answering the ones you're sure you know. But don't rush; it's important to read every part of a true–false question, because keywords such as "never," "always," and "sometimes" often determine the appropriate response.

  If you don't have a clue about whether a statement is true or false, here's a last-resort principle: Choose "true." In general, more statements on a true–false test are likely to be true than false.

- **Matching Questions.** Matching questions typically present you with two columns of related information, which you must link, item by item. For example, a list of terms or concepts may be presented in one column, along with a list of corresponding definitions or explanations in the second column. The best strategy is to reduce the size of both columns by matching the items you're most confident about first; this will leave a short list in each column, and the final matching may become apparent.

- **Short-Answer and Fill-In Questions.** Short-answer and fill-in questions basically require you to *generate and supply* specific information in your own words. Unlike essays, which are more free-form and may have several possible answers, short-answer and fill-in questions are usually quite specific, requiring only one answer.

  Use both the instructions for the questions and the questions themselves to determine the level of specificity that is needed in an answer. Try not to provide too much or too little information. Usually, brevity is best.

About Academic Honesty   It might be tempting: A glance at a classmate's test may provide the one piece of information that you just can't remember. But you owe it to yourself not to do it. Copying from a classmate's paper is no different from reaching over and stealing that classmate's calculator or watch. It is a violation of **academic honesty,** one of the foundations of civility in the classroom, as well as in society. Unless the work you turn in under your own name is your work, you are guilty of academic dishonesty.

Academic honesty
Completing and turning in only one's own work under one's own name

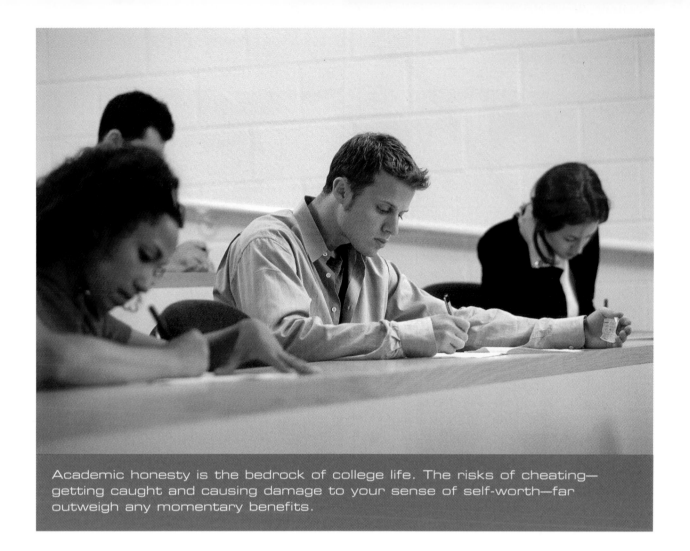

Academic honesty is the bedrock of college life. The risks of cheating—getting caught and causing damage to your sense of self-worth—far outweigh any momentary benefits.

Violations of academic honesty can take many forms. They may involve *plagiarism,* copying another's work and passing it off as your own. (We'll talk more about plagiarism in Chapter 7). Academic dishonesty may also include using a calculator when it's not allowed, discussing the answer to a question, copying a computer file when it's unauthorized, taking an exam for another person, or stealing an exam. It can take the form of ripping a page out of a book in the library, or lying to an instructor about the reason for a late paper.

Whatever the form, academic dishonesty is wrong. It lowers the level of civility in the classroom, it makes the grading system unfair, and it ultimately reduces the meaning of your grade. It certainly damages academic and personal growth. It can't help but reduce one's self-esteem, and it robs the cheater of self-respect.

Finally, academic dishonesty violates the rules of every college and university. (You should familiarize yourself with your own college's academic honesty policy.) Violations of honesty policies will lead to any number of unpleasant scenarios: failing the exam on which the cheating has taken place, failing the entire course, being brought before a disciplinary board, having a description of the incident permanently placed on your grade transcript, being placed on academic probation, or even being thrown out of school. Cheating is simply not worth it.

Evaluate: Taking Your Own Final Exam

The last few minutes of a test may feel like the final moments of a marathon. You need to focus your energy and push yourself even harder. It can be make-or-break time.

Save some time at the end of a test so you can check your work. You should have been keeping track of your time all along, so plan on stopping a few minutes before the end of the test period to review what you've done. It's a critical step, and it can make the difference between a terrific grade and a mediocre one. It's a rare person who can work for an uninterrupted period of time on a test and commit absolutely no errors—even if he or she knows the material backward and forward. Consequently, checking what you've done is crucial.

Start evaluating your test by looking for obvious mistakes. Make sure you've answered every question and haven't skipped any parts of questions. If there is a separate answer sheet, check to see that all your answers have been recorded on the answer sheet and in the right spot.

If the test has included essay and short-answer questions, proofread your responses. Check for obvious errors—misspellings, missing words, and repetitions. Make sure you've responded to every part of each question and that each essay, as a whole, makes sense.

Check over your responses to multiple-choice, true–false, and matching questions. If there are some items that you haven't yet answered because you couldn't remember the necessary information, now is the time to take a stab at them. As we discussed earlier, it usually pays to guess, even randomly if you must. On most tests, no answer and a wrong answer are worth the same amount—nothing!

What about items that you initially guessed at? Unless you have a good reason to change your original answer—such as a new insight or a sudden recollection of some key information—your first guess is likely your best guess.

Know When to Stop   After evaluating and checking your answers, you may reach a point when there is still some time left. What to do? If you're satisfied with your responses, it's simply time to tell yourself, "Let it go."

Permit yourself the luxury of knowing that you've done your best, and hand the test in to your instructor. You don't have to review your work over and over just because there is time remaining and some of your classmates are still working on their tests. In fact, such behavior is often counterproductive, because you might start overinterpreting and reading things into questions that really aren't there.

Disaster! I've run out of time! It's a nightmarish feeling: The clock is ticking relentlessly, and it's clear that you don't have enough time to finish the test. What should you do?

Stop working! Although this advice may sound foolish, in fact the most important thing you can do is to take a minute to calm yourself. Take some deep breaths to replace the feelings of panic that are likely welling up inside you. Collect your thoughts, and plan a strategy for the last moments of the test.

If there are essays that remain undone, consider how you'd answer them if you had more time. Then write an outline of each answer. If you don't have

Career Connections

Tests for a Lifetime

If you think the last tests you'll ever have to take are the final exams just before you graduate from college, you're probably wrong.

For one thing, increasing numbers of professions require initial licensing exams and some even require periodic exams to remain in good standing within the profession. For example, in some states, people who wish to become teachers must pass an exam, as in the case of Imani Brown described at the beginning of the chapter. Even experienced teachers are required to take periodic tests throughout their careers to remain in the teaching field.

In addition, you may have to take tests to continue your course of study for some professions. For example, if you are thinking about a career in medicine, law, or business, you'll need to take a national, standardized test to enroll in a postundergraduate program. How well you do on the test will determine whether you can go to graduate school and which graduate schools will accept you.

In short, good test-taking skills won't just bring you success in college. They're something that may benefit you for a lifetime as you pursue your career.

> "The test of any man lies in action."
>
> Pindar, *Odes*

time even for that, write a few keywords. Writing anything is better than handing in a blank page, and you may get at least some credit for your response. The key principle here: Something is better than nothing, and even one point is worth more than zero points.

The same principle holds for other types of questions. Even wild guesses are almost always better than not responding at all to an item. So rather than telling yourself you've certainly failed and giving up, do as much as you can in the remaining moments of the exam.

R ethink: Reflecting on The Real Test of Learning

Your instructor is about to hand the graded exams back. All sorts of thoughts run through your head: How did I do? Did I do as well as my classmates? Will I be happy with my results? Will the results show how much I studied? Will I be embarrassed by my grade?

Most of us focus on the evaluative aspects of tests. We look at the grade we've received on a test as an end in itself. It's a natural reaction.

But there's another way to look at test results: They can help guide us toward future success. By looking at what we've learned (and haven't learned) about a given subject, we'll be in a better position to know what to focus on when we take future exams. Furthermore, by examining the kinds of mistakes we make, we can learn to do better in the future.

When you get your test back, you have the opportunity to reflect on what you've learned and to consider your performance. Begin by looking at your mistakes. Chances are they'll jump out at you since they will be marked incorrect. Did you misunderstand or misapply some principle? Was there a certain aspect of the material covered on the test that you missed? Were there particular kinds of information that you didn't realize you needed to know? Or did you lose some points because of your test-taking skills? Did you make careless errors, such as forgetting to fill in a question or misreading the directions? Was your handwriting so sloppy that your instructor had trouble reading it?

Once you have a good idea of what material you didn't fully understand or remember, get the correct answers to the items you missed—from your instructor, fellow classmates, or your book. If it's a math exam, rework problems you've missed. Finally, summarize—in writing—the material you had trouble with. This will help you study for future exams that cover the same material.

Finally, if you're dissatisfied with your performance, talk to your instructor—not to complain, but to seek help. Instructors don't like to give bad grades, and they may be able to point out problems in your test that you can address readily so you can do better in the future. Demonstrate to your instructor that you want to do better and are willing to put in the work to get there. The worst thing to do is crumple up the test and quickly leave the class in embarrassment. Remember, you're not the first person to get a bad grade, and the power to improve your test-taking performance lies within you. (Now, take a deep breath before completing Try It 5.)

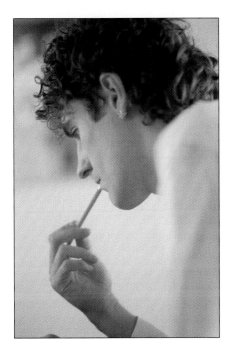

Take a Test-Taking Test

Take the following test on test-taking skills, which illustrates every question type discussed in this chapter. Answers to all questions except short-answer and essay questions are provided at the end of the test.

Before taking the test, think of the test-taking strategies we've discussed in the chapter and try to employ as many of them as possible.

Multiple-Choice Section

Choose *one* of the possible responses following each question.

1. Tests are useful tools for which of the following purposes?
   a. Determining people's likely level of future career success.
   b. Indicating strengths and gaps in people's knowledge.
   c. Defining people's fundamental abilities and potentials.
   d. Evaluating people's individual worth and contributions.

2. One of the main advantages of study groups is that:
   a. Every individual must contribute equally to the group.
   b. Group members can help each other during the test.
   c. Each member has to memorize only a fraction of the material.
   d. Groups motivate their members to do good work.

3. Which of the following is a good way to deal with test anxiety?
   a. Visualizing success on the test.
   b. Drinking coffee or other stimulants.
   c. Telling yourself to stop worrying.
   d. Focusing on the importance of the test.

Matching Section

____	1. Essay question	A.	A question in which the student supplies brief missing information to complete a statement.
____	2. Multiple-choice question	B.	Hurried, last-minute studying.
____	3. Matching question	C.	A question in which the student must link information in two columns.
____	4. Fill-in question	D.	A question requiring a lengthy response in the student's own words.
____	5. Guessing penalty	E.	Deduction of points for incorrect responses.
____	6. Cramming	F.	Representing another's work as one's own.
____	7. Academic dishonesty	G.	A question that requires selection from several response options.

Fill-In Section

1. Fear of testing that can interfere with test performance is called _____.

2. The primary source of error on machine-scored tests is incomplete _____.

True–False Section

1. The best way to prepare for an essay test is to review detailed factual information about the topic. T _____ F _____

2. True–false questions require students to determine whether given statements are accurate or inaccurate. T _____ F _____

3. You should never permit yourself to feel panicky during a test. T _____ F _____

4. A good evaluation strategy toward the end of a test is to redo as many questions as time permits. T _____ F _____

5. In a multiple-choice question, the words "always" and "never" usually signal the correct response. T _____ F _____

6. If you run out of time at the end of a test, it is best to write brief notes and ideas down in response to essay questions rather than to leave them completely blank. T _____ F _____

Short-Answer Section

1. What are five things you should find out about a test before you take it?

2. What is academic honesty?

Essay Section

1. Discuss the advantages of using a study group to prepare for an examination.

2. Why is academic honesty important?

Answers. Multiple-choice: 1b, 2d, 3a; Matching: 1D, 2G, 3C, 4A, 5E, 6B, 7F; Fill-in: test anxiety, erasing; True–False: 1F, 2T, 3F, 4F, 5F, 6T.

After you have completed the test, consider these questions: Did you learn anything from taking the test that you might not have learned if you hadn't been tested? How effective were the test-taking strategies you employed? Were any types of strategies easier for you to employ than others? Were any types of questions easier for you to answer than others? **Working in a Group:** Exchange your essay responses with a classmate, and critique the essay. How do the responses of your partner compare with your own?

To Try It online, go to **www.mhhe.com/power**.

Speaking of Success

Name: *Theresa Winebrenner*
Education: *AA, Austin Community College*
Home: *Austin, Texas*

There's nothing like a test to create anxiety in students—we've all felt it. Theresa Winebrenner, a student at Austin Community College, is no different, except that her techniques for coping with test anxiety are a bit specialized. Both blind and hearing-impaired, Winebrenner combines technological solutions with her own ingenuity to cope with the task of preparing for the approximately 16 tests she has to take each semester.

Winebrenner's preparation begins with careful notetaking. "In class, I have a notetaker, called a Type and Speak, which is like a laptop computer. When I get home, I can download the lecture into my other computer, which has a synthesized voice capability," she notes. "Then, as the computer speaks the lecture for me, I take notes in braille.

"I also have a machine called a Reading Edge that reads to me. If I place a book face down on its screen, it reads the page while I take braille notes.

"Because of my hearing impairment, I have to take notes in braille; the audible signal doesn't always stick in my memory. Reading my notes in braille is very helpful; it forces me to have a clear understanding of what I'm saying," Winebrenner says.

As for taking tests, "that's more a matter of motivation and human help than technological assistance," Winebrenner says.

"I usually start about a week early to study for a test," Winebrenner explains. "I prepare a schedule for myself so I have a set of clear deadlines that I need to meet. Then I collect my notes, take them home, and review them.

"For the actual tests, the college's Special Services Department provides students who read the tests for me and write down my answers," she says. "One of the problems I run into is that some students are not familiar with the academic background of the course I'm taking and don't read the test well or write the answers appropriately.

While she prefers multiple-choice tests, Winebrenner has been successful on many different kinds of tests, using different techniques to study for each type.

"If it's a test with multiple-choice questions, I focus more on the end-of-chapter reviews. I go through those and make notes on the questions in the text. If it's an essay test, I look more at the examples in the book or in my notes and use the essay-type questions and solutions at the end of the chapter as a guideline.

"Finally," she adds, "it gets to the point where you have to stop memorizing the material and start understanding it. There's no substitute for understanding the content of what you learn and its applications."

Looking Back

What kinds of tests will I encounter in college?

- Although tests are an unpopular fact of college life, they can provide useful information about one's level of knowledge and understanding about a subject.

- There are several types of tests, including brief, informal quizzes; more substantial tests; and even more weighty exams, which tend to be administered at the midpoint and end of a course.

What are the best ways to prepare for and take various kinds of tests?

- Good test preparation begins with doing the course assignments, attending class regularly, and paying attention in class. It also helps to find out as much as possible about a test beforehand and to form a study group to review material.

- If cramming becomes necessary, focus on summarizing factual information broadly, identifying key concepts and ideas, and rehearsing information orally.

- When you first receive the test, skim it to see what kinds of questions are asked, figure out how the different questions and sections will be weighted, and jot down complex factual information that is likely to be needed for the test.

- Answer the easiest questions first, write legibly, use only one side of each sheet of paper, mark answer sheets carefully, and record answers in the test book as well as the answer sheet.

What are the best strategies for answering specific kinds of test questions?

- For essay questions, be sure to understand each question and each of its parts, interpret action words correctly, write concisely, organize the essay logically, and include examples.

- For multiple-choice questions, read the question very carefully and then read all response choices. Educated guessing based on eliminating incorrect response choices is usually a reasonable strategy.

- For true–false and matching questions, answer all the items that you are sure of quickly and then go back to the remaining items.

- The best strategy for short-answer and fill-in questions is to be very sure what is being asked. Keep answers complete but brief.

Key Terms and Concepts

Resources

On Campus

Colleges often provide a variety of resources for students having difficulties with test-taking. Some offer general workshops for students, reviewing test-taking strategies. Furthermore, if you are planning to take a specific standardized test, such as the tests required for admission to business, law, or medical school, you may be able to sign up for a course offered through your college (or through such commercial organizations as *Princeton Review* or *Kaplan*).

If you find that you are experiencing significant test anxiety when taking a test or in the days leading up to it, talk to someone at your campus counseling center or health center. They can help you learn relaxation techniques and can provide counseling to help make your anxiety manageable.

In Print

In *'Ace' Any Test* (3rd ed., Career Press, 2000), Ron Fry provides a variety of techniques designed to improve your performance on any kind of test. Eileen Tracy's *The Student's Guide to Exam Success* (Open University Press, 2001) gives an overview of strategies for test-taking success. Finally, *Taking the Anxiety Out of Taking Tests* (New Harbinger Publications, 1997) by Susan Johnson is a step-by-step guide to dealing with test anxiety, providing a variety of concrete suggestions for dealing with the problem.

On the Web

The following material on the World Wide Web provides opportunities to extend your learning about the material in this chapter. (Although the Web addresses were accurate at the time the book was printed, check the P.O.W.E.R. Learning website [**www.mhhe.com/power**] for any changes that may have occurred.)

* "The Multiple Choice Exam," an online handout from the University of Victoria's Learning Skills Program (**www.coun.uvic.ca/learn/program/ hndouts/multicho.html**), offers some valuable suggestions on how to approach multiple-choice exams. Several types of multiple-choice questions are described and strategies for answering them are explained. There are also helpful hints about what to look for in the wording of both the questions and the answer choices.

* "Simplified Plans of Action for Common Types of Question Words," another online handout from the University of Victoria's Learning Skills

Program (**www.coun.uvic.ca/learn/program/hndouts/simple.html**), gives examples of question words that are often found in essay assignments or in essay questions on exams. Possible plans of action for each of the question types are outlined. These outlines can be useful as a starting point for understanding how to approach essay questions.

- "Tactics for Managing Stress and Anxiety," a "virtual pamphlet" from the University of Victoria's Counselling Services (**www.coun.uvic.ca/personal/stress.html**), offers several suggestions that you might find helpful in managing and reducing your level of stress and anxiety. The techniques may help you deal with test-related anxiety as well as academic anxiety in general. Not all of the techniques work for everyone. Try them and use the ones that work best for you.

Taking It to the Net

1 Seeing exams from other classes can help you get an idea of the kinds of questions that are often asked on exams. Use an Internet search engine to locate examples of exams from other colleges and universities. (One strategy would be to use the Google search engine—**www.google.com**—and type "examples of exams" [including the quotes] at the search prompt.) Look at several exams. How many of the questions on these exams were true–false? How many were multiple-choice? How many were essays?

2 Practice answering essay questions by comparing and contrasting the information different websites offer about the same topic. For example, go to AltaVista (**www.altavista.com**) and enter the phrase "essay exams" (using quotes). Read the strategies for essay exams offered in the first two websites. Then write a paragraph describing the information both sites had in common, and another paragraph describing the information that was unique to each site.

The Case of . . .

Too Many Questions, Too Little Time

There was no reason to panic, said Mia Varela to herself at the start of the test. The exam, a midterm in her Greek civilization class, contained 50 multiple-choice questions (each worth 1 point) and two short-answer essays (worth a total of 50 points). And she had 75 minutes to complete the test.

"Let's see," she said to herself. "At one and a half minutes per multiple-choice question, that would take 75 minutes. Hmm . . . that's no good. How about a minute for each one? Fifty minutes for the multiple-choice questions, leaving 25 minutes for the essays. That ought to work. I'll get the multiple-choice questions out of the way first."

But things didn't work out the way she planned. After an hour she had completed only 40 of the multiple-choice questions and hadn't even started on the essay questions. With only 15 minutes left, panic began to set in. She had trouble thinking. She began to be certain that she'd fail the test. She thought about how she hadn't studied enough. If only she'd worked harder. How could she explain this failure to her friends . . . to her parents . . . to herself? The thoughts kept coming, and time kept ticking away.

1. Is there evidence that Mia didn't study effectively for this type of test?

2. What was right about Mia's initial approach to the test?

3. What should Mia have done differently in calculating the amount of time to devote to each portion of the test? Why?

4. What should Mia have done to be aware of and address her timing problem sooner?

5. How should Mia have dealt with her panic? Were her thoughts productive or counterproductive? Why?

6. If you were in Mia's shoes, what would you do with only 15 minutes left in the test?

Building Your Reading Skills

"Read the first two chapters in your text by next Thursday." "I've put three articles on reserve in the library. You'll need to have them read by our next class." "Take a look at the first three Shakespeare sonnets in your book, and see if you can derive the major themes."

For Chris O'Hara, these reading assignments—handed down by different instructors on the same day in early October—felt like nails in his coffin. How was he supposed to finish all this reading in the next 2 days, in addition to studying for a Spanish test, writing a paper for history, and putting in 8 hours at his part-time job?

Although the papers and tests were hard enough to deal with, it was the constant reading that was proving the most difficult challenge for Chris during his first term of college. He was a conscientious student who attempted to get everything done, but no matter how hard he tried, he just couldn't get everything read on time. When he pushed himself to read quicker and absorb more, he actually read and retained less. Thoughts about falling behind crowded out the meaning of whatever he was reading, and he had to go through the material all over again, slowing him down even more.

Looking Ahead

For students like Chris, reading assignments are the biggest challenge in college. The amount of required reading is often enormous. Even skilled readers may find themselves wishing they could read more quickly and effectively.

Fortunately, there are ways to improve your reading skills. In this chapter, we'll go over a number of strategies for reading more effectively. You'll assess your reading style and your attention span, consider what you should do before you even start reading an assignment, discover some ways of getting the most out of your reading, and learn how to retain what you've read.

In short, after reading this chapter, you'll be able to answer the following questions:

- **How does my reading style and attention span affect my reading?**

- **How can I improve my concentration and read more effectively?**

- **How can I best retain what I have read?**

Sharpen Your Reading Skills

What kind of reader are you? Ask yourself first of all about your reading *preferences:* what do you *like* to read, and why? What makes you pick up a book and start reading—and what makes you put one down?

Second, what's your reading *style?* Do you read at a comfortable pace and feel reasonably satisfied with how much you retain? Or do you plod through reading assignments, novels, and magazines and, like Chris, end up feeling that you're taking far too long? Perhaps you whip through chapters, devour books, and fly through the daily newspaper, but then find you can't recall the information as precisely as you'd like?

Before going any further, think about your own reading preferences by completing the Journal Reflections, and then consider your reading style—your characteristic way of approaching reading tasks—by completing Try It 1.

Read for Retention, Not Speed

You may have seen advertisements promoting reading "systems" that promise to teach you to read so quickly that you'll be reading entire books in an hour or so and whizzing through assigned readings in a few minutes.

Forget it: It's not going to happen. For one thing, certain biological facts relating to the eye movements involved in reading simply prevent people from reading (and ultimately comprehending) so rapidly. Claims of speed reading are simply groundless; it is unlikely that any system will overcome the built-in limitations of the human eye.

But even if it were physically possible to read a book in an hour, ultimately it probably doesn't matter very much. Reading is not a race, and faster readers are not necessarily better readers.

The act of reading is designed to increase our knowledge and open up new ways of thinking. It can help us achieve new levels of understanding and get us to think more broadly about the world and its inhabitants. Speed matters far less than what we take away from what we've read. The key to good reading is understanding—not speed.

In describing how you can use the principles of P.O.W.E.R. Learning to become a better reader, we'll focus on the type of reading that is typically called for in academic pursuits—textbook chapters, articles, handouts, and the like. However, the same principles will help you get more benefit and enjoyment out of your recreational reading as well.

repare: Approaching the Written Word

Preparation to begin reading isn't hard, and it won't take very long, but it's a crucial first step in applying P.O.W.E.R. Learning (summarized in the P.O.W.E.R. Plan below). Your aim in preparation is to become familiar with **advance organizers**—outlines, overviews, section objectives, or other clues to the meaning and organization of new material—provided in the material you are reading. Most textbooks have them built in; for an example, look at the start of every chapter in this book, which includes a chapter outline, plus a set

Advance organizers
Broad, general ideas related to material that is to be read or heard, which pave the way for subsequent learning

Try It! 1

Personal Styles: Discover Your Reading Style

Use the following questions to learn *how* you read—that is, your characteristic reading style. Rate how well each statement below describes you. Use this rating scale:

1 = Doesn't describe me at all

2 = Describes me only slightly

3 = Describes me fairly well

4 = Describes me very well

	1	2	3	4
1. I often reread passages in books that I particularly like.				
2. I often read good passages aloud to whomever is around.				
3. I often stop while reading to check that I understood what I just read.				
4. If I come across a long, unfamiliar name, I try to sound it out and pronounce it correctly.				
5. If there's a word I don't understand, I look it up in a dictionary right away or mark it so I can look it up later.				
6. Before I start reading a textbook or other serious book or article, I look for clues about how it is organized.				
7. I often question what I'm reading and "argue" with the author.				
8. I often try to guess what the chapter I'm about to read will cover.				
9. I often write comments or make notes in books that I own.				
10. I'm always finding typographical errors in books and articles I read.				

Reading styles range from a very holistic (i.e., broad-brushstroke, noncritical) style to a very analytic (i.e., detailed, critical) style. Add up the points you assigned yourself. Use this informal scale to find your reading style:

10–12 = Very holistic reading style

13–20 = Mostly holistic reading style

21–28 = Mostly analytic reading style

29–40 = Very analytic reading style

How do you think your reading style affects the way you learn material in textbooks? Is your style related to the kinds of subjects you prefer? Do you think your reading style affects your leisure reading?

To Try It online, go to **www.mhhe.com/power**.

of questions at the end of the "Looking Ahead" section. You can also create your own advance organizers by skimming material to be read and sketching out the general outline of the material you'll be reading. Advance organizers pave the way for subsequent learning, and ultimately they can help us recall material better after we've read it. (To prove the value of advance organizers, take a look at Try It 2, "Discover How Advance Organizers Help.")

What's the Point of the Reading Assignment? Before you begin an assignment, think about what your goal is. Will you be reading a textbook on which you'll be thoroughly tested? Is your reading supposed to provide background information that will serve as a context for future learning but that won't itself be tested? Is the material going to be useful to you personally? Realistically, how much time can you devote to the reading assignment?

Your goal for reading will help you determine which reading strategy to adopt. You aren't expected to read everything with the same degree of intensity. Some material you may feel comfortable skimming; for other material you'll want to put in the maximum effort.

Understand the Point of View of the Material Itself What are you reading—a textbook, an essay, an article? If it is an essay or article, why was it written? To prove a point? To give information? To express the author's personal feelings? Knowing the author's purpose (even if his or her specific point and message aren't yet clear) can help you a great deal as you read.

Start with the Frontmatter If you'll be using a text or other book extensively throughout the term, start by reading the preface and/or introduction and scanning the table of contents—what publishers call the **frontmatter.** Instructors often don't formally assign the frontmatter, but reading it can be a big help because it is there that the author has a chance to step forward and explain, often more personally than elsewhere in an academic book, what he or she considers important. Knowing this will give you a sense of what to expect as you read.

By reading the frontmatter, you can get inside the author's head, obtaining insight into the author's goals, values, and strategies in writing the book. You

Frontmatter

The preface, introduction, and table of contents of a book

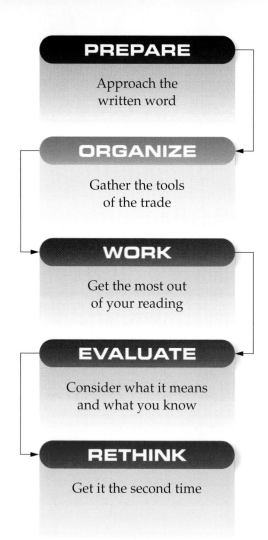

PREPARE

Approach the
written word

ORGANIZE

Gather the tools
of the trade

WORK

Get the most out
of your reading

EVALUATE

Consider what it means
and what you know

RETHINK

Get it the second time

P.O.W.E.R. Plan

might also find information about the author's background, and perhaps even a photo. Use this material to "personalize" the author, to gain some insight into the kind of person he or she is. The information you obtain from the frontmatter will provide a mental "hook" on which you can hang the new ideas to which you'll be exposed. (For practice with frontmatter, do Try It 3 on page 152.)

Create Advance Organizers To provide a context for your reading, create your own advance organizers by skimming through the table of contents, which provides the main headings of what you will be reading. Textbooks often have chapter outlines, listing the key topics to be covered, which also provide a way of previewing the chapter content. As you read over the outline, you can begin to consider how the new material in the book may relate both to what you know and to what you expect to learn—from the reading assignment itself and from the course.

Textbooks also often have end-of-chapter summaries, and many articles include a final section in which the author states his or her conclusions. Take a look at these ending sections as well. Even though you haven't read the material yet and the summary probably won't make complete sense to you, by reading the summary, you'll get an idea of what the author covers and what he or she considers important.

Your instructor may also provide an advance organizer for readings. Sometimes instructors will mention things to pay particular attention to or to look for, such as "When you read Thomas Paine's *Common Sense*, notice how he lays out his argument and what his key points are." Sometimes they will say why they assigned a reading. Such information provides clues that can help you develop a mental list of the reading's key ideas.

However you construct advance organizers, be sure they provide a framework and context for what you'll be reading; this framework and context can spell the difference between fully comprehending what you read and misunderstanding it.

Now it's time to put all this practice to good use. Create an advance organizer for this chapter in Try It 4 on page 153.

ry It! 2

Discover How Advance Organizers Help

Read this passage. What do you think it means?

> The procedure is actually quite simple. First you arrange items into different groups. Of course, one pile may be sufficient, depending on how much there is to do. If you have to go somewhere else due to lack of facilities, that is the next step; otherwise, you are pretty well set. It is important not to overdo things. That is, it is better to do too few things at once than too many. In the short run this may not seem important but complications can easily arise. A mistake can be expensive as well. At first, the whole procedure will seem complicated. Soon, however, it will become just another facet of life. It is difficult to foresee any end to the necessity for this task in the immediate future, but then one can never tell. After the procedure is completed, one arranges the materials into different groups again. Then they can be put into their appropriate places. Eventually, they will be used once more and the whole cycle will then have to be repeated. However, this is a part of life.[1]

If you're like most people, you don't have a clue about what this all means. But suppose you had been given some context in advance, and you knew before reading it that the description had to do with washing laundry. Now does it all fall into place? Read the passage once more, and see how having an advance organizer (in this case, *washing laundry*) helps out.

To Try It online, go to **www.mhhe.com/power**.

Organize: Gathering the Tools of the Trade

It's obvious that the primary item you'll need to complete a reading assignment is the material that you're reading. But there are other essential tools you should gather, potentially including the following:

- A pencil or pen to write notes in the margin.
- A highlighter to indicate key passages in the text.
- A copy of the assignment, so you'll be sure to read the right material.
- A pad of paper and/or index cards for notetaking if the material is particularly complex. If you routinely use a word processor to take notes, get it ready.
- A dictionary. You never know what new words you'll encounter while you're reading. If a dictionary is not handy, you'll be tempted to skip over unfamiliar words—a decision that may come back to haunt you. Note that some word-processing software includes a dictionary; there are also many good dictionaries available online (e.g., Merriam-Webster's at **www.m-w.com**, where you will also find an online thesaurus). The point is to use what's available—but use something!

Try It! 3

Read the Frontmatter

Have you read the frontmatter of *this* book? Go there now. If you've already read it, review it. If you haven't, read it now. Then answer the following questions:

What are the goals of this book? _____

_____

_____

Who is the author, and what qualifies him to write this book? _____

_____

_____

Do you think the author has an understanding of students? _____

_____

_____

Do you think the author has an understanding of what students should do to become
successful in their studies? _____

_____

Is there anything in the frontmatter that made you curious? Does anything seem particularly
interesting? _____

_____

After reading the frontmatter, do you feel confident that you can learn what the author wants to
teach? Do you feel that you *want* to learn it?_____

_____

To Try It online, go to **www.mhhe.com/power**.

Give Yourself Time There's one more thing you need to prepare successfully for a reading assignment: enough time to complete it. The length of reading assignments is almost never ambiguous. You will typically be given a specific page range, so you will know just how much material you will need to cover.

Now get a watch and time yourself as you read the first three pages of your assignment, being sure to pay attention to the material, not the time! Timing how long it takes to read a representative chunk of material provides you with a rough measure of your reading speed for the material—although it will vary even within a single reading assignment, depending on the complexity of the material.

You'll also need to consider an aspect of your personal learning style: your reading attention span. **Attention span** is the length of time that a person usually is able to sustain attention. People with long attention spans can read for

Attention span
The length of time that
attention is typically
sustained
_____

Chapter 6 Building Your Reading Skills

Create an Advance Organizer

Use any information you have available to create an advance organizer for this chapter. Feel free to return to the frontmatter, skim the section headings, read the "Looking Back" chapter summary, or recall anything your instructor may have said about the chapter.

(If you come across words, phrases, or ideas that seem unfamiliar or incomprehensible, it may be helpful to think of several questions you would ask me if you had the opportunity.)

Complete the following statements to prepare your organizer:

The key topics that will be covered in the rest of this chapter are . . .

_____

_____

_____

I think I will be most interested in . . .

_____

_____

_____

I think I will be least interested in . . .

_____

_____

_____

I hope the chapter covers this topic . . .

_____

_____

_____

Words, phrases, and ideas that are unfamiliar to me include . . .

_____

_____

_____

If the author were here, I would ask . . .

_____

_____

_____

Note: You may want to use this Try It as a starting point for advance organizers for each chapter in this book.

To Try It online, go to **www.mhhe.com/power**.

relatively lengthy periods without getting jumpy, while those with shorter ones can only maintain attention for a short while. You can get a general sense of this by using Try It 5, "Discover Your Attention Span."

Use the three pieces of information you now have—the length of the assignment, your per-page reading speed at full attention, and your typical attention span—to estimate roughly how long it will take you to complete the reading assignment. For example, if you are asked to read 12 pages, you have found that you need approximately 4 minutes to read a page, and your reading attention span is, on average, 25 minutes long, you can expect your reading to take at least 60 minutes, assuming you'll take a short break when your attention begins to fade after 25 minutes.

In addition, you may need to interrupt your reading to look up words in the dictionary, get a drink, stretch, or answer the phone. You may also decide to break your reading into several short sessions, in which case your total reading time may be greater since you will have to get reacquainted with the reading assignment each time you sit down again.

W ork: Getting the Most Out of Your Reading

Finally, it's time to get down to work and start reading.

Obviously—because it's what you're doing at this very moment—you know how to read. But what's important is what you do *while* you're reading. Here are several things that will help you get the most out of the process of reading:

Stay Focused The TV show you watched last night . . . your boyfriend forgetting to meet you at the bus stop . . . your father's health . . . your grumbling stomach. There are a million and one possible distractions that can invade your thoughts as you read. Your job is to keep distracting thoughts at bay and focus on the material you are supposed to be reading. It's not easy, but there are things you can do to help yourself stay focused:

Despite the throngs of students walking by on the campus of the University of Texas in Austin, the student seated on the bench seems to have no trouble concentrating on what she's reading. Though this might work for her, if you are easily distracted, choosing an isolated location to read is a wise strategy.

- **Read in small bites.** If you think it is going to take you 4 hours to read an entire chapter, break up the 4 hours into more manageable time periods. Promise yourself that you'll read for 1 hour in the afternoon, another hour in the evening, and the next 2 hours spaced out during the following day. One hour of reading is far more manageable than a 4-hour block.

Personal Styles: Discover Your Attention Span

You should be aware of your attention span, the length of time you usually are able to sustain attention to a task, as you prepare for reading assignments. To get an idea of the length of your current attention span for reading, perform this exercise over the next few days.

1. Choose one of the textbooks that you've been assigned to read this semester.

2. Start reading a chapter, without any preparation, noting in the chart below the time that you start reading.

3. As soon as your mind begins to wander and think about other subjects, stop reading and note the time on the chart below.

4. Using the same textbook, repeat this process four more times over the course of a few days, entering the data on the chart below.

5. To find your reading attention span, calculate the average number of minutes across the five trials.

Trial #1:   Starting time:_____   Ending time:_____
                   Number of minutes between start and end times: _____

Trial #2:   Starting time:_____   Ending time:_____
                   Number of minutes between start and end times: _____

Trial #3:   Starting time:_____   Ending time:_____
                   Number of minutes between start and end times: _____

Trial #4:   Starting time:_____   Ending time:_____
                   Number of minutes between start and end times: _____

Trial #5:   Starting time:_____   Ending time:_____
                   Number of minutes between start and end times: _____

Reading attention span (the average of the number of minutes in the last column, found by adding up the five numbers and dividing by 5) = _____ minutes

---

Ask yourself these questions about your reading attention span:

1. Are you surprised by the length of your reading attention span? In what way?

2. Does any number in the set of trials stand out from the other numbers? For instance, is any number much higher or lower than the average? If so, can you account for this? For example, what time of day was it?

3. Do the numbers in your trials show any trend? For instance, did your attention span tend to increase slightly over the course of the trials, did it decrease, or did it stay about the same? Can you explain any trend you may have noted?

4. Do you think your attention span figures would be very different if you had chosen a different textbook? Why?

To Try It online, go to **www.mhhe.com/power**.

- **Take a break.** Actually, plan to take *several* short breaks to reward yourself while you're reading. During your break, do something enjoyable—eat a snack, watch a bit of a ball game on television, play a video game, or the like. Just try not to get drawn into your break activity to the point that it takes over your reading time.

- **Deal with distractions.** Sometimes problems have a way of popping into our minds and repeatedly distracting us. If a particular problem keeps interrupting your concentration—such as a difficulty you're having on the job—try to think of an action-oriented strategy to deal with it. You might even write your proposed solution down on a piece of paper. Putting it down in words can get the problem off your mind, potentially making it less intrusive.

Write While You Read Writing is one of the most important aspects of reading. If you haven't underlined, jotted notes to yourself, placed check marks on the page, drawn arrows, constructed diagrams, and otherwise defaced and disfigured your book while you're reading, you're not doing your job as a P.O.W.E.R. reader.

The idea of writing on a book page may go against everything you've been taught in the past. (And of course you should never write on a library book or one that you've borrowed.)

However, once you've bought your book, *you own it and you should make it your own.* Don't keep your textbooks spotless so they will fetch a higher price if you sell them later. Instead, think of textbooks as documents recording your active learning and engagement in a field of study. In addition, you should look at your textbooks as the foundation of your personal library, which will grow throughout your lifetime. In short, writing extensively in your book while you're reading is an important tactic for achieving success.

> "What is reading but silent conversation?"
>
> Walter Savage Landor, "Aristoteles and Callisthenes," *Imaginary Conversations*

The ability to add your own personal notes, underlining, and other annotations to a clean text while you're reading is one of the reasons it usually pays to buy new, rather than used, textbooks. Why would you want a stranger's comments on something you own? Can you really trust that person's judgment over your own regarding what's important to underline? New books allow you to mark them up in your own, personal style, without the distraction of competing voices.

What should you be writing while you are reading? There are several things you should write down:

- **Rephrase key points.** Make notes to yourself, in your own words, about what the author is trying to get across. Don't just copy what's been said. Think about the material, and rewrite it in words that are your own.

  Writing notes to yourself in your own words has several consequences, all good. First, you make the material yours; it becomes something you now understand and part of your own knowledge base.

  Second, trying to summarize a key point in your own words will make it very clear whether you truly understand it. It's easy to be fooled into thinking we understand something as we're reading along. But the true test is whether we can explain it to ourselves (or someone else) on our own, without referring to the book or article.

  Third, the very act of writing engages an additional type of perception—involving the physical sense of moving a pen or pressing a keyboard. This will help you learn the material in a more active way.

Finally, writing notes and phrases will help you study the material later. Not only will the key points be highlighted, but your notes will also quickly bring you up to speed regarding your initial thoughts and impressions.

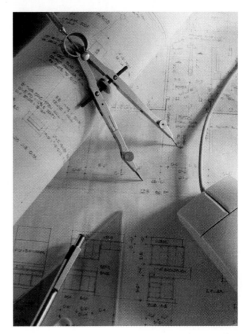

- **Highlight or underline key points.** Very often the first or last sentence in a paragraph, or the first or last paragraph in a section, will present a key point. (Remember those lessons about "topic sentences" you had in high school English classes? Writers really use them.)

    Before you highlight anything, though, read the whole paragraph through. Then you'll be sure that what you highlight is, in fact, the key information. Topic sentences do not always fall at the beginning of a paragraph.

    Be selective in your highlighting and underlining. A page covered in yellow highlighter may be artistically appealing, but it won't help you understand the material any better. Highlight only the key information. You might find yourself highlighting only one or two sentences or phrases per page. That's fine. *In highlighting and underlining, less is more.* One guideline: No more than 10 percent of the material should be highlighted or underlined.

- **Use arrows, diagrams, outlines, tables, time lines, charts, and other visuals to help you understand and later recall what you are reading.** If there are three examples given for a particular point, number them. If a paragraph discusses a situation in which an earlier point does not hold, link the original point to the exception by an arrow. If a sequence of steps is presented, number each step.

    For example, after you have annotated this page, it might look something like what is shown on page 160.

    Particularly if your learning style is a visual one, representing the material graphically will get you thinking about it—and the connections and points in it—in new and different ways. Rather than considering the material solely in verbal terms, you now add visual images. The act of creating visual annotations will not only help you to understand the material better but it will also ease its later recall. Practice this technique in Try It 6.

- **Look up unfamiliar words in a dictionary.** Even though you may be able to figure out the meaning of an unfamiliar word from its context, use a dictionary anyway. This way you can be sure that what you think it means is correct. A dictionary will also tell you what the word sounds like, which may be important if your instructor uses the word in class.

- **Use specialized strategies for special subjects.** Although the approaches to reading we've discussed cut across different subject areas, certain disciplines warrant specialized strategies. Consider the following:

    Reading mathematics texts. With their many formulas, math books can be especially intimidating. Although it may be tempting to skip over the formulas, that's a mistake. Look at them, think about them, annotate them, and make them concrete by substituting actual numbers for abstract letters.

Working in a Group:
Mark Up a Book Page

First, working alone, read the excerpt on the following page. Then use the techniques we've discussed for marking up a page to highlight its key points.

Next, working in a group, compare and contrast your annotations with those of some classmates, and answer the following questions:

1. How do others' annotations differ from yours?

2. Why did they use the annotations they did?

3. Which annotation techniques worked best for you? Which did others prefer? Why?

4. How might these annotations help you to remember what is important?

5. If there were different sorts of material presented on the page, such as mathematical formulas, would you use different kinds of annotations?

The more parents speak to their children, the better their children's language skills.

Understanding Language Acquisition: Identifying the Roots of Language

Anyone who spends even a little time with children will notice the enormous strides that they make in language development throughout childhood. However, the reasons for this rapid growth are far from obvious. Two major explanations have been offered: one based on learning theory and the other on innate processes.

The **learning-theory approach** suggests that language acquisition follows the principles of reinforcement and conditioning discussed in Chapter 6. For example, a child who utters the word "mama" is hugged and praised by her mother, which reinforces the behavior and makes its repetition more likely. This view suggests that children first learn to speak by being rewarded for making sounds that approximate speech. Ultimately, through a process of shaping, language becomes more and more like adult speech (Skinner, 1957).

learning-theory approach: The theory suggesting that language acquisition follows the principles of reinforcement and conditioning

The learning theory approach is supported by research that shows that the more parents speak to their young children, the more proficient the children become in language usage (see Figure 8-11). In addition, higher levels of linguistic sophistication in parents' speech to their young children are related to a greater rate of vocabulary growth, vocabulary usage, and even general intellectual achievement by the time the children are 3 years of age (Hart & Risley, 1997).

On the other hand, the learning theory approach is less successful when it comes to explaining the acquisition of language rules. Children are reinforced not only when they use proper language, but also when they respond incorrectly. For example, parents answer the child's "Why the dog won't eat?" as readily as they do the correctly phrased question "Why won't the dog eat?" Both sentences are understood equally well. Learning theory, then, has difficulty in providing the full explanation for language acquisition.

Pointing to such problems with learning theory approaches to language acquisition, Noam Chomsky (1968, 1978, 1991), a linguist, provided a ground-breaking alternative. Chomsky argued that humans are born with an innate linguistic capability that emerges primarily as a function of maturation. According to his analysis, all the world's languages share a similar underlying structure called a **universal grammar.** Chomsky suggests that the human brain has a neural system, the **language-acquisition device,** that both permits the understanding of the structure of language and provides strategies and techniques for learning the unique characteristics of a given native language.

universal grammar: Noam Chomsky's theory that all the world's languages share a similar underlying structure
language-acquisition device: A neural system of the brain hypothesized to permit understanding of language

tion—involving the physical sense of moving a pen or pressing a keyboard. This will help you learn the material in a more active way.

Finally, writing notes and phrases will help you study the material later. Not only will the key points be highlighted, but your notes will also quickly bring you up to speed regarding your initial thoughts and impressions.

use highlighter – but less is more Not more than 10% highlighted.

topic sentence

① Highlight or underline key points. Very often the first or last sentence in a paragraph, or the first or last paragraph in a section, will present a key point. (Remember those lessons about "topic sentences" you had in high school English classes? Writers really use them.)

Before you highlight anything, though, read the whole paragraph through. Then you'll be sure that what you highlight is, in fact, the key information. Topic sentences do not always fall at the beginning of a paragraph.

Be selective in your highlighting and underlining. A page covered in yellow highlighter may be artistically appealing, but it won't help you understand the material any better. Highlight only the key information. You might find yourself highlighting only one or two sentences or phrases per page. That's fine. *In highlighting and underlining, less is more.* One guideline: No more than 10 percent of the material should be highlighted or underlined.

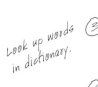

use visuals

② Use arrows, diagrams, outlines, tables, time lines, charts, and other visuals to help you understand and later recall what you are reading. If there are three examples given for a particular point, number them. If a paragraph discusses a situation in which an earlier point does not hold, link the original point to the exception by an arrow. If a sequence of steps is presented, number each step.

For example, after you have annotated this page, it might look something like what is shown on page 160.

Particularly if your learning style is a visual one, representing the material graphically will get you thinking about it—and the connections and points in it—in new and different ways. Rather than considering the material solely in verbal terms, you now add visual images. The act of creating visual annotations will not only help you to understand the material better but it will also ease its later recall. Practice this technique in Try It 6.

Look up words in dictionary.

③ Look up unfamiliar words in a dictionary. Even though you may be able to figure out the meaning of an unfamiliar word from its context, use a dictionary anyway. This way you can be sure that what you think it means is correct. A dictionary will also tell you what the word sounds like, which may be important if your instructor uses the word in class.

Special strategies for particular subjects e.g., math.

④ Use specialized strategies for special subjects. Although the approaches to reading we've discussed cut across different subject areas, certain disciplines warrant specialized strategies. Consider the following:

Reading mathematics texts. With their many formulas, math books can be especially intimidating. Although it may be tempting to skip over the formulas, that's a mistake. Look at them, think about them, annotate them, and make them concrete by substituting actual numbers for abstract letters.

Reading in a foreign language. Use of a dictionary may be a big help when reading in a foreign language. But don't rely on it too much: if you can't remember the meaning of a word, first try to figure out what is being said from the context, and only then look it up. Also keep in mind this fundamental rule of language study: the more you immerse yourself in a language, the easier it will become.

Reading in the sciences. Be aware that the *scientific method* is the basis for much writing about scientific topics. In particular, scientists conduct experiments to support *hypotheses*, specific predictions that are derived from a theory. When reading about scientific research, try to identify the hypothesis that is being tested, and what alternative hypotheses might be used.

Dealing with Learning Disabilities

If you, like millions of people in the United States, have a learning disability of one sort or another, reading may prove to be particularly challenging. **Learning disabilities** are defined as difficulties in processing information when listening, speaking, reading, or writing; in most cases, learning disabilities are diagnosed when there is a discrepancy between learning potential and actual academic achievement.

One of the most common kinds of learning disabilities is *dyslexia,* a reading disability that produces the misperception of letters during reading and writing, unusual difficulty in sounding out letters, spelling difficulties, and confusion between right and left. Although its causes are not yet completely understood, one likely explanation is a problem in the part of the brain responsible for breaking words into the sound elements that make up language.

People with learning disabilities are sometimes viewed as unintelligent. Nothing could be further from the truth: There is no relationship between learning disabilities and I.Q. For instance, dozens of well-known and highly accomplished individuals suffered from dyslexia, including physicist Albert Einstein, U.S. General George Patton, poet William Butler Yeats, and—as we discuss in "Speaking of Success" later in this chapter—writer John Irving.

By the time they reach college, most people with learning disabilities have already been diagnosed. If you do have a diagnosed learning disability and you need special services, it is important to disclose your situation to your instructors and other college officials.

In some cases, students with learning disabilities have not been appropriately evaluated prior to college. If you have difficulties such as mixing up and reversing letters frequently and suspect that you have a learning disability, there is an office on campus that can provide you with guidance. One place to start is your college counseling or health center.

However, just because you are having trouble with reading assignments doesn't automatically mean that you have a learning disability. Not only is the kind of reading you do in college more difficult than what you did in high school, but there's also more of it. It's only when reading represents a persistent, long-term problem—one that won't go away no matter how much work you do—that a learning disability becomes a possible explanation.

Learning disabilities
Difficulties in processing information when listening, speaking, reading, or writing, characterized by a discrepancy between learning potential and actual academic achievement

E valuate: Considering What It Means and What You Know

Evaluation is a crucial step in reading. You need to be able to answer the seemingly simple question: "What does all this mean?"

But there's another aspect to evaluation. You need to evaluate, truthfully and honestly, your own level of understanding. What do you know as a result of your reading? Evaluation, then, consists of the following steps:

- **Identify the main ideas and themes and their value *to you personally*.** Try to determine the take-home message of the material you've read. For example, the take-home message of a chapter of an American history text might be, "Although Abraham Lincoln eventually called for the end of slavery, initially he was hesitant because of political considerations."

  Sometimes the main ideas and themes are spelled out, and at other times you will have to deduce them for yourself. Evaluating the main ideas and themes in terms of how they relate to you personally will help you understand and remember them more easily.

- **Prioritize the ideas.** Of all the information that is presented, which is the most crucial to the main message and which is the least crucial? Make a list of the main topics covered and try to rank them in order of importance.

- **Think critically about the arguments presented in the reading.** Do they seem to make sense? Are the author's assertions reasonable? Are there any flaws in the arguments? Would authors with a different point of view dispute what is being said? How would they build their own arguments?

- **Pretend you are explaining the material (talking—out loud!—about the material) to a fellow classmate who missed the assignment.** This is one time when talking out loud when no one is around is not only normal but also beneficial. Summarize the material aloud, as if you were talking to another person.

  Talking out loud does two things. First, it helps you identify weak spots in your understanding. Talking to yourself will help you nail down concepts that are still not clear in your own mind. Second, and equally important, because you are transforming the written word into the spoken word, you are thinking about the information in another way, which will help you remember it better.

- **Be honest with yourself.** Most of us are able to read with our minds on cruise control. But the net result is not much different from not reading the passage at all. If you have drifted off while you've been reading, go back and reread the passage.

- **Pat yourself on the back.** Just as you've done during each of your reading breaks, reward yourself for completing the reading passage. But keep in mind that there's one more step before you can really relax, and it's a crucial one: rethinking what you've read.

R ethink: Getting It the Second Time

You're human, so—like the rest of us—when you finish a reading assignment you'd probably like nothing more than to heave a sigh of relief and put the book away.

By now you know that there's a crucial step you should take that will assist you in cementing what you've learned into memory: rethinking what you've read. If you do it within 24 hours of first reading the assignment, it can save you hours of work later.

The best way to rethink an assignment is to reread it, along with any notes you've taken. "Yeah, right," you're probably thinking. "Like I have time for that." The benefits of rereading can't be overstated. Rereading transfers material from your short-term memory to your long-term memory. It solidifies information so that it will be remembered far better over the long haul.

Rereading will take far less time than did reading the first time. In fact, it isn't necessary to reread word for word. You already know what's important and what's not important, so you can skim some of the less important material. But it is wise to reread the more difficult and important material carefully, making sure that you fully understand what is being discussed and why.

Rethinking should be the central activity as you reread the passage and your notes. You need to be sure that your understanding is complete and that you're able to answer any questions that you had earlier about the material.

The Concept Map As a Rethinking Tool As we saw in Chapter 4, **concept mapping** is a method of structuring written material by graphically grouping and connecting key ideas and themes. Each key idea is placed in a different part of the map, and related ideas are placed near it—above, below, or beside it. A concept map looks similar to a graphic of the solar system, with the central idea (the "sun") in the center, surrounded by related concepts (the "planets").

Concept maps help you to rethink material you've read about, especially if you have used a more traditional outline earlier. Furthermore, once you have developed a concept map for a particular aspect of the material, you can create additional, expanded concept maps involving related information.

Concept maps are particularly useful for people with learning styles that depend on spatial relationships. Furthermore, students with certain kinds of learning disabilities—a topic we discussed earlier in this chapter—can also benefit from the use of concept maps.

An example of a concept map involving the material we've discussed so far is illustrated at the right. Note how it summarizes the material and shows how it is related to the central topic of "Reading with Understanding."

> "Reading furnishes the mind only with materials of knowledge; it is thinking that makes what we read ours."
>
> John Locke, *Of the Conduct of the Understanding* (1706), p. 20

Concept mapping
A method of structuring written material by graphically grouping and connecting key ideas and themes

This concept map illustrates the key ideas of reading with understanding.

Career Connections

The Job of Reading

Memos. Annual reports. Instructions. Continuing education assignments. Professional journals.

Each of these items illustrates the importance of developing critical reading skills for on-the-job success. Virtually every job requires good reading expertise, and for some professions, reading is a central component. Polishing your reading skills now will pay big dividends when you enter the world of work. The better you are at absorbing written information, the better you'll be at carrying out your job.

For instance, in many corporations, vital information is transmitted through the written word, via e-mails, hard-copy memos, technical reports, or Web-based material. The person who repairs your broken washing machine or automobile has probably read numerous service manuals while attending continuing education classes required to master the complex computer diagnostic systems that are now standard equipment. The physician who gives you a physical may have taken an online distance learning class that required reading about the newest medical technologies. And every one of your college instructors probably spends hours each month reading about the newest developments in his or her field.

Furthermore, because not all supervisors are effective writers, you'll sometimes need to read between the lines and draw inferences and conclusions about what you need to do. You should also keep in mind that there are significant cultural differences in the way in which people write and the type of language they use. Being sensitive to the cultural background of colleagues will permit you to more accurately interpret and understand what you are reading.

In short, reading is a skill that's required in virtually every profession. Developing the habit of reading critically while you are in college will pave the road for future career success.

Speaking of Success

Name:	*John Irving*
Education:	*BA, University of New Hampshire*
Home:	*New Hampshire*

The author of such novels as *The World According to Garp* and *The Cider House Rules,* John Irving is one of America's foremost storytellers. But his road to success was not always smooth, particularly because he suffers from the learning disability dyslexia, which makes both reading and writing difficult.

While attending Exeter Academy, his high school, Irving knew something was wrong. But in the 1950s, there was little known about learning disabilities.

"I was a mediocre student—as it turned out, I was dyslexic, but no one knew this at the time,"[2] Irving noted. "To say that Exeter was hard for me is an understatement. I was the only student in my genetics class who failed to control his fruit-fly experiment. The Red Eyes and the White Eyes were interbreeding so rapidly that I lost track of the generations."

While at Exeter, Irving developed a love of wrestling, which became an important part of his life. As a member of the wrestling team, he learned from his coach how he could compensate for his shortcomings as

an athlete: by being dedicated. "Talent is overrated," said his coach. "That you're not very talented needn't be the end of it. . . . An underdog is in a position to take a healthy bite."

Irving continued, "This was a concept of myself that I'd been lacking. I was an underdog; therefore, I had to control the pace—of everything. . . . The concept was applicable to my creative writing—to all my schoolwork, too.

"If my classmates could read our history assignments in an hour, I allowed myself two or three. If I couldn't learn to spell, I would keep a list of many most frequently misspelled words, and I kept the list with me; I had it handy even for unannounced quizzes," Irving said.

Irving's hard work and dedication permitted him to overcome his learning disability. Ultimately, he became one of the most prominent authors of our time. To what does he attribute his success? "Writing is one-eighth talent and seven-eighths discipline," he believes.

How does my reading style and attention span affect my reading?

- The most important aspect of reading is understanding, not speed. People have different reading styles that can be modified to improve their ability to read with understanding.

- One problem people have with reading is a limited attention span. However, attention span can be increased with self-awareness and practice.

How can I improve my concentration and read more effectively?

- Reading should be approached with a clear sense of purpose and goals, which will vary from assignment to assignment. Examining the front-matter of a book and creating advance organizers is also useful.

- Maintain focus by breaking down the reading into small chunks, taking breaks as needed, dealing with distractions, and writing while reading.

How can I best retain what I have read?

- Understanding of reading assignments can be cemented in memory by identifying the main ideas, prioritizing them, thinking critically about the arguments, and explaining the writer's ideas to someone else.

- Quickly rereading assignments and notes taken on them can greatly help in solidifying memories of what has been read. Concept maps that structure and relate ideas can also help.

Key Terms and Concepts

Advance organizer (p. 147)
Attention span (p. 152)
Concept mapping (p. 163)

Frontmatter (p. 149)
Learning disabilities (p. 161)

Resources

On Campus

If you are experiencing unusual difficulties in reading, and the problem is one you encountered in high school, you may have a learning disability. If you suspect this is the case, take action. Many colleges have an office that deals specifically with learning disabilities. You can also talk to someone at your college's counseling center; he or she will arrange for you to be tested, which can determine whether you have a problem.

In Print

The third edition of Joe Cortina and Janet Elder's book, *Opening Doors: Understanding College Reading* (McGraw-Hill, 2002), provides a complete set of guidelines for reading textbooks and other kinds of writing that you will encounter during college. Another useful volume is the sixth edition of *Breaking Through: College Reading* (Longman, 2001) by Brenda Smith.

On the Web

The following sites on the World Wide Web provide the opportunity to extend your learning about the material in this chapter. (Although the Web addresses were accurate at the time the book was printed, check the P.O.W.E.R. Learning website [**www.mhhe.com/power**] for any changes that may have occurred.)

- The "Great Books Index: An Index to Online Great Books in English Translation" (**www.mirror.org/books/**): Check out this lengthy list of books. While it is one person's interpretation of what constitutes great books, it nevertheless contains a variety of 20th-century works, as well as older classics, written by a very diverse collection of writers.

- "Increasing Textbook Comprehension by Using SQ3R" is one of several online study skills workshops sponsored by the Cook Counseling Center of the Virginia Polytechnic Institute and State University (**www.ucc.vt.edu/**). This site introduces the SQ3R approach to reading, and retaining, textual material. A summary of the method can be found at **www.ucc.vt.edu/stdysk/sq3r.html**.

Taking It to the Net

1 Read a historical document. Choose a document that interests you by going to the Netscape search site (**www.netscape.com**) and conducting a search by entering the phrase "historical documents." After finding a document, read it, and summarize it in a short essay.

2 Go to a newspaper's website, such as that of *The New York Times* (**www.nyt.com**) or the *Atlanta Constitution* (**www.ajc.com**), and read one of the current editorials. Take notes on the editorial, concentrating on evaluating the strength of the argument(s). How persuasive was the editorial, and why?

The Case of . . .

War and Peace

One thousand four hundred eighty-four.

That's all Chenille Lawrence could think about when she got to the bookstore to purchase *War and Peace,* which her instructor said they'd be reading over the next 4 weeks. Sure, she thought to herself, it's great literature, as her instructor had said. It's undoubtedly a classic that every well-educated person should read some time in his or her life. Sure, maybe reading it would change her life in unimaginable ways, as her instructor had also argued (although she had strong doubts that its immediate effect would be anything but pain).

All she could think about, though, was its length—1,484 pages, not even counting the introduction. How would she ever get through such a giant book?

1. How would you advise Chenille to prepare for her reading of *War and Peace*? What sort of advance organizers would you suggest she create?

2. How would you suggest Chenille organize her time so that she could finish the book in the allotted 4 weeks?

3. How might Chenille stay focused on her reading? How might she most effectively use writing as a way to accomplish her task?

4. Why is evaluation important for effectively reading a long book such as *War and Peace*? How might Chenille evaluate the book and her understanding of it as she reads?

5. In what ways can Chenille use rethinking techniques to improve her understanding of the book?

Writing and Speaking

7

taring at the blank computer screen, Maria Ramos felt another surge of anxiety wash over her. She was beginning to panic.

The paper she was trying to get started on was due in 2 days, and she had not yet put a word down on paper. The problem was . . . well, that was just it: she didn't *know* what the problem was. The topic was completely hazy; she had no idea what her instructor was looking for.

As the minutes turned into hours, Maria was becoming increasingly desperate. Finally, for lack of a better idea, she

decided to start writing down whatever came to mind, producing a flurry of stream-of-consciousness thoughts, recollections, and ideas.

Although most of the things that found their way to her computer screen had nothing to do with the paper topic, she was surprised to come up with a few thoughts that were relevant. And suddenly, she had an idea about how she could approach the assigned topic. Things gradually began to fall into place.

Maria had found her writing voice.

Looking Ahead

Few activities raise so many concerns and anxieties as writing and public speaking. Yet few skills are as important to your success, not only in college but also in the world outside the classroom. Taking time now to learn how to write well and speak well will not only increase your chances of success, but it will also improve your peace of mind!

This chapter focuses on writing and speaking. We begin by considering how to write, with a focus on composing college-level papers. We'll talk about how to get started and how you can move from a rough first draft to a final draft of which you can be proud.

The second part of the chapter looks at oral presentations. We'll discuss ways of getting over stage fright and how to engage listeners from the very start of your talk. We consider the importance of practicing neither too little nor too much.

After reading this material, you'll be able to answer these questions:

- **What are the best techniques for getting started and writing a first draft?**

- **How can I move from my first draft to my final draft?**

- **How can I conquer my fear of public speaking and make effective oral presentations?**

The Writing Process

What happens when you sit down to write? Does the sight of a blank page or blank screen leave your mind blank as well? Do your fingers, which move so quickly when you're playing a game on the computer, become sluggish when poised over a keyboard to write a paper?

Writing is not easy, and for many students, writing assignments raise more anxieties than any other academic task. There are many reasons for this anxiety. For one thing, papers often have a large impact on your final course grades. If you do all your writing at the last minute, with a deadline looming, writing is almost certainly a tense experience. Perhaps you've never really been taught how to write well. Or maybe you believe that there's some sort of special writing gene that you just weren't born with.

Stop! Delete from your memory any negative preconceptions you may have about writing. There is no mystery to writing; it's a skill that can be taught and a skill that, with practice, anybody can learn. Writing is not a product you read; it is a thinking and reasoning *process* that is the means of producing that product, a skill that can be learned like any other.

Using strategies based on P.O.W.E.R. Learning (summarized in the P.O.W.E.R. Plan on the next page), you will be able to achieve the goal of writing clearly and competently. These strategies will help you to build upon your strengths and maximize your abilities. They will permit you to translate what's inside your head into words that communicate your experience or thoughts directly.

Journal Reflections

How I Feel about Writing

Reflect on the feelings you have about writing by answering the following questions:

1. When I receive a writing assignment, my initial reaction is . . .

2. Do you ever write for pleasure? When? Under what circumstances?

3. Which writing experiences are particularly pleasant for you? Which are unpleasant?

4. Are you particularly good at finding ways to put off writing tasks? Do you do anything to prevent this?

5. When faced with a lengthy writing assignment, how do you decide what to write? How do you organize your thoughts?

Prepare: Confronting the Blank Page

There is nothing more intimidating than a blank piece of paper (or computer screen!). It is something that every writer faces, no matter how proficient. Shakespeare, Jane Austen, Mark Twain, Anna Akhmatova, Ralph Ellison, and Sandra Cisneros all felt the challenge of having to fill that void with words.

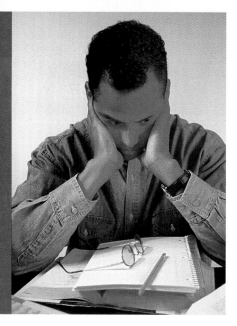

Nothing is more intimidating than a blank piece of paper—or a blank computer screen. On the other hand, it can also be liberating, offering you the freedom and opportunity to say what *you* want to say.

Looked at another way, though, there is nothing more liberating than a blank page. It offers every possibility, and it gives you the freedom to say whatever you want to say. And therein lies one of the keys to good writing: deciding what it is you want to say.

Preparation will help you decide. Writing is a process, and preparation for it encompasses the following steps:

Deciding What Your Goal Is

To write successfully, you need to think about the end product. Is it a long research paper, based on information you must gather? An essay arguing a particular point of view? A fictional short story? A critique of someone else's work or argument? A book or movie review?

Most often, you'll be working to complete a class assignment that will explain what the goal is. But sometimes the assignment will provide you with several choices; it may even be vague or imprecise. If this is the case, your first step will have to be to decide what your goal is.

If there is a choice among different types of writing, decide which will make you most comfortable. If one choice is to prepare an essay, and you are creative and enjoy expressing your opinions, choose that option. If you enjoy gathering information and drawing a conclusion from your findings, a research paper might well be the best choice.

Choosing Your Topic

Once you've determined the specific type of writing you are going to do, the next step is to choose a topic. Although instructors often assign a particular topic, in some cases the choice will be left to you. However, the freedom to choose a topic does not come without a price. In fact, many students find that choosing what to write about is harder than actually writing the paper itself. Here are some things you can do to help pick an appropriate topic:

- **Use freewriting.** According to Peter Elbow, a writing expert who has revolutionized the teaching of writing, one of the reasons we find writing so hard is that we have a set of censors inside our heads[1]. Just as we set pen to paper, those censors are ready to spring up and whisper, "That's no good."

    However, there is a way to keep these internal voices at bay. You can use a technique called **freewriting.** In freewriting, you write continuously for a fixed period of time—say, 5 or 10 minutes. The only rule that governs freewriting is to write continuously, without stopping. It doesn't matter whether the product is bad;

PREPARE
Approach writing as a process

ORGANIZE
Write a flexible outline and construct a thesis statement

WORK
Get it down in the first draft; refine it in the second draft

EVALUATE
Be your own best critic: fine-tune your work

RETHINK
Reflect on the writing process: what worked, what didn't

P.O.W.E.R. Plan

it doesn't matter whether it's good. The only principle you must follow in freewriting is to get something—anything—down on paper.

Try it, and you'll see how liberating freewriting can be. Of course the product will not be perfect, but you'll most likely find that you've written something of value to you.

Suppose, for example, you are stuck for a topic. Through freewriting you can explore your feelings about the course you are going to be writing for, what you like and don't like, and from there go on to get some rough ideas down on paper. What's more, you'll probably form an "attitude" toward one or more potential topics, which can be used to add a personal voice and authenticity to your writing.

Once the freewriting session is completed, you may want to write a single sentence that captures the main point of what you have written—the "center of gravity," Elbow calls it. You can then use this sentence as a springboard for further exploration of ideas the next time you write. (Test this method by completing Try It 1.)

- **Use brainstorming.** The oral equivalent of freewriting is **brainstorming.** While freewriting is done alone, brainstorming is most often done with others. In brainstorming, you say out loud as many ideas as you can think of in a fixed period of time. Although brainstorming works best when you do it with a group of friends or classmates, you can also do it by yourself. (This is one of those times when talking to yourself has its benefits.) Initially, the goal simply is to produce as many ideas as possible, no matter how implausible, silly, or irrelevant. Jot down the ideas that intrigue you as they come up, so you don't forget them.

As with freewriting, the point is to temporarily silence the censors that prevent us from saying whatever comes into our heads. In brainstorming, the initial goal is not to produce high-quality ideas, but a high quantity of ideas. You can revisit and evaluate the ideas you've come up with later (see Try It 2).

Deciding Who Your Audience Is That's easy, you may be thinking: it's my instructor. Not so fast. Although the instructor is the most obvious reader for what you write, you should think of your audience in terms of the ultimate purpose of the writing assignment. For example, if you're writing a paper about the dangers of global warming, are you directing it to a layperson who knows little about the issue? Or are you writing it for someone with a good understanding of science, someone who already knows about atmospheric pressure, *El Niño,* and the ozone layer? Clearly, the answer to this question will make a difference in how and what you write.

In short, it's crucial to know—and to keep in mind—the persons to whom you are writing. What is their level of knowledge about the topic? Are they already predisposed to a particular position? What do you think they would like to take away with them after reading what you've written?

Keeping an audience in mind serves another purpose: It personalizes your writing. Rather than targeting your writing to a nondescript group of individuals ("all the people who might be worried about global warming"), you individualize your audience. Think of the reader as your sister, or a friend, or your next-door neighbor. Think of how that individual would feel after reading what you've written, and what you would say to convince him or her.

Freewriting
A technique involving continuous, nonstop writing, without self-criticism, for a fixed period of time

Brainstorming
A technique for generating ideas by saying out loud as many ideas as can be thought of in a fixed period of time

Try It!

1

Set Yourself Free: Freewriting

Use this space to practice freewriting for a 5-minute period. Optional guidance is offered below, but if you want to go ahead and "just do it," simply start writing. Be sure to keep your hand moving; stop controlling yourself. Write only for yourself; forget about what others might think.

If you need a little more guidance, you are not alone; most people need help the first time they try to freewrite. There are actually two kinds of freewriting: plain vanilla freewriting (like that above) and *focused* freewriting. Focused freewriting gives you a starting point.

Here are some starting points for focused freewriting:

Today I feel . . .

I remember . . .

I don't like . . .

I really like . . .

I get sick when . . .

I know . . .

I am . . .

I am not . . .

Using one of these lead-in phrases as a starting point, return to the blank space and begin your freewriting.

What is the main point of what you wrote? Was freewriting effective in helping you get something down on paper? Was it easy or difficult for you? Can you think of how the process of freewriting might help you when it's time to write a paper?

To Try It online, go to **www.mhhe.com/power**.

Researching the Topic To write most papers, you must do research, either in the library or on the World Wide Web (something we'll discuss further in Chapter 10). To put the information you find in a useable form, consider using a file folder and note-card system, a proven technique that involves three steps:

ry It!

2

🏃 Working in a Group:
Get Your Brain Storming: Using Brainstorming to Generate Ideas

Your American history professor has asked you to come up with 10 ideas for a five-page paper on some aspect of the 1960s. Brainstorm in a group and come up with a list of possible topics, assigning one member of the group to record ideas below.

As you brainstorm, keep the length of the paper assigned and the sort of topic suited to American history generally in mind. Remember, the idea is to produce as many possibilities as you can, without evaluating how realistic or feasible they may be. Think quantity over quality.

After your group has concluded brainstorming, go back to your answers and circle each that you think is realistic for a paper topic. Did brainstorming work? Did you surprise yourself with the number of alternative possibilities you generated for each item?

To Try It online, go to **www.mhhe.com/power**.

1. **Assemble information folders.** Break down material you've found into subtopics by placing the raw information you've located (photocopies, computer printouts, and computer disks) into different multicolored file folders. Label each folder with a stick-on Post-It type label, which will permit you to easily modify the topic of the folder if necessary in the future.

   This system can work on the computer, too: you can create a file-folder structure into which you put your notes and related material, assuming the information is in electronic form. For many of us this might not yet be completely practical—we still rely too heavily on handwritten notes and hard copies—but as more and more research material becomes available online, this will likely change.

2. **Create note cards.** Taking notes on index cards is the best way of making information easy to use. *The key is to place no more than one major idea on each card.* If you stick to this rule, you will later find it easy to sort the cards and put them in logical order. It often helps to write the relevant subtopic (such as "Early Influences" or "Husband" or "Politics") at the top right-hand corner of the card for easy reference. (Once again,

it is also possible to type notes directly into your computer and store them in a subfolder labeled "Early Influences," "Husband," "Politics," etc.)

Be sure to write the ideas on the note card in your own words, unless you are directly quoting from a source—in which case you must remember to use quotation marks. It's also a good idea to mark a note card with the word "paraphrase" when you put someone else's unique idea in your own words, as in the sample note cards below. (A **paraphrase** is a restatement of a passage using different words.) Using your own words will prevent you from accidentally copying others' words and passing them off as your own—which, as we'll discuss, is the gravest of academic sins.

Paraphrase
A restatement of a passage using different words

3. **Place source information on every note card.** Make sure every note card contains information that clearly identifies its source. It is extremely important that you know where the idea on the note card came from so you can credit this source when you write your paper. You do not need to include complete bibliographical information on every note card, but you must keep a master list—either on a separate set of note cards or in a computer file—with the full citation. (Examples of citations for different kinds of sources are listed in Table 7.1. Your instructor will tell you which citation style he or she prefers.)

Source, page # ("n.p." = no page #)

Gallup n.p.   *Terrorism in U.S.* — Subtopic

In the month following the terrorist attacks on the World Trade Towers in New York City, public approval of the president and the Congress were at the highest levels ever seen in previous polls. (Paraphrase.) — Paraphrase

"There has never been a time in the last 25 years when over eight out of 10 Americans approved of the job being done by both the president and the Congress." — Quote

Note Card

Source abbreviation

Gallup

The Gallup Organization. "Latest Summary: American Public Opinion and the War on Terrorism." Gallup Poll Analyses 17 Oct. 2001. 23 Oct. 2001 ‹http://www.gallup.com/poll/releases/pr010926b.asp›. — Full citation

Bibliographic (Source) Card

Table 7.1

Sample Citations for Different Types of Sources[2]

Book with One Author	Daddario, Gina. *Women's Sport and Spectacle.* Westport, CT: Praeger, 1998.
Book with More Than One Author	Spring, Anita, and Barbara E. McDade. *African Entrepreneurship: Theory and Reality.* Gainesville, FL: University Press of Florida, 1998.
Magazine or Newspaper Article	Gladstone, Valerie. "The Flame of Flamenco' Keeps Alive a Tradition." *The New York Times* 12 Oct. 1997: AR-6.
Scholarly Journal Article	Jaasma, Marjorie A. "Classroom Communication Apprehension: Does Being a Male or Female Make a Difference?" *Communication Reports* 10 (1997): 219–228.
Article with No Author Named	"Friends Don't Let Friends Drive Tired." *Health* Oct. 1997: 18.
Article from CD-ROM Collection	Schrag, Peter. "The Near-Myth of Our Failing Schools." *Atlantic Monthly* Oct. 1997. SIRS CD-ROM database. Retrieved 4 Nov. 1997.
Article Reproduced on Internet	Nothaft, Mark A. "New Trend in Temping Has Benefits." *Arizona Republic* 6 Oct. 1997. Available on Internet (www.newsworks.com). Retrieved 19 Oct. 1997.
Internet Site with Author Listed	Gomez, Crystal. "Hot Spots to Visit." Ecotourism Explorer (Internet site at www.ecotourism.org). Retrieved 13 Nov. 2002.
Internet Site with No Author Listed	Mahidol University. "Welcome to Thailand." Guide to Thailand (Internet site at www.mahidol.ac.th/Thailand/Thailand-main.html). Retrieved 28 Nov. 1997.
Newsgroup Posting	Dundjerovic, Nemanja. "Can Tennis Be Made More Interesting?" Online posting: alt.rec.tennis (17 Oct. 1997). Retrieved 20 Nov. 1997.
E-mail	Graham, Heather, former editor, Purdue University student newspaper. "Censorship of Student Newspapers." E-mail to Terry West. 13 Dec. 1997.
Interview	Harris, Jonathan, M.D., dermatologist. Personal interview. 15 Nov. 2002.
TV Program	Sawyer, Diane, narrator. "The Truth About Lying." *Primetime Thursday.* ABC News. 15 March 2001.
Video Recording	*The Military in the Movies.* Videocassette. Center for Defense Information, 1997.

For Items Lacking Full Identification—for example, pamphlets, charts, and handouts—put as much data as you can find:

> *Dangers of Chewing Tobacco.* New York: American Cancer Society. Undated booklet.

Organize: Constructing a Scaffold

When we read and listen to information, the author or speaker has (hopefully!) already constructed a framework for presenting the information to us. Our job as readers and listeners is to figure out what that organization is, like detectives following a trail of clues.

When we're writing, however, we're creating something new. Consequently, it's up to us to come up with the scaffolding for our written product.

Construct an Outline (and Be Ready to Change It!)

The key to organizing an extended piece of writing is the outline. Outlines provide a roadmap to follow when we're writing, a set of sequential steps that show us where we are heading and how we are going to get there.

The secret of successful outlining is flexibility: It is essential to keep an open mind about sequencing and to avoid getting "locked in" too early to a pattern that might later prove unworkable. The best approach is to write possible subtopics, based on your research, on index cards—or simply to type all of them into your computer. Then try to place them in a logical order. (If you use the computer, the program's outlining feature will even renumber the outline as you make changes.) Ask yourself how the subtopics build into a complete and convincing presentation. In doing so, always remember your audience: consider what a reader would have to know already to understand a given fact or argument. Then try out several sequences and determine which order works best.

ABBCC structure

The structure of the typical research paper, consisting of argument, background, body, counterarguments, and conclusion

Thesis

The main point of a paper, typically stating the writer's opinion about the topic of the paper

Develop the Paper's Structure Although instructors sometimes provide a structure for a paper, you will ordinarily have to construct one yourself. One way to do this is to follow the **ABBCC structure.** "ABBCC" stands for the five parts of a typical research paper: Argument, Background, Body, Counterarguments, and Conclusion. Each of these plays a specific role:

- **Argument.** Just as we introduce ourselves when we meet someone for the first time, a writer needs to introduce a reader to the main argument being put forward in the paper. Every paper should have a main argument or **thesis,** a one- or two-sentence description of the main point of the paper. For instance, your thesis might make the argument that "Personal character does not matter in leaders; what matters is their effectiveness in accomplishing the goals for which they were elected."

  A thesis should be stated as an assertion ("people are their own worst enemies"). An effective thesis statement takes a position on some issue; many times this is signaled by use of an action verb ("the current technological revolution *requires* that people receive computer training") or the use of such keywords as "should" or "ought." For instance, "Smoking should be banned from restaurants and bars" presents a thesis statement. "This paper will discuss smoking in restaurants and bars," on the other hand, simply states the topic: we have no idea what stand the writer takes on smoking in restaurants and bars. Try It 3 will help you to turn ideas into thesis statements.

  The thesis or argument need not be the first sentence of the paper. In fact, it is usually wise to start off with something that grabs readers' attention. Begin with a controversial quote, an illustrative story, or a personal encounter—anything that is likely to make a reader sit up and take notice.

  In addition to presenting the main thesis of the paper, the first section should lay out the areas that you will cover and the general scope of the paper. You should use this section to present the paper's overall perspective and point of view. For example, "Taxpayers have every right to expect . . ." signals the writer's perspective on campaign finance reform—he or she is thinking about it as a taxpayer, as opposed to a legislator or political candidate.

- **Background.** You'll need to provide readers with a context in which to place your paper's arguments, and the background section is the place to do it. Provide a brief history of the topic, talking about different schools of thought on it. Introduce any unusual terms you might need to

Make Your Point: Write a Thesis Statement

Write a thesis statement for each of the topics below. Remember that the thesis should be an *assertion*.

restrictions on access to particular World Wide Web pages in school libraries

the death penalty

same-sex marriages

cloning

global warming and modern technology

campaign finance reform

prayer in schools

bank charges for using an ATM

Evaluate each of the thesis statements that you wrote. Do they all contain an assertion? Is there a relationship between how controversial a topic is and how easy it is to write a thesis statement?

 Working in a Group: Each group member should generate three potential topics for a paper and compose a thesis statement for each. Then, as a group, evaluate each of the thesis statements.

To Try It online, go to **www.mhhe.com/power**.

use. If the topic is highly controversial, discuss the reasons for the controversy. For example, if you are arguing that capital punishment should be abolished, you could briefly review the history of its use and of opposition to it.

- **Body.** The body makes up the bulk of most papers. In the paper's body, you provide evidence as to why your thesis is correct.

    This evidence should be presented in a logical order. Exactly what this means depends upon your topic. You may need to work chronologically if you are discussing a historical event. In other cases, you will want to start with the least controversial arguments and gradually move into the ones that are most debatable.

    When deciding on the order, keep your audience firmly in mind. For instance, a paper on the dangers of electromagnetic radiation written for a community law class would be very different from one written for a physics class.

- **Counterarguments.** You will also need to touch on the counterarguments to your position: acknowledge them and then go on to systematically refute each one. This section need not be long, but it is crucial. By doing this you help reinforce your own position and strengthen your argument, showing that you have arrived at your point of view fully aware of—and unconvinced by—opposing views.

- **Conclusion.** A good ending to a paper is as important as a good beginning. It's where you pull everything together. And it is your last chance to drive home your thesis.

    The conclusion should summarize the thesis and the arguments that you have made regarding it. Do not introduce new information: The conclusion is a recap. Do make an effort to close with a flourish. You might cite a quotation, present an anecdote that is linked to one you presented at the start of the paper, or pose a rhetorical question ("If the government turns its back on welfare recipients, how can we claim to have a just society?"). However you choose to conclude the paper, make sure that it ties the various pieces together.

W ork: Writing the Work

Now comes the moment that so many dread: It's time to face that blank page or screen and actually start writing. However, if you've followed the steps above and carefully prepared and organized, this phase is likely to be easier than you expect.

In fact, you should be so well prepared that you know just how to proceed: Your outline offers a clear roadmap, and your research notes will help you explain your ideas along the way. Your outline, if carefully composed, will actually provide you with the major headings of your paper. The job of writing the paper then becomes a matter of matching up the research to the appropriate outline heading. Looked at in this way, that blank page isn't so blank after all.

Don't try to do too much at one sitting.

Professional authors writing a 500-page book don't think about the 500 pages they need to write; such thoughts are at best mind-numbing and at worst totally unproductive and paralyzing. Instead, professionals break their task down into smaller, more manageable pieces. They might decide that they'll write a certain number of pages in a given period of time—perhaps four or five pages a day. Or maybe they plan on writing one chapter per month.

You probably don't have as much time to devote to your writing as a professional writer, so the chunks you break your writing into should be shorter. For instance, if you have to write a 10-page paper, don't think of it as 10 pages. Instead, break it down into chunks of two pages a day, spread out over 5 days. Or think of it in terms of the major sections: an introduction, a description of the background of an issue, arguments in favor of a position, arguments against a position, and a conclusion. You could then schedule writing each of those five sections on a different day.

It's also helpful to divide the actual work of writing into two stages: writing the first draft and revising your draft.

Writing the First Draft Starting a first draft is like diving into a cold lake. You know the initial plunge will be painful because the water is icy cold, but you know that once you're *in*, it won't feel so bad.

It's the same thing with writing a first draft. Getting started is often the hardest part. However, once you've put even a few words on paper, it gets easier.

When you set pen to paper or fingers to keyboard to begin writing, don't feel that you are carving your words in stone. Permit yourself to be less than perfect. Don't worry about word choice, grammar, sentence structure, spelling, or punctuation. That can come later. The first draft is meant to give you something to go on. The important thing is to fill up that blank space with *something*.

There are several strategies you can use to make writing the first draft less painful:

- **Start where you like.** You need not follow the order of the outline when you write. For example, some writers start a paper by writing the conclusion first. By keeping the end in mind, they know just where they are headed, making the journey a little easier. Similarly, other writers save the beginning of the paper for last, reasoning that they'll be better able to tell their readers where the paper is going after it has actually gotten there.

    Write whatever part of the paper you feel most comfortable writing,

If you've ever gone white-water rafting, you know that following the water's rhythm permits you to remain afloat. In the same way, on those occasions when you achieve a steady rhythm while writing and the words are coming rapidly, stick with it and go with the flow. Revising can come later.

because just having something on paper will encourage you to write the rest.

- **Turn off your inner critic.** If you're anything like most people, with every word you write, there's probably a voice somewhere in your head that's whispering, "Terrible sentence. Dumb idea. Forget it, you idiot, you'll never finish this paper." Your job is to turn off the voice of that inner critic, at least for now. (You'll want to use it later, when the nagging may come in handy as you revise your work.) While you're working on your first draft, you want to give yourself permission to be creative. As long as you write things down, you'll be able to go back later and make your paper better. But you can't revise what isn't there.

- **Go with the flow.** When you're writing your first draft, try to write quickly. Writing often takes on a rhythm, and you should try to write in sync with that rhythm. If you're on a roll, go with it: Don't stop (yet) to edit your work.

    On the other hand, if you're having trouble getting into a rhythm, and each word is like pulling teeth, take a break. Do something entirely different for a few minutes and then return with a fresh mind.

    If you're really having trouble, try rearranging your note cards (or scrambling your outline). Placing them in a new or even a random order may provide a fresh way of looking at your topic, and this may in turn free you enough to get your writing started.

Voice

The unique style of a writer, expressing the writer's outlook on life and past writing experiences

- **Don't be afraid to modify your outline.** When you start writing, it's easy to fall into the trap of viewing an outline as a rigid, unbending framework. Your outline is a living document, and you should feel free to rearrange headings and to deviate from it as you're creating your first draft.

    Many writers find that their outlines need to be revised, and so might you. That's fine; that's why you're writing a first draft and not pretending to start with a final one.

- **Use your own voice.** Just as you have a distinctive speaking voice, each of us has a distinct *writing* voice. That voice represents our own unique style, a reflection of our outlook on life and of our past writing experiences.

    Novice writers sometimes get hung up trying to use a voice that isn't their own. For example, they may use words they would never normally use when speaking.

"I spend a great deal of my time thinking about the power of language—the way it can evoke an emotion, a visual image, a complex idea, or a simple truth."

Author Amy Tan

Avoid the temptation to write as if you were someone else. Instead, use your own natural voice and vocabulary, and don't use big words in an effort to impress your audience. If you'd feel foolish saying "heretofore" in a conversation, you shouldn't use it when you're writing a paper. Don't scan the thesaurus in search of unusual words to use in place of simple ones. (Just because you *can* do something doesn't mean you should.)

- **Forget about it.** The last step in creating a first draft is the easiest: When you have finished your sketch of the entire paper, from introduction through conclusion, put it aside.

You need to let your mind idle in neutral for a while so that it will be at full strength when you move on to the next phase of writing: revision.

Revising Your Draft   Remember that inner critic—that voice in your head—that you tuned out while you were writing the first draft? It's time to tune it back in.

The fact is that most of writing is *re*writing. Sure, it's possible to hand in a first draft, and sometimes you'll even get a passable grade. But if you want to reach your own potential as a writer, you *must* revise.

Don't feel that revising is something that only students have to do. Professional writers may go through dozens of drafts—and still not be completely satisfied. Virtually no one has the ability to write a first-draft paper that is so lucid and compelling that it stands on its own.

Following several basic rules can make the revision process work smoothly for you:

- **Read the first draft out loud.** Read your paper out loud—to yourself, a friend, or your computer. It doesn't matter who's listening.

    Reading out loud does several things. You'll more easily discover missing words, verbs that don't match the subject of the sentence, shifts in tense, missing transitions, and other things that you might have to fix. This is partly because speaking takes longer than silent reading; the slowed pace of reading out loud can help you identify problems that you'd otherwise miss.

- **Take the long view.** Start off by taking the broadest perspective possible and asking yourself a series of questions:

    What is the purpose of my paper? Has that purpose been fulfilled?

    Have I addressed every aspect of the assignment?

    Does the paper tell its readers everything they need to know?

    Will readers be able to follow its logic?

    Does the paper make its points clearly?

    Are the transitions between sections clear?

- **Be ruthless.** Words that we've put on paper tend to take on a life of their own—a life that we have created and so are often reluctant to change or part with.

    It is natural to feel a bit parental toward our first draft, but it is important to fight this instinct. You need to be merciless and unforgiving with passages, paragraphs, phrases, and words that don't sound right or that do not ultimately add to your argument. Don't tear *yourself* down, but, like a coach demanding the best from his or her players, be demanding of your performance.

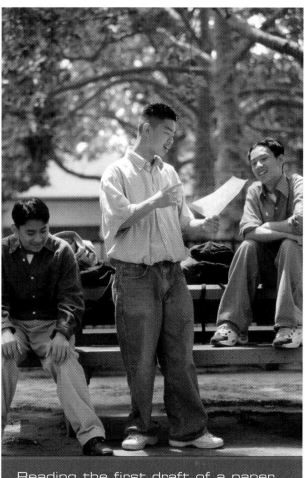

Reading the first draft of a paper aloud can help you identify problems that need to be addressed in a revised draft.

Start pruning at the paragraph level. Assess each paragraph to make sure that it adds to the final message, that it flows from the previous paragraph logically, and that it is consistent with what you are trying to accomplish.

Then move to the level of sentences and words. Evaluate each sentence, and then each word, to make sure that it adds to the clarity of your message.

"Wrestling with words gave me my moments of greatest meaning."

Author Richard Wright

By paring down your writing, you let your ideas shine through. If you are extremely fond of a phrase or a group of words that you suspect are unnecessary, write down or print out the sections and phrases, put them into an envelope, and toss the envelope into the top drawer of your dresser. You never know when you might need them. More important, knowing that you can save the cut material may make it easier to do the necessary cutting.

- **Check sequence and logic.** It's now time to reverse course. Whereas before the focus was on cutting extraneous material, you now need to check for what's *missing*.

  For example, earlier cuts might have made it necessary to add or modify transitions between sections and paragraphs. You might also need to improve logic by reordering your ideas, by reordering sentences within paragraphs, and reordering paragraphs within sections.

- **Check punctuation and spelling.** Check for the obvious stuff: Sentences should start with capital letters and end with the appropriate punctuation, commas should set off dependent clauses, and the like. Use a handbook or style manual if you're unsure.

  Check your spelling carefully. This is one of the areas in which word processors earn their keep best. The spell-check feature will not only identify every misspelled word (that is, every word not in its dictionary), but it will also prompt you with alternative spellings.

  Be careful not to rely completely on the spell-checker, however. Such programs can find only misspellings that do not form recognized words; if what you typed is a word, the spell-checker will ignore it, even if it is not the word you wanted to use. *Foe instants, know spelt-cheek pogrom wood fined eras inn thus sent-tense.* And yet every word in the preceding "sent-tense" is spelled incorrectly in this context.

- **Check that all quotes are cited and referenced correctly.** As we'll discuss in detail later, it is critical that you give proper credit to others' ideas and words. Make sure that you haven't directly quoted or paraphrased a source without acknowledging it.

- **Make it pleasing to the eye.** Instructors are human. They can't help but react differently to a paper that is neatly typed compared with one that is handwritten in a difficult-to-read scrawl.

  A neat paper conveys a message: I'm proud of this paper. I've put time and effort into it. This is my best work.

  A sloppy paper says something different.

  Take the time, then, to make sure your paper looks good. This doesn't mean that you need to invest in a fancy plastic cover, or worry about the alignment of the staples, or spend a lot of time deciding which font to use on your word processor. But it does mean that the quality of the paper's appearance should match the quality of the writing.

Evaluate: Acting as Your Own Best Critic

Because you've already put so much work into your paper, you might be tempted to rush through the final stages of the P.O.W.E.R. process. Avoid the temptation. If you've carefully revised your paper, the last stages will not be time-consuming, and they may have a significant impact on your paper's ultimate quality—and your success.

Take these steps to *evaluate* what you've written:

- **Ask yourself if your paper accomplishes what you set out to do.** The beginning of your paper contains a thesis statement and the argument that you intended to make. Does your paper support the thesis? Is your argument upheld by the evidence you've reported? Would an impartial reader be convinced by what you've written?

- **Put yourself in your instructor's shoes.** Does the paper precisely fit the assignment requirements? Does it meet the instructor's underlying goals in giving the assignment?

- **Check the mechanical aspects of the paper.** The grammar and spelling must be correct; the paper should also look good. If your instructor requires that citations or references be reported in a certain style, make sure you've followed it.

If you've revised the paper with care, it will likely pass muster. If it doesn't, though, go back and work on it once again. By this point, it should require only minor tinkering to get it into shape.

Rethink: Reflecting on Your Accomplishment

Rethinking is the homestretch of the writing process. It's a moment to savor, because it permits you take a long view of what you've accomplished. You've gone from a blank page to words on paper that tell a story. You've turned nothing into something—an achievement in and of itself.

Rethinking occurs on several levels: rethinking the message, mechanics, and method. But don't address them until a little time has passed: Wait a day or so to reread the paper. Then, bringing your critical thinking skills to bear, reflect on the following:

- **Rethink the message.** Be sure that the overall message your paper conveys is appropriate. A paper is like an advertisement. In most papers, you are seeking to communicate information to convince someone of a particular opinion. Make sure that the message is what you wish to communicate, and that ultimately the paper is successful in making the case.

- **Rethink the mechanics.** A television commercial filled with fuzzy images and annoyingly unsteady camera shots would not be very compelling, no matter how good the underlying product. In the same way, a paper with mechanical errors will not impress your readers or persuade

Career Connections

Write Away

The first step in getting a job is putting pen to paper (or, probably more accurately, finger to keyboard). Whether you receive a lead for a job from a college career center, read an ad in the paper, or see a job listing on the Internet, you'll need to communicate in writing to the potential employer.

You are selling yourself in a letter of application. To be effective, keep these guidelines in mind:

- **Brief is better.** Employers are likely to get many letters, and long ones are least likely to be read.

- **State what you can do for the employer, not what the employer can do for you.** Don't tell a potential employer you really, really need a job to pay off your credit card bills. Instead, explain how your skills can help further an organization's goals.

- **Summarize your qualifications.** Respond specifically to the skills required for the job. List specific experiences you've had that are relevant to what the employer is looking for.

- **Enclose a résumé.** Your résumé should contain a detailed summary of your educational background and work experience, as well as other relevant qualifications.

- **Ask for an interview.** Close your letter with a request to meet and discuss the job. Provide your telephone number and e-mail address.

- **Proofread!** You must have zero tolerance for errors. Any mistake is likely to put you at the bottom of the pile of applications.

them. Take another look at your writing style; look at grammar, punctuation, and word usage to make sure the choices you've made are appropriate.

- **Rethink the method.** Every time you finish a paper, you learn something—something about the topic of your writing and something about yourself. Ask yourself what you have learned to help you become a better writer in the future. What might you have done to improve the writing process? What could have gone better? What will you do differently the next time you write? Above all, remember what you've accomplished: You've transformed what's inside your head—your thoughts, your ideas, your values—into something that can potentially influence other people. You have exercised the ability to move others and get them to think in new ways. You've made a difference. That's the real power of writing.

Acknowledging Others' Ideas in Your Paper

As you move through the process of writing a paper, there are many temptations to cut corners. A friend may have written a paper the previous year on the same topic and offer to "lend" it to you . . . you may find a paper on the Web that addresses just what you intended to write . . . you and a friend may be enrolled in a very large class, and he may suggest that you each write part of the paper and "share" sections.

Don't yield to temptations such as these. Not only is honesty the best policy, but it's also the *only* policy in the world of academics. There's no greater academic sin than **plagiarism,** taking credit for someone else's words, thoughts, or ideas. In the academic world, plagiarism is about the same as stealing a stranger's car. Even if you just mean to "borrow" a passage, passing another person's work off as your own is totally wrong.

Furthermore, penalties for plagiarism are severe. In many colleges, plagiarism results in expulsion. You could even face legal charges, because almost all published material is copyrighted, which means that it is someone's *intellectual property*. If an author learns that you have used his or her writing as your own, the author has the right to take you to court and sue for damages.

The best way to avoid plagiarism is to be extremely careful. If you are writing a paper that requires the use of source materials from the library or the Web, *always* note the source, and distinguish between your ideas, quotations, and your paraphrases of others' ideas. When you quote directly from the work of another, use quotation marks.

When you paraphrase, be careful: It's not just a matter of rearranging the words and choosing synonyms for them. For instance, consider the following passage from the book *Nation of Nations*[3]:

> In the 1860s they had come in a trickle; in the 1870s they became a torrent. They were farmers from the East and Midwest, black freedmen from the rural South, and peasant-born immigrants from Europe. What bound them together was a craving for land.

Here's one way of rephrasing the passage, but one that is so close to the original that it amounts to plagiarism:

> In the 1860s they had come in a drizzle; in the 1870s, they became a deluge. There were crop-growers from the East and Midwest; former black slaves from the rural South, and common people from Europe. Holding them together was a hunger for land.

A more appropriate rewording of the original passage would be the following, which more clearly paraphrases the authors' ideas:

> There was a great deal of growth in the number of settlers from 1860 to 1879. The settlers represented several groups, including farmers from the eastern and midwestern United States, former Southern slaves, and poor Europeans who had come to the United States to better their lives. They all shared a dream of obtaining land.*

Note that *it is still necessary to cite the source* of the facts or ideas that you are paraphrasing: one way to cite here would be to add a footnote reference similar to the one at the bottom of this page (and those at the end of this book). Citation is necessary for two reasons: (1) to give credit where credit is due; and (2) to allow your readers to follow up for more information on a subject. Facts and ideas that are unique to a source or even those that are infrequently heard should be cited. It is probably advisable to cite too much rather than risk plagiarizing, but it is *not* necessary to have a citation after every sentence. Some facts are so basic ("Japan and Germany were the enemies of the United States in World War II") that no source is necessary.

Keep in mind, too, that you must cite material that you find on the World Wide Web: It was produced by someone else and that someone must be given credit. The rules for how to cite material found on the Web are still in flux, but you should at the very least include the site name, Web address (URL), and author, as well as the date you accessed the site.

Plagiarism
Taking credit for someone else's words, thoughts, or ideas

* Davidson, J. W., Gienapp, W. E., Heyrman, C. L., Lytle, M. H., & Stoff, M. B. (1996). *Nation of nations. A concise narrative of the American republic.* New York: McGraw-Hill.

Try It! 4

Summarize, Don't Plagiarize

Try to capture in your own words the meaning of the following quoted passages, without plagiarizing them in any way. Assume that you intend to reflect the main points of each author in a paper of your own, summarizing the arguments. In each case, ask yourself: Would I need to cite the author and work?

1. From *No Ordinary Time* by Doris Kearns Goodwin (New York: Simon & Schuster, 1995), pp. 628–629, on the political relationship between President Franklin D. Roosevelt and his wife, Eleanor.

   > It was said jokingly in Washington during the war years that Roosevelt had a nightly prayer: "Dear God, please make Eleanor a little tired." But in the end, he often came around to her way of thinking. Labor advisor Anna Rosenberg had been one of those who criticized Eleanor's unceasing pressure on the President, but years later she changed her mind. "I remember him saying, 'We're not going to do that now. Tell Eleanor to keep away; I don't want to hear about that anymore.' And then 2–3 weeks later he would say, 'Do you remember that thing Eleanor brought up? Better look into it, maybe there's something to it—I heard something to indicate that maybe she's right.' I'm not sure she would have had the opportunity to bring things to his attention unless she pressured him—I mean he was so involved and in retrospect it was never anything for herself. . . . He would never have become the kind of President he was without her."

2. From "The Streak of Streaks" in *Bully for Brontosaurus* by Stephen Jay Gould (New York: W. W. Norton & Company, 1991), pp. 466–467, on baseball player Joe DiMaggio's 56-game hitting streak in 1941.

   > Ed Purcell, Nobel laureate in physics but, for purposes of this subject, just another baseball fan, has done a comprehensive study of all baseball streak and slump records. His firm conclusion is easily and swiftly summarized. Nothing ever happened in baseball above and beyond the frequency predicted by coin-tossing models. The longest runs of wins or losses are as long as they should be, and occur about as often as they ought to. . . .
   >
   > But "treasure your exceptions," as the old motto goes. Purcell's rule has but one major

And remember this: In your research on the Web you might come across sites that offer to sell you term papers. Don't even think about it: The academic and legal consequences would be severe. Some instructors routinely use Web-based computer programs to check students' papers for plagiarism. Such programs work.

Try It 4, above, will give you some practice in the proper use of other people's information and ideas. Before we turn to the topic of public speaking, which we consider next, make sure the distinction between summarization and plagiarism is clear in your mind.

Speaking Your Mind

Surveys find that most people are more afraid of public speaking than of dying! In a way, it's not surprising. How often are we so totally exposed to others' scrutiny? Not only do we have to worry about the message we're communicating—just as with our writing—but each of us also has to be concerned exception, one sequence so many standard deviations above the expected distribution that it should never have occurred at all: Joe DiMaggio's 56-game hitting streak in 1941. . . . Purcell calculated that to make it likely (probability greater than 50 percent) that a run of even 50 games will occur once in the history of baseball up to now (and 56 is a lot more than 50 in this kind of league), baseball's rosters would have to include either four lifetime .400 batters or 52 lifetime .350 batters over careers of 1,000 games. In actuality, only three men have lifetime batting averages in excess of .350, and no one is anywhere near .400 (Ty Cobb at .367, Roger Hornsby at .358, and Shoeless Joe Jackson at .356). DiMaggio's streak is the most extraordinary thing that ever happened in American sports.

3. From "General Relativity" in *Who's Afraid of Schrodinger's Cat?* by Ian Marshall and Danah Zohar (New York: William Morrow and Company, 1997), pp. 170–171.

In 1916, Albert Einstein proposed an interaction between mass-energy and the structure of space-time. Mass-energy produces "curvature" in space-time—i.e., it deviates from flat, Euclidean space. Curved space-time in turn changes the paths of mass-energy through it . . .

One test of the worth of any new scientific theory is whether it offers us additional predictions. How do the predictions of General Relativity differ from those of Newtonian gravity? One obvious one is that curved space will deflect not only matter but also light rays passing through it. Thus, light from a distant star should be deflected if it passes near the sun. Newtonian gravitation predicts a similar effect, but only half as much. During an eclipse of the sun in 1919, the measured deflection of light from a distant star won international acclaim for Einstein's theory. Given the technology of the time, one other experimental verification was possible, an explanation for an anomaly in the orbit of Mercury, and this, too, was achieved successfully.

Working in a Group: After you summarize the passages on your own, compare your answers to those of other classmates in your group. What different approaches did others in your group take? Which passages did people find particularly hard to summarize? Why? Did your group arrive at one best way to capture the authors' main points?

To Try It online, go to: **www.mhhe.com/power**.

about nonverbal behavior and the impression we are making. . . . *Is my hair sticking out? . . . This sweater was a big mistake. . . . Are they bored? . . . I wish my hands would stop shaking.*

Although you may be self-conscious about public speaking (complete Try It 5 to see where you stand), it's important to keep several points in mind:

* Audiences are generally sympathetic. They've all been where you are and probably share your fears about public speaking. They're on your side and are rooting for you to succeed.

* Once you start speaking, it will become easier. Anxiety tends to be highest *before* you start talking. Most people find that after they start to talk, their nervousness declines.

* Practice helps. Practice and preparation for the talk will go a long way toward easing your tension.

Keep in mind, too, that in many fundamental ways, speaking is like writing. You need to consider who your audience is, muster your arguments, and decide how to sequence those arguments.

Try It! 5

Personal Styles: Determine Your Level of Self-Consciousness

One of the main reasons people feel nervous when speaking in public is their self-consciousness. To explore your own level of self-consciousness, answer the following questions,[4] choosing the phrase from the rating scale that is closest to your feelings.

0 = Extremely uncharacteristic

1 = Generally uncharacteristic

2 = Equally characteristic and uncharacteristic

3 = Generally characteristic

4 = Extremely characteristic

1. I'm concerned about my style of doing things. _____

2. I'm concerned about the way I present myself. _____

3. I'm self-conscious about the way I look. _____

4. I usually worry about making a good impression. _____

5. One of the last things I do before I leave the house is look in the mirror. _____

6. I'm concerned about what other people think of me. _____

7. I'm usually aware of my appearance. _____

Scoring: Add up the numbers to get a total score. If you score below 16, you are unusually low in self-consciousness, and public speaking should be less of a burden than it is for most other people. If you score between 16 and 22, you have a medium level of self-consciousness. Public speaking is not necessarily easy for you, but it does not provoke too many fears. If you score above 22, your level of self-consciousness is relatively high. Public speaking is likely to be particularly challenging for you.

To Try It online, go to **www.mhhe.com/power**.

The P.O.W.E.R. writing framework that we presented earlier in the chapter applies to speaking as well:

- **Prepare** what you will say and how you will say it. Think about your audience and the occasion on which you will speak, and try to be sure your words match both audience and occasion.

- **Organize** your thoughts, using notes to cue you to the main parts of your presentation and making logical connections for your audience to follow.

- **Work** carefully during your presentation by speaking clearly and calmly to your audience and avoiding distracting mannerisms or body language.

- **Evaluate** your performance after you finish your presentation and ask others to evaluate it, too. Take notes on the feedback.

- **Rethink** your entire approach to preparing for and delivering presentations each time you make one. Make the changes you feel you should make to improve your performance over time.

Meeting the Challenge of Public Speaking

Although speaking and writing share many features, speaking presents several unique challenges. Among the factors that you need to take into account when you are speaking are these:

- **The first minute counts—a lot.** If you can get your audience's attention, arouse their interest, and engage them in the first few minutes, you're on your way to a successful speech. On the other hand, let them drift off early on and you've lost them—potentially for good.

  How do you get them interested? There are several ways:

  Begin with an anecdote. *"It was a scientist's dream, experienced as he dozed off in front of a fire, that led to one of the most important biological discoveries of all time."*

  Start with a quotation. *"'I have seen the enemy, and he is us.' But are we really the enemy? I believe . . . "*

  Arouse their curiosity. *"I have a secret, one that I've kept hidden for many years—until now."*

  Talk about the significance of the topic. *"If you think that global warming is not a problem, take a look at what's happening to the beachfront up and down the Atlantic coast this year."*

  Ask a question. *"Have you ever wondered how you could save enough money to buy a new car?"*

  Use humor. *"My introduction to gardening was not promising: Seeking to surprise my mother, I 'weeded' her garden so enthusiastically that I pulled up all her flower seedlings."*

  Try It 6 will help get you started.

- **Provide oral transition points.** When we're reading a textbook selection, we usually have the luxury of knowing exactly when a transition point occurs. It's marked by a title, section heading, or new paragraph. These markers help us construct a mental map that permits us to understand the overall structure of the piece we're reading.

  Listeners don't have the same advantage. Unless the speaker orally signals that he or she is moving to a new part of a talk, listeners might get lost.

  However, there are several ways to erect verbal signposts throughout a speech. By using phrases such as the following, you can alert listeners that a twist in the journey lies ahead:

  "To understand the problem, we need to consider . . . "

  "The problems are clearly daunting. But there are solutions. Let's consider some of them. . . . "

Try It! 6

Let's Talk

Devise a 1-minute opening to a talk about the thing you know most about in this world: you. The topic can be about one of your experiences or about anything that concerns you or reveals a little bit about your past, your feelings, or your opinions. Use any of the opening strategies that we've considered.

Which opening strategy are you going to employ? _____

Now write your opening:

_____

_____

_____

_____

_____

_____

_____

_____

_____

_____

Now try it out on a friend or classmate. Remember: Limit what you say to the 1-minute opening.

When you're finished, ask yourself how well you think your strategy worked. Why? Would another strategy have worked as well or better? What did your audience think of your opening? Why do you think it had the effect it did? Did your opening make your audience want to hear more? Did your opening make you want to *write* more?

To Try It online, go to **www.mhhe.com/power**.

"Now that we've considered the solutions, we need to take a look at their costs. . . . "

"Let's go back for a moment to an earlier point I made. . ."

"To sum up, the situation offers some unexpected advantages. . . . "

- **Make your notes work for you, not against you.** A speaker is giving a talk, and suddenly she loses her place in her notes. She fumbles around, desperately trying to find her place and figure out what comes next.

  It's a painful situation to watch—and even worse for the person experiencing the problem. How do you avoid finding yourself in such a predicament?

  One way is by thoroughly acquainting yourself both with what you are going to say *and* with your notes. Once again, practice is your best friend. But the type of notes you have also makes a big difference.

  Some speakers write out their entire talk in advance; others use no notes at all, counting on memorizing their talk. Avoid either extreme. If you write out your complete speech in advance, you'll experience an overwhelming urge to read it to your audience. Nothing could be more deadly. On the other hand, if you memorize your talk and have no notes at all, you'll be susceptible to a memory lapse that can make you feel completely foolish. Even if you can remember your talk successfully, you may end up sounding mechanical, like an amusement park guide who has given the same speech about the "jungle cruise" a thousand times.

Choose a middle ground. Develop an outline that includes the major points you wish to cover and have this outline in front of you when you speak. It might be written or typed on a sheet of paper, or you might use index cards (number them!). In addition, write out and memorize your opening and closing statements.

By memorizing the opening and closing statements, you'll have the opportunity to look your audience in the eye and engage them nonverbally at two of the most crucial junctures in your talk—the beginning and the end. Using an outline for most of your talk permits you to sound natural as you speak. You'll probably use slightly different words every time you give your talk, which is fine.

Audio-visual aids, such as pictures, are not only worth a thousand words, they will keep your audience more interested in what you are saying. They also take the focus away from you, making the enterprise of public speaking less nerve-wracking.

- **A picture can save you a thousand words.** Maps, charts, photos, drawings, figures, and other illustrations add another dimension to a presentation, helping to engage listeners. Computer programs, such as PowerPoint, permit you to create graphics relatively painlessly (as we'll discuss further in Chapter 10).

  You can even use props. For example, if you are talking about a series of Supreme Court rulings, you might incorporate a gavel into your talk. Effective visual aids make abstract concepts more concrete and immediate.

- **Use the right amount and kind of practice.** After you've written your opening and closing statements, constructed an outline, and decided what visual aids to use, it's time to practice. It's not just the amount of practice that is critical: *How* you practice is as important as *how much* you practice.

  Running through your speech mentally will help you to familiarize yourself with your presentation, but you really need to give the speech out loud. Only by hearing yourself speak can you actually get a sense of how the presentation works as an oral presentation.

  Practice in front of a friend or classmate. It is only by actually trying your talk out in front of a warm body that you'll be able to approximate the experience of actually speaking in public, and your audience can provide you with feedback regarding what is working and what is not.

  How much practice is enough practice? You've probably done enough when you do a good job giving a talk twice in a row. If you practice your talk too many times, you'll become so bored with it that the actual talk will sound canned and unconvincing.

"I could have been a big celebrity but for my fear of public speaking."

Fight stage fright. As you know, for many people, the mere thought of speaking in front of others causes a knot of fear to form deep in their gut. Even those who routinely speak in front of others experience some degree of anxiety. (Ask one or two of your course instructors if they ever feel nervous when teaching a class. Their answers may surprise you.)

Although you won't be able to alleviate your stage fright completely, several techniques can reduce the anxiety that public speaking produces. First, make sure you're wearing clothes that are comfortable and that make you feel pleased with your appearance. If you feel good about your appearance, you'll be more relaxed.

Five minutes before you get up to speak, take three slow, deep breaths. Concentrate on the feeling of the air going in and out of your body. If a particular part of your body feels tense, tighten it up even more and then relax it. Do it several times. Finally, visualize yourself giving the speech successfully and the relief that you'll feel afterward.

Monitor your nonverbal behavior. Anxiety about public speaking can do strange things to people's bodies. Their hands may shake or feel icy cold. They may pace back and forth like a caged lion. They may sweat profusely. They may stand rigidly while speaking, looking like stiff toy soldiers. Or they may slump over a podium as if they wished they could dissolve into thin air.

To avoid appearing as if you were scared to death—even if you are—stand up straight and tall. Look directly at different members of your audience, shifting your gaze from one person to the next. Eye contact engages audience members, making them feel that your words are directed straight toward them.

If the thought of eye contact scares you, try a trick that some speakers use. Look directly at the *hairline* of different audience members; to your listeners, this is generally indistinguishable from eye contact.

Speaking Off-the-Cuff: Extemporaneous Speaking

What do you do when an instructor calls on you in class and asks, "What do you think the point of this poem is?" Just as anxiety-producing as giving a prepared talk (and probably a lot more common) is public speaking that is extemporaneous. **Extemporaneous talks** are unprepared presentations that require you to speak on a moment's notice.

Extemporaneous talk

An unprepared, off-the-cuff oral presentation

Extemporaneous speaking happens far more frequently than you may think: your professor asks you to explain why some historians consider Reconstruction a failed enterprise; a co-worker or classmate asks you to explain how a software program works; you visit your landlord to complain about the water heater that keeps breaking, and the landlord asks you for details. The response you give in each of these situations (and many others) is an exercise in extemporaneous speaking.

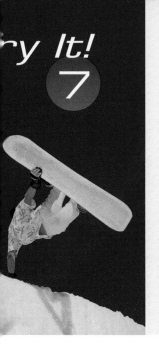

Working in a Group:
Put Yourself on the Spot

Each member of a class group should write two questions on separate note cards. Some examples: "Are basketball players paid too much?" "What's the best way to wash dishes?" "How can you get people to exercise more?"

Place the cards, face down, on a table. Have the first group member choose one of the cards at random, and immediately answer the question using the PREP system. Every person should take a turn answering a question.

After each person gives his or her extemporaneous speech, evaluate the responses by answering the following questions as a group: Generally, how effective was the person's response to the question? What were its greatest strengths? What could have been done better?

To Try It online, go to **www.mhhe.com/power**.

"PREPing" to speak extemporaneously Just because extemporaneous speaking is, by definition, unplanned, it does not have to be totally off the top of your head. There is a simple process that you can use when you're put on the spot. Known as the PREP formula,[5] it consists of breaking down an answer into four parts:

- **Point of view.** Initially provide your point of view or your stand on the issue.

- **Reasons.** Provide the chief reasons why you believe your position is correct.

- **Evidence or examples.** Give specific evidence to support your point of view.

- **Point of view, restated.** Restate your point of view.

Here's an example:

Professor Fiske: Who can tell me if racism is a uniquely American problem? Stephanie, why don't you take a stab at the question.

Stephanie: I don't believe racism is uniquely American at all. **[point of view]** If we look at other times in history or other parts of the world today, we find all sorts of racial problems. **[reasons]** For example, consider Bosnia and the Middle East. Or look at the difficulties that South Africa had. Or look at Nazi Germany. **[evidence or examples]** So it's hard for me to understand how anyone could contend that racism is uniquely American. Racism, unfortunately, is a universal fact of life. **[point of view, restated]**

Although using the PREP system may seem awkward at first, you'll find it easy to learn. And with sufficient practice, it will become automatic, saving you lots of mental scrambling the next time you're called on in class (see Try It 7).

Speaking of Success

Name: *ThaoMee Xiong*
Education: *Mt. Holyoke College, South Hadley, Massachusetts; major in community and identity in culture*
Home: *Appleton, Wisconsin*

I t's a long way from the Southeast Asian country of Laos to Mt. Holyoke College, but for ThaoMee Xiong it's been a journey of success. The high point so far was being named to *USA Today*'s All-USA College First Academic Team. Xiong's success is all the more remarkable given that she immigrated with her family from Laos to Thailand and then to Wisconsin. In Wisconsin she not only entered a totally different culture, but she also faced the challenge of learning to speak and write the language of that culture.

"I've always struggled with writing and have never been confident with it," she says. "Once I get an idea for a paper, I try to do some research on the subject to see if there's enough information on the topic before I start writing about it. Then I just start writing," she adds. "I feel better when I get something down on paper."

Although writing may be difficult for Xiong, speaking before groups of people is more comfortable.

"I find speaking a lot easier and feel far more confident than when I write," she explains. "In high school I took up forensics and participated in mock trials. I found this helped me a lot with language and speaking. It taught me not to be fearful of speaking in public.

"In high school I was one of the few students of color. I always felt it was my responsibility to speak up and get my issues out there," Xiong notes. "I had some concerns about my community, and I was dealing with the feeling of always being put on the spot. Speaking up helped."

Xiong has continued to speak out, although this time in a different way: Her most recent accomplishment is co-authoring an article on Hmong refugee women that will be published in the book *Outside the Master Narratives: Women's Untold Stories*.

Remember: You're Already an Accomplished Public Speaker

Speaking in front of others is something you've done all your life. It might have been a heart-to-heart with a friend. It might have been with a group of friends deciding on what kind of pizza to order, with you arguing against anchovies and your friends arguing in favor. It might have been as a sports team member, with you shouting encouragement to your fellow athletes. The point is that you've already spoken in front of others—lots of times.

When you are faced with giving a formal presentation, then, give yourself credit for the times you've already spoken publicly. Let go of your fears and enjoy your moment in the spotlight. You may well find the experience satisfying and rewarding.

Looking Back

What are the best techniques for getting started and writing a first draft?

- Freewriting and brainstorming can help you choose a topic.

- Identifying the audience for writing is essential.

- Breaking down large writing tasks into smaller, more manageable pieces helps pave the way to completing a writing assignment.

- Good organization, which is essential to both writer and reader, often follows the ABBCC structure: argument, background, body, counterarguments, and conclusion.

How can I move from my first draft to my final draft?

- Use your outline as your roadmap

- The best way to begin writing the first draft is to plunge in, starting anywhere in the paper.

- Revision is an essential part of writing: Most of writing is rewriting.

How can I conquer my fear of public speaking and make effective oral presentations?

- Although public speaking can be intimidating, audiences are generally sympathetic, speaking becomes easier once it is underway, and practice leads to success.

- The first minute of the presentation, oral transition points, visual aids, and having enough practice are important.

- Use the PREP system for giving extemporaneous (unrehearsed) talks.

Key Terms and Concepts

ABBCC structure (p. 178)   Paraphrase (p. 176)
Brainstorming (p. 173)   Plagiarism (p. 186)
Extemporaneous talk (p. 194)   Thesis (p. 178)
Freewriting (p. 172)   Voice (p. 182)

Resources

On Campus

If you are having difficulties with writing, the first place to turn to is a cooperative classmate. Ask someone to read a draft of a writing assignment. He or she may be able to make enough constructive comments to allow subsequent drafts to come more easily. In addition, some colleges have writing clinics where you can bring a draft of your paper and work with a counselor. Finally, your instructors may be willing to read preliminary drafts of your work.

In Print

Peter Elbow's book *A Community of Writers* (McGraw-Hill, 2001) presents a fine introduction to the art and practice of writing, with specific suggestions for how to get started and for refining and polishing first drafts.

Another excellent guide to writing is William Zinsser's classic, *On Writing Well: The Classic Guide to Writing Nonfiction* (Harperreference, 1998). A widely used guide to writing, Zinsser's book is helpful both for beginners and for more experienced writers.

Finally, Hamilton Gregory's book *Public Speaking for College and Career* (McGraw-Hill, 2002) provides an excellent introduction to public speaking. It is filled with tips for planning and delivering a talk.

On the Web

The following sites on the World Wide Web provide the opportunity to extend your learning about the material in this chapter. (Although the Web addresses were accurate at the time the book was printed, check the P.O.W.E.R. Learning website [**www.mhhe.com/power**] for any changes that may have occurred.)

- The "Reference Shelf" from the Veterinary Education and Information Network (**www.library.usyd.edu.au/VEIN/elibrary/grammar.html**) offers a large collection of links to a variety of college sites providing information on utilization of grammar and effective writing.

- "Preparing a Speech: A Step-by-Step Guide" (**all.successcenter.ohio-state.edu/speech/speech-steps.htm**), from the Academic Learning Lab at Ohio State University, outlines four major steps to preparing a speech. It can also be used for preparing a paper.

- Bartleby.com offers E. B. White's *The Elements of Style* (**www.bartleby.com/141/**), a 1918 edition of the classic text recommended by writing instructors for many years. This text is filled with helpful hints on word usage, punctuation, and avoiding common mistakes. It's a must for writers serious about improving their writing.

Taking It to the Net

1 Write a brief summary of a news story. Go to Yahoo! (**www.yahoo.com**) and click on "Today's News." Select one of the available categories (e.g., for example, "Top Stories") and read the first story. Summarize the news story, including only the most important facts.

2 Practice public speaking. Again, go to Yahoo! (**www.yahoo.com**) and click on "Today's News" and then on "Top Stories." Read the two top stories and write brief notes for each on an index card. Now find a willing classmate or friend and explain the details of each story using your index cards for reference. Did your listener follow the story? Did he or she find it interesting? Were you able to answer any questions that your listener had?

The Case of . . .

The Reluctant Speaker

"No one," thought Erik Phillips, "could hate public speaking more than I do."

Erik was horrified at the thought of giving a presentation. Not only did he not like standing up in front of others, exposing himself to their scrutiny, but he was also embarrassed by his thick Louisiana accent, which his friends at the northern college he attended teased him about constantly.

He was sure he'd never be able to do it. Erik made up his mind to ask his instructor if he could write a paper instead of making the oral presentation. But before he could, one of his friends in the class told him that he had already asked for an alternative assignment and that the instructor had flatly refused, saying that it would be a "good experience" to give the talk.

Erik was stuck.

1. How would you advise Erik to prepare and organize for his talk?

2. Erik expressed a willingness to write a paper instead of giving a talk. Should he prepare the paper and read it for his presentation? Why or why not? How might he use the research for his paper to help with his talk?

3. Erik is especially nervous about speaking because he believes that his accent interferes with understanding. How might he deal with this particular anxiety? How could friends or classmates help him?

4. Do you think props would be helpful for Erik? What purpose might they serve?

5. What advice would you give Erik to reduce his anxiety?

Memory

8

The stack of note cards kept getting higher and higher.

And as it grew, so did Rosa Carlozzi's sense of frustration. Taking a class on the biology of the human body, Rosa had described the functions of the major organs of the body on separate note cards, hoping that would help her to memorize them. But all that was happening was that the number of cards was increasing each week.

Rosa decided that drastic measures were called for. She began to take her stack of cards

with her everywhere she went. Whenever she had a spare moment, she would shuffle through the cards, trying to memorize them. She sometimes felt a little silly walking around with her thick stack of cards. But as she spent more time going over them, she became more confident, and she began to recall more and more.

It worked! By the final, Rosa realized that she had succeeded in memorizing most of the information on the cards. She ended the semester with an A in the course.

Looking
Ahead

Most of us have experienced the challenge of memorizing a seemingly impossible amount of information, and we tend to focus on our failures far more than on our successes. But the truth is that our memory capabilities are truly astounding. If you are like the average college student, your vocabulary contains some 50,000 words. You know hundreds of mathematical facts, and you can recall detailed images from scenes you saw years ago. In fact, simply cataloging the memories you already have might well take a lifetime.

In this chapter, you'll learn how you can improve the memory skills you already have. We'll examine what memory is and why it sometimes fails us. Finally, you will become acquainted with specific ways to learn information so that you can recall it when you need to.

In short, after reading this chapter, you'll be able to answer these questions:

- **What is memory and how does it function?**

- **Why might I have problems with memory, and how can I deal with those problems?**

- **What are some techniques I can use for memorizing information?**

The Secret of Memory

Sure, sometimes you have trouble recalling information that you know you've learned. Or maybe you don't recall that you learned it, even though in fact you did. But this is not because information has disappeared from your head. The problem is one of *retrieval*. **Retrieval** entails finding information stored in memory and making it conscious so that it can be used. Every piece of information that you've ever learned is buried somewhere in your brain. The trick is to find it when you need it.

Retrieval
The process of finding information stored in memory and returning it to consciousness for further use

The proof of this assertion comes from the biology of memory. Consider what happens when you're exposed to some new material. Say your geometry instructor spends a class talking about the Pythagorean formula in geometry, which maintains that the square of the length of the hypotenuse of a right triangle is equal to the sum of the squares of the two other sides. (You may recall this formula as $a^2 + b^2 = c^2$.)

When you first learn the formula, the wiring connecting a handful of the 70 trillion or so brain cells in your head is changed—forever. The information on the Pythagorean formula is etched into some tiny part of your brain, and unless that part of the brain is damaged in some way through injury or disease, it will stay there for the rest of your life.

The practical outgrowth of this biological process is straightforward: You already remember everything you need to know, and a lot more. With some effort, you could remember the names of everyone in your third-grade class. You know what you ate when you went to the eighth-grade dance. You remember the name of the body of water that borders Iraq. And you could even have remembered where you left your keys the last time you misplaced them.

The key to successful recall is to learn the material initially in a way that will allow you to recall it *easily* later. By using the strategies summarized in the P.O.W.E.R. Plan, you'll be able to do that.

P repare: Remembering the Right Stuff

Memorize what you need to memorize. Forget about the rest.

The average textbook chapter has something like 20,000 words. If you had to recall every word of the chapter, it would be nearly impossible. Furthermore, it would be a waste of time. Being able to spew out paragraphs of material is quite different from the more important ability to recall and deeply understand academic material in meaningful ways.

Within those 20,000 words, there may be only 20 different concepts that you need to learn. And perhaps there are only 10 keywords. *Those* are the pieces of information that should be the focus of your efforts to memorize.

In short, the first step in building a better memory is to

PREPARE
Determine what you need to remember

ORGANIZE
Relate new material to what you already know

WORK
Use proven strategies to memorize new material

EVALUATE
Test your recall of new information

RETHINK
Consolidate memories through repeated review

P.O.W.E.R. Plan

POWER

Remember This

Read the following story. Pay attention to the details, but don't take notes or make lists.

Demain entered the marketplace slowly, feeling his way. He had never seen such confusion.

Hundreds of wagons, caravans, booths, and carts were drawn up in a broad U, occupying three sides of the enormous town square, their awnings and curtains open and inviting. The colors and odors were a sensual assault; he perceived them not just through his eyes and nose, but as if they were pressing forcibly against his skin. And the sounds! He could scarcely keep himself from bolting back the way he had come, to the safety of the countryside.

A sense of wonder pushed him forward. He walked past gold merchants, with their gray cloaks and watchful eyes, and a potter, her shop filled three shelves high with vases, bottles, and jars of deep blues, reds, and yellows that Demain—accustomed to the brown clay that adorned his mother's kitchen—had never even imagined possible. Cloths were on sale in the booth next to the potter's—shamelessly long bolts of impossibly patterned prints, depicting herons, bulls, schools of fish, a field of wheat, great bowls of fruit, and men and women engaged in the pursuits he knew from stories: They danced in bold colors and graceful postures, harvested vast fields of bounty, fought battles of intricate strategy, and drank and courted in riotous taverns.

Past the dealers in rugs, chairs, hats, shoes, and wagons; past the blacksmith's huge muddy arms beating out rugged tools and fine weapons; past the fortune tellers and musicians, Demain at last came to the vendors of food and drink. Never had he felt so hungry. He was lifted off his feet—he swore he was floating—by the aroma of long lines of sausages, sides of beef, whole lambs, chickens on spits the length of spears, bacon and hams, fried potatoes, great vats of boiling vegetables, stewing tomatoes, and breads—all shapes and sizes of loaves, twisted into braids, curled into circles, flattened, puffed, elongated, pocketed, and glazed.

Demain felt the two coppers in his pocket—his holiday bounty—and hoped they would be enough.

Note: We'll return to the story of Demain later. For now, read on.
To Try It online, go to **www.mhhe.com/power**.

---

determine just what it is that you wish to recall. By extracting what is important from what is less crucial, you'll be able to limit the amount and extent of the material that you need to recall and you'll be able to focus, laserlike, on what you need to remember.

It's not easy. We're all victims of information overload. We're exposed to more information in a year than our grandparents were exposed to in their entire lifetimes.

To determine what is important, look at

> "A retentive memory may be a good thing, but the ability to forget is the true token of greatness."
>
> Elbert Hubbard, *The Note Book* (1927)

the big picture. Don't get lost in minute details. Instead, prepare yourself by taking a broad overview of the material, and decide what your goal is going to be. (To begin testing your memory, complete Try It 1.)

O rganize: Relating New Material to What You Already Know

Don't think of memorization as pumping gasoline (new information) into an almost-empty gas tank (your brain). You're not filling something that is empty. On the contrary, you are filling a container that already has a lot of things in it, that is infinitely expandable, and that never empties out.

If you approach each new memorization task as something entirely new and unrelated to your previous knowledge, you'll have enormous difficulty recalling it. On the other hand, if you connect it to what you already know, you'll be able to recall it far better. The way to get your brain to do this organizational work for you is by thinking about the associations the new material has with the old.

Say, for example, you need to remember information about the consequences of global warming, such as the fact that the level of the oceans is predicted to rise. You might think

> "Human memory works its own wheel, and stops where it will."
>
> William Saroyan, *Chance Meetings* (1978)

about the rising level of the ocean as it relates to your personal memories of visits to the beach. You might think what a visit to the beach would be like with dramatically higher water levels, visualizing a shrunken shoreline with no room for sunbathing. Then whenever you think about global warming in the future, your mind is likely to associate this fairly abstract concept with its concrete consequences for beaches. The association you made while rehearsing the information makes it personal, long-lasting, and useful. (You can see this for yourself in Try It 2.)

Memories can also be organized by place. *Where* you learn something makes a difference in how well you can recall it. Memory researchers have found that people actually remember things better in the place where they first studied and learned them. Consequently, one of the ways to jog your memory is to try to re-create the situation in which you first learned what you're trying to remember. If you memorized the colors that litmus paper turns when it is placed in acids and bases while you were lying in bed, it might be helpful during a test to recall the correct colors by imagining yourself lying on your bed thinking about the colors.

Another effective place-related strategy is to introduce new data into your mind in the place that you know you're going to need to recall it at some future moment.

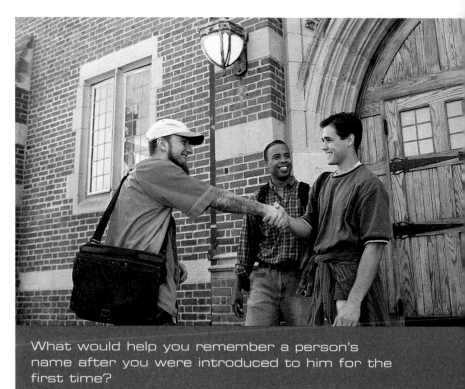

What would help you remember a person's name after you were introduced to him for the first time?

Organize Your Memory

As critical thinking expert Diane Halpern points out, having an organized memory is like having a neat bedroom: Its value is that you know you'll be able to find something when you need it. To prove the point, try this exercise she devised.[1]

Read the following 15 words at a rate of approximately one per second:

girl

heart

robin

purple

finger

flute

blue

organ

man

hawk

green

lung

eagle

child

piano

Now, cover the list, and write down as many of the words as you can on a separate sheet of paper. How many words are there on your list? _____

For instance, suppose you know that you're going to be tested on certain material in the room in which your class is held. Try to do at least some of your studying in that same room.

W ork: Using Proven Strategies to Memorize New Material

One of the good things about the work of memorization is that you have your choice of literally dozens of techniques. Depending on the kind of material you need to recall and how much you already know about the subject, you can turn to any number of methods.

As we sort through the various options, keep in mind that no one strategy works by itself. (And some strategies don't work at all: for example, forget about drugs like ginko biloba—there's no scientific evidence that they are ef-

After you've done this, read the following list:

green

blue

purple

man

girl

child

piano

flute

organ

heart

lung

finger

eagle

hawk

robin

Now cover this second list and write down as many of the words as you can on the other side of the separate sheet of paper.

How many words did you remember this time? Did you notice that the words on both lists are identical? Did you remember more the second time? (Most people do.) Why do you think most people remember more when the words are organized as they are in the second list?

Working in a Group: Discuss with your classmates ways in which you can organize material from this book to make it easier to remember.

To Try It online, go to **www.mhhe.com/power**.

fective.) Instead, try the following proven strategies and find those that work best for you. Feel free to devise your own strategies or add those that have worked for you in the past.

Rehearsal Think it again: rehearsal. Say it aloud: rehearsal. Think of it in terms of the three syllables that make up the word: re—hear—sal. OK, one more time—say the word "rehearsal."

If you're scratching your head over the last paragraph, it's to illustrate the point of **rehearsal**: to transfer material that you encounter into memory. If you don't rehearse information in some way, it will end up like most of the information to which we're exposed: on the garbage heap of lost memory.

To test if you've succeeded in transferring the word "rehearsal" into your memory, put down this book and go off for a few minutes. Do something entirely unrelated to reading this book. Have a snack, catch up on the latest sports scores on ESPN, or read the front page of the newspaper.

Rehearsal

The process of practicing and learning material to transfer it into memory

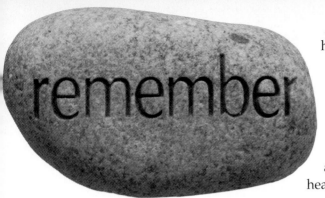
remember

Are you back? If the word "rehearsal" popped into your head when you picked up this book again, you've passed your first memory test. You can be assured that the word "rehearsal" has been transferred into your memory.

Rehearsal is the key strategy in remembering information. If you don't rehearse material, it will never make it into memory. Repeating the information, summarizing it, associating it with other memories, and above all thinking about it when you first come across it will ensure that rehearsal will be effective in pushing the material into memory.

Mnemonics
Formal techniques used to make material more readily remembered

Mnemonics This odd word (pronounced in an equally odd fashion, with the "m" silent—"neh MON ix") describes formal techniques used to make material more readily remembered. **Mnemonics** are the tricks-of-the-trade that professional memory experts use, and you too can use them to nail down the sort of information you will often need to recall for tests.

Among the most common mnemonics are the following:

- **Acronyms.**

  FACE

  Roy G. Biv

  P.O.W.E.R.

Acronym
A word or phrase formed by the first letters of a series of terms

  You're already well acquainted with **acronyms,** words or phrases formed by the first letters of a series of terms. For instance, FACE spells out the names of the notes that appear in the spaces on the treble clef music staff ("F," "A," "C," and "E," starting at the bottom of the staff.) Roy G. Biv is a favorite of physics students who must remember the colors of the spectrum (red, orange, yellow, green, blue, indigo, and violet.) And P.O.W.E.R. stands for—well, by this point in the book, you probably remember.

  The benefit of acronyms is that they help us to recall a complete list of steps or items. The drawback, though, is that the acronym itself has to be remembered, and sometimes we may not recall it when we need it. For instance, Roy G. Biv is not exactly the sort of name that readily comes to mind. And if we're unable to remember an acronym, it won't be of much use to us. Even if we do remember Roy G. Biv, we might get stuck trying to recall what a particular letter stands for. (For example, we'd probably prefer not to spend a lot of time during a test trying to remember if the "B" stands for brown, or beige, or blue.)

- **Acrostics.** After learning to use the acronym "FACE" to remember the notes on the spaces of the music staff, many beginning musicians learn that the names of the lines on the staff form the acrostic, "Every Good Boy Deserves Fudge." **Acrostics** are sentences in which the first letters spell out something that needs to be recalled. The benefits—as well as the drawbacks—of acrostics are similar to those of acronyms. (You can explore acronyms and acrostics in Try It 3 on page 210).

Acrostic
A sentence in which the first letters of the words correspond to material that is to be remembered

- **Rhymes and jingles.** "Thirty days hath September, April, June, and November . . ." If you know the rest of the rhyme, you're familiar with one of the most commonly used mnemonic jingles in the English language. Similarly, some of us learned the main theme of Schubert's Unfinished Symphony by singing the words "This is the symphony that Schubert wrote and never finished" when the theme first appears. For those who learned to recognize the symphony by using this mnemonic, it is virtually impossible to hear the symphony without recalling the words.

Although mnemonics are helpful, keep in mind that they have a number of significant shortcomings. First, they don't focus on the meaning of the items being remembered. Because information that is learned in terms of its surface characteristics—such as first letters that form a word—is less likely to be retained than information that is learned in terms of its meaning, mnemonic devices are an imperfect route to memorization.

There's another problem with mnemonics: Sometimes it takes as much effort to create a mnemonic device as it would to memorize the material in the first place. And because the mnemonic itself has no meaning, it can be forgotten.

Despite their drawbacks, mnemonics can be useful. They are particularly helpful when the material being memorized includes a list of items or a series of steps.

The Method of Loci and the Peg Method: Special Help for Recalling Sequences and Lists The ancient Greeks had a way with words. Their orators could deliver speeches that went on for hours, without notes. How did they remember what they wanted to say?

They used a procedure called the **method of loci.** *Loci* is the Latin word for "places," and it helps describe a procedure in which items in a sequence you wish to remember—such as the sections of a speech or a series of events—are thought of as "located" in a different place in a building.

Consider, for example, a speech that has three major sections: an introduction, a main body, and a conclusion. Each of the three sections has various points that you need to recall also.

To use the method of loci, you'd first visualize the living room, kitchen, and bedroom of a house with which you were familiar. Next, you'd mentally "place" the introduction of the speech into the living room of the house. You would mentally place each of the *parts* of the introduction on a different piece of furniture, following the way in which the furniture was laid out in the room

What Sort of Memory Do I Have?

1. What kinds of information do you remember best: faces, shapes, colors, smells, names, dates, or facts? Why do you think this is?

2. What kinds of information do you have the greatest difficulty remembering? Why do you think this type of information is hard for you to remember?

3. Is there any particular source of information about which you can remember exceptional amounts, such as baseball records or movie trivia? Why do you think you remember this information so readily?

4. Do you use any memorization techniques now? Have you ever tried any in the past? What do you think you could do to improve your memory recall?

Method of loci
A memory technique by which the elements in a list are visualized as occupying the parts of a familiar place

Try It!
3

Working in a Group:
Do-It-Yourself Acronyms and Acrostics

In the first part of this Try It, work individually to create an acronym and an acrostic.

1. Figure out an acronym to remind you of the names of the five Great Lakes, using the first letters of their names (which are Erie, Huron, Michigan, Ontario, Superior).

2. Devise an acrostic for the nine planets in order of their average distance from the sun. Their names, in order, are Mercury, Venus, Earth, Mars, Jupiter, Saturn, Uranus, Neptune, Pluto

After you've tried to create the acronym and acrostic, meet in a group and discuss these questions: How successful were you in devising effective acronyms and acrostics? Do some of the group members' creations seem more effective than others? Why? Is the act of creating them an important component of helping to remember what they represent, or would having them created by someone else be as helpful in recalling them? For your information, a common acronym for the Great Lakes is HOMES (**H**uron, **O**ntario, **M**ichigan, **E**rie, **S**uperior), and a popular acrostic for the order of the planets is **M**y **V**ery **E**ducated **M**other **J**ust **S**erved **U**s **N**ine **P**izzas.

To Try It online, go to **www.mhhe.com/power**.

(for example, you might proceed clockwise from the door). The easy chair might contain the first point of the introduction, the sofa the next point, and an end table the last point. Then you'd move into the kitchen and do the same thing with the body of the paper, laying out your arguments on different pieces of kitchen furniture or appliances. Finally, you'd end up in the bedroom, where you'd "place" the conclusion.

A close cousin of the method of loci is the **peg method.** The peg method uses a series of keywords tied to numbers to help in the recall of numeric information. For instance, a set of "pegs" that you could use would link numbers with these words:

Peg method

A memory technique by which a series of memorized words is linked by images to a list of items to be remembered

One is a sun,

Two is a zoo,

Three is me,

Four is a store,

Five is a dive,

Six are sticks,

Seven is heaven,

Eight is a gate,

Nine is a pine,

Ten is a den.

By thinking of exotic images using the peg words tied to the numbers, you can recall specific numbers that you need to memorize. For instance, suppose you had trouble remembering the value of *pi,* used to calculate the circumference of a circle (3.14, in case you don't remember). Translate the number into the relevant peg words—me (three), sun (one), and store (four)—and imagine an image linking the three. One obvious possibility is an image of yourself wearing sunglasses, heading out to a store on a sunny day. A less obvious and more exotic possibility is an image of yourself bowling a large sun into the front of a store.

The peg system can also be used to memorize ordered lists of items, when the sequence in which they appear is important. In this use, the peg system is very similar to the method of loci. You simply link images of the ordered set of items to the 10 "numbers." The first item is linked with the sun, the second with a zoo, and so on.

Involve Multiple Senses The more senses you can involve when you're trying to learn new material, the better you'll be able to remember. Here's why: Every time we encounter new information, all of our senses are potentially at work. For instance, if we witness a car crash, we receive sensory input from the sight of the two cars hitting each other, the sound of the impact, and perhaps the smell of burning rubber. Each piece of sensory information is stored in a separate location in the brain, and yet all the pieces are linked together in extraordinarily intricate ways.

What this means is that when we seek to remember the details of the crash, recalling a memory of one of the sensory experiences—such as what we heard—can trigger recall of the other types of memories. For example, thinking about the *sound* the two cars made when they hit can bring back memories of the way the scene looked.

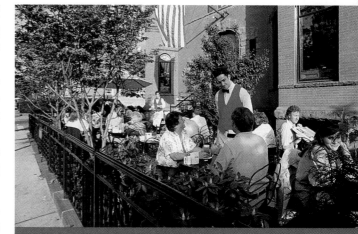

In fact, many of us have a favorite memory style—one that we use most often when trying to recall information. Take a moment to learn about your own memory style by completing Try It 4.

You can make use of the fact that memories are stored in multiple ways by applying the following techniques:

- **When you learn something, use your body.** Don't sit passively at your desk. Instead, move around. Stand up; sit down. Touch the page. Trace figures with your fingers. Talk to yourself. Think out loud. It may seem strange, but doing this increases the number of ways in which the information is stored. By involving every part of your body, you've increased the number of potential ways to trigger a relevant memory later, when you need to recall it.

Have you ever wondered how some waiters can remember what their customers have ordered without writing anything down? They use the same simple memory strategies that you can use to recall information you'll need to remember for tests.

Try It!
4

Personal Styles: Determine Your Memory Style

What's your dominant memory style? Do you most easily remember sounds, sights, or the way things feel? Read the statements below and circle the response choice that most closely describes your habits.

To help recall lectures, I . . .

  V. Read the notes I took during class.

  A. Close my eyes and try to hear what the instructor said.

  K. Try to place myself back in the lecture room and feel what was going on at the time.

To remember a complex procedure, I . . .

  V. Write down the steps I have to follow.

  A. Listen carefully and repeatedly to the instructions.

  K. Do it over and over again.

To learn sentences in a foreign language, I do best if I . . .

  V. Read them on paper to see how they're written.

  A. Hear them in my head until I can say them aloud.

  K. See someone speaking them and then practice moving my mouth and hands the way the speaker did.

If I have to learn a dance move, I like . . .

  V. To see a diagram of the steps before trying it.

  A. Someone to coach me through it while I try it.

  K. To watch it once and then give it a try.

When I recall a very happy moment, I tend to . . .

  V. Visualize it in my head.

  A. Hear the sounds that I heard when experiencing it.

  K. Feel with my hands and body what I felt at the time.

When I have to remember driving directions, I usually . . .

  V. See a map of the route in my mind.

  A. Repeat the directions aloud to myself.

  K. Feel my hands steering and the car driving along the correct route.

Answer key:

If you chose mostly Vs, your main memory style is visual; your preference is to remember things in terms of the way they appear.

If you chose mostly As, your main memory style is auditory; your preference is to recall material in terms of sound.

If you chose mostly Ks, your main memory style is kinesthetic; your preference is to remember using your sense of touch.

Keep in mind that this questionnaire only gives a rough idea of how we usually use our memories. Remember: All of us use all of the memory styles during the course of each day.

Consider these questions: How do you think your memory style affects the way you recall academic information? How does it affect the way you learn things initially? How could you make greater use of your less-preferred styles?

To Try It online, go to **www.mhhe.com/power**.

And when one memory is triggered, other related memories may come tumbling back.

- **Draw and diagram the material.** We've already considered (in Chapter 4) the power of concept maps, the method of structuring written material by graphically grouping and connecting key ideas and themes. When we create a concept map, one of the things we're doing is expanding the modalities in which information can be stored in our minds.

  Other types of drawing can be useful in aiding later recall. Creating drawings, sketches, and even cartoons can help us remember better. Your creations don't have to be great art, or detailed, involved illustrations. Even rough sketches are effective, because creating them gets both the visual and tactile senses involved.

- **Visualize. Visualization** is a technique by which images are formed to ensure that material is recalled. For instance, you now know that memory requires three basic steps: the initial recording of information, the storage of that information, and, ultimately, the retrieval of the stored information. As you read the three steps, you probably see them as logical and straightforward processes. But how do you remember them?

  You might visualize a computer, with its keyboard, disks, and monitor (see Figure 8.1). The keyboard represents the initial recording of information. The disk represents the storage of information. And the monitor represents the display of information that has been retrieved from memory. If you can put these images in your mind, it will help you to remember the three basic memory steps later.

  Visualization serves several purposes: it helps make abstract ideas concrete; it engages multiple senses; it permits us to link different bits of information together; it provides us with a context for storing information.

  What kind of visualization works best? There's a simple rule: Weird is good. The more extreme, outlandish, and eccentric the image you create, the more notable it will be and so the easier it will be to remember. And if you can remember the image, you'll probably remember the information that's attached to it (see Try It 5).

Visualization
A memory technique by which images are formed to help recall material

Think Positively Emotions matter. If you're in a negative frame of mind when you try to memorize something, your negative feelings can become attached to the memory, making you less likely to recall it because you'll automatically tend to avoid those bad feelings. The opposite is also true: If you think positively about the process of memorization, those more-positive feelings will end up being etched into your memory.

Of course, feelings can't be turned off in the same way we're able to turn off a light. If you feel nervous and scared about memorizing all the formulas you need to for your chemistry midterm, you can't just tell yourself it's great fun. But if you recognize your feelings, they lose much of their power to influence you and to block memories.

Figure 8.1

Recording of information

Storage of information in memory

Display of information retrieved from memory

Try It!
5

Visualize the Possibilities

You may have noticed how important visualization is to memory. In fact, many of the techniques we've discussed in this chapter rely in some measure on visualization, especially your visualization of extreme or absurd images.

Test the truth of this statement by drawing a concept map—itself a visual form of organizing material—of the concept of visualization. Place the word "Visualization" in the center of the map and link as many other memory and mnemonic techniques to it as you can. You may be surprised at the richness of your map.

How well does the concept map reflect what you know about visualization? Is it a useful tool for you? Do you think that the act of creating a concept map itself is helpful in memorizing the material? Would using someone else's concept map be less helpful than creating your own?

 Working in a Group: Compare your concept map with those of your classmates. What are the major similarities and differences? How do you account for them? Are some of the participants' concept maps more likely to help recall information than others?

To Try It online, go to **www.mhhe.com/power**.

Overlearning Think back to when you were learning your basic multiplication facts ($1 \times 1 = 1$; $2 \times 2 = 4$; and so forth). Let's suppose you had put each multiplication problem on a flash card, and you decided to go through your entire set of cards, trying to get every problem right.

The first time you went through the set of cards and answered all the problems correctly, would you feel as if you'd memorized them perfectly and that you'd never again make an error? You shouldn't. You would need several instances of perfect performance to be sure you had learned the multiplication facts completely.

Lasting learning doesn't come until you have overlearned the material. **Overlearning** consists of studying and rehearsing material past the point of initial mastery. Through overlearning, recall becomes automatic. Rather than searching for a fact, going through mental contortions until perhaps the information surfaces, overlearning permits us to recall the information without even thinking about it.

To put the principle of overlearning to work, don't stop studying at the point when you can say to yourself, "Well, I'll probably pass

"Don't let those few Einsteins who can ace a test by never attending class and by sleeping on the textbook the night before trick you into using their study methods. My roommate tried to convince me that studying by osmosis was a proven method. Trust me, it isn't."

Keith Vernon, University of Puget Sound[2]

this test." You may be right, but that's all you'll do—pass. Instead, spend extra time learning the material until it becomes as familiar as an old pair of jeans.

Evaluate: Testing Your Recall of New Information

The memory strategies just described can bring you to a point where you probably feel comfortable in your ability to remember the material you've been learning. Once you've used one or more of them to help you, it's time to test yourself—to evaluate whether you'll be able to recall the material when you need it. There are several ways to evaluate your memory:

- **Use in-text review questions and tests.** Many textbook chapters end with a quiz or a set of review questions about the material. Some have questions scattered throughout the chapter. Don't avoid them! Not only do such questions indicate what the writer of the book thought was important for you to learn and memorize, but they can also provide an excellent opportunity for evaluating your memory.

  Even if you've answered the review questions earlier, while you were first reading the material (which is always a good idea), answer them again later as you study for the test and then the final.

- **Test yourself.** Temporarily transform yourself into your instructor, and prioritize what you're most likely to be tested on. Then create your own test, writing out some questions.

  Later, after as little as a few hours, take the test, and then grade it. How have you done? If you've achieved a grade that you're satisfied with, then fine. If, on the other hand, you've missed some key pieces of information, then you'll want to return to work and spend more time on memorization.

Career Connections

Memory on the Job

- Military genius Julius Caesar could dictate as many as seven letters at a time to his secretaries.

- Conductor Arturo Toscanini memorized every note of 400 different musical pieces. When a musician told him, just before a concert, that his instrument had just broken and he was unable to play a particular note, Toscanini paused a moment, but then told him not to worry, because that note was not in the piece they were about to play.

- Warren Buffett, one of the world's most successful investors, could recall sales figures from companies in which he had invested dozens of years earlier.[3]

Improving your memory is not something that will only help you do better in college. Whatever your future job—be it military general, musician, business tycoon, or anything else—a good memory will further your career success.

Not all professionals need the same kind of memory skills, of course. A camera operator at a television network must remember lighting combinations; lawyers need to recall the details of witness testimony; elementary school teachers must remember what kinds of exercises work best for certain students; physicians need to keep track of a host of medical conditions and medicines. But in each of these professions, memory abilities are an important aspect of job performance.

Memory is also important in terms of keeping track of people's names and functions. Being able to recall the names of those with whom you work, professional colleagues from other companies, and clients is an important skill. People are flattered when you remember their names. It says you think they are important and worth noticing.

In short, remember this: The strategies that you learn in college to improve your memory will pay big dividends in the world of work.

- **Team up with a friend.** When it comes to evaluating your memory, two heads are often better than one. Working with a classmate can help you test the limits of your memory and assess areas in which you need work.

    For instance, you and a friend can take turns testing yourselves, switching back and forth between asking and answering questions. Turn it into a contest: One of you can be Alex Trebek of *Jeopardy*, and the other, a contestant. You can even work in groups. The important thing is to switch who's asking and who's answering the questions. Even when you're directing questions to others—officially evaluating their memory—you're giving your own memory a workout. (Put your memory to the test in Try It 6.)

ry It!
6

Remember Demain

Remember the passage earlier in this chapter (Try It 1) about Demain, who found himself in the midst of a colorful, aromatic bazaar of booths and shops? Without turning back to the passage, write down everything you can remember about what Demain experienced in the marketplace—the shops, sights, and foods.

_____

_____

_____

_____

_____

_____

_____

_____

_____

Now reread the passage, trying to remember its details by using one or more techniques from this chapter. You might use the method of loci, the peg method, the method of organizing ideas into chunks, or other techniques. Then answer these questions about the passage:

1. What scenes were depicted on the cloths?

   _____

   _____

2. What were the gold merchants wearing?

   _____

   _____

3. After the cloth shop, what businesses did Demain pass to arrive at the vendors of food and drink?

   _____

   _____

4. What foods did Demain see and smell at the fair?

   _____

   _____

How would you assess your performance on these questions? Do you think you would have remembered more initially if you had used some of the memory techniques in this chapter? Do you see how you could employ these techniques in your own studying? Did one seem to work better for you than others?

To Try It online, go to **www.mhhe.com/power**.

Speaking of Success

Name: Lamar Heckstall

Education: Virginia Commonwealth University, Richmond, Virginia; major in art illustration and communication arts

Home: Richmond, Virginia

For college sophomore Lamar Heckstall, an art major, developing memory skills has required proceeding along two fronts simultaneously. It has been important for him to remember not only the written word but also the many images and visuals that are the stock-in-trade of an art major.

"For me visual memorization is actually easier," says Heckstall. "When it comes to remembering verbal information, like artists' names or titles of paintings, I try to create associations with the images. If the name of the artist is hard to pronounce, I try to put it into a rhyme or think of something I like that I can associate with the name. When we're viewing slides of artwork, I sometimes redraw the figure and then write the title underneath, and that helps. Most of the time I get

them all right, or maybe miss only one or two."

Heckstall says he started developing his memory skills toward the end of high school, but the larger

VCU
Virginia Commonwealth University

intellectual demands of college forced him to intensify his approach.

"Basically what I do when I'm studying is to take a word or definition and say it to myself five times," he explains. "I then write it down five times and actively try to recall it later on.

"I do have problems with

memorizing long definitions or long descriptions of people. In the past I found myself trying to memorize too much and not learning anything, so what I've been doing is concentrating on one or two main things about the definition or individual," he says.

In conjunction with memorization techniques, Heckstall says that his study habits have changed dramatically since high school, and now he finds that getting an early start on studying reaps rewards.

"In high school the work was easier, and while I took it seriously, I didn't put in as much time as I should have," he admits. "Now that I'm in college, I have to use my time wisely every day. As soon as I find out a test is scheduled, I start studying for it and generally put in about two or three hours a day until the day of the test."

Rethink: Consolidating Memories

Memory consolidation

The process by which the physical links between brain cells that represent memory become fixed and stable over time

Like fine wines, memories need time to age. Psychologists talk about this as the process of **memory consolidation.** What this means is that the physical links between brain cells that represent memory in the brain need time to become fixed and stable. This process explains why information is not suddenly and permanently established in memory the first time we're exposed to it. In fact, the process of consolidation may continue for days and even—in some cases—for years.[4]

Obviously you don't have years to wait. But it does pay to try to memorize material in advance of the time that you'll really need to use it. Then, when you go back to reconsider it, it will become even more well-established in your mind.

The phenomenon of memory consolidation explains why cramming is not a great idea. As we discussed in the chapter on taking tests, cramming is the process of spending the preceding evening or even the hours just before a test trying to memorize as much as possible. The memories that come from cramming simply don't last, because they aren't rehearsed and processed sufficiently. It's far more effective to distribute studying over many shorter sessions.

The best way to ensure good recall is to return to the material even after your personal evaluation tells you that you've got it down. Wait several days, if possible, and then review it again. You'll be able to identify the aspects of the material that you know well, as well as the things that just haven't jelled yet in memory. Rethinking the material, then, not only permits you to consolidate memory but also helps you to identify where you need more work.

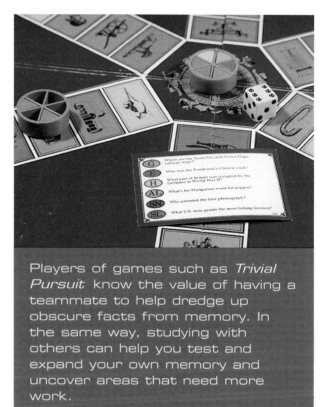

Players of games such as *Trivial Pursuit* know the value of having a teammate to help dredge up obscure facts from memory. In the same way, studying with others can help you test and expand your own memory and uncover areas that need more work.

Looking Back

What is memory and how does it function?

- Information we actively process is permanently etched into the brain, but it is not always readily available for retrieval.

- The challenge is to recall information when we need it, and the key to effective recall is learning material in a way that makes recall easy.

Why might I have problems with memory, and how can I deal with those problems?

- The problems we have with memory are mostly related to the inability to recall or retrieve information when it is needed. However, if information is rehearsed carefully, you can usually recall it more easily.

- Memory can be improved through careful preparation, by selecting in advance the pieces of information that are worthy of memorization and rehearsal.

- Another key to effective memorization is linking new information to information that is already in memory.

What are some techniques I can use for memorizing information?

- Many memory techniques are available to improve memorization. Rehearsal is a primary one, as is the use of mnemonics such as acronyms, acrostics, and rhymes.

- Other memory techniques are the method of loci, the peg method, visualization, and the use of multiple senses while learning new material.

- Overlearning is a basic principle of memorization.

- Memory takes some time—days or even longer—to reach the point of consolidation, when the physical links between brain cells that represent memory become stable. The need for consolidation explains why cramming is ineffective for long-term recall.

Key Terms and Concepts

Acronym (p. 208)
Acrostic (p. 208)
Memory consolidation (p. 219)
Method of loci (p. 209)
Mnemonics (p. 208)

Overlearning (p. 215)
Peg method (p. 210)
Rehearsal (p. 207)
Retrieval (p. 203)
Visualization (p. 213)

Resources

On Campus

If you have considerable difficulty in memorizing material compared with your classmates, it's possible that you might have a learning disability. If you suspect this, visit the college learning disabilities office or counseling center.

In Print

In *Memory: How It Works and How to Improve It* (Marlowe, 2001), Kenneth Higbee provides insight into the functioning of memory and how to improve it. Jerry Lucas's *Learning How to Learn: The Ultimate Learning and Memory Instruction* (Lucas Educational Systems, 2001) offers a simple system for improving memory. Finally, *Total Memory Workout* (Bantam Doubleday Dell, 1999), by Cynthia Green, provides an overview of techniques to maximize your memory.

On the Web

The following sites on the World Wide Web provide the opportunity to extend your learning about the material in this chapter. (Although the Web addresses were accurate at the time the book was printed, check the P.O.W.E.R. Learning website [**www.mhhe.com/power**] for any changes that may have occurred.)

- "Concept Mapping" (**www.coun.uvic.ca/learn/program/hndouts/map_ho.html**), an online "handout" from the University of Victoria's Learning Skills Program, outlines this memory aid, which improves recall by building meaning structures around key concepts.

- "Mnemonics" (**www.coun.uvic.ca/learn/program/hndouts/mnemon.html**), another "handout" from the same learning skills program, offers some good examples of mnemonics.

- Mind Tools, a bookstore specializing in works on memory, offers a number of free online articles (**www.mindtools.com/memory.html**) detailing methods for improving memory. It includes examples of how each technique can be applied to such topics as remembering lists and foreign languages.

Taking It to the Net

1 Practice the rehearsal technique for storing information in memory. Go to Yahoo! (**www.yahoo.com**) and click on "Regional" and again on "U.S. States." Click on your state, then on "Government," and finally on "elected officials" to find the names of your state's U.S. Senators. Repeat the names several times. Now explore another, unrelated site on the Web. After a few minutes, write down the names of your state's U.S. Senators from memory. How did you do?

2 Practice the visualization memory technique. Go to MovieWeb's site listing the top 50 all-time highest grossing movies (**www.movieweb.com/movie/alltime.html**). Try to memorize the top 10 movies by creating weird visual images based on the titles.

The Case of . . .

Remember the Alamo

For Kyle Dupree, history had always been a hard subject. Although he had no trouble learning general historical trends and concepts, he had difficulty keeping names, dates, and places sorted out.

Consequently, when his American history instructor, Ms. Teeler, announced that a major history exam was scheduled for the following week, Kyle panicked. He hadn't finished 100 pages of the assigned reading (300 pages altogether!), and here he was expected to learn what seemed to be virtually everything there was to know about the United States' western expansion during the 1800s. Ms. Teeler had said that the test would focus in particular on the Battle of the Alamo and its significance in U.S. history. When Kyle couldn't even recall where the Alamo was located, he knew he'd better get started memorizing. But where to begin?

1. How should Kyle prepare for the history exam? Should he simply get the history text and start reading? Why or why not?

2. How can Kyle prevent the facts of history from appearing to be a jumble of random words and numbers? How should he use his existing knowledge to structure historical information? Why might this become easier the more often Kyle does it?

3. Suppose Kyle is expected to remember the names of several officers in the two armies involved in the Battle of the Alamo, names that seem unusual to him and very hard to remember. Which memory technique is likely to be most effective? How would it work?

4. To remember lists of events in the western expansion movement, what technique would you recommend that Kyle use? How would it work?

5. How could Kyle use multiple senses while learning about the western expansion and the Battle of the Alamo?

Choosing Your Courses and Major

9

SCIENCE

"**P**hysics for Poets."

The course title jumped out at Gwen Izell. She had never liked science much, but she was intrigued by this title. Here was a class that seemed designed with her in mind. "Physics for Poets," the description began, "is designed for nonscience majors. It presents the links between physics and the arts." Gwen decided to take a chance and enroll in the class.

It turned out to be one of the best

decisions she ever made. She loved the course. The instructor was terrific, making physics fascinating. Not only did she begin to like the subject matter but she was good at it also.

Gwen was hooked. She took several other science courses over the next semesters. And during her senior year she found herself in an interview with a middle school principal, telling him—a bit to her surprise—that she'd be glad to teach ninth-grade physics.

Looking

Ahead

Our academic and professional careers are propelled by many forces, not the least of which is chance. Gwen Izell, like many other students, found a new direction while leafing through her course list. Although she never would have predicted at the start of college that she would end up taking a variety of science courses and teaching physics, her willingness to take a chance in selecting a course led to a new passion and to a career opportunity.

In this chapter we focus on choosing an academic course of study, one of the central challenges of college life. Not only do the choices we make color our entire college experience, but they also may determine the path we follow once we graduate.

This chapter begins by considering the many choices that you'll have to make as a routine part of attending college, including the choice of courses, instructors, and especially majors—each of which has long-term implications. You'll learn ways to select courses each term that meet your personal needs and maximize your chances of getting the courses you want.

Ultimately, the degree to which your college education benefits you is in your hands. By learning various strategies, you can act decisively to get the most out of your college experience. After reading this chapter, you'll be able to answer these questions:

- **How can I prepare for the academic choices that college demands?**

- **What is the best way to choose courses and ensure I'm getting the most out of my studies?**

- **How can I choose a major?**

Making Academic Choices

It's a moment filled with promise.

A list of courses for the upcoming term lies on the table in front of you. Many of them sound interesting. Each offers the possibilities of new knowledge and therefore has the potential for changing your life in significant ways.

As you leaf through the course catalog and begin to make your decisions, you will likely be feeling a wide range of emotions: anticipation over what you'll learn; hope that the course can bring you closer to your dreams; fear that you won't be able to do well; and excitement that you're proceeding with your college career, taking another of the many small steps that will eventually add up to a complete journey through college.

Choosing the right set of courses can be intimidating. But if you approach the problem thoughtfully, your final choices will make the best of the possibilities offered. Let's consider how to proceed, using the P.O.W.E.R. system as a guide (see the P.O.W.E.R. Plan).

repare: Becoming Familiar with Your Options and Requirements

Choosing which courses to take requires that you take several significant preparatory steps before you jump in. These include the following:

Familiarize Yourself with Your College Catalog Think of your college catalog as a kind of mail-order catalog. Like a mail-order catalog, it provides you with information about the merchandise that's offered, its cost, and the steps you need to take in placing an order. In this case, though, instead of a new pair of pants or a rug, the merchandise offered in the catalog is a college degree.

College catalogs are actually legal documents that offer you a contract. If you are admitted to the college and you fulfill certain requirements (such as taking a particular set of courses, maintaining a certain level of grades, and—let us not forget—paying your tuition bills on time), you'll get something in return. That something is a college degree.

Because they outline contractual obligations, college catalogs are important documents. They provide a summary of what your institution expects and offers in a number of areas:

1. **Academic regulations.** Every college has strict rules, requirements, and policies; these are all spelled out in the college catalog. For example, to graduate you need a certain number of courses or course credits. Similarly, if you wish to add or drop a course, you must do so by a certain date.

   In addition, colleges often require that you maintain a certain grade point average. A **grade point**

P.O.W.E.R. Plan

PREPARE

Become familiar with your options and requirements

ORGANIZE

Examine what you have done and what you need to do

WORK

Choose the next term's courses

EVALUATE

Decide whether you are in the classes you need

RETHINK

Learn what you love and like what you learn

Grade point average (GPA; also known as quality point average)
A numeric average in which letter grades are transformed into numbers

Major
A specialization in a particular subject area, requiring a set course of study

Prerequisites
Requirements that must be fulfilled before a student may enroll in a course or discipline

College advisor
An individual who provides students with advice about their academic careers

average (or **GPA;** also known as a *quality point average*) is a numeric average in which letter grades are transformed into numbers. Most colleges use a four-point scale in which A = 4, B = 3, C = 2, D = 1, and F = 0.

2. **Academic programs.** Most of the college catalog is a description of the school's academic departments and its **majors**—specializations in a particular subject area, each requiring a set course of study.

Requirements for majors generally fall into two or three categories. First, typically, are collegewide requirements that every student enrolled in the college must fulfill. Second are specific requirements for each particular major; to major in an area, you must take a specified number of courses or credits in that area. Finally, if the major falls within a broader academic unit (such as a school of education), that broader entity may have its own requirements for a degree.

For instance, a psychology major might be required to fulfill collegewide requirements that apply to all students enrolled in the college, such as a specified number of English, writing, math, and science courses. The Department of Psychology will have its own separate requirements for its majors to complete, such as taking no fewer than six psychology courses. Finally, because the Department of Psychology may be housed in a more general Division of Social Sciences, there may be divisional requirements to fulfill (perhaps a course in social science methodology or a foreign language requirement).

The college catalog also provides information for students who have transferred from another college. For instance, transfer students may receive credit for only a certain number of courses or credits earned at their first institution. Or they may be required to take particular courses even if they already took them at their previous school.

3. **Course listings.** The college catalog usually lists all the courses the school offers, even though not all of them may be offered every term. Courses are listed by department, and the descriptions typically include the course name, the number of credits the course provides, and a short description. Some courses have **prerequisites**—requirements that must be fulfilled before one can enroll. If the course has a prerequisite, this will also be stated. Sometimes the description will also name the instructors who teach the course and the time and place the class meets, although this information may also be published separately.

Make an Appointment with Your College Advisor Your **college advisor**'s job is to give you good, clear-headed advice. Your advisor will be someone who knows the ins and outs of the college's regulations, and whose experience in working

College advisors can play an important role in your academic career, providing valuable advice, helping you to overcome problems, and making sure that you meet all the requirements needed to graduate.

Table 9.1

Advisor Visit Checklist

_____ Check the college catalog for information about the advisor, noting any potential links or conversational topics that might be used to open the meeting.

_____ Be on time, be aware of how much time is scheduled for your appointment, and check the time frequently during the appointment.

_____ Summarize who you are (e.g., hometown, high school, grades in high school, interests, high school or community activities, etc.) to begin the more formal part of the meeting.

_____ List some or all of the courses you plan to take in the first semester.

_____ Prepare some questions about your course choices (e.g., difficulty of the courses, whether they match your interests, whether they will fulfill your requirements, what future courses or career choices they might lead to, personality of the instructors, etc.).

_____ List the extracurricular activities you're considering.

_____ Prepare some questions about these activities (e.g., how time-consuming, how interesting, what sorts of students participate in them, etc.).

_____ Be prepared to ask about the advisor's impressions of the college.

_____ Be prepared to ask the advisor to recommend activities, events, and the like on campus or off, and which to avoid.

_____ List any other issues you would like to raise (e.g., impressions of the college so far, roommate issues, personal issues, etc.).

_____ Be prepared to ask about the availability of the advisor in the future (e.g., office hours, policy on calling outside office hours, etc.).

_____ Remember to thank the advisor before leaving.

with other students provides a good deal of knowledge in other areas as well. Advisors can help you figure out what classes to take, how to overcome academic bureaucracies, whom to go to about a problem, and generally how to prepare yourself for graduation and beyond. They can even provide information on extracurricular activities, volunteer opportunities, and part-time jobs.

Advisors are usually very busy at the beginning of each term, so find out their office hours, schedule an appointment early, and be sure to keep your scheduled appointment. Don't go unprepared when you do go. Table 9.1 provides a checklist you should go through before your appointment.

Advisors can be tremendously valuable resources. Take some time to get to know your advisor as a person—and to let him or her get to know you. To get a better sense of who your own advisor is, complete Try It 1, "Get to Know Your College Advisor."

> "It can be no dishonor to learn from others when they speak good sense."
>
> Sophocles, _Antigone_

If you find that you and your advisor aren't a good match and you know of another advisor who is willing and qualified to advise you, you might consider making a switch. Just be sure you have given your original advisor a chance. It is not your advisor's fault, for example, that you missed your only chance this year to take astronomy. Similarly, even though you may not like your advisor's message ("You still need to take a science course"),

> "Choosing courses can make or break you in college. The better you are at it, the better your grades and the less your aggravation."
>
> Junior, University of Colorado[1]

this doesn't mean that he or she doesn't have your best interests at heart. If you feel you can trust and speak with your advisor frankly, you and your college career will have gained a valuable ally.

Try It!
1

Get to Know Your College Advisor

It is helpful to get a feel for who your advisor is, so schedule an appointment with him or her. Before you meet with your advisor, do some background research by looking at your college catalog. College catalogs usually provide information on the background of faculty and staff, listing their titles, where they went to college and graduate school, what departments they teach in, and what their areas of academic interest are. In addition, you can search the Web; some instructors have their own home pages that describe their background.

To learn more about your advisor, cover some of these topics when you meet:

Philosophy of college advising:

Words of advice:

Things to try at the college:

Things to avoid at the college:

After you have met with your advisor, consider the following questions: Do you have a better sense of your advisor as an individual? What things did you learn that can help you? How can you use your advisor's responses to take better advantage of what your college has to offer?

To Try It online, go to **www.mhhe.com/power**.

No matter how helpful your advisor is (or unsupportive, for that matter), remember that ultimately *you* are responsible for your academic career. Advisors provide guidance, but you need to take charge of your own college experience.

Organize: Examining What You Have Done and What You Need to Do

Where Are You?   If you've prepared well, you have a basic understanding of how the courses you are taking now or have already taken fulfill your college requirements. To figure out what you still need to do, you should organize a complete list of the requirements you need to fulfill to graduate. Try It 2, "Create a List of Course Requirements," provides a form that you can complete if your college doesn't provide one for you. Even if you have yet to decide on a major, you might now be taking courses to satisfy requirements for a major you are considering. Noting this on your list will help you plan.

If this is just the start of your college career, you'll probably have completed only a few of the requirements. Don't let the blank spaces on the form overwhelm you; the credits have a way of adding up quickly.

If you are further along in your college career and have trouble remembering what courses you've taken, get a copy of your transcript from the registrar. The **registrar** is the official designated to oversee the scheduling of courses, the maintenance of transcripts, and the creation and retention of other official documents. (A **transcript** is the official record of the courses you've taken and the grades you received in them.)

As you're recording the courses you've taken, remember that meeting graduation requirements may not be the same as meeting your major's requirements. For instance, some schools not only require that you take and pass certain courses, but sometimes you also have to achieve a certain minimum grade in your courses as a whole. Or you may have to get a grade of C or better in a course for it to be counted toward your major. In this case, if you received a C– in the course, you'd still get credit toward graduation, but the course wouldn't count toward the number of credits you need in your major.

Confusing? You bet. That's why it's important to keep track of where you stand from the very start of your college career. (It's a good idea to keep all relevant information together on your computer, in a file folder, or even in a shoebox.) There's no worse surprise than finding out a month before you thought you'd be graduating that you lack some critical requirement. Don't count on others to keep track of this information for you. No one knows more about what you've done than you do.

Where Are You Going?   You should also use the information you have recorded to help determine which courses you should take in the upcoming term. Once you have declared a major, you can add those requirements to your record.

Now that you know where you are and where you are going, you are ready to start selecting courses to take you there.

Work: Choosing the Next Term's Courses

The course listings for the next term are published in a *course schedule.* It is organized by department, with each course in the department having a number,

Registrar
The college official designated to oversee the scheduling of courses, the maintenance of grades and transcripts, and the creation and retention of other official documents

Transcript
A college's official record of courses taken and grades received by students

Try It! 2

Create a List of Course Requirements

Use the form below to list all of your course requirements. The form covers both prerequisite courses (i.e., courses you must take before you can take other courses) and requirements imposed by your college, the division of which your department is a part, and your department. In addition, the form allows you to indicate both credit requirements and grade requirements.

List of Course Requirements					Whose Requirement?		
Type of Course	Credits Required	Credits Completed	Grade Required	Grade Achieved	College	Division	Department
I. Prerequisite Courses							
Total Prerequisite Courses							
II. Required Courses							
Total Required Courses							

What does the information in the chart tell you? How can you use it to plan your future course selections? What courses do you wish to take that are not requirements? How much leeway do you have to take nonrequired courses?

To Try It online, go to **www.mhhe.com/power**.

such as "History 204: The French Revolution." Generally, the higher the number, the more advanced the course. The course catalog will tell you when and where the class meets and whether there are any prerequisites for the course.

Go with What You Know   Chances are, you already know of at least one or two courses you need to take in a given term. Perhaps this is the term you plan to fulfill your natural science or your foreign language requirement. There may be some courses you have been waiting to take, since some courses are only taught once a year. A good place to begin is to find out when these courses are given and where.

Draft a Personal Schedule for the Term   First, write down when the courses you absolutely have to take are scheduled. If, as is the case for many introductory courses in large colleges, you have a choice of times, choose one you prefer. In choosing times, take into consideration whether you are a "morning person," at your best first thing in the morning, or whether you usually drag yourself out of bed in the morning and don't fully function until 11:00 A.M. This will be the beginning of your time management for the upcoming term.

Next, choose **electives**—courses that are not required. Keep in mind broad considerations about the kinds of courses you need to take for your major and for graduation. But also explore courses that simply sound interesting to you. College offers the opportunity to discover who you are and what you like and do best, but the only way that can happen is by taking intellectual risks.

To get started in deciding which courses to take for the upcoming term, complete Try It 3, "Choose Your Courses."

Electives
Courses that are not required
_____

Register for Courses   The rest of the work of choosing courses consists of **registering,** or completing the college's paperwork to become formally enrolled in your chosen classes.

Meeting with your advisor is an essential step. Sometimes, in fact, it's mandatory, and you won't be allowed to register without your advisor's signature. But even if it's not required, it's a good idea to go over your proposed course of studies. You may have overlooked something, or your advisor may be able to suggest some alternative courses that will work better for you.

Remember, though, that the ultimate responsibility for taking the right courses rests with you. Advisors sometimes make mistakes and overlook a requirement; ultimately, you know best what's right for you.

After meeting with your advisor, your next step will be to register. Course registration varies significantly from one school to another. In some cases, it's a matter of listing course numbers on a form, along with some alternatives.

In some schools, you will be expected to register for your courses over the telephone or through the World Wide Web. If your college uses a telephone registration system, you will probably be given a specific time period in which to call. When you do call, you'll receive voice prompts to enter your course choices using your telephone's touch-tone key pad (see Figure 9.1 on page 233).

If your college uses the newest form of registration, the World Wide Web, you will be prompted to enter course information on a Web form, and your registration will be accomplished completely online.

Register
To enroll formally in courses
_____

Try It!
3

Choose Your Courses

Use the form below to make your course selections for the coming term. The form will allow you to verify that you are meeting course requirements, avoiding schedule conflicts, and signing up for instructors you want.

Course Selections

Term: _____

Course Name and Number	Credits	Required Course or Just for Fun?	Prereq-uisites Met?	Meeting Grade Required	Days and Time	Schedule Conflicts	Instructor	Instructor OK?

After completing the chart, answer these questions: How does the next semester seem to be shaping up? Will you be able to take courses you *want* to take, as opposed to those you *need* to take? Have you made any choices that open you to new intellectual possibilities?

To Try It online, go to **www.mhhe.com/power**.

Evaluate: Deciding Whether You Are in the Classes You Need

Picture this horror story:

You receive your grade report from the previous term. You're excited because you know you've done well. You're especially looking forward to seeing your Spanish grade because you know you were on the borderline between an A– and a B+. Instead you're astounded to see that there is no grade listed for the Spanish class, but you've received an F in a French class that you didn't even take. That F pulls down your grade point average, and at the bottom of your grade report is an announcement that you are on academic probation.

Here's the explanation: Because of an error during registration, you were never formally enrolled in the Spanish course, even though you actually spent the entire term attending classes in the course. To compound the mistake, your instructor never noticed that you weren't on her class roster. At the end of the term, when she was filling out her

Figure 9.1

Telephone Course Registration Worksheet

Before you begin your telephone call, fill in this entire worksheet, listing all courses you wish to add, drop, or change including laboratory and discussion sections, and the appropriate "action codes" you will enter. Be sure to fill in all boxed areas properly and to enter '##' at the end of your call.

1. Call the system at (555) 444-3214 (From On-Campus, call 4-3214)

2. Enter your student ID number [1][2][6] - [0][4] - [9][8][1][1]

3. Enter your branch code [1] (Undergraduate = 1, Graduate = 2)

4. Enter your personal ID number (PIN) [6][7][7][5]

5. If the Schedule Confirmation you receive in the mail instructs you to get from your advisor a Registration Approval Code before add/drop, enter that code [ ][ ][ ][ ]

6. For each add, drop, or change you want to make, enter the appropriate action code from the list below and the schedule number for the course you want affected by that action.

Action Code*	Schedule Number of Course Requested	Dept	Course #	Section #	Crd	Day/Time
[1][0]	[7][8][2][8][4][0]	Psych	102	1	3	T-T 11:15-12:30
[1][0]	[6][7][2][9][9][7]	Engl	231	1	3	M-W-F 9:05-9:55
[1][0]	[2][6][0][4][6][3]	Phed	102	2	1	M 4:00-4:50
[1][0]	[1][2][0][3][0][9]	Latn	124	1	3	T-T 9:00-10:15
[1][0]	[8][8][0][1][8][1]	Hist	102	1	3	M-W-F 10:10-11:05
[1][0]	[7][2][4][9][6][2]	Phys	101	3	3	T-T 2:30-3:45
[ ][ ]	[ ][ ][ ][ ][ ][ ]					
[ ][ ]	[ ][ ][ ][ ][ ][ ]					
[ ][ ]	[ ][ ][ ][ ][ ][ ]					
[ ][ ]	[ ][ ][ ][ ][ ][ ]					

7. After entering your course requests, enter # # instead of an action code to terminate your call.

*Action Code	Action
10	ADD a course or Swap between sections of a course (To SWAP, simply add the new section; the old section will automatically be dropped from your schedule.)
30	ADD a course with Pass/Fail option or CHANGE existing course to Pass/Fail
90	DROP a course
80	REMOVE Pass/Fail or Audit option from existing course
50	CHANGE variable credit for an existing variable credit course
40	ADD a course with AUDIT grading option or CHANGE existing course to AUDIT grading
60	LIST your course schedule (press any key to end listing)
*	ERASE an entry error before completion

Note: Action Codes 30 and 80 are not available to graduate students. 40 is not available to undergraduates.

grade report, she didn't notice that your name wasn't listed. So no grade was reported for Spanish.

At the same time, the instructor of the French class in which you were erroneously enrolled had to give you a grade at the end of the semester. Because you never completed any assignments or took any tests, your average for the semester was 0—warranting an F for the term. That F is what appeared on your grade report.

The situation—which is far more likely to occur at a large university than a small college—might be seen as a comedy of errors if it weren't so painful. Fortunately, if this were actually your story, it would most likely have a happy ending— eventually. You would go to your college registrar, who would be able to tell you what to do to get the F erased and the appropriate grade added. Still, undoing the cascade of errors would take time and a considerable amount of effort.

Difficulties such as these are encountered by a surprising number of students every term. Many problems, however, can be avoided with a bit of "due diligence" on the part of the student. One key is to evaluate your success in registering.

Before the term starts, your school will provide you with a list of courses in which you are enrolled for the upcoming term. Immediately look it over. Use the following checklist to determine how successful your efforts to register have been:

- Are the courses to which you are assigned the ones you wanted?
- Are the times accurate? Are there any conflicts?
- Have any substitutions been made?
- Are you registered for the number of credits that you wanted to be registered for?

If there are any problems, try to correct the situation immediately. If there has been a clerical error, you should pay a visit to the registrar's office. Sometimes, though, you'll find that there was no mistake. Class sizes are almost always limited, and not every student who wants to enroll can do so, either because of physical limitations (the room can hold only a certain number of students) or because of educational considerations (learning may be maximized when only a small number of students are in the class).

When a course is overbooked, you have several alternatives. One is to sign up for another section of the course that is not overbooked. Another is to attempt to register for an entirely different course.

Finally, you may appeal directly to the course instructor. Instructors sometimes will permit particularly interested or motivated students to enroll in the class, even if the official capacity has been reached. You may find that approaching an instructor with a polite request may yield you a slot in the course after all.

If none of these alternatives works, you will have to add a course to the ones you have already registered for. How do you add courses after the registration period has ended? Typically, you'll need to complete a special form. Depending on the timing of your request, the form may require the signature of the instructor whose course you are adding.

Also keep in mind that if you drop a class during a term, you must do it officially, through the registrar. Simply ceasing to attend doesn't mean you'll be dropped from the class list. Instead, you'll probably end up with a failing grade in the course unless you complete the necessary paperwork to officially drop the course.

"Help—I Can't Get into the Courses That I Need to Graduate!" For some students, their efforts to register result in utter disaster. Sometimes most or all of their first choices are unavailable, and they end up enrolled in only a few of the courses they had requested. Or perhaps they cannot get into the one crucial course required for graduation.

Whatever the problem, there are several steps you can take to improve the situation:

- **Don't despair—act!** There is virtually no academic problem that can't be solved in some way. Focus your energies on finding a creative solution to the problem.

- **Identify classes that are still available and enroll in them.** There are probably many classes offered at your college that are still available. Registrars or departments often maintain lists of classes that have many openings.

- **Talk with your advisor.** Perhaps what you think of as an absolute requirement can be waived or appealed. Or maybe some other course can substitute for a particular required course.

- **Speak with individual course instructors.** It may be that the instructor of the course you need will make an exception and permit you to enroll; it can't hurt to ask.

- **Consider taking a must-have, re-quired course at another college.** If you live in an area where there are other schools in the vicinity, it may be possible to enroll in a course that you simply must take at another school. It also may be possible to take the course using distance learning. As we'll discuss further in Chapter 10, **distance learning** courses are taught at some other institution, and students participate via either video technology or the World Wide Web.

  Before you take a course offered by a college other than your own, make sure that you'll receive credit for the course at your school. Also keep in mind that you'll probably have to pay for courses offered by other schools over and above what you've already spent for your own school's tuition.

Distance learning
The teaching of courses at another institution, with student participation via video technology or the World Wide Web

R ethink: Learning What You Love and Liking What You Learn in College

Take one step back. No, make that two steps back.

Stepping back and taking stock of where you are in your course of studies and where you're headed are absolutely essential tasks. In fact, they are among the most important things you can do during your college career. They can spell the difference between plodding through your courses, focused only on day-to-day deadlines and tribulations, and, alternatively, gaining a sense of satisfaction as you progress toward your own goals and see yourself growing as a person.

Taking stock of your course of studies is not something you need to do every day, or once a week, or even once a month. But you should do it, without fail, at least once every term. Circle a date on your calendar so you'll be

Try It! 4

Reflect on Your College Experience

As you proceed in college, take a few moments at regular intervals (e.g., once a semester, once a year) to rethink your entire college experience. With a small group of classmates, discuss your reactions to the following topics and questions:

Course Work

- Are my courses moving me toward my educational, career, and personal goals?
- Are the classes I'm taking helping me to meet my short- and long-term goals?
- Are the classes I'm taking meeting my expectations?

Personal Commitment

- Am I working hard to get the most out of the classes I'm taking?
- Am I doing my best in every class?
- Am I keeping the goal of learning—apart from doing well in classes—in mind as I progress through my classes?

Personal Growth

- What personal growth am I experiencing?
- Am I becoming closer to the person I want to be?
- Are my critical thinking abilities growing?

College

- Is my school providing me with the best educational experience possible?
- Am I learning not only in the classroom but outside the classroom?
- Am I learning from my fellow students as well as my instructors?

Changes

- Is there anything (my course selections, my major, or my college) that I should consider changing?
- Have I made the best choices in the past? How can I remedy mistakes that I have made?

To Try It online, go to **www.mhhe.com/power**.

sure to do it, and treat it no differently than any other deadline you simply can't miss.

When you do take stock, answer the questions in Try It 4. If you're satisfied with your answers, feel affirmed in the choices you've made. You're on the right track, and you should feel secure in the knowledge that you're getting from college what you want to.

On the other hand, if you're less than satisfied with the answers you come

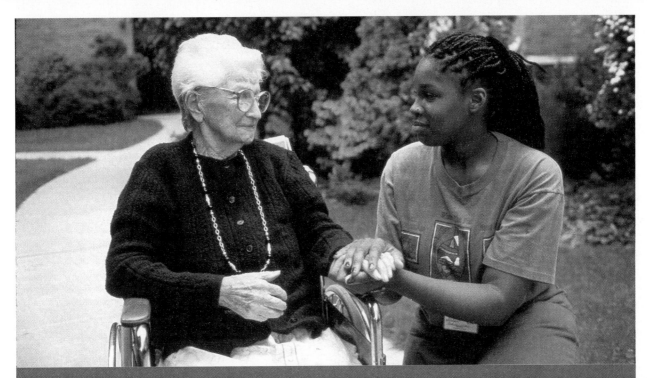

If you're having trouble choosing a major, one strategy is to consider the kinds of activities you most like doing outside the academic arena. For example, if you've enjoyed doing community service work as a volunteer, you might want to consider a major such as education, psychology, or social work.

up with, take action. Choose courses in the future that better match your goals. Consider changing your major to one that more closely reflects what you want to get out of college. And, if you're truly unhappy with the way your college career is proceeding, consider changing colleges.

Whichever course you choose, don't simply accept dissatisfaction with your college career. There are few times in our lives when we have the opportunity to partake of an experience that has the potential to raise us to new intellectual and emotional heights. College should be intellectually enlightening and exciting. We should be able to see how our education is preparing us for the rest of our lives. The worst thing we can do is let the time slip away without being confident that our college experience is the best experience possible.

Taking stock of your choice of courses and academic career also helps you with another important choice you will have to make (if you haven't already): choosing your major.

Choosing a Major

You attend a family gathering and encounter relatives you haven't seen for a while. What's the first question they ask when you say you're attending college? You can bet on it: "What's your major?"

Although one could argue that there are lots of other important questions that you could be asked—"What interesting things have you learned?" comes

Try It! 5

Personal Styles: Identify Major Attractions

To complete this assessment, check off each of the characteristics that applies to you. Then use the pattern of results to determine how closely your interests and personality style match with the characteristics of others who are already in a particular field of study.

Characteristic	Is This Me?	Possible Field of Study
• High interest in creative expression. • Appreciation of nonverbal communication. • Understanding of aesthetics. • Commitment to perfection. • Ability to manipulate form and shape.	_____ _____ _____ _____ _____	Arts (e.g., dance, drama, music, art, creative writing)
• Interest in organization and order. • Ability to lead and manage people. • Interest in practical problem solving. • Ambition and interest in financial incentives. • Can-do attitude. • Ability to simplify complexity.	_____ _____ _____ _____ _____ _____	Business
• Intense interest in solving real problems. • "Tinkerer" mentality a plus. • Extreme ability to focus on minute details. • Commitment to exactness and perfection. • Strong logical ability. • Ability to work alone for long stretches.	_____ _____ _____ _____ _____ _____	Engineering sciences (e.g., engineering, computer science)
• Interest in people. • Desire to solve real human problems. • Commitment to people more than money. • Tolerance of "messy" situations with multiple, partial solutions. • Insight and creativity. • Ability to work with people.	_____ _____ _____ _____ _____ _____	Helping professions (e.g., nursing, counseling, teaching, many areas of medicine)
• Interest in human emotions and motivations. • Interest in cultural phenomena. • Ability to integrate broad areas of study and inquiry. • Good skills of human observation. • Interest in the panorama of human life.	_____ _____ _____ _____ _____	Humanities (e.g., English literature, history, theater, film)

to mind—having a major focus of study is an important part of college. A major is important because it focuses what we study, leading us to become experts in a specific area.

Some students know what they want to major in when they begin college; some don't have a clue. That's fine. No one says you should know right away.

In fact, using your first year in college to explore a range of possibilities is

Characteristic	Is This Me?	Possible Field of Study
• Interest in words, word origins, and speech. • View of language as a science. • View of literature as human expression. • Appreciation of cultural differences as scientific phenomena.	_____ _____ _____ _____	Languages and linguistics
• Interest in physical performance. • Enjoyment of sports and athletics. • Commitment to helping others appreciate physicality. • Patience and perseverance. • Commitment to perfection through practice.	_____ _____ _____ _____ _____	Physical education
• Enjoyment of research questions; high level of curiosity about natural phenomena. • Quantitative thinking a requirement; high comfort level with mathematics and statistics. • Minute problem-solving skills; attention at great level of detail. • Strong logical ability. • Ability to work with others.	_____ _____ _____ _____ _____	Physical, biological, and natural sciences (e.g., physics, astronomy, chemistry, biology, some areas of medicine)
• Interest in people as individuals or groups. • Ability to think quantitatively and qualitatively. • High comfort level with mathematics and statistics. • High level of creativity and curiosity. • Ability to work with others. • Interest in theory as much as problem solving.	_____ _____ _____ _____ _____ _____	Social sciences (e.g., psychology, communication, sociology, education, political science, economics)
• Interest in the inner life. • Interest in highly theoretical questions. • Ability to think rigorously about abstract matters. • Appreciation of the human search for meaning.	_____ _____ _____ _____	Spiritual and philosophical studies

Use the results to focus on the kinds of courses and educational experiences that are involved in potential fields of study. Examining your responses may lead you toward some unexplored territory.

After you complete the chart, consider how you can use the information. Did you learn anything new about yourself or about various courses of study? Do your responses direct you toward a particular major? Do they direct you away from any major?

To Try It online, go to **www.mhhe.com/power**.

a very good idea. You might find after taking a civics course that you have a passion for legal studies. Or a physics class may lead you to consider a major in engineering. College is meant to be a time of exploration, and leaving yourself open to the future—and the unknown—is a completely reasonable thing to do. (To begin your own exploration of majors, complete Try It 5, "Identify Major Attractions.")

But what if you don't have any idea which major you wish to pursue? If you are still in your first year of college, you have plenty of time to make up your mind. But here are some approaches that should help. You may also want to look ahead to the discussion of decision making in Chapter 11 as the time to declare a major (usually by the end of your sophomore or the beginning of your junior year) draws nearer.

> "I sat back thinking that the right major would just pop into my head. It didn't."
>
> Senior, University of Connecticut[2]

1. **Celebrate your indecision.** If you don't have to make a decision for some time, take advantage of the situation. Enjoy the fact that you're uncommitted and that you have an uncommon degree of freedom.

> "He who hesitates is sometimes saved."
>
> Author James Thurber

2. **Focus on your interests.** Take a long look inward, paying attention to what your interests are. What do you most like to do in life? What are your strengths and weaknesses? What do you want to get out of life? The more you know about yourself, the easier it will become to narrow down the choices for a major. Completing the Journal Reflections, "Focus on Your Interests," is a good place to start.

3. **Seek the help of others.** College campuses provide many resources to help their students choose a major (and also to help narrow the choices for potential careers). Talk to other students majoring in areas that interest you. Find out what they like and don't like about the field and its requirements. You will probably find your interest in the major grows or diminishes depending on how you feel about the issues they mention.

Double-major
A course of study that fulfills all the requirements for two majors

Unique major
A course of study that is geared to your own needs

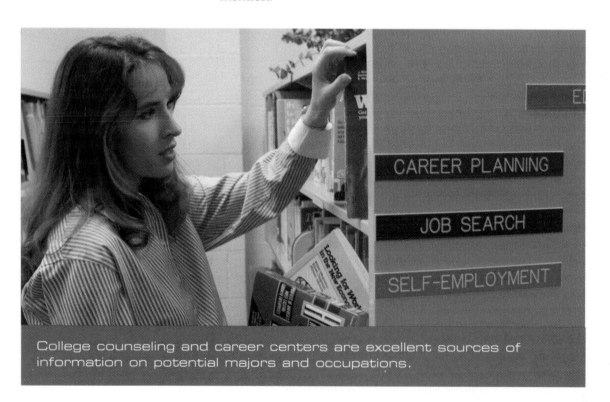

College counseling and career centers are excellent sources of information on potential majors and occupations.

Speak with your advisor. If you've gotten to know your advisor, he or she can often provide reasonable, helpful information. For instance, you may be able to find out about the strengths and weaknesses of various departments.

You can also turn to your college counseling or career center. Most colleges have offices that can provide information about the different majors, including information about career opportunities typically available to graduates with the various majors. Sometimes it's possible to take tests that will help focus your choices, pinpointing how your interests, values, and personality type fit with particular careers.

4. **Consider double-majoring—or inventing your own major.** Although it's not easy, there are paths you can take if you know clearly what you want to do, but find it doesn't fit a single existing major.

A **double major** is a course of study that fulfills all the requirements for each of two majors. If you can't decide between two majors, or if you are interested in a career that overlaps two majors, this is a reasonable solution. The downside: It can be an awful lot of work. Because both majors usually carry a number of their own requirements, you may have very little freedom to pick courses other than those directly relating to one of the two majors.

Another option that some, although not all, colleges permit is the creation of a **unique major** geared to your own needs. Again, this is not an easy road to take because you must put together a cohesive set of courses that centers upon a discipline not normally offered through a major. Furthermore, you must also get the support of a faculty member or a committee of faculty members to oversee the process.

Journal Reflections

Focus on Your Interests

The following questions are intended to lead you to explore areas of personal preference and interest that should inform your choice of a major. These questions are informal and designed to be answered briefly; more-extended and formal "interest inventories" are available in your college's counseling office.

1. Do you think you would enjoy being told exactly what to do and how to do it, or would you rather work things out by yourself, without extensive instructions or supervision? What implications might your answer have for a choice of majors?

2. Are you ambitious and success-oriented and not ashamed to admit that you'd like to earn a lot of money, or are success and money of secondary importance to you? What implications might your answer have for a choice of majors?

3. Are you the artistic type and do you enjoy performing, creating, and viewing/listening to artistic works, or is art of relatively little interest to you? What implications might your answer have for a choice of majors?

4. Do you enjoy working with others, or do you prefer to work on your own? What implications might your answer have for a choice of majors?

Career Connections

Choosing a Job That's Right for You

It's a question no parent can resist asking, and one that you've probably asked yourself: What kind of work are you going to do when you graduate?

Happily, it's a question you don't have to answer, at least not yet. Many students—perhaps most—don't decide which career they want until late in their academic career. After all, one of the reasons you are in college is to expose yourself to the universe of knowledge. In one sense, keeping your options open is a wise course. You don't want to prematurely narrow your options and discard possibilities too early.

In the Career Connections boxes in previous chapters, we've discussed various strategies for exploring future professions. Here, in summary, are some steps to take to identify a career:

1. **Clarify the goal of your search.** There's no single perfect career choice. Some people search for the ideal career, assuming that they need to identify the one, and only one, career for which they have been destined. The reality is, though, that there are many careers that they could choose that would make them equally happy and satisfied.

   Start with what you already know about yourself. You've already done a lot of mental work toward narrowing down a profession. Do you hate the sight of blood? Then you're probably well aware you're not cut out to be a surgeon or a veterinarian. Does the sight of a column of numbers bring an immediate yawn? Count out accounting and statistics.

Awareness of your likes and dislikes already puts you on the road to identifying a future career. Knowing what you don't want to do helps identify what you do want to do and to narrow down the kinds of occupations for which you're more suited.

2. **Gather information.** The more you know about potential careers, the better. Examine career-planning materials, read industry profiles, and visit relevant websites. Talk with career counselors. Discuss your options with people who work in professions in which you're interested. Find out how they chose their career, how they got their current job, and what advice they have for you. In addition, consider participating in an internship in a profession that you think might be attractive. As an intern, you'll gain firsthand experience—possibly college credit as well—for the work that you do.

3. **Narrow down your choices.** Once you've gathered enough information to give yourself a reasonable comfort level, narrow down the choices. If it's early in your college career, you don't need to make up your mind. If it's late and you feel the pressure to choose, then make the decision. Just do it. Remember, there's no single, absolutely correct decision; there are many right decisions.

   Whatever it is you ultimately choose as a career, think of it only as a first step. As the average life span continues to lengthen due to advances in medical technology, most people will pass through several careers during the course of their life. By periodically taking stock of where you are and considering your goals, you'll be in a position to make career changes that bring you closer to your ideal.

If double-majoring or inventing a major seems too daunting, there's another option that may resolve the difficulty of choosing between two majors: majoring in one field and *minoring* in another. A **minor** is a secondary specialization in a discipline different from one's major. Typically students must take at least four courses in a discipline for their study to qualify as a minor.

"Actually, I'm hoping what I'm going to be when I grow up hasn't been invented yet."

5. **Be career-oriented, but not too career-oriented.** If you have a good idea about what career you wish to embark upon once you graduate, you can easily find out which skills are required to be successful in that field. Knowing what you'll need to gain entry into a field can help you determine a good major that will set you on the road toward your desired profession.

Don't narrow your options too much, however. Students sometimes fear signing up for classes that don't seem to lead directly toward a career. Or they may avoid courses that seem to point them in the direction of a career that would be "unacceptable" to their parents or friends. One of the greatest sources of indecision in choosing a major stems from the mistaken notion that when you choose your major, you're also choosing a career.

Don't fall into that trap. Follow your heart—not always your head—and pursue courses without regard to how they may broaden or narrow your future job opportunities. You may discover a passion—and an aptitude—that you never knew you had.

Minor

A secondary specialization in a discipline different from one's major

6. **Always keep in mind that education is a lifelong enterprise.** Educational opportunities will continue to present themselves not just through the undergraduate years, but for the rest of your life.

Consequently, no matter what your choice of major, you're not precluding the

> "Far and away the best prize that life offers is the chance to work hard at work worth doing."
>
> President Theodore Roosevelt

possibility of taking courses in other areas in the future. You may eventually end up in a graduate school pursuing a masters degree, a doctorate, or an MD. You also may take courses periodically at local colleges even after you graduate, enrolling in them because they will help you advance in your career or simply because they interest you.

In short, choosing a major is not a decision that places your life on a set, unchangeable course. Instead, it's one step in what can be a lifetime of learning.

Speaking of Success

Name: *Catalina Angeles*
Education: *BA, California State University at San Marcos*
Home: *San Marcos, California*

Catalina Angeles has accomplished many things since she came to the United States 13 years ago from Michoacan, Mexico. But the most important has been achieving a college education.

"My parents brought us to the United States to get an education," she said. "It was difficult, but we've been able to do it," she said.

Overcoming a language barrier and raising a child were two major obstacles that confronted Catalina. But a combination of self-discipline and careful planning helped her to finish her degree in 4 years, becoming the first person in her family to graduate from college.

"I definitely have self-discipline," Angeles noted. "I believe that was one of the things that held me together. I had to set goals and plan everything carefully.

"In high school I never thought I would forget things, but when you need to do a thousand different things you do forget. That's why you need to have things written down," she said, and this is why she believes

Cal State San Marcos

so strongly in setting goals and arranging what needs to be done.

But sometimes things would not go according to plan.

"I had to be very flexible," she said. "When you plan things, they don't always work out. When I would set up my schedule I knew that some things wouldn't take as long as

others, so if I didn't finish something I could take the time from elsewhere."

Weekends were devoted to her family, with the rest of the week slated for school requirements, according to Angeles. Despite her goal-setting and careful time management, however, overcoming the language barrier required her to put more time and effort into her studies than other students, according to Angeles.

"I had to study extra hard because I didn't know the meaning of many words and was constantly using a dictionary," she said. "My first semester was difficult. However, I took a basic composition course that involved a lot of reading and writing, and I took full advantage from tutors at the writing lab. That helped me enormously."

Accepting Responsibility for Your Academic Performance

You received the highest grade in your class . . . you received an A on a paper . . . your instructor tells you your class participation was the best in the course.

Take pride in your success, and reflect on what you did to achieve it. If you're doing well academically, it's not an accident. It's because you've worked hard and put your intellectual capacities to full use.

On the other hand, each of us has moments of academic disappointment. When you get a poor grade in a course, it hurts. But even if you feel tempted to shrug it off publicly, don't make that mistake privately. It's just as important to take responsibility for and reflect on your academic disappointments as it is to accept your successes.

There is, of course, a great difference between reflecting on what has happened and blaming ourselves. When things go wrong, it's reasonable to reflect to understand what went wrong. It is *not* useful, however, to spend time and energy blaming ourselves.

Learn from your mistakes. Consider why something went wrong, analyze what you could have done—or avoided doing—to prevent it, and seek ways of preventing a similar outcome in the future.

Remember, success occurs because we want it to and because we've worked hard to make it happen. It can happen every day if we allow it. And success is not just reaching an end-point, such as when we're handed our diploma. Success is a process. Any achievement that brings us closer to fulfilling our goals and dreams is a success.

Looking Back

How can I prepare for the academic choices that college demands?

- Making course choices involves finding out as much as possible about what your college has to offer. The college catalog is the best initial source of this information.

- An important source of information and personal guidance in college is your college advisor, who has training and experience in advising students on courses, instructors, requirements, and regulations.

What is the best way to choose courses and ensure I'm getting the most out of my studies?

- In choosing courses, check out your selections with your academic advisor and then register for the courses. You should be prepared to choose different courses or course sections if your initial selections are unavailable.

- Verify that you have received your chosen courses, that the schedule of courses makes sense, and that your course schedule will help provide the number of credits needed to graduate.

- Be prepared to deal with errors during registration or to cope with the unavailability of courses that you need to take.

- Reflect on your college experience regularly, verifying that course choices, academic performance, personal growth, choice of major, and your overall educational experience are satisfactory.

How can I choose a major?

- Choosing a major first involves accepting a period of indecision, finding out more about yourself, seeking the help and advice of others, considering going beyond the traditional structure of your college major, trying out unusual courses, and taking career plans into account.

Key Terms and Concepts

College advisor (p. 226)   Minor (p. 243)
Distance learning (p. 235)   Prerequisites (p. 226)
Double-major (p. 241)   Register (p. 231)
Electives (p. 231)   Registrar (p. 229)
Grade point average (GPA) (p. 225) Transcript (p. 229)
Major (p. 226)   Unique major (p. 241)

Resources

On Campus

The obvious choice for information about courses is your advisor. Sometimes your advisor will be associated with a general program, such as liberal arts; sometimes with a particular department, such as English or Sociology; or sometimes with a collegewide academic advising center. Your course instructors also can often give good advice about what future courses to sign up for. Finally, don't forget about your fellow students; they can be an excellent source of information about the most interesting and exciting courses.

If you'd like advice about future careers, visit your college career center. Not only will they have pamphlets and books on different jobs, but they also can often provide tests that can help you see how your personal strengths fit with potential majors and careers.

In Print

Paul Phifer's *College Majors and Careers: A Resource Guide for Effective Life Planning* (Ferguson, 2000) provides a good overview of college majors, as does Richard Blumenthal and Josepha Despres's *Major Decisions: A Guide to College Majors* (Wintergreen, 1996). Probably the most popular guide to careers is *What Color Is Your Parachute?* (Ten Speed Press, 2001). In it you'll find ways to make decisions about choosing (and changing) professions, as well as ways to obtain a job.

On the Web

Many sites on the World Wide Web provide the opportunity to extend your learning about the material in this chapter including the following. (Although the Web addresses were accurate at the time the book was printed, check the P.O.W.E.R. Learning website [**www.mhhe.com/power**] for any changes that may have occurred.)

- "Selecting College Courses" (**www.es.wayne.edu/uac/hndbk/courses.html**), a guide offered by the Advising Center at Wayne State University, provides a solid list of questions to ask yourself when choosing your courses.

- Wesleyan University offers "A Guide to Choosing a Major" (**www.wesleyan.edu/deans/sophmajor.html**) online. Though some of the information is tailored specifically to Wesleyan, many of the ideas are helpful for students at any college or university. Even if you've already decided on a major, this site can help you to examine and reevaluate your academic priorities.

- The University of Waterloo online Career Development Manual at **www.adm.uwaterloo.ca/infocecs/CRC/manual-home.html** includes self-assessments that will help you start thinking about career issues.

Taking It to the Net

1 Colleges usually have a set of core courses that each student must take to fulfill the liberal arts education requirement. Visit a college website (*not* your own) and see if you can determine the core requirements for that school. How many science courses are required? How many math courses? Are any other types of courses required?

2 Use different search engines to help locate information about selecting classes or majors. Go to Excite (**www.excite.com**), Yahoo! (**www.yahoo.com**), and AltaVista (**www.altavista.com**) and type in the phrase "choosing college classes." Look over the first few pages in each search. Did they offer any helpful information on choosing classes or majors? Are there any common tips that are offered by most or all of the sites?

The Case of . . .

Major Problems

As Chen Lee began his junior year, he still was unsure which major to choose. He had come to college as an "undeclared major" and that was still his official designation—although he thought "clueless major" would be a more accurate label.

Chen had thought seriously about several possibilities, including communications and marketing, but none seemed to offer just what he was looking for. Part of the trouble was, of course, that he really didn't know what he was looking for. In fact, he was a lot clearer about what he didn't want to major in than what he did want to major in.

The clock was ticking away, and he felt lost. His parents offered many suggestions, but that just seemed to increase the pressure. And now he was getting warnings from the school that he had to make a decision.

1. What seems to be Chen's main problem in coming to grips with the choice of a major?

2. How can Chen's prior consideration of majors such as communications and marketing help him move closer to a decision?

3. How would you advise Chen to make use of his understanding of what he doesn't want to major in?

4. How can Chen find out more about himself? Why is this important in choosing a major?

5. Do you think Chen is taking this decision too seriously or not seriously enough? What advice would you give him about the importance of the choice of a major?

Making the Most of Technology

10

Information

rian Sullivan had never really gotten into computers. Unlike most of his friends, he didn't even use e-mail much, preferring to keep in touch by phone.

So when his psychology instructor announced on the first day of class that her course required extensive use of the Internet, Brian was not very enthusiastic. He was even less enthusiastic when the instructor said the class was going to be paperless. Assignments would be provided on the class website, and papers had to be "handed in" electronically.

For the first month, Brian had a hard time seeing the point to the system. Then, in the middle of the term, his best friend from high school was in a serious car accident. Brian rushed home to see him; his friend was in pretty bad shape. Brian wanted to stick around for a while, but he worried that if he did, he would fall behind in his classes.

Then he found out that the hospital offered visitors Internet access. Though he was hundreds of miles away, Brian could get his psychology and other assignments and e-mail his responses back to the instructors.

The Internet probably saved his academic career that semester.

Looking Ahead

The technology that permitted Brian to keep up with his classes didn't even exist a dozen years ago. Education is changing, as it takes increasing advantage of "virtual" resources—e-mail, the Internet, and other evolving technologies. In fact, at some point, you might be taking a course entirely on the Web, never setting foot in the same room as your instructor or your classmates.

Technology is making a profound difference in how we are taught, the ways we study and carry out our work, and how we communicate with our professors and other students. It is changing the way you can access the vast quantities of information published each year—tens of thousands of books, journals, and other print materials, and literally millions of Web pages.

In this chapter we discuss how technological advances increase your opportunities to achieve success in college. We'll consider the basics of computers and the ways in which they can be used to manipulate data and present it. We'll also talk about distance learning, an approach to education that involves studying with an instructor who may be thousands of miles away. Finally, we'll consider how you can use technology for information management—locating and using both the information traditionally held in libraries *and* information created for and in the virtual world of cyberspace.

In short, after reading this chapter, you'll be able to answer these questions:

- **What are the basic components of computers?**
- **What is available on the Internet?**
- **What is distance learning?**
- **What are the basic sources of information?**
- **What do I need to keep in mind as I use the Web to gather information?**

You and Computers

They are an amazing time-saver. They're a great tool that can help you achieve success in your classes. They're the remarkable equivalent of a typewriter, archive, printing press, calculator, and proofreader, all rolled into one.

They can also, at times, be extremely frustrating, annoying, and maddening.

"They," of course, are computers. And you'll need to be able to use them to maximize your success in college. These days it's as much a necessity to learn to use a computer as it was for you to learn to use a calculator earlier in your schooling. No one facing the job market in the 21st century will want to leave college without basic computer skills.

If you are not yet at ease with computers, relax. No one is born with computer skills. With sufficient practice, however, using a computer will become second nature.

(To explore your feelings about computers, complete the *Journal Reflections*.)

Computer Basics

At its most basic, a computer is just an overgrown calculator. It has a bigger display, a lot more keys, and its capacity is millions of times larger than that of a calculator, but at heart it's simply another way of inputting, manipulating, and outputting information. Computers are a lot smarter than calculators due to the complexity of the hardware and software of which they are made up.

- **Hardware** is the physical part of a computer—the metal, glass, plastic, and other substances that can be touched and seen. The most obvious pieces of hardware are the *display*, which is the screen that shows what you are working on; the *keyboard* and *mouse*, which allow you to input information and navigate around the screen; and the *computer unit*, typically housed in a case that sits on your desk or the floor.

Journal Reflections

How I Feel about Computers

1. If you had to characterize your general reactions when you hear the words "computer" and "the Internet," what would you say?

2. Do you use e-mail? Do you use the Internet much? Do you use a computer for other things? If so, what have your experiences been like?

3. How satisfied do you feel with your level of *expertise* in using computers/the Internet? Do you intend to take any steps to increase it?

4. How do you feel about people who are expert in using computers? Do you ever use the term "computer geek" to describe them? If so, what do you mean by it? What do you think others mean by it?

5. Do you think it is harder for older adults to learn about computers? Why or why not?

Hardware
The physical part of a computer, the metal, glass, plastic, and other substances that can be touched and seen such as the display, keyboard, and mouse

- **Software** tells the computer what operations it needs to carry out. Several different kinds of software are used to run computers. The *operating system* provides the ground rules by which a computer operates. The most popular operating systems are *Windows* (Microsoft), *Macintosh* (Apple), and *Linux,* a free system.

    Application programs make computers perform specific kinds of functions: word-processing software that produces nice-looking documents, games like *Myst,* and programs that calculate your income tax are just a few of the huge number of common applications. As we'll discuss next, the three main types of application that you'll use for your classes are word-processing programs, presentation programs, and spreadsheets.

Word-Processing Programs:
Spreading the Word

A **word-processing program** turns a computer into a smart typewriter—a very smart typewriter. With a word-processing program, everything you write can be stored in a computer's memory, and you can check the spelling of the words you type, automatically keep track of your footnotes, and "cut and paste" material with incredible ease. Most important, word processors take much of the drudgery out of revision. You can quickly delete words and sentences that you don't want, substitute new material in place of what you deleted, and rearrange words, sentences, and entire paragraphs.

Some of the most important things you can do with a word-processing program include:

- *Inserting and deleting text.* After you have created a document, you can easily add material—simply move the cursor to the appropriate spot and type. It's equally easy to delete text, even large blocks of it, simply by selecting (highlighting) the text and hitting "delete."

- *Moving and copying text.* Want to change the order of two paragraphs? It can be done simply by highlighting one of the paragraphs and dragging it with the mouse. Alternately, you can use a cut-and-paste function, highlighting the paragraph, "cutting" it so that it's temporarily stored on a virtual "clipboard," and then "pasting" the paragraph into the appropriate spot.

- *Changing the appearance of text.* You can easily type **bold,** *italic,* or <u>underlined</u> text, as well as change the style and size of the type (known as the *font*) to any look you prefer. Common fonts include Helvetica, Century Expanded, Optima, Times New Roman, and *Handwriting,* and each comes in different sizes, measured in *points.* For instance, type can be 16-point, 12-point, or 10-point.

    Obviously, before you use an exotic-looking or extra-large or extra-small font size for a paper, consider your instructor's requirements. (And don't expect font size to rescue a paper that's too short: instructors are likely to notice if you use an oversized font to extend the page count of a paper!) Probably the most common font—primarily because it is so easy to read—is Times New Roman at 12-point.

(Express yourself typographically in Try It 1.)

ry It!

1

Express Yourself

Type the following sentences on a computer. Use word-processing software to make the appearance of each sentence match the message it conveys (i.e., by using different fonts, different sizes, punctuation marks, symbols, etc.).

Do unto others as you would have them do unto you.

If you can read this, you're too close.

Step right up and see the Amazing Shrinking Man.

That's one small step for a man, one giant leap for mankind.

Keep off the grass. This means you.

Give me liberty or give me death.

Question authority.

Danger. Explosives.

Fourscore and seven years ago our fathers brought forth on this continent a new nation conceived in liberty and dedicated to the proposition that all men are created equal.

Don't worry. Be happy.

After you've completed this exercise, share your results with others in your class or with your study group. Is there a particular approach that works most effectively?

To Try It online, go to **www.mhhe.com/power**.

- *Adding footnotes or endnotes.* Word processors are extremely helpful if you are writing a paper that requires footnotes (citations at the bottom of the page) or endnotes (citations listed on a single page at the end of a paper). You can insert a footnote or endnote anywhere in a document, and the program will automatically number it correctly—and renumber it if you add or delete a footnote before it.

- *Verifying the spelling of every word.* At the press of a button, a word-processing program will check the spelling of every word you have typed. If it finds a misspelling, it will alert you and provide alternatives with correct spellings. But spell-checking is not foolproof: all the program can do is check to see whether your spelling matches that of any word in its dictionary. For example, if you type "hear" when you meant "here," or "gong" when you mean "going," the word-processing program will not flag it.

- *Checking for basic grammatical errors.* If you wish, your word processor will check the grammar of passages in a document. It may be able to catch simple problems such as errors in subject-verb agreement (for instance, you may have mistakenly written "Recent studies has found" instead of "Recent studies have found"). As with spell checks, grammar checks don't work perfectly: They sometimes miss errors that exceed their grammatical "knowledge," and they will sometimes tell you that something is wrong when it isn't. Consequently, you *must* always carefully edit and proofread your work yourself.

- *Saving what you write.* As you use a word-processing program, the computer stores your document in a temporary memory. If you turn off the computer, however, or if the power goes off, or if the computer freezes up, the material you've worked on can disappear, possibly forever.

  That's why it's crucial to actively save your work. You can save a document to a computer's hard drive, a disk, or a network drive (if you have space on one). However you do it, *make sure you save material frequently and make back-up copies onto floppy disks.* Nothing is more frustrating than laboring over a document for hours and having it disappear into cyberspace.

Presentation Programs: Looking Good

Presentation programs
Computer application software that helps you create impressive, professional-looking visual materials that include words, charts, maps, and other graphical elements

Sometimes *how* you present material is as important as *what* you're presenting. **Presentation programs** such as PowerPoint help you put your best foot forward by allowing you to create impressive, professional-looking visual materials, including charts, maps, animations, and other graphical elements. The resulting output can be printed onto paper, made into overhead transparencies or slides, run as a "slide show" from your computer, or projected directly from your computer onto a screen through a projector.

There are several keys to developing an effective presentation:

- **Include graphics.** Most presentation programs have an array of graphics that can be added to a slide. A globe, a cap-and-gown, a shooting star, or other objects can add visual spice to your presentation.

PowerPoint slide background graphics add visual interest; large font and bullets direct attention to key statistics.

Microsoft PowerPoint - [Technology in the Classroom.ppt]

File Edit View Insert Format Tools Slide Show Window Help

Technology in the Classroom*

- Number of Post-Secondary Students Who Own PC's--5.3 Million
- Number of Students Attending Brick and Mortar Institutions--13 Million
- Number Taking On-Line Courses--1 Million
- Percentage of Students Who Obtain Class Assignments Electronically-- 40
- Percentage of Institutions Reporting Student Resistance--2; Faculty Resistance--55!

*Data from PBS's 1998 documentary net LEARNING (www.pbs.org/netlearning)

Slide 1 of 1   Azure

Presenting . . .

Type the following key points about using presentation programs into a presentation program, one per page (or "slide"). Use the features of the presentation program to make the points more striking. Work with others in your study group.

Key points:

      Include graphics

      Remember: less is more

      Standardize

      Avoid errors

      Use animation

How satisfied are you with your presentation? How easy was it to accomplish what you wanted to do? What other things might you have done in creating your presentation?

    To Try It online, go to **www.mhhe.com/power**.

- **Remember: Less is more.** Don't try to cram too much information on a particular slide. Avoid putting too many words on a line or using too many colors. Just because you *can* do all sorts of cool things with graphics doesn't mean that you *should*—at least not all at the same time.

- **Unify your presentation.** Individual slides or other presentation materials should have a similar look. Using similar fonts and font sizes unifies your presentation.

- **Check for spelling errors.** Most presentation programs have built-in spell checks. Use them! It's embarrassing to have a 1-foot-high spelling mistake projected onto a screen.

- **Use *animation* if you are using a projector that connects directly to a computer.** Animation allows you to add movement to your presentation. Graphics, sentences, words, or even letters can be made to slide in from the left or right of the screen, or appear (or disappear) as you choose.

To test out using a presentation program, complete Try It 2.

Spreadsheet Programs:
Crunching the Numbers

Whether you love or hate math, you're going to like spreadsheet programs, for they take the drudgery out of crunching numbers. **Spreadsheet programs** like Excel help you with budgeting and financial projections and are necessary for accounting and engineering courses. They allow you to perform calculations with complete accuracy.

    Spreadsheet programs contain files that are divided into *cells*, which is where you input information. Each cell has an "address" which pinpoints its

Spreadsheet programs
Application programs that help with budgeting and financial projections and are necessary for accounting and engineering courses

location by column (designated by a letter) and row (designated by a number). After you input data, you can instruct the program to perform an amazing array of calculations with a simple formula or command. For example, you can have the program add up a range of cells; subtract the value of one cell from a second cell; or find the square roots of the numbers in three cells and add the results together. Revisions are easy with spreadsheets. Change a number in any cell, and a revised result will be displayed.

Spreadsheet programs also offer easy ways of creating graphs. By entering the appropriate information, you can create a variety of graphs, ranging from bar graphs to pie charts.

Expense report generated by Excel spreadsheet software. Numerical calculations are embedded as formulas in the spreadsheet, simplifying the task of figuring totals.

Moving beyond Your Computer:
The Internet and the World Wide Web

Be prepared: If you haven't already become acquainted with the Internet, your first encounter with it may permanently alter the way in which you interact with others.

The **Internet** is a network connecting millions of computers together. Hooking up to this network permits a user to share information with virtually anyone else who has a computer. Internet resources available to users are vast; from your home desktop you can access information from institutions at the farthest-flung corners of the Earth. In fact, that's an understatement: Live images from as far away as the planet Mars have been transmitted to users via the Internet. Many experts believe the Internet will become the central storehouse for information in the 21st century

Because the Internet is constantly evolving, the best place to learn about it is on the Internet itself. Here are a few of the features that you are most likely to find useful:

- **E-mail.** The most widely used feature of the Internet is **e-mail,** short for "electronic mail." E-mail offers a way for people to send and receive

Internet
A vast network of interconnected computers that share information around the world

E-mail
Electronic mail, a system of communication that permits users to send and receive messages via the Internet

messages with incredible speed. On some college campuses, e-mail is the most common form of communication among students and faculty. (We'll discuss e-mail in detail later in the chapter.)

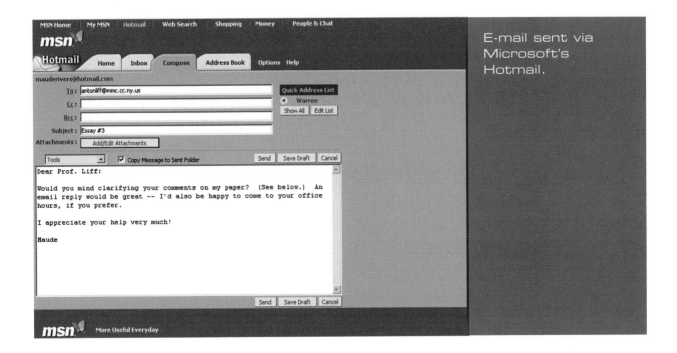

E-mail sent via Microsoft's Hotmail.

- **Newsgroups.** The Internet contains thousands of electronic **newsgroups,** where people can read and post messages relevant to a particular topic. For example, there are newsgroups devoted to the stock market, snowmobiles, *Ally McBeal,* the Boston Celtics, Ricky Martin, and Shakespeare's sonnets.

- **Listservs.** A **listserv** is a subscription service that automatically e-mails messages on general topics of shared interest to people who have added their names to its mailing list. Members can respond to messages by replying to the listserv, and their responses will be distributed automatically to everyone on the mailing list. (In most cases it's also possible to respond directly to an individual who posts a message of interest, without sending that response to all members of the listserv.) Among the thousands of listservs online are those relating to jazz, tourism, privacy issues, and libertarianism.

- **World Wide Web.** Want to know how to order flowers for your girlfriend in Dubuque? Find a long-lost friend? Hear the opening theme of Schubert's Unfinished Symphony? Read the latest health bulletin from the Centers for Disease Control?

    There is one way you can look for all this information—and stand a good chance of finding it: by using the World Wide Web. The **World Wide Web (WWW)** is a highly graphical means of locating and browsing through information on the Internet. Using the Web is rapidly becoming the standard way to find and use such information. The Web provides a way to transmit not just typewritten text but visual and auditory information—graphics, photos, music, soundbites, video clips, and much more.

Newsgroup
An electronic Internet area in which users may post and read messages relevant to a particular topic of the group's choosing

Listserv
A subscription service through which members can post and receive messages via e-mail on general topics of shared interest

World Wide Web
A highly graphical interface between users and the Internet that permits users to transmit and receive not only text, but pictorial, video, and audio information

Telnet

A dial-up communication system that permits users at remote locations to use computer databases and other resources housed on distant computers

• **Telnet. Telnet** is another means of getting access to the computers that make up the Internet. It is a character-based system, an ancestor of the more user-friendly, graphics-driven World Wide Web. One other major difference between the WWW and Telnet is that Telnet requires that you log on directly to the computer you want to access. Usually you will be told what username and password to use to log in. You will find some databases and institutions that are accessible only via Telnet, and many more that are moving from Telnet to the Web. Though your school library's catalog may not (yet) be accessible via the WWW, you may be able to access it via Telnet from your dorm room. You'll still have to go over there to get the books, but you will arrive with a list of sources in hand and won't have to wait for a terminal in the library itself.

Using E-Mail Effectively

What's the first thing you do when you turn on a computer? If you're like most people, you check first for new e-mail messages.

E-mail has become the preferred means of written communication for many of us. Quick, efficient, and (usually) reliable, e-mail is the most widely used feature of the Internet.

Every person using e-mail has at least one address, consisting of these elements:

• **Mailbox name.** The mailbox name—the name assigned to your account on an e-mail system—is often some variant of your own name (e.g., conan_obrien), though it may also be totally fictitious (e.g., hepcat9).

• **@.** The *at* sign.

• **Domain name.** The domain name is the name of the organization that hosts the e-mail "post office" to which the user subscribes—often an institution (e.g., umass.edu or mcgraw-hill.com), an Internet service provider (e.g., aol.com or earthlink.net), or a multifaceted system such as yahoo.com or hotmail.com. *Host computers* are connected directly to the Internet. You can usually tell what kind of an organization hosts an e-mail account by the last part of the address (the *extension*): for example, *.edu* is an educational organization, *.com* is a commercial organization, and *.gov* is a governmental organization (see Table 10.1).

Many e-mail providers (e.g., Yahoo! Mail and America Online) have their own, unique e-mail systems on which e-mail can be retrieved anywhere you have access to the Web. Others use particular software pro-

Table 10.1

Domain Extensions

The last three letters of an e-mail address indicate the type of organization that hosts a sender's e-mail account.

E-mail address	Extension	Type of Organization
jasper.johns@asu.edu	.EDU	Arizona State University—Educational
dowd@nytimes.com	.COM	The New York Times—Commercial
send.help@redcross.org	.ORG	American Red Cross—Charitable or nonprofit
general@army.mil	.MIL	United States Army—Military
head.counter@census.gov	.GOV	U.S. Census Bureau—Government

grams such as Microsoft's Outlook to send and receive mail; you must have that software installed on your computer to retrieve your e-mail.

Writing and Responding to E-mail

Writing e-mail messages is simple. First, type the address of the person to whom you are writing (or, if you've gotten that far already, select it from your e-mail address book). Next, type a brief description of the message in the subject line. Always use the subject line; it allows recipients to get a preview of what the message is about and to easily distinguish that message later from other messages that they may have received from you.

Finally, write the message itself. E-mail messages have several features that are not part of more traditional, formal "snail-mail" letters. For instance, writers frequently include abbreviations. Some common ones are AFAIK ("as far as I know"), BTW ("by the way"), CYA ("see ya"), OIC ("oh, I see"), and WTG ("way to go"). They may also include **emoticons** (or **smileys**), which signal the emotion that the writer is trying to convey. Emoticons often look like faces on their side, with facial expressions related to the meaning of the emoticon. A list of the most common emoticons is shown in Table 10.2.

One of the ways that e-mail quickens the pace of communication is the ease with which you can respond to a message you've received. To respond you simply click an on-screen button marked "reply." A new message window appears on screen, and you type in your reply and send off the message.

You can also *forward* messages that you've received to another person who was not an original recipient of the message.

E-mail messages can also contain *attachments,* files that do not appear in the body of the message but that can be opened separately. Attachments can take the form of word-processing documents, audio files, movies, and video clips.

You can use attachments to submit a paper to an instructor. A paper sent as an attachment will be an exact copy of the original file that you produced using a word processor. (Of course, make sure that your instructor accepts assignments via e-mail before you send it.)

Not every message deserves a response. For example, you may receive *spam,* which is the equivalent of junk mail. Spam may range from get-rich-quick schemes to advertisements for body enhancements or pornography. Spam is more than a nuisance; it takes up valuable transmission resources ("bandwidth"), disk space, and computer time. Some e-mail systems allow users to apply a *filter* that uses a few simple rules to separate the wheat (e-mail you actually want to read) from the chaff (spam). Unfortunately, these systems are not perfect: they sometimes let junk through and can even at times dispose of messages you want. The only absolutely reliable way to deal with spam is to delete it yourself as quickly as possible.

Meaning	Symbol
angry	(:-&
bored	:|
crying	:,(
exhausted	:-6
frown	:-(
funny	:-D
happy	:^D
hug	[], ()
kiss	*
mad	>:-<
sad	:(
sarcasm	:-]
sleepy	|-(
smile	:)
surprised	:-0
tear	:'-(
wink	;)
yawn	:-0

Table 10.2

Emoticons

This is a brief listing of the most frequently used emoticons (or smileys).

Emoticons (or smileys)

Abbreviations used in e-mail messages that provide information on the emotion that the writer is trying to convey. Emoticons usually look like faces on their side, with facial expressions related to the meaning of the motion

Finally, *never* open an attachment from someone you don't know. Computer viruses, which can ruin everything on your hard drive, are often spread through e-mail attachments.

Netiquette: Showing Civility in E-mail

Although e-mail communication is usually less formal than a letter, you still need to maintain civility. Here are some rules:

- **Don't write anything in an e-mail message that you'll regret seeing on the front page of the campus newspaper.** Yes, e-mail is usually private; but the private message you write can easily be forwarded by the recipient to another person or even scores of other people. Worse yet, it's fairly easy to hit "reply [to] all" when you mean simply to "reply": in this case, you might think that you are responding to an individual, when in fact the e-mail will go to everyone who received the message along with you.

- **Be careful of the tone you convey.** It is harder on e-mail to convey the same kind of personality, and often the same degree of subtlety, that our voice, our handwriting, or even our stationery can add to other forms of communication. This means that attempts at humor and especially sarcasm can backfire. If you're using humor, consider adding an emoticon to clarify the intent of your message.

- **Don't use all capital letters.** Using all caps MAKES IT LOOK AS IF YOU'RE SHOUTING.

- **Never send an e-mail when you are angry.** No matter how annoyed you are about something someone has written in a message, don't respond in kind—or at least wait until you've cooled down. Take a deep breath, and wait for your anger to pass.

Distance Learning: Classes Without Walls

Distance learning
A form of education in which students participate via the World Wide Web or other kinds of technology

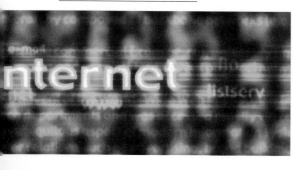

Do you find that your schedule changes so much from one day to the next that it's hard to fit in a course that meets at a regularly scheduled time? Interested in an unusual course topic that your own college doesn't offer? Want to take a class during the summer, but find yourself summering too far from a college campus?

The solution to your problem may be to enroll in a distance learning course. **Distance learning** is a form of education in which students participate via the World Wide Web or other kinds of technology. Although most distance learning courses are taught via the Web, some use teleconferencing, fax, and/or express mail.

The key feature of distance learning courses is the mediated interaction between instructor and students. Rather than meeting in a traditional classroom, where the instructor, you, and the other students are physically present, distance learning classes are most often virtual. Although some schools are experimenting with "Webcasts" of lectures and with virtual discussion rooms, many students in distance learning courses will never sit through a lecture or even participate in a real-time conversation with students in the class. They may never even know what their instructor or classmates look like or hear their voices.

Typically, if you take a distance learning course today, you may read lecture notes posted on the Web, search and browse websites, write papers, post replies to discussion topics on a *message board,* and take online quizzes and exams. You will see your instructor's and classmates' responses through comments they post on the Web. You may be expected to read a textbook entirely on your own.

Distance learning is not for everyone. Whether you're a good candidate for it or not depends on your preferred style of course-taking. Complete Try It 3 to see whether you are suited to learn at a distance.

Distance learning classes have both advantages and disadvantages. On the plus side, distance learning courses offer the following:

- **You can take a Web-based distance learning course anywhere that you have access to the Web.** You can be at home, at the college library, or on vacation at the beach and still participate.

- **Distance learning classes are more flexible than traditional classes.** You can participate in a course any time of the day or night. You set your own schedule.

In distance education, you can take classes at another institution without physically having to be on that campus. Although taking courses online can help you fulfill graduation requirements, make sure before you register that your own college will accept the course credits. What do you think the future of distance education will be?

Try It! 3

Personal Styles: Assess Your Course-Taking Style

Your preferred course-taking style—how you participate in classes, work with your classmates, interact with your teachers, and complete your assignments—may make you more or less suitable for distance learning. Read the following statements and indicate whether you agree or disagree with them to see whether you have what it takes to be a distance learner.

	Agree	Neutral	Disagree
1. I need the stimulation of other students to learn well.			
2. I need to see my teacher's face, expressions, and body language to interpret what is being said.			
3. I participate a lot in class discussions.			
4. I prefer to hear information presented orally rather than reading it in a book or article.			
5. I'm not very good at keeping up with reading assignments.			
6. I'm basically pretty easily distracted.			
7. I'm not very well organized.			
8. Keeping track of time and holding to schedules is NOT a strength of mine.			
9. I need a lot of "hand-holding" while I work on long assignments.			
10. I need a close social network to share my feelings, ideas, and complaints with.			
11. I'm not very good at writing.			
12. Basically, I'm not very patient.			

The more you disagree with these statements, the more your course-taking style is suited to distance learning. Interpret your style according to this informal scale:

Disagreed with 10–12 statements = Excellent candidate for distance learning

Disagreed with 7–9 statements = Good candidate for distance learning

Agreed with 6–9 statements = Probably better taking classes on campus

Agreed with 10–12 statements = Avoid distance learning

To Try It online, go to **www.mhhe.com/power**.

- **Distance learning classes are self-paced.** You may be able to spread out your work over the course of a week, or you may do the work in a concentrated manner on one day.

- **You may have more contact with your instructor than you do with a traditional class.** Even though you may not have face-to-face contact, you may have greater access to your instructor, via e-mail and the Web, than in traditional classes. You can leave messages for your instructor any time of the night or day; most instructors of distance learning classes respond in a timely way.

- **Shy students may find it easier to "speak up" in a distance learning class.** You can think through your responses to make sure you are communicating just what you wish to say. You don't have to worry about speaking in front of other people. For many people, distance learning is liberating.

- **You can become a better writer.** Because distance learning usually involves more writing than traditional courses, you receive more practice writing—and more feedback for it—than in traditional classes.

On the other hand, distance learning has disadvantages that you should keep in mind. You won't have direct, face-to-face contact with your instructor or other students. It may feel isolating to be alone at your computer, and you can feel lost in cyberspace.

In addition, you won't get *immediate* feedback. In a distance learning class, it may be hours, or sometimes days, before you receive feedback on what you have posted to a message board, depending on how well the pace of other students matches your own.

Finally, distance learning classes require significant personal responsibility and time management skills. You won't have a set time to attend class as you do in traditional courses. You must carve out the time yourself. Although instructors provide a schedule when things are due, *you* have to work out the timing of getting them done.

Despite these potential drawbacks to distance learning courses, they are becoming increasingly popular. More and more colleges are offering them. Many companies encourage employees with crowded schedules to take distance learning as a way of providing continuing education.

If you are considering taking a distance education course, follow these steps, which are summarized in the P.O.W.E.R. Plan at the right.

P repare: Identifying Distance Learning Course Possibilities

How do you find a distance learning course? In some cases, your own college may offer courses on the Web and list them in your course catalog. In other cases, you'll have to find courses on your own.

The best place to look is on the Web itself. By searching the Web, you can find distance learning courses ranging from agronomy to zoology. Don't be deterred by the physical location of the institution that offers the course; it doesn't matter where the college is located, because you'll never have to go to the campus itself.

PREPARE

Identify distance learning course possibilities

ORGANIZE

Obtain access to technology

WORK

Participate in a distance learning class

EVALUATE

Consider your "classroom" performance

RETHINK

Reflect on what and how you have learned

P.O.W.E.R. Plan

🏂 **Working in a Group:** Get Some Distance on the Problem

Working by yourself initially, see if you can find distance learning courses of interest to you: start by checking your school's course catalog to see what might be offered there. If you're already comfortable online, you might also try the following:

- *The Chronicle of Higher Education*'s Distance Education: Daily Updates (**www.chronicle.com/distance/**).

- The World Lecture Hall (**www.utexas.edu/world/lecture/index.html**), hosted by the University of Texas, which provides a list of distance learning courses offered worldwide.

- Distance Learning Newsgroup (**alt.education.distance**).

- distance_ed: Distance Education Mailing List (To subscribe, send an e-mail to **majordomo@email.rutgers.edu** with "subscribe distance_ed" in the subject line.)

Try to find five courses you would be interested in. After you have completed your list, share your list with others in a group. How diverse were the courses you were able to find? Were particular subject areas better represented than others? Why?

To Try It online, go to **www.mhhe.com/power**.

But before you sign up for a potential course that you would like to count toward your degree, *make sure that your own college will give you credit for it.* Check with your advisor and registrar's office to be certain.

You should also find out what the requirements of a course are before you actually sign up for it. Check the syllabus carefully and see how it meshes with your schedule. If it is a summer course and you are going to be away from your computer for a week, you may not be able to make up the work you miss.

Finally, try to talk with someone who has taken the course before. Was the instructor responsive, providing feedback rapidly? If necessary, could you speak with the instructor by phone? Was the course load reasonable? (Try It 4 will help you to work through the process.)

Organize: Obtaining Access to Technology

Although you don't need to be a computer expert, you will need some minimal e-mail and Web skills to take a distance learning course. If you don't have sufficient technological expertise, beef up your computer skills by taking a computer course or workshop *before* you actually sign up for the course.

You'll also need access to a computer connected to the Internet. It doesn't have to be your own computer, but you will certainly need regular and convenient access to one. Make sure that the computer you plan to use has sufficient internal resources to quickly connect to the Internet; a very slow connection is frustrating.

Be sure to make all your arrangements for computer access prior to the start of a course. It can take several weeks to set up Internet service on a home computer if you don't have it already.

W ork: Participating in a Distance Learning Class

Successfully participating in a distance learning course involves several skills that are distinct from those needed for traditional classes. To get the most out of a distance learning course, you'll need to do the following:

- **Manage your time carefully.** You won't have the luxury of a regular schedule of class lectures, so you'll have to manage your time carefully. No one is going to remind you that you need to sit down at a computer and work.

- **Check in frequently.** Instructors may make crucial changes in the course requirements. Make sure to check for any changes in due dates or class expectations.

- **Find a cyberbuddy.** At the start of the semester, try to make personal contact with at least one other student in the class. You can do this by e-mailing, phoning, or actually meeting the student if he or she is geographically nearby. You can share study strategies, form a study group, and share notes. Connecting with another student can help you avoid feelings of isolation that may interfere with your success.

- **Make copies of everything.** Don't assume everything will go well in cyberspace. Make a printed copy of everything you submit, or alternatively have a backup stored on another computer.

- **Have a technology backup plan.** Computers crash, your connection to the Internet may go down, or an e-mailed assignment may be mysteriously delayed or sent back to you. Don't wait until the last minute to work on and submit assignments, and have a plan in place if your primary computer is unavailable.

E valuate: Considering Your "Classroom" Performance

As with any class, you'll be receiving feedback from your instructor. But unlike many courses, in which almost all the feedback comes from the instructor, much of the feedback in a distance learning course may come from your fellow students. What can you learn from their comments?

At the same time you'll be receiving feedback, you will likely be providing feedback to your classmates. Consider the nature of feedback you provide, and be sure that you use the basic principles of classroom civility.

R ethink: Reflecting on What and How You Have Learned

Distance learning is not for everyone. If your preferred learning style involves extensive, face-to-face interaction with others, you may find that your experience is less than satisfying. On the other hand, if you are at ease with computers and enjoy working on your own, you may find distance learning highly effective.

As you reflect on your distance learning experience, go beyond the technology and think about the learning outcomes. Ask yourself whether you learned as much as you would have in a traditional class. You should also consider ways that the experience could have been more effective for you. And think about whether you were so absorbed by the technology that you lost sight of the real goal of the course: learning new material.

Most educational experts believe that distance learning will play an increasingly important role in higher education. Furthermore, because it offers an efficient way of educating people in far-flung locales, it is a natural means of promoting lifelong learning experiences. In short, the first distance learning class you take is likely not to be your last.

Finding Facts: Locating the Information You Need

One of the greatest advances brought about by developments in technology is in the area of research. We'll now consider some of the ways in which you can search the two primary repositories of knowledge for any student. One you can walk or drive to—the library. The other—the Internet—doesn't have a physical location. Both are indispensable in anyone's quest for information.

Libraries

No matter how humble or imposing their physical appearance, whether they contain only a few hundred volumes or hundreds of thousands of them, libraries are a good place to focus your efforts as you seek out and gather information. Although every library is different, all share two key elements: the material they hold—their basic collections—and tools to help you locate the material you need.

> "Knowledge is of two kinds: we know a subject ourselves, or we know where we can find information upon it."
>
> Samuel Johnson

What Can Be Found in a Library's Basic Collection? Libraries obviously contain books, but they typically have a lot more than that, including some or all of the following:

- **Periodicals.** *Periodicals* include magazines published for general audiences, specialized journals for professionals in a field, and newspapers. Magazines and journals are often bound and stored by year; newspapers are usually kept in **microform,** in which documents have been photographed and stored on either microfilm (reels of film) or microfiche (plastic sheets).

Microform
A means of storing greatly reduced photographs of printed pages, which can be read using special microform readers; the two main types of microform are microfiche and microfilm

- **Indexes to Periodicals and Other Information Sources.** An index provides a listing of periodical articles by title, author, and subject. Some indexes also provide a short summary, or **abstract,** of the contents of each article. Some indexes, such as the *Reader's Guide to Periodical Literature,* cover a variety of general circulation magazines of the type you'd find at a decent newsstand, such as *Newsweek, Ebony,* and *Rolling Stone.* Others are more specialized (e.g., the *Music Index* and the *Business Periodicals Index*).

  Most indexes come in both print and electronic form. Although some people prefer to use indexes in book form, computerized indexes are considerably easier and quicker to use. Furthermore, you can often download the results of electronic searches at a library onto your own floppy disks.

Abstract
A short summary of the contents of a journal article

- **Encyclopedias.** Some encyclopedias, such as the *Encyclopaedia Britannica* or *World Book Encyclopedia,* attempt to cover the entire range of knowledge, and they may take up several volumes. Others are more specialized, covering only a particular field, such as the *Encyclopedia of Human Behavior* or the *Encyclopedia of Religion.* Most are printed as multivolume sets of books, although an increasing number are available electronically, on CD-ROM or online. Encyclopedias provide a good general view of a topic, but they lack depth: use them at the earliest stage of your hunt for information for an overview of key issues, and move from there to more specific and current sources.

- **Government documents.**

- **Musical scores.**

- **Reserve collections.** Reserve collections hold heavily-used items that instructors assign for a class. Sometimes reserve material can be checked out for only an hour or two and used in the same room; in other cases the material can be used overnight or for a few days.

Locating Information in a Library The place to begin searching for information in a library is the library catalog. Catalogs list all materials that are held in the library and provide their location. Most library catalogs are computerized, though a few still use paper cards filed in drawers or microform (microfiche or microfilm). You may be able to access your school's computerized catalog from home as well as from computers housed in the library itself.

Library catalogs traditionally allow searches by title, author name, and subject; electronic catalogs also typically allow searching by keyword. Individual catalog entries generally include additional information about the material, such as the publisher, date of publication, number of pages, and similar information.

Say, for example, you're writing a paper on Ernest Hemingway. To find books *he wrote* in an electronic catalog, you would enter his name in the "author" field. You may be presented with the following listing:

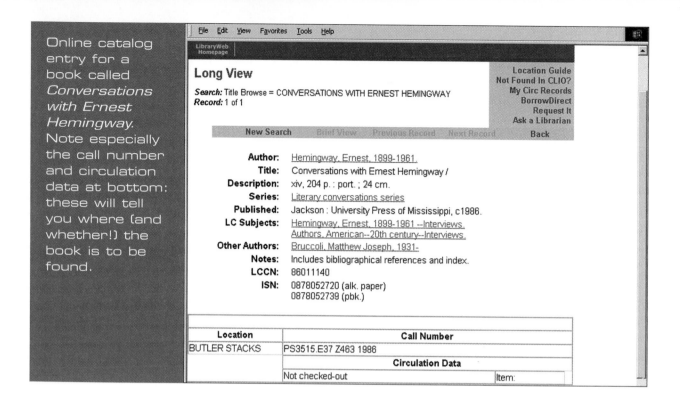

Online catalog entry for a book called *Conversations with Ernest Hemingway.* Note especially the call number and circulation data at bottom: these will tell you where (and whether!) the book is to be found.

Call number

A unique classification number assigned to every book (or other resource) in a library, which provides a key to locating it

Stacks

The shelves on which books and other materials are stored in a library

Recall

A way to request library materials from another user who has them

Interlibrary loan

A system by which libraries share resources, making them available to patrons of different libraries

Of course, you could also search on "Hemingway" as the subject, which would yield a list of books *about* him and his work; if you entered his name in a "keyword" search, the catalog would return a more comprehensive list of books both by *and* about him.

The key piece of information in a catalog entry is the book's **call number,** a code that tells you exactly where to find it. Most college libraries use the Library of Congress classification system, which assigns to each book a unique combination of letters and numbers.

Because the record illustrated above is from an electronic search, it contains further helpful information. The word "available" under "status" tells you that the book has not been checked out by another patron and should be sitting on the shelf. You'll need to familiarize yourself with your library's particular system to know precisely how you can make most efficient use of the catalog. Chances are there's a handout or posted set of instructions nearby.

Once you have identified the material you need and where it is located, you'll need to go find it. In all but the biggest libraries, you can simply go into the **stacks,** the place containing shelves where the books and other materials are kept, and—using the call number—hunt for it. In libraries with closed stacks, you must fill out a form with the call numbers of the books you want. A library aide will find and deliver the material to a central location.

What if you go to the location in the stacks where the material is supposed to be and you can't find it? The material may be checked out, in use by someone else at that time, incorrectly shelved, or simply lost. Whatever the reason, *don't give up.* If the material is checked out to another user, ask a librarian if you can **recall** the material, a process by which the library contacts the person who has the book and asks him or her to return it.

If the librarian informs you that the material is not checked out, wait a few days and see if it appears on the shelf. Someone may have been using it while you were looking for it. If it was misshelved, the librarian may be able to find it. If the material is truly lost, you may be able to get it from another library through **interlibrary loan,** a system by which libraries share resources.

Finally, even if you do find exactly what you were looking for, take a moment to scan the shelves. Because books and other materials are generally grouped by topic, you may find other useful titles in the same place. One of the pleasures of libraries is the possibility of finding an unexpected treasure—material that your catalog search did not initially identify but that may provide you with exactly what you need.

The World Wide Web

As its name implies, the Web is vast—sometimes frustratingly so. In fact, no one knows how much material exists on the Web. Not only is more information added to the Web every day, but the information also resides on thousands of individual computers. Anyone with minimal Web savvy and access to a *server* (a computer with a permanent Internet connection) can set up a personal website.

The fact that anyone can put information on the Web is both the biggest asset and greatest disadvantage of using the Web as an information source. Because minimal computer skill is the only expertise a person needs to set up a Web page, there may be as much misinformation on the Web as there is information. Consequently, keep the usual consumer rule in mind: Buyer beware. Unless the website has been established and is maintained by a reliable organization, the information it contains may not be accurate.

There are a number of key factors involved in each Web search. They include a browser, Web pages, links, and search engines.

- **Browsers.** To use the World Wide Web, your computer has to have a browser. A **browser,** as its name implies, is a program that provides a way of looking at the information on the Web. Among the major browsers are Microsoft's Internet Explorer and Netscape's Navigator.

  Using a browser is a bit like taking a taxi: once you get in, you get to where you want to go by providing an address. The address, also known as a URL (Uniform Resource Locator), identifies a unique location on the Web, a *website* or a *Web page* (one of the parts of a site).

Browser

A program that provides a way of navigating around the information on the World Wide Web

Searching for materials in the library stacks can be frustrating if they are not on the shelves. However, you may unexpectedly find relevant and interesting material.

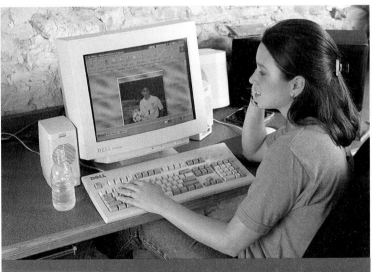

It is becoming increasingly easy for anyone to put material on the World Wide Web, and many students are creating their own personal Web pages containing information and photos about their lives.

Web addresses are combinations of letters and symbols. They typically start off with "www.[domain_name].[xxx]"—the address of the hosting website (e.g., **www.umass.edu**, the home page for the University of Massachusetts). If you're looking for a subsite or a particular page on the site, the address becomes increasingly specific: **www.umass.edu/visitors** will take you to a "visitors" site—a collection of pages—hosted by umass.edu. A *page* on that site—for example, **www.umass.edu/visitors/directions.html**, which offers directions to campus—ends with a specific name, usually followed by ".htm" or ".html." Because most addresses begin with "http://," this part of the address is often dropped in references to a site.

You can often get a decent idea of what kind of site you're going to by taking a careful look at the Web address: you can tell that **www.mhhe.com/power**, for example, is a site that has something to do with "power" and is hosted by a commercial entity (which you might or might not recognize as McGraw-Hill Higher Education). (Hmm, might be worth checking out. . . .)

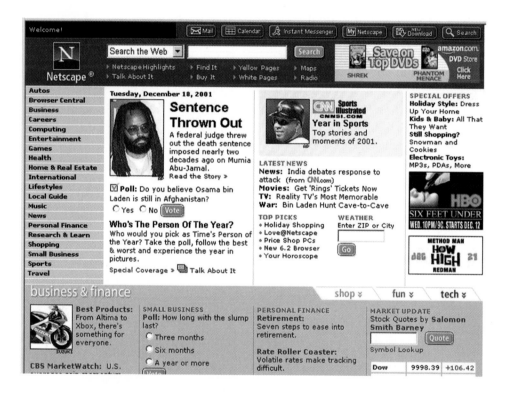

Web page

A location (or site) on the World Wide Web housing information from a single source, and (typically) links to other pages

Link

A means of "jumping" automatically from one Web page to another

- **Web pages.** Web pages are the heart of the World Wide Web. A **Web page** is a document that presents you with information. The information may appear as text on the screen, to be read like a book (or more accurately, like an ancient scroll). It might include a video clip, an audio clip, a photo, a portrait, a graph, or a figure. It might offer a news service photo of the president of the United States or a backyard snapshot of someone's family reunion.

- **Links.** Web sites typically provide you with **links**—embedded addresses to other sites or documents that, at a click, cause your browser automatically to "jump" there. Just as an encyclopedia article on forests might say at the end, "See also *Trees*," Web pages often refer to other sites on the Web—only it's easier than with a book. You just have to click on the link with your mouse and—*poof!*—you're there.

- **Search engines.** A **search engine** is simply a computerized index to information on the Web. When you know what information you want to find but don't have an address for it, a search engine can often steer you toward relevant sites.

"Go ask your search engine."

The various parts of the Web are similar to the components of traditional libraries. A Web browser is equivalent to a library card; it gives you access to vast quantities of material. Websites are like the books of a library; Web pages are the book pages, where the content resides. Links are analogous to "see also" portions of books that suggest related information. And search engines are like a library's card catalog, directing you to specific locations.

Search engine
A computerized index to information on the World Wide Web

Traditional Library

Library card

Book

"See Also" pages

Library catalog

World Wide Web

Web browser

Web site

http://www.nbcnews.com
http://www.whitehouse.gov
http://www.umass.edu
http://www.ama-assn.org

Web links

Search engine

Locating Information on the World Wide Web There is no central catalog of the contents of the World Wide Web: instead, there are a number of different search engines. Furthermore, depending on the search engine you use and the type of search you do, you'll identify different information.

Search engines themselves are located on the Web, so you have to know their addresses. After you reach the "home" address of a search engine, you enter your search terms. The search engine then provides a list of websites that may contain information relevant to your search.

Some search engines, such as Yahoo!, specialize in organizing information by subject, making it easy to search for information on, say, different dog breeds, the Islamic religion, or car repair. Using Yahoo! for its subject directories is like searching for information using the subject entries in a library catalog.

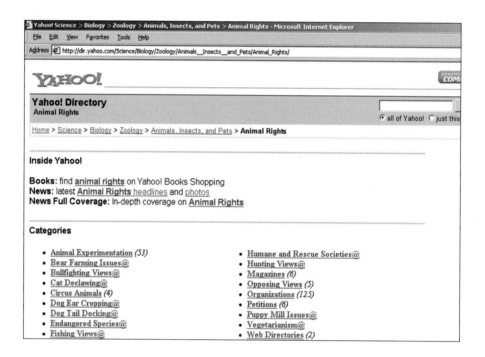

Other search engines, such as Google or AltaVista, catalog many more pages than Yahoo! but don't group them by subject: due to the breadth of their coverage, they might be more useful when you are looking for obscure pieces of information or for numerous sources for different perspectives on a topic. Using Google or AltaVista is like performing a keyword search in a library catalog.

Finally, a third type of search engine is exemplified by Ask Jeeves and Dogpile. Known as metasearch tools, these sites send your search commands to other search engines, compiling the results into a single, unified list.

There's no single search engine that works best. Most people develop their own preferences based on their experience. The best advice: Try out several of them (some pros and cons are summarized in Table 10.3) and see which works best for you. To get started, try, "Information, Please!" (Try It 5 on page 274).

Becoming a Savvy Surfer of the Web The process you use to search the Web couldn't be easier—or more difficult. The vast amounts of material online and the relative ease of navigation afforded by the Web

Table 10.3

Major Search Sites on
the Web

Search Site	Comments
Alta Vista www.altavista.com	Powerful engine returns high-quality results; advanced features take time to learn; lots of clutter
Ask Jeeves www.ask.com	This natural-language site returns too many home page links and not enough direct links to the information. It has no advanced search features
Excite www.excite.com	Busy home page makes search engine seem like an afterthought; help section is vague; doesn't specify how many links it found
Fast Search www.alltheweb.com	Fast and relevant, but lacks Google's uncanny accuracy; simple and streamlined; has relatively few advanced features; no directory
Dogpile www.dogpile.com	Unlike other metasearch engines, Dogpile divides results by the sites it gathered them from, which makes them less useful
Google www.google.com	Returns highly relevant results; very easy to use; few advanced features, but you may not need them to find what you're looking for
HotBot www.hotbot.com	Good choice for serious searchers who like lots of options; basic queries may not return super relevant results; few broken links or duplicates
LookSmart www.looksmart.com	Solid directory with better descriptions than Yahoo! but it seemed slower than most, with more broken links
Lycos www.lycos.com	Lots of features, but relevance of results was erratic; more broken links and duplicates than most; few advanced search options
Northern Light www.northernlight.com	Powerful and unique, but the topic folders don't always sort results effectively; better for business searches than for fun stuff; no directory
MetaCrawler www.metacrawler.com	This metasearch site struggled with sample search terms. It works better when searching for general information
Yahoo www.yahoo.com	Still the best portal, and easier to use than most

make finding information quite simple: what is hard is finding *appropriate* information.

Consider the search illustrated on page 275. It is the result of entering "How do I use the World Wide Web?" into the home page of Google. The search identified more than two million websites related to the topic.

Using the list of sites generated by the search is simple. With a computer mouse, click on the site address of the relevant document, and the home page of the site will (eventually) appear on your computer screen. You can then take notes on the material, in the same way you'd take notes on material in a book.

> "Don't let that little glowing screen become an adversary. If you plan correctly, the computer can become your most useful tool at college—next to your brain."
>
> Greg Gottesman

Many of the million sites Google returned, however, may well be of little use. It's easy in such a search to end up in a virtual dead end, in which the information you have found is only minimally related to the topic you're researching. If you do find yourself at a site that's of no use to you, simply hit the "back" command on your browser until you return to where you started.

Try It! 5

Work the Web: Information, Please!

Try to find the answer to the first question below on Yahoo! (**www.yahoo.com**), Google (**www.google.com**), *and* Dogpile (**www.dogpile.com**). Then use whichever search engine you prefer to find answers to the remaining questions.

1. What was the French Revolution and when did it occur? _____
   _____
   _____

2. Who is Keyser Soze? _____
   _____
   _____

3. What are the words of Dr. Martin Luther King, Jr.'s, "I Have a Dream" speech? _____
   _____
   _____

4. Is the birthrate in the United States higher or lower than that in Brazil? _____
   _____
   _____

5. What is the ecu? _____
   _____
   _____

How easy was it for you to find the answers to the questions? Which search engine(s) did you prefer, and why?

To Try It online, go to **www.mhhe.com/power**.

But how to limit your search in the first place, so that you find sites more directly relevant?

The following tips can help you to get the most from a search[2]:

1. **Before turning to your computer, phrase your search as a question.**

2. **Identify the important words in that question.** Then think of words that are related to the important words. Write all the words down.

3. **Go to your favorite search engine.**

4. **Type in two or three words from your list,** making sure they are spelled correctly, then search. Note: You can do a few things here to limit the number of results returned, thus making your search more efficient: most search engines allow you to use the following:

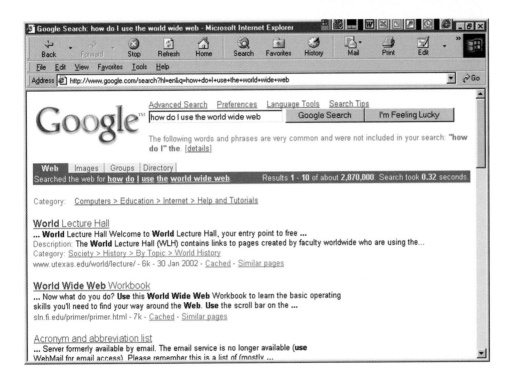

- *Quotation marks,* to denote a phrase—words that should appear together, in a specific order (e.g., "animal rights").

- *Plus signs,* used before terms that *must* appear in all results returned (+"animal rights" +experimentation).

- *Minus signs,* before terms you do *not* want to appear in results (+"animal rights" +experimentation –fur).

- *Boolean operators*—words like AND, OR, AND NOT, and NEAR (e.g., "animal rights" AND experimentation NOT fur).

Check the "Help" section of your preferred search engine for more precise information on limiting your searches.

5. Open a new window, type in a different arrangement of your terms, and search again.

6. Identify the common links between the two searches. Read the very brief summaries provided.

7. When you choose a website, open the page in a new window so that you can go back to your list of hits.

8. Open a text editor window. Copy and paste the site's address into that window and follow it with an annotation of your own. Do that for five sites.

9. See if you have found the answer you were looking for. If not, reformulate your question to come up with new key words.

"First, they do an on-line search."

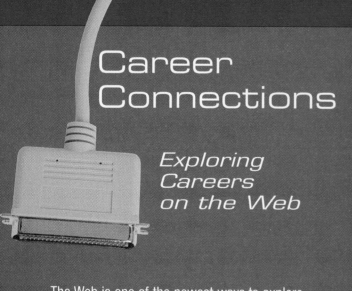

Career Connections

Exploring Careers on the Web

The Web is one of the newest ways to explore careers that may interest you. You can begin to gather information by going to a website devoted to jobs, such as "The Catapult" on JobWeb (**www.jobweb.org/catapult/catapult.htm**). The Catapult site presents a variety of career-related sites. You can also find other sites using the various search engines we've been discussing.

In addition, you can find help wanted advertisements for many jobs on the Web. In fact, it is possible to apply directly for jobs using the Web. Some firms advertise their job needs on their company sites, and you can e-mail a cover letter and a résumé listing your education and experience. An increasing number of jobs are obtained in this way.

Keep this in mind, too: The computer expertise you develop during college will later help you in your professional life. Already, more and more jobs require at least minimal computer skills, and every projection of the future suggests that computers will become a central facet of the workplace.

Evaluating the Information You Find on the Web In most instances, you'll find more information than you need, and you'll have to evaluate the information you have found. Some of the important questions you must address before you can feel confident about what you've found include the following:

- **How authoritative is the information?** It is absolutely essential to consider the source of the material. Approach every piece of information with a critical eye, trying to determine what the author's biases might be. The best approach is to use multiple sources of information. If one source diverges radically from the others, you may reasonably question the reliability of that source.

  Another approach is to consider the publisher of the material or sponsoring institution. For instance, sites established by well-known publishers and organizations are more likely to contain accurate information than those created by unknown (and sometimes anonymous) authors. Remember, the Web is completely unregulated: *anyone* can put *anything* on the Web.

  One way of evaluating Web information is to consider a site's host. Commercial Web pages (whose address includes the letters *.com,* short for commercial) often tend to include the least objective material. On the other hand, addresses including the letters *.gov* (government), *.org* (nonprofit organization), *.mil* (military), and *.edu* (educational and research institutions) generally include more objective information. Still, each site must be evaluated on its merits.

- **How current is the information?** No matter what the discipline, information is changing at a rapid rate. Even a field like Chaucerian English, which concentrates on poetry written in the 14th century, advances significantly year by year as scholars make new discoveries, come to new insights, and reach new conclusions.

  Consequently, don't assume that, because you're researching a historical topic, old sources will suffice. Consider whether what you've found is the most recent and up-to-date approach. Compare older sources to newer ones to identify changes in the ways in which the topic is considered.

- **How well are claims documented?** Are there references and citations to support the information? Are specific studies identified?

- **Is anything missing?** One of the hardest questions to answer is whether your research is complete. Have you found all the relevant sources? Have you missed anything that is important?

Although there is no way to answer these questions definitively, you can do a couple of things. One way to ensure that you haven't missed anything important is to check out the sources that you have found. Many will have bibliographies and lists of suggested additional readings. By carefully considering this information, you'll be able to get a good sense of the important work in your topic area and verify that you haven't overlooked some critical source.

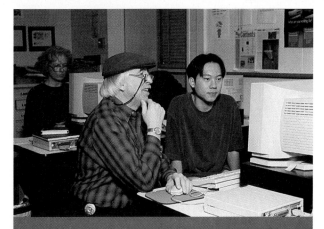

Despite any initial difficulties people experience when learning to use the computer, most ultimately master them. Here an instructor at Pasadena City College in California works with a student on a computer lab assignment.

You can also talk to your course instructor, describing generally what you've found. Probably the best person to turn to, however, is a reference librarian.

The stereotype of a librarian as someone whose main job is to stop people from talking in the library is dead. Librarians today are masters at information management and technology—people who can help you find your way through a huge range of data sources and steer you to the right material.

Make use of librarians—but do it properly. Start by looking for material yourself. Then, if you're having trouble sorting through what you've found (or can't find material in the first place), ask for help.

The better the question, the better the answer. Don't ask vague, unfocused questions (e.g., "Where are the books about nuclear power?"). Instead, sharpen your question, being as precise as possible ("I'm writing a paper on the environmental effects of using nuclear power to generate electricity. I've found two books and several websites, but they're not quite right. I wonder if you have any ideas about where I might find additional material?").

Don't be afraid to ask. Think of librarians as highly trained guides who can save you hours of aimless wandering in an increasingly dense forest of information.

A Final Word

The Information Age presents us with great promise and opportunity. Through the use of media such as e-mail and the Internet, we have at our fingertips the ability to communicate with others around the world. We can break the bounds of our physical location and reach across geography to learn about others. The computer keyboard truly can be said to contain keys to the entire earth and its peoples.

Speaking of Success

Name: *Naison Nyamatutu*
Education: *Carthage College*
Home: *Kenosha, Wisconsin*

hen Naison Nyamatutu arrived on the campus of Carthage College for the first time, he came with a duffel bag, jet lag, and no money. What he did have was the conviction that somehow he would be able to get a college education.

That belief came from a fleeting encounter at a train station in Bulawayo, the second-biggest city in Zimbabwe, with a professor from Carthage. At the end of a 15-minute conversation, the professor wrote his name and address on a slip of paper and casually told Naison to get in touch if he ever happened to be in the United States.

That chance meeting eventually led to $60,000 in scholarships and a college education for Naison.

It was not an easy journey from

Zimbabwe to a U.S. college. Naison had to convince a government official to give him a visa, and then he had to raise the funds for the plane ticket. He tried to buy and sell potatoes to

finance the trip; it didn't work, because the potatoes rotted before he could sell them. Finally, his father used most of his pension for the plane ticket.

Naison arrived at Carthage in the middle of the semester, along with enormous drive and the conviction that he could succeed. He convinced the admissions office to give him a shot at college and to give him a scholarship. In the end, Naison graduated in only 3 years, because he took classes year-round. He was an energetic student, motivated to learn things that would help him throughout his life. "I worried about learning something that I could use in business, not about learning what would help me on tests," he said.[3]

What next? Because of the political instability in Zimbabwe, Naison has not decided whether he will return. "I have a very aggressive mentality," he noted. "If I go home now, I might end up getting in trouble."[4]

What are the basic components of computers?

- Computers consist of hardware (the physical components including the display, keyboard, mouse, and the computer unit) and software (programs that tell computers what to do).

- Word processing, presentation, and spreadsheet are the basic kinds of programs.

What is available on the Internet?

- The Internet is a vast network that connects millions of computers. It has numerous useful features, including e-mail, telnet, newsgroups, listservs, and the World Wide Web.

- E-mail and the World Wide Web are the most frequently used features of the Internet.

- E-mail permits instant communications across the world. Users can reply to messages, forward them, and include attachments.

What is distance learning?

- Distance learning is a form of education that does not require the physical presence of a student in a classroom. It is usually conducted over the World Wide Web.

- Distance learning requires some adjustments, but it is likely to increase in popularity in future years.

What are the basic sources of information?

- There are two main sources of information today: libraries and the World Wide Web.

- Information in libraries is available in print form, electronic form, and microform.

- Library resources can be found through the use of the library catalog, which may be print-based but is increasingly likely to be computerized.

- The World Wide Web is another major source of information. Web users access Web pages (or sites) by using a browser, locate information by using search engines, and move from site to site by following links on each Web page.

What do I need to keep in mind as I use the Web to gather information?

- Using the Web effectively to find information can be tricky. It has many dead ends, false trails, and distractions, and the accuracy of the information presented as fact can be difficult to assess.

- Information on the Web must be carefully evaluated by considering how reliable the source is, how current the information is, how well the source's claims are documented, and how complete the information is.

Key Terms and Concepts

Abstract (p. 267)
Browser (p. 269)
Call number (p. 268)
Distance learning (p. 260)
E-mail (p. 257)
Emoticons (or smileys) (p. 259)
Hardware (p. 251)
Interlibrary loan (p. 269)
Internet (p. 256)
Link (p. 270)
Listserv (p. 257)
Microform (p. 267)

Newsgroup (p. 257)
Presentation programs (p. 254)
Recall (p. 268)
Search engine (p. 271)
Software (p. 252)
Spreadsheet programs (p. 255)
Stacks (p. 268)
Telnet (p. 258)
Web page (p. 270)
Word-processing program (p. 252)
World Wide Web (p. 257)

Resources

On Campus

If you are having difficulty in gaining access to the World Wide Web, you may find help at the college computer center. Most campuses have consultants who can help you with the technical aspects of computer usage.

The librarians at your college library are the people to whom you should turn first if you need help in locating information. In recent years, librarians—most of whom hold advanced degrees—have undergone a significant change in what they do, and most are now equally at home using traditional print material and searching electronic information storehouses.

In Print

A good beginner's guide to computers is Ruth Maran's *Computers Simplified* (Hungry Minds Publisher, 2000). The fifth edition of *Find It Fast: How to Uncover Expert Information on Any Subject* by Robert Berkman (HarperCollins, 2000) provides a step-by-step guide to locating information of all sorts. Finally, Danny Goodman's *Living at Light Speed: Your Survival Guide to Life on the Information Superhighway* (Random House, 1995) provides clear instruction and explanations for using the information superhighway.

On the Web

Many sites on the World Wide Web provide the opportunity to extend your learning about the material in this chapter. (Although the Web addresses were accurate at the time the book was printed, check the P.O.W.E.R. Learning website [**www.mhhe.com/power**] for any changes that may have occurred.)

- Imperial College (London)'s Department of Computing offers FOLDOC (Free Online Dictionary of Computing) at **wombat.doc.ic.ac.uk/foldoc/index.html**. If you're having a hard time trying to figure out some computer jargon, this site—a dictionary of computer terminology—might help. Topics are listed alphabetically and a search engine helps locate specific information.

- The WWW Virtual Library (**www.vlib.org/**) is one of the oldest catalogs of the Web, providing useful links to thousands of subjects.

- Yahoo! (**www.yahoo.com**) is a very popular Internet search engine and subject directory; unlike Google and AltaVista, as subject directory, Yahoo! allows browsing through prearranged categories (e.g., education, health, social science, and more). It also offers easy access to news, weather, maps, the Yellow Pages, and much more.

Taking It to the Net

1 Using the search engine of your choice, find the address for the website of the libraries of the University of California at Berkeley. Once there, try to find "Finding Information on the Internet: A Tutorial." (If you're stumped, you can find the precise URL at the bottom of this page.*) Try the tutorial, which will help you understand many of the basic skills needed to use the Internet effectively. (Would taking the tutorial *first* have helped you to find it?)

2 To see for yourself how the Web can be a great resource for locating information on important issues, try to find the answer to this question: "What are the effects of media violence on children?" Go to a search engine (try **www.northernlight.com**) and type in the phrase: "media violence and children" (being sure to include the quotation marks). Look over the first page of documents that the search engine turns up. Are they in fact about the effects of media violence on children? Do they answer the question you are asking? What *is* the answer to the question?

* www.lib.berkeley.edu/TeachingLib/Guides/Internet/FindInfo.html.

The Case of . . .

the Missing File

Katrisha was almost done with her paper. She'd been working in a marathon session, sitting in front of her computer screen with only a couple of breaks over the course of an afternoon.

She'd begun work just after noon, when the sky was bright and clear. By now, some 4 hours later, it was dark and gray and she heard thunder in the distance. But who cared about the weather? The main thing was that she was almost done.

She didn't usually put things off, but this time she'd gotten behind and was forced to do the work at the last minute. She was writing a report on software that blocks "adult" sites from home computers. Luckily she'd been able to find what she needed using various search engines and incorporating the information into her paper.

The assignment was due by 5:00 P.M., but the professor accepted papers submitted via e-mail. As long as the message was sent before 5:00, she would be OK. She still had an hour to put the final touches on the paper and send it off.

Suddenly, there was a bright flash of lightning, followed by a clap of thunder. At the same moment, her computer screen went black as the electricity was cut.

Much to Katrisha's relief, the outage lasted only a few seconds. Her computer began to reboot, and the screen powered up again. In a few moments, she figured, she could continue her work.

But when the computer had fully restarted, the file with the paper that she'd been working on all day was nowhere to be found. She searched frantically through the various files on the computer, but to no avail. Her heart sinking, she realized that everything she had done over the afternoon was lost.

1. How well did Katrisha use her time to work on her paper? What advice would you give her about the preparation stage of working on a paper?

2. Did Katrisha organize her work well? What would you tell her to do next time?

3. Clearly, Katrisha should have saved her work frequently while she was working. What else should she have done while working on her paper to help her recover from such a catastrophe?

4. What should Katrisha do first to start solving her immediate problem with her professor?

5. What should she do next to begin reconstructing her paper and recovering as much of her work as possible?

Making Decisions That Are Right for You

11

or Rich Rinkowski, the moment of truth was fast approaching. He had to make up his mind and decide what he was going to do when he graduated.

Throughout his college career he had intended to go to law school, and he had majored in criminal justice. He'd already been accepted to law school by the middle of his senior year and it seemed that his future was well in hand.

Except for one thing: He was no longer sure he wanted to be a lawyer.

The reason for his indecision was an internship he held working for a film director during the summer between his junior and senior years.

Although Rich spent a good deal of his time photocopying and making coffee, he learned a lot about the film industry. In fact, after talking several times at length with the director, Rich began to wonder seriously if he might build a career in the movie industry.

Rich's girlfriend and family were dead set against it: they argued that law was a far safer choice.

As his final term went by, Rich knew he had to make up his mind. But how?

Looking
Ahead

Like Rich, all of us face important decisions in our lives at one time or another. How can we make the *right* decisions? The best way is to employ some basic techniques that can help improve the quality of our decision making.

This chapter will give you a sense of what decision making is and is not, and it discusses a structured process that can help make your decisions the right ones. We'll also consider the related issue of problem solving. You'll confront a variety of problems as you proceed through college. We'll look at a number of proven techniques that will help you solve them.

Neither making decisions nor solving problems is easy. Sometimes the best decision or solution to a problem is one that we don't see at first; we all have mental blind spots. The best problem solvers and decision makers have learned how to use critical thinking to see around these blind spots. To help you improve your critical thinking skills, we'll examine some common problems that can affect our thinking and discuss several biases that can make us jump too quickly to conclusions.

In sum, after reading this chapter you'll be able to answer these questions:

- **How can I improve the quality of my decisions?**

- **What strategies can I use for problem solving?**

- **What are some problems that affect critical thinking and how can I avoid them?**

Making Good Decisions: A Framework

Decision making is the process of deciding among various alternatives. Whether you are trying to decide between a Ford or a Honda; between an apartment that is close to your job or one that is close to campus; or simply between a hamburger or pizza—every one of these choices requires a decision. Some decisions are easily made and have few consequences, but others, such as whether to major in music composition or follow a pre-med course of study, can involve the deepest examination of our beliefs and values.

Decision making
The process of deciding among various alternatives

> "Nothing is more difficult, and therefore more precious, than to be able to decide."
>
> Napoleon I, *Maxims* (1804–15)

Whatever the decision you face, it is possible to map out a strategy for making the choice that is best for you. Every decision can benefit from your systematically thinking through the options involved, based on the P.O.W.E.R. Plan illustrated below.

P repare: Identifying Your Goals

Every decision starts with the end you have in mind: the goals you wish to accomplish by making the decision.

For example, suppose you are trying to decide between enrolling in one of two classes next term, neither of which is required: swimming or psychology. To decide, you need to consider both your short- and long-term goals. For instance, the swimming class may raise your level of fitness, and you'll end up with a certificate that will allow you to be a lifeguard during the summer. The psychology class may provide you with some useful information—perhaps information you can use in other classes, perhaps techniques that will help you learn and remember better—but this is by no means certain. In terms of short-term goals, then, the swimming class may be the better choice. On the other hand, while the psychology class may not provide as clear-cut an immediate payoff, it may help you meet your longer-term goal of graduating with honors and becoming a successful teacher.

In short, every decision should start with a consideration of what our short- and long-term goals are. Identifying the goals that underlie decisions ensures that we make decisions in the context of our entire lives and not just to provide short-term answers to immediate problems.

O rganize: Considering and Assessing the Alternatives

Every decision is based on weighing various alternatives. Determining what those alternatives are, and their possible consequences, is often the most difficult part of decision making.

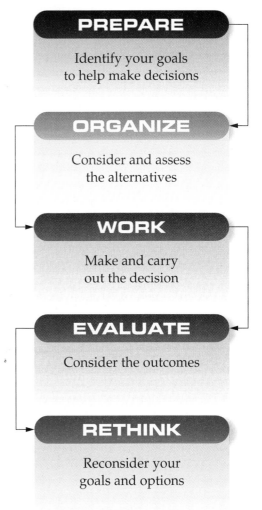

PREPARE

Identify your goals
to help make decisions

ORGANIZE

Consider and assess
the alternatives

WORK

Make and carry
out the decision

EVALUATE

Consider the outcomes

RETHINK

Reconsider your
goals and options

P.O.W.E.R. Plan

We've all been there: facing a mind-boggling array of similar choices. However, by systematically assessing the alternatives, it's possible to make an informed decision that will satisfy us.

Develop a List of Flexible Alternatives   It's important not only to think thoroughly about the obvious alternatives, but also to consider those that are less obvious. For instance, if you are trying to obtain additional funds to support your college theater group, you might consider raising ticket prices for productions, holding a raffle to raise funds, or asking for sponsorship from a local business. After additional thought, though, you might reframe the issue, considering how best to place pressure on the college administration to increase funding for your group.

In short, the way you develop and frame alternatives is critical to the solution that you ultimately reach. The more alternatives you have, the better able you will be to come to a good solution.

How can you be sure that you've considered all the alternatives? You can't. But using the freewriting technique described in Chapter 7 can help you maximize your efforts.

In *freewriting*, one writes continuously for a fixed period of time, perhaps 5 or 10 minutes. During this period, the idea is to write as many different ideas as possible, without stopping. It makes no difference whether the alternatives are good or bad or even whether they make sense. All that matters is that you let yourself brainstorm about the topic for a while and get it down on paper.

With freewriting, evaluating the worth of the ideas you've generated comes later. After you have produced as many possibilities as you can, then you go back and sift out the reasonable ones from those that are truly unlikely or just

Try It! 1

Use Freewriting

Use freewriting to think of as many answers as you can to each of the following questions. The ground rules are that you should spend 3 minutes on each question, generating as many ideas as possible—regardless of whether they are feasible. To give yourself maximum freedom, write each answer on a separate page.

1. How can you make room in your schedule to take one more course next term than you're taking this term?

2. How can someone get from the 3rd floor to the 20th floor of a building?

3. What should you do if you suspect that one of your instructors is a space alien?

4. What would happen if the average life span were extended to 125 years?

After generating ideas, go back and evaluate them. How many were actually feasible or realistic? Do you think freewriting led to the production of more or fewer ideas than you would have come up with if you hadn't used the process? Did the quality of ideas change? **Working in a Group** After you have answered the questions above, form a group of classmates and compare your answers to those of others. As a group, try to identify the best answers to each question.

To Try It online, go to **www.mhhe.com/power**.

plain wacky. It's OK if you have to delete quite a few alternatives from your list; the process is likely to have liberated some truly reasonable alternatives that you might not otherwise have come up with. (Try the technique in the "Use Freewriting" exercise—see Try It 1.)

Assess Alternatives Once you have generated as extensive a list of alternatives as possible, assess them. You need to follow three key steps when assessing each alternative:

1. *Determine the possible outcomes for each alternative.* Some outcomes are positive, some negative. Consider as many as you can think of. For example, if you are considering ways of solving transportation problems, one alternative might be to purchase a car. That alternative produces several potential outcomes. For example, you know that it will be easier to get wherever you want to go, and you might even have a better social life—clearly positive outcomes. But it is also true that buying and owning a car will be expensive, or it may be difficult to find convenient parking—both significant negative outcomes.

2. *Determine the probability that those outcomes will take place.* Some outcomes are far more likely than others. To take this into account, make a rough estimate of the likelihood that an outcome will come to pass, ranging from 100 percent (it is certain that it will occur) to 0 percent (it is certain that it will never occur). For instance, consider the possible outcomes to buying a car this way:

**Alternative:
Purchase car**

Outcome	Probability
Easier transportation	100%
Greater expense	100
Greater opportunities for part-time job	75
Difficulty finding parking	40
Improve social life	30

Obviously, the probabilities are just guesses, but going through the exercise of estimating them will make the outcomes more real and will permit you to compare the various alternatives against one another more easily.

3. *Compare the alternatives, taking into account the potential outcomes of each.* Systematically compare each of the alternatives as illustrated above. Then ask yourself the key question: Which alternative, on balance, provides the most positive (and most likely) outcomes?

Obviously, not every decision requires such an elaborate process. In fact, most won't. But when it comes to major decisions, those that could have a large impact upon you and your life, it's worthwhile to follow a systematic process.

Take a look at Career Connections on page 290 for another process that you can follow to help you make a career decision.

W ork: Making and Carrying Out the Decision

Working through the previous steps will lead you to the point of decision: choosing one of the alternatives you've identified. Having carried out the steps will make the actual decision easier, but not necessarily easy.

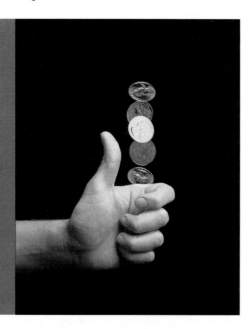

If all else fails, toss a coin to decide what alternative to follow. Tossing a coin at least brings you to a decision. Then, if you find you're unhappy with the result, you'll have gained important information about how you really feel regarding a particular choice.

Choosing among Alternatives The reason that important decisions are difficult is that the alternatives you have to choose from carry both benefits and costs. Choosing one alternative means that you have to accept the costs of that choice and give up the benefits of the other alternatives.

What if, after going through the steps of the process laid out here, you still can't make up your mind? Try these strategies:

- **Give the decision time.** Sometimes waiting helps. Time can give you a chance to think of additional alternatives. Sometimes the situation will change, or you'll have a change in viewpoint.

- **Make a mental movie, acting out the various alternatives.** Many of us have difficulty seeing ourselves in the future and envisioning how various options would play out. One way to get around this difficulty is to cast yourself into a series of "mental movies" that have different endings depending on the decision you make. Working through the different scripts in your head makes potential outcomes far more real and less abstract than they would be if you simply left them as items on a list of various options.

- **Toss a coin.** This isn't as crazy as it sounds. If each alternative seems equally positive or negative to you, pull out a coin—make option A "heads" and B "tails." Then flip it.

  The real power of the coin-toss strategy is that it might help you discover your true feelings. It may happen while the coin is in the air, or it may be that when you see the result of the coin toss, you won't like the outcome and will say to yourself, "No way." In such a case, you've just found out how you really feel.

- **Learn to view indecision as a decision.** Sometimes we spend so much time making a decision that our indecision becomes a decision. It works like this: Suppose a friend asks you to help her work on a student government task force that is studying the use of alcohol on campus. You'd like to participate, but, because you'll have to commit to a term-long series of meetings, you're worried about the amount of time it will take up.

  Because the first meeting isn't going to occur for a few weeks, you have some time to make up your mind. But you just can't seem to decide. Finally, it's the day of the meeting, and you still don't know what to do.

  The truth is, you've made the decision: You don't really want to be on the committee. Your indecision is telling you that—bottom line—you don't have sufficient interest to make the commitment.

- **Go with your gut feeling.** Call it what you like—gut feeling, intuition, hunch, superstition—but sometimes we need to go with our hearts and

Journal Reflections

My Decision Crossroads

Have you ever made a decision that proved to be of great importance in terms of the direction your life would take? For example, perhaps you broke off a romantic relationship, or decided to quit a sports team because practice took up so much time, or participated in an act of civil disobedience during a protest rally. Reflect on that decision by answering these questions.

1. What was an important decision that you made that had significant effects on your life?

2. What have been the main benefits and disadvantages that you derived from the decision?

3. Every decision to do something is also a decision not to do other things. What did your decision keep you from doing?

4. Considering both the benefits and disadvantages of the decision, would you say that you made a good decision?

Career Connections

Weighing Career Possibilities

One of the most important decisions you'll ever make is choosing a career. Here's one method that can help you:

- **Generate a selection of choices to consider after graduation.** Make a list of possibilities—including work (e.g., computer programming, banking, teaching, law, business, insurance, computer software development, etc.), further study (e.g., graduate school, business school, law school, etc.), and even some pie-in-the-sky possibilities (e.g., jazz musician, circus performer).

- **Determine life-satisfaction considerations that are important to you.** Generate a list of criteria to use in weighing these postgraduation possibilities. For instance, you might want to consider the following:

   Benefit to society.

   Income.

   Parents' opinions.

   Friends' opinions.

   Interest in the activity.

   Prestige.

   Job security/ job openings.

   Benefits (vacation, health insurance, etc.).

   Time off.

   Practicality/attainability.

   Everyday working conditions.

- **Determine how well a particular option fulfills each of the life-satisfaction factors you consider important.** By systematically considering how a potential postgraduation path fulfills each of the criteria you use, you'll be able to compare different options. One easy way to do this is to create a chart like the one in Table 11.1 (which shows an example of how computer programming might fulfill the various criteria).

- **Compare different choices.** Using the chart, evaluate your possibilities. Keep in mind that this is just a rough guide and that it's only as accurate as (a) the effort you put into completing it and (b) your understanding of a given choice. Use the results in conjunction with other things you find out about careers—and yourself.

Table 11.1

Making Career Decisions

Life-Satisfaction Considerations	Possible Choice #1 *Computer programming*	Possible Choice #2	Possible Choice #3	Possible Choice #4
Benefit society	✓			
Income	✓			
Parents' opinions	✓			
Friends' opinions				
Interest in the activity	✓			
Prestige				
Job security/job openings	✓			
Benefits	✓			
Time off				
Practicality/attainability	✓			
Everyday working conditions				
Other				
Other				
Other				
Other				
Other				

not our minds. If you've thought rationally about a decision and have been unable to determine the best course of action but have a gut feeling that one choice is better than another, follow your feelings.

Following a gut feeling does not mean that you don't need to consider the pros and cons of a decision rationally and carefully. In fact, generally our "intuitions" are best when informed by the thoughtfulness of a more rational process.

> "Each of us has the right and the responsibility to assess the roads which lie ahead and . . . if the future road looms ominous or unpromising . . . then we need to gather our resolve and . . . step off . . . into another direction."
>
> Maya Angelou, poet

Carrying Out the Decision Ultimately, decisions must move from thought to action—they have to be carried out. Consequently, the final stage in making a decision is to act upon it. You need to turn your decision into behavior.

E valuate: Considering the Outcomes

Did you make the right decision?

Even if you've spent time and mental effort in thinking through a decision, you still need to consider the results. Even well-considered decisions can end up being wrong, either because you neglected to consider something or because something has changed: either you or the situation.

For instance, suppose you were trying to decide between a major in management or one in biology. If you decide to go into management, it means that you'll be taking more courses related to finance and economics. As you take these courses, you will find out whether you're enjoying them. If you find you are consistently unhappy with them, you should allow yourself to reevaluate your decision to major in management and reconsider the alternatives. It's not too late to change your mind.

In fact, even major life decisions are often reversible. That's why it's so important to evaluate your choices. If you chose the wrong alternative, reverse course and reconsider your options.

Remember: It's not a bad thing to change your mind. In fact, admitting that a decision was a mistake is often the wisest and most courageous course of action. You don't want to be so rigidly committed to a decision that you're unable to evaluate the consequences objectively. Give yourself permission to be wrong.

R ethink: Reconsidering Your Goals and Options

We can get to most places by multiple routes. There's the fastest and most direct route, which will get us to our destination in the least amount of time. Then there's the longer, more scenic route, where the trip itself provides pleasure. You can "take the long way home," as the song goes.

Is one route better than the other? Often not. Both take us to our destination. However, the experience of reaching our goal will have been very different.

Decisions about how to achieve a goal are similar to traveling down different routes. There's often no single decision that is best, just as there's often no single road to a particular place. Consequently, it's important to periodically reconsider the major decisions that we've made about our lives.

Ask yourself these questions:

- Are my decisions still producing the desired consequences?
- Are my decisions still appropriate, given my circumstances and changes in my life?
- Are my decisions consistent with what I want to get out of life?
- Do my decisions fit with my mission statement (a written, guiding philosophy of life, discussed in Chapter 3)?

Periodically taking stock like this is the best way to make sure that your decisions are taking you where you want to go. Taking stock also helps you to be more effective in making future decisions.

Transferring
Changing colleges

Deciding to Change Colleges   One of the biggest decisions you'll potentially face involves changing colleges, or **transferring.** You may be changing from a 2-year to a 4-year school. Or you may find that your current school doesn't offer the course of study you want or meet some other important need. Whatever the reason, there are several questions to keep in mind when making such an important decision:

- **Do I meet the minimum requirements for admission?** Every college has its own requirements for admission. For example, you'll probably be required to have a minimum grade point average for admission.

- **What new requirements will I have to meet at another school?** Because every school has its own particular set of requirements, you'll want to know the courses you'll have to take to graduate.

- **What courses have I taken that the other school will accept as meeting its requirements?** You'll need to determine the degree of *course equivalency*, in which courses you've already taken substitute for courses at another college.

- **Is there an** *articulation agreement* **between my current school and the school I'm considering transferring to?** *Articulation agreements* are official pacts between schools that set out course equivalency.

Problem Solving: Applying Critical Thinking to Find Solutions

Two trains are approaching one another, each moving at 60 miles an hour. If the trains continue moving at the same speed, how long will it be before . . .

If this is what comes to mind when you think of problem solving, think again. **Problem solving** encompasses more than the abstract, often unrealistic situations portrayed in math texts. It involves everyday, commonplace situations: How do we divide the grocery bill so that each person pays a fair share? How do I keep my 1-year-old from tumbling down the stairs when there seems to be no way to fasten a gate at the top? How can I stop a faucet from dripping? How do I manage to study for a test and complete a paper the same evening?

While decision making is most focused on choosing among various alternatives, the central issue in problem solving is *generating* alternatives. Since many problems require that decisions be made regarding alternatives, decision making and problem solving are often related.

Problem solving
The process of generating alternatives to work on

What's the Problem?

The first step in solving any problem is to be as clear as you can about what the problem is. This may sound easy, but often it isn't. In fact, it may take some time to figure out just what is at stake. The reason is that some problems are big and hard to define, while others are quite precise, such as mathematical equations or the solution to a jigsaw puzzle. Determining how to stop terrorism or finding peace in the Middle East are big, ill-defined problems. Simply determining what information is required to solve such problems can be a major undertaking.

To determine what the problem is and set yourself on a course for finding a solution, ask yourself these questions:

1. What is the initial set of facts?

2. What is it that you need to solve?

3. Which parts of the problem appear to be most critical to finding a solution?

4. Is there some information that can be ignored?

As you clarify what the problem is, you may find that you have encountered similar problems before. Your experience with them may suggest the means to the solution of the current problem. For example, consider the problem of the trains rushing toward one another. If you have worked on this kind of problem before, you might know a fairly simple equation you can write to determine how long it will take before they meet. If someone asks you about the problem they have keeping their toddler from tumbling down the stairs, you might offer your experience in keeping your puppy from visiting an off-limits area of your house.

> "Problems are only opportunities in work clothes."
>
> Henry J. Kaiser, *Maxim*

On the other hand, to solve many of the problems we face in our daily lives, we have to do more than reach into our memories of prior situations. Instead, we need to devise novel approaches. How do you do this? There are several strategies you might use.

Strategies for Working on Life's Messier Problems

- **Break the problem down into smaller, more manageable pieces.** Break a problem down into a series of subgoals. As you reach each subgoal, you get closer to your overall goal of solving the problem. For example, if your goal is to spend your junior year in your school's program in St. Petersburg, a subgoal would probably be to learn some basic Russian. By reaching this subgoal, you move closer to reaching your ultimate goal—a year abroad in a country that interests you.

- **Work backward.** Sometimes you know the answer to the problem, but not how to get there. Then it's best to work backward. A **working backward** strategy starts at the desired solution or goal and works backward, moving away from the goal. For example, consider this problem:

Working backward

The strategy of starting at the desired solution or goal and working toward the starting point of the problem

> Water lilies on a certain lake double in area every 24 hours. From the time the first water lily appears until the lake is completely covered takes 60 days. On what day is the lake half covered?

Most people solve this problem readily if they work backward. Here's how: If the pond is fully covered on day 60, how much is it covered the day before? Because the water lilies double each day, there had to be half as many the day before day 60. The answer, then, is that half the lake is covered on day 59. Only by moving backward could one see the solution clearly.

Some kinds of academic problems can be solved using the same strategy. For example, if you know what courses you must have completed to graduate, it's sometimes easiest to work backward from that point, determining the courses you need to take each year.

- **Use a graph, chart, or drawing to redefine the problem.** Transforming words into pictures often can help us to devise solutions that otherwise would elude us. One good example is this problem:

  > A man climbs a mountain on Saturday, leaving at daybreak and arriving at the top near sundown. He spends the night at the top. The next day, Sunday, he leaves at daybreak and heads down the mountain, following the same path that he climbed the day before. The question is this: Will there be any time during the second day when he will be at exactly the same point on the mountain as he was at exactly that time on the first day?

  Trying to solve the problem through the use of algebra or words is quite difficult. However, there's a simpler way: drawing the two paths. As you can see from Figure 11.1, the drawing provides a clear solution.

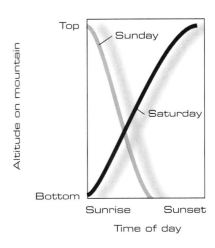

Figure 11.1

Up and Down the Mountain: The Paths to a Solution

- **Consider the opposite.** Problems can sometimes be solved by considering the opposite of the problem you're seeking to solve. For example, to define "good mental health" you might try to define "bad mental health."

- **Use analogies.** Some problems can be solved through the use of **analogies,** comparisons between concepts or objects that are alike in some respects, but dissimilar in most others. For instance, if you liken a disastrous experience attending summer camp to a voyage on the *Titanic,* you're using an analogy.

  Analogies may help us gain additional insight into the problem at hand, and they may provide an alternative framework for interpreting the information that is provided. For instance, the manufacturers of Pringles potato chips found that they could cut packaging costs if they slightly moistened the chips before packaging them—an idea that came when researchers noticed that dry tree leaves, which normally crumble easily, could be packed together tightly when they were wet.

Analogy

A comparison between concepts or objects that are alike in some respects, but dissimilar in most others

- **Take another's perspective.** By viewing a problem from another person's point of view, it is often possible to obtain a new perspective on the problem that will make the problem easier to solve.

- **Forget about it.** Just as with decision making, sometimes it's best simply to walk away from a problem for a while. Just a few hours or days away from a problem may give us enough of a break to jar some hidden solutions from the recesses of our minds. The idea of "sleeping on it" also sometimes works; we may wake up refreshed and filled with new ideas.

Test these problem-solving skills in Try It 2 on the next page.

Assessing Your Potential Solutions

If a problem clearly has only one answer, such as a math problem, this step in problem solving is relatively easy. You should be able to work the problem and figure out whether you've been successful. In contrast, messier problems

Try It! 2

🌴 **Working in a Group:** Exercise Your Problem-Solving Skills

Working in a group, try to solve these problems.[1] To help you devise solutions, a hint regarding the best strategy to use is included after each problem.

1. One cold, dark, and rainy night, a college student has a flat tire on a deserted stretch of country road. He pulls onto the shoulder to change it. After removing the four lug nuts and placing them into the hub cap, he removes the flat tire and takes his spare out of the trunk. As he is moving the spare tire into position, his hand slips and he upsets the hub cap with the lug nuts, which tumble off into the night where he can't find them. What should he do? (*Hint:* Instead of asking how he might find the lug nuts, reframe the problem and ask where else he might find lug nuts.)

2. Cheryl, who is a construction worker, is paving a walk, and she needs to add water quickly to the concrete she has just poured. She reaches for her pail to get water from a spigot in the front of the house, but suddenly realizes the pail has a large rust hole in it and cannot be used. As the concrete dries prematurely, she fumbles through her toolbox for tools and materials with which to repair the pail. She finds many tools, but nothing that would serve to patch the pail. The house is locked and no one is home. What should she do? (*Hint:* When is a pail not a pail?)

3. What day follows the day before yesterday if 2 days from now will be Sunday? (*Hint:* Break it up or draw a diagram.)

4. A caterpillar has to climb up the muddy wall of a well that is 12 feet deep. Each day the caterpillar advances 4 feet, but each night as he sleeps, he slips back 2 feet. How many days will it take him to get out? (*Hint:* Draw it.)

5. Carrie has four chains, each three links long. She wants to join the four chains into a single, closed chain. Having a link opened costs 2 cents and having a link closed costs 3 cents. How can Carrie have the chains joined for 15 cents? (*Hint:* Can only end links be opened?)

6. What is two-thirds of one-half? (*Hint:* Reverse course.)

7. Juan has three separate large boxes. Inside each large box are two separate medium-sized boxes, and inside each of the medium boxes are four small boxes. How many boxes does Juan have altogether? (*Hint:* Draw it.)

After working to solve these problems, consider these questions: Which problems were the easiest to solve, and which were more difficult? Why? Were the hints helpful? Do you think there was more than one solution to any of the problems? Did your initial assumptions about the problem help or hinder your efforts to solve it? (*Note:* Answers to the problems are found at the end of the chapter.)

To Try It online, go to **www.mhhe.com/power**.

have several possible solutions, some of which may be more involved and costly than others. In these cases, it's necessary to compare alternative solutions and choose the best one. For example, suppose you want to surprise your best friend on her birthday. She is working in Omaha, about 90 miles from you, and you need to find a way to get there. Perhaps you could rent a car, take a bus, or find some other way. Money is an issue. You will want to figure out how much each alternative costs before choosing one as your solution to the problem. Since every penny you spend getting there is a penny less that you will have to celebrate, you will want to weigh the options carefully.

Finally, spend a bit of time seeing whether there is a way to refine the solution. Is the solution you've devised adequate? Does it address all aspects of the problem? Are there alternative approaches that might be superior? Answering these questions, and refining your solution to address them, can give you confidence that the solution you've come up with is the best. For example, if you're trying to get to Omaha, you might decide to use the ride board at your school to try to find a ride with someone going to Omaha that day. Maybe your friend's family is going to be driving in and could pick you up or could even lend you a car for the trip.

Remember that not every problem has a clear-cut solution. Sometimes we need to be satisfied with a degree of uncertainty and ambiguity. For some of us, such a lack of clarity is difficult, making us uneasy, and it may push us to choose solutions—any solution—that seems to solve the problem. Others of us feel more comfortable with ambiguity, but this may lead us to let problems ride, without resolving the situation.

Either way, it's important to consider what your own problem-solving style is when you seek to identify solutions. And keep in mind that often there is no perfect solution to a problem—only some solutions that are better than others. (To find out whether you have a high need for clarity in problem-solving or whether you tolerate ambiguity more easily, complete Try It 3.)

Reflect on the Process of Problem Solving

It's natural to step back and bask in the satisfaction of solving a tough problem. That's fine—but take a moment to consider your success. Each time we solve a problem we end up a couple steps ahead, but only if we've thought about the process we went through to solve it.

Go back and consider what it took to solve the problem. Can the means you used to come up with your solution be applied to more complex kinds of problems? If you arrived at a solution by drawing a chart, would this work on similar problems in the future? Taking a moment to rethink your solution can provide you with an opportunity to become an expert problem solver and, more generally, to improve your critical thinking skills. Don't let the opportunity slip away.

Don't Fool Yourself: Avoiding Everyday Problems in Critical Thinking

Being able to think clearly and without bias is the basis for critical thinking. As you have probably noticed already, the quality of the thinking you do regarding problems and decisions plays a crucial role in determining how successful you are.

Unfortunately, it is sometimes the alternative you *didn't* think of that can end up being the most satisfactory decision or solution. So how can we learn

Personal Styles: Find Your Problem-Solving Style

To get a sense of how much you prefer ambiguity versus clarity in the problems you face, rate how much you agree with each of the statements in the questionnaire[2] below. Use this rating scale:

1 = Strongly disagree

2 = Disagree

3 = Not sure, but probably disagree

4 = Not sure, but probably agree

5 = Agree

6 = Strongly agree

1. An expert who doesn't come up with a definite answer probably doesn't know too much. _____

2. There is really no such thing as a problem that can't be solved. _____

3. A good job is one where what is to be done and how it is to be done are always clear. _____

4. In the long run, it is possible to get more done by tackling small, simple problems than large and complicated ones. _____

5. What we are used to is always preferable to what is unfamiliar. _____

6. A person who leads a well-organized, routine life in which few surprises or unexpected happenings arise really has a lot to be grateful for. _____

7. I like parties where I know most of the people more than ones where all or most of the people are complete strangers. _____

to think critically and avoid blind spots that hinder us in our decision making and problem solving? We can start by considering the common obstacles to critical thinking.

Here are some of the decision-making and problem-solving pitfalls to look out for. Avoiding them will improve your critical thinking greatly.

- **Don't assume that giving something a name explains it.** The mere fact that we can give an idea or problem a name doesn't mean we can explain it. Yet we often confuse the two.

    For instance, consider the following sequences of questions and answers:

    Q. Why do I have so much trouble falling asleep?

    A. Because you have insomnia.

8. The sooner we all acquire similar values and ideals, the better. _____

9. I would like to live in a foreign country for a while. _____

10. People who fit their lives to a schedule probably miss most of the joy of living. _____

11. It is more fun to tackle a complicated problem than to solve a simple one. _____

12. Often the most interesting and stimulating people are those who don't mind being different and original. _____

13. People who insist upon a yes or no answer just don't know how complicated things really are. _____

14. Many of our most important decisions are based upon insufficient information. _____

15. Teachers or supervisors who hand out vague assignments give opportunities for individuals to show initiative and originality. _____

16. A good teacher is one who makes you wonder about your way of looking at things. _____

To score this questionnaire, you'll first need to change the numbers you have in items 9 to 16 in this way: If you've put a 1, change it to a 6; change 2 to 5; change 3 to 4; change 4 to 3; change 5 to 2; and change 6 to 1. (Items 1 to 8 don't need to be changed.) Now add up your total score.

If you scored below 30, you have a low tolerance for ambiguity in problem-solving. You prefer problems to be clear-cut and dislike uncertainty.

If you scored between 30 and 60, you have an average tolerance for ambiguity. Most of the time problems that are vague don't present you with any particular difficulty, although you generally prefer things to be fairly concrete.

If you scored above 60, you have a high tolerance for ambiguous problems. You don't mind—and in fact prefer—problems that are unclear.

To Try It online, go to **www.mhhe.com/power**.

Q. Why is he so unsociable?
A. Because he's an introvert.

Q. Why did the defendant shoot those people?
A. Because he's insane.

Q. How do you know he's insane?
A. Because only someone who was insane would shoot people in that way.[3]

It's clear that none of these answers is satisfactory. All use circular reasoning, in which the alleged explanation for the behavior is simply the use of a label.

- **Don't accept vague generalities dressed up as definitive statements.** Read the following personality analysis and think about how well it applies to you:

> You have a need for other people to like and admire you and a tendency to be critical of yourself. You also have a great deal of unused potential that you have not turned to your advantage, and although you have some personality weaknesses, you are generally able to compensate for them. Nonetheless, relating to members of the opposite sex has presented problems to you, and while you appear to be disciplined and self-controlled to others, you tend to be anxious and insecure inside.

> If you believe that these statements provide an amazingly accurate description of your unique qualities, you're not alone: Most college students believe that the descriptions are tailored specifically to them.[4] But how is that possible? It isn't. The reality is that the statements are so vague that they are virtually meaningless. The acceptance of vague but seemingly useful and significant statements about oneself and others has been called the *Barnum Effect,* after showman and circus master P. T. Barnum, who coined the phrase "there's a sucker born every minute."

- **Don't confuse opinion with fact.** Opinions are not fact. Although we may be aware of this simple formula, almost all of us can be fooled into thinking that someone's opinion is the same as a fact.

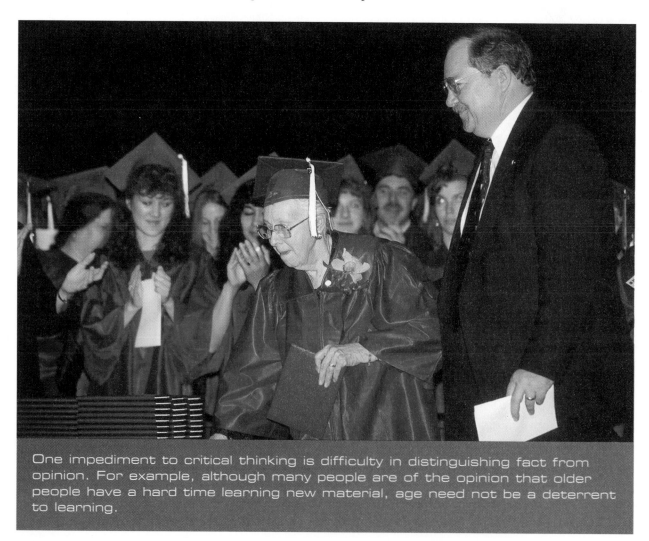

One impediment to critical thinking is difficulty in distinguishing fact from opinion. For example, although many people are of the opinion that older people have a hard time learning new material, age need not be a deterrent to learning.

ry It!

4

Distinguish Fact from Opinion

Read the following statements and try to determine which are facts and which are opinions.

1. College students should get at least 7 hours of sleep every night. _____

2. The average college student sleeps less than 7 hours a night. _____

3. Nikes offer better styling and comfort than any other brand of shoe. _____

4. Two out of five sports figures surveyed preferred Nikes over Converse shoes. _____

5. The U.S. government spends too much money on guns and missiles and not enough money on education. _____

6. Government figures show spending is much higher for guns and missiles than for education. _____

7. In general, U.S. high school students receive less classroom instruction in foreign languages than their counterparts in Europe and Asia. _____

8. No student in the United States should graduate without having studied a language other than English for at least 4 years. _____

9. Michael Jordan is the most outstanding, most exciting, and certainly most successful basketball player who ever stepped onto a court. _____

To Try It online, go to **www.mhhe.com/power**.

A fact is information that is proven to be true. In contrast, an opinion represents judgments, reasoning, beliefs, inferences, or conclusions. If we accept some bit of information as a fact, we can use it to build our opinions. But if we are presented with an opinion, we need to determine the facts on which it is built to judge its reliability.

The difference between fact and opinion can sometimes be subtle. For instance, compare these two statements:

1. Every college student needs to take a writing course during the first term of college.

2. Many college students need to take a writing course during the first term of college.

The first statement is most likely an opinion, because it is so absolute and unqualified. Words such as "every," "all," and "always" are often evidence of opinion. On the other hand, the second statement is more likely a fact, since it contains the qualifier "many." In general, statements that are qualified in some way are more likely to be facts.

Complete Try It 4 to see the difficulties sometimes involved in distinguishing between fact and opinion.

- **Avoid jumping to conclusions.** Read this riddle and try to answer it:

    A father and his son were driving along the interstate highway when the father lost control of the car, swerved off the road, and crashed into a utility pole. The father died instantly, and his son was critically injured. An ambulance rushed the boy to a nearby hospital. A prominent surgeon was summoned to provide immediate treatment. When the surgeon arrived and entered the operating room to examine the boy, a loud gasp was heard. "I can't operate on this boy," the surgeon said. "He is my son."[5]

    How can this be?

    If you find this puzzling, you've based your reasoning on an assumption: that the surgeon is a male. But suppose you had assumed that the surgeon was a female. Suddenly, the riddle becomes a lot easier. It's far easier to guess that the surgeon is the son's *mother* if we don't leap to embrace a faulty assumption.

    Why is it so easy to jump to conclusions? One reason is that we sometimes aren't aware of the assumptions that underlie our thinking. Another is our reliance on "common sense."

- **Don't believe in the myth of common sense.** Much of what we call common sense makes contradictory claims. Which are we to believe? For example, if you believe in the notion "Absence makes the heart grow fonder," you may assume that your high school girlfriend, now in college across the country from you, will arrive home at Christmas even more in love with you than before. But what about "Out of sight, out of mind," which suggests a less positive outcome?

    Common sense often presents us with such contradictory advice. To see this for yourself, take a look at the statements in Try It 5, "Explore the Myth of Common Sense" and see if you can come up with their opposites.

- **Don't assume that just because two events occur together one causes the other.** Just because two events appear to be associated with one another—or, in the language of social science, are *correlated* with one another—we cannot conclude that one event has caused the other to occur. It's a basic rule: *Correlation does not prove causation.*

    For example, suppose you read that a study showed that 89 percent of juvenile delinquents use marijuana. Does this mean that smoking marijuana *causes* juvenile delinquency?

    No, it doesn't. It is pretty safe to say that 100 percent of juvenile delinquents grew up drinking milk. Would you feel comfortable saying that milk causes delinquency? With correlations such as marijuana use and delinquent behavior, it is very likely that there's some third factor—such as influence of peers—that causes people both to (a) try drugs and (b) engage in delinquent behavior. The bottom line: we do not know the cause of the correlation.

    In short, we need to be careful in assuming causality. Even if two events or other kinds of variables occur together, it does not mean that one causes the other.

Explore the Myth of Common Sense

Read the list of proverbs—which represent the common sense of our culture—and see if you can recall another proverb that advises exactly the opposite course of action. Which of the opposing views of common sense is really sensible? Clearly, for any given situation, only hindsight can tell us.

1. A stitch in time saves nine.

Opposite: _____

_____

2. He who hesitates is lost.

Opposite: _____

_____

3. Birds of a feather flock together.

Opposite: _____

_____

4. You're never too old to learn.

Opposite: _____

_____

5. It's no use beating a dead horse.

Opposite: _____

_____

6. A taste of honey is worse than none at all.

Opposite: _____

_____

Answers:

1. Haste makes waste.
2. Look before you leap.
3. Opposites attract.
4. You can't teach an old dog new tricks.
5. If at first you don't succeed, try, try again.
6. 'Tis better to have loved and lost than never to have loved at all.

To Try It online, go to **www.mhhe.com/power**.

Speaking of Success

Name: *Dr. Ben Carson*

Education: *BA, Yale University; MD, University of Michigan Medical School*

Home: *Baltimore, Maryland*

Few who knew Ben Carson as a fifth grader would have guessed that he would become a surgeon whose skills would save the lives of hundreds of patients.

Dr. Carson grew up in a poor, single-parent household in Detroit. His mother, who had only a third-grade education, worked two jobs cleaning bathrooms.

To his classmates—and even to his teachers—he was thought of as "the dumbest kid in the class," according to his own not-so-fond memories. He had a terrible temper and once tried to stab another child.

Dr. Carson was headed down a path of self-destruction until a critical moment in his youth: His mother, convinced that she had to do something dramatic to prevent him from leading a life of failure, laid down some rules. He could not watch television except for two programs a week, could not play with his friends after school until he finished his

homework, and had to read two books a week and write book reports about them.

His mother's strategy worked. As he wrote his weekly book reports for his mother, worlds opened to him.

"Of course, we didn't know she

couldn't read, so there we were submitting these reports," he says. "She would put check marks on them like she had been reading them. As I began to read about scientists, economists, and philosophers, I started imagining myself in their shoes."[6]

As he got in the habit of hard work, his grades began to soar. Ultimately, he received a scholarship to attend Yale University, and later he was admitted to the University of Michigan Medical School. He is now head of pediatric neurosurgery at Johns Hopkins University, one of the most prestigious medical schools in the world; he is also the author of three books.

Dr. Carson tries to pass on to others the lessons he learned as a child. He has established a fund for students in grades 4 through 12 who maintain a 3.75 grade point average. Each month, 800 children come to his hospital, where he underscores the importance of education. As he says, "There is absolutely nothing in this world that you can't become simply through the acquisition of knowledge, because knowledge creates power and you make yourself into a more valuable person."[7]

How can I improve the quality of my decisions?

- A structured process of decision making can clarify the issues involved, expand our options, and improve the quality of our choices.

- Good decision making begins with understanding your short- and long-term goals.

- Decision making is improved if you have a large number of alternatives.

- For difficult decisions, strategies include giving the decision time, acting out alternatives, tossing a coin to test our feelings, understanding that indecision is often a decision itself, and acting on gut feelings.

What strategies can I use for problem solving?

- Problem solving entails the generation of alternatives to consider.

- We need to first understand and define the problem and to determine the important elements in coming to a solution to a problem.

- Approaches to generating solutions include breaking problems into pieces, working backward, using pictures, considering the opposite, using analogies, taking another's perspective, and "forgetting" the problem.

- Problem solving ultimately requires the evaluation and refinement of the solutions that have been generated.

What are some problems that affect critical thinking, and how can I avoid them?

- Labeling, using vague generalities, accepting opinion as fact, jumping to conclusions, mistaking common sense, and assuming correlation all pose threats to critical thinking.

- Awareness of the biases that may affect our thinking can help us avoid them.

Key Terms and Concepts

Analogy (p. 295)
Decision making (p. 285)
Problem solving (p. 293)

Transferring (p. 292)
Working backward (p. 294)

Resources

On Campus

Some colleges offer courses in critical thinking, and they are a good bet to help increase decision-making and problem-solving skills. In addition, courses in logic and philosophy will help improve critical thinking skills.

If you are having a personal problem that is difficult to solve, you can turn to staff at the campus counseling center, mental health center, or residential life office. Even if the person with whom you speak initially is not the right one, he or she can direct you to someone who can help.

In Print

If you have trouble making good decisions, J. Edward Russo and Paul Schoemaker's *Winning Decisions: Getting It Right the First Time* (Doubleday, 2001) is for you. Another approach to decision making is found in H. W. Lewis book *Why Flip a Coin? The Art and Science of Good Decisions* (Wiley, 1998), which shows how to make a rational decision based on the information at hand. For a general overview of thinking critically, read Alec Fisher's *Critical Thinking* (Cambridge University Press, 2002).

On the Web

The following sites on the World Wide Web provide the opportunity to extend your learning about the material in this chapter. (Although the Web addresses were accurate at the time the book was printed, check the P.O.W.E.R. Learning website [**www.mhhe.com/power**] for any changes that may have occurred.)

- Mind Tools, Ltd. (**www.psychwww.com/mtsite/index.html**) offers links to other sites that can help with setting goals, time management, and stress control and to numerous other helpful sites. It also includes shareware for setting up life plans.

- "Basic Guidelines to Problem Solving and Decision Making" (**www.mapnp.org/library/prsn_prd/prb_bsc.htm**) by Carter McNamara, PhD, provides basic guidelines to problem solving and decision making in seven steps. This site is rich in links to comprehensive approaches to decision making, critical and creative thinking, time management, and organizing yourself.

- "Critical Thinking Core Concepts" (**www.kcmetro.cc.mo.us/longview/ctac/corenotes.htm**), by Lauren Miller and Michael Connelly of Longview Community College, presents principles of critical thinking with exercises and examples. The site contains a short history of logic and answers the question: "What is the point of studying critical thinking?"

- "Effective Decision Making: How to Decide What to Do Next" (**www.geodex.com/decmak.html**) provides a general outline of steps to follow in helping you to make better decisions.

Taking It to the Net

1 Making good decisions can depend on distinguishing legitimate appeals (good reasons) from fallacious appeals (bad reasons). Go to San Jose State University's "Mission: Critical," an interactive tutorial in critical thinking (**www.sjsu.edu/depts/itl/graphics/adhom/appeal.html**). After reading the description of the different kinds of fallacious appeals, do the related exercises.

2 Locate three problem-solving strategies on the Internet. Possible strategy: Go to Yahoo! (**www.yahoo.com**) or AltaVista (**www.altavista.com**), and enter the key phrase "problem solving." Search the results until you find at least three different problem-solving strategies. Are these strategies similar to the ones described in the book? If not, how are they different?

Answers to Try It 2 problems:

1. Remove one lug nut from each of the other three tires on the car and use these three to attach the spare tire. This will hold until four more lug nuts can be purchased.

2. Dump the tools out of the toolbox and use it as a pail.

3. Thursday.

4. Five days; on the fifth day the caterpillar will reach the top and will not have to slide down again.

5. Open all three links on one chain (cost = 6 cents) and use them to fasten the other three chains together (cost = 9 cents; total cost = 15 cents).

6. It is the same as one-half of two-thirds, or one-third.

7. 33 boxes (3 large, 6 medium, 24 small).

The Case of . . .

Left Holding the Lease

Erica had a problem.

In the spring of her first year of college, she and her friend Shira had found a two-bedroom apartment to share for the upcoming school year. The apartment was on the expensive side, but they had decided that it was worth it because it was so close to campus. She and Shira had jointly paid the security deposit on the apartment. However, because Shira hadn't been around when it came time to sign the lease, only Erica had signed it. Consequently, Erica was legally responsible for fulfilling the terms of the lease.

Now, only 2 weeks before the start of the fall term, Shira told Erica that she had realized she couldn't afford the rent and that she had decided she had to live with her parents. Erica was simultaneously furious with Shira and panicky at the thought of having to pay the rent by herself.

How was she going to deal with the problem?

1. Is the problem a purely financial and legal one, or are there personal and social considerations that should be taken into account in solving the problem?

2. Is the problem solely Erica's problem, or should Shira take responsibility for solving it as well?

3. What alternatives does Erica have for dealing with the situation?

4. How should Erica go about evaluating the outcomes for each alternative?

5. Based on your analysis of the problem, what advice would you give Erica for dealing with the situation?

Getting along with Others

12

C ablinasian.

That's the word coined by star golfer Tiger Woods to describe his racial heritage. "Cablinasian" means a mix of Caucasian, Black, Indian, and Asian, and it was a label he didn't find on forms asking for his racial identity when he began college.

But Woods did not want to fit himself into some arbitrary racial category. His mother is from Thailand and his father is African-American, and none of the standard racial categories were appropriate to describe him.

But to Woods, it didn't matter. His background is less important than who he is now and where he is going in the future. "I'm just who I am," he told one interviewer, "whomever you see in front of you."[1]

Looking Ahead

Whether you have skin that is black or white or brown, are Jewish or Muslim or Greek Orthodox, were born in Cuba or Vietnam or Boise, are able-bodied or physically challenged, college presents a world of new opportunities. Because almost every college draws students from a wider sphere than the average high school, college permits you to encounter people with very different backgrounds from your own. If you take the opportunity to form relationships with a variety of individuals, you will increase your understanding of the human experience and enrich your life.

In this chapter, we consider how social diversity and relationships affect your college experience. We examine the increasing diversity of college campuses, which reflects that of society at large, and consider the meanings and social effects of race, ethnicity, and culture. We look at practical strategies for acknowledging—and shedding—prejudice and stereotypes and being receptive to others on their own merits.

We next discuss relationships from a broader perspective, exploring ways that you can build lasting friendships with others. Finally, the chapter discusses the conflicts that can arise between people and what you can do to resolve them.

In short, after reading this chapter you'll know the answers to these questions:

- **Why is the increasing racial, ethnic, and cultural diversity of society important to me?**

- **How can I become more at ease with differences and diversity?**

- **How can I build lasting relationships and deal with conflict?**

Becoming Comfortable in a World of Diversity

No matter where we live, our contacts with others who are racially, ethnically, and physically different from us are increasing. The Internet and World Wide Web are bringing people from across the globe into our homes, as close to us as the computer sitting on our desk. Businesses now operate globally, so co-workers are likely to come from many different countries and cultures. Being comfortable with people whose backgrounds and beliefs may differ from our own is not only a social necessity, but it is virtually a requirement for career success.

By the mid-21st century, the percentage of people in the United States of African, Latin American, Asian, and Arabic ancestry will be greater than the percentage of those of Western European ancestry—a profound statistical, and social, shift. College enrollments will mirror these changes, as populations that were minority become the majority. (You can examine the diversity of your own campus by completing Try It 1.)

Race, Ethnicity, and Culture

Are you African-American or black? Caucasian or white or Euro-American? Hispanic or Latino? American Indian or Native American?

The language we use to describe our ethnic and racial group membership, and those of other people, is in constant flux. And what we call people matters. The subtleties of language affect how people think about members of particular groups, and how they think about themselves.

One of the difficulties in understanding diversity is that many of the terms we use are ill-defined and often are overlapping. The term **race** is generally used to refer to obvious physical differences that set one group apart from others. According to such a definition, whites, blacks, and Asian Americans are typically thought of as belonging to different races, determined largely by biological factors.

Ethnicity refers to shared national origins or cultural patterns. In the United States, for example, Puerto Ricans, Irish, and Italian Americans are

Race
Traditionally, biologically determined physical characteristics that set one group apart from others

Ethnicity
Shared national origins or cultural patterns

Our cultural heritage plays an important role in shaping who we are.

Try It! 1

Determine the Diversity of Your Campus Community

Try to assess the degree of diversity that exists at your college, and the overall attitude toward diversity on your campus, by answering these questions. When thinking of diversity, remember to include the many different ways in which people can be different from one another, including race, ethnicity, culture, sexual orientation, physical challenges, and so on.

Overall, how diverse would you say your campus is?

What is the nature of your college's *student* diversity in terms of statistics regarding membership in different racial, ethnic, or cultural groups?

What is the nature of your college's *faculty* diversity in terms of statistics regarding membership in different racial, ethnic, or cultural groups?

Are many courses available that directly address diversity as an issue? (A good place to check is your college catalog listing of courses in the social sciences and humanities.)

Does your college have an explicit statement of policy and principles relating to diversity and/or the avoidance of discrimination?

Was diversity discussed during your orientation to the campus?

How does the diversity on your campus compare to the following statistics on diversity in the United States as of the 2000 census: white 75 percent; Hispanic or Latino 13 percent; black or African-American 12 percent; Asian 4 percent; two or more races 2.4 percent; American Indian and Alaska Native .9 percent; Native Hawaiian and other Pacific Islander .1 percent; other race 6 percent. (Note: Percentages add up to more than 100 percent because Hispanics may be of any race and are therefore counted under more than one category.)

Look back at your answer to the first question ("Overall, how diverse would you say your campus is?") and answer the question again. Did your response change?

To Try It online, go to **www.mhhe.com/power**.

Culture
The learned behaviors, beliefs, and attitudes that are characteristic of an individual society or population, and the products that people create

categorized as ethnic groups. However, ethnicity—like race—is very much in the eye of the beholder. For instance, a Cuban American who is a third-generation citizen of the United States may feel few ties or associations to Cuba. Yet whites may view her as "Hispanic," and blacks may view her as "white."

Finally, **culture** comprises the learned behaviors, beliefs, and attitudes that are characteristic of an individual society or population. But it's more than that: Culture also encompasses the products that people create, such as architecture, music, art, and literature. Culture is created and shaped by people, but at the same time it creates and shapes people's behavior.

Race, ethnicity, and culture shape each of us to an enormous degree. They profoundly influence our view of others, as well as who we are. They affect how others treat us, and how we treat them in turn. They determine whether we look people in the eye when we meet them, how early we arrive when we're invited to dinner at a friend's house, and even, sometimes, how well we do in school.

Building Cultural Competence

We're not born knowing how to drive a car or cook. We have to learn how to do these things. The same is true of developing a basic understanding of other races, ethnic groups, cultures, and minority groups. Called **cultural competence,** this knowledge of others' customs, perspectives, background, and history can teach us a great deal about others, as well as ourselves. Cultural competence also provides a basis for civic engagement, permitting us to act with civility toward others and to make the most of our contributions to society.

Building cultural competence proceeds in several steps, outlined in the P.O.W.E.R. Plan on the next page.

repare: Accepting Diversity as a Valued Part of Your Life

In the title of her book on social diversity, psychologist Beverly Tatum asks, "Why Are All the Black Kids Sitting Together in the Cafeteria?"[2] She might just as well have asked a similar question about the white kids, the Asian-American kids, and so forth. It often appears as if the world comes already divided into separate racial, ethnic, and cultural groups.

It's more than appearances: We form relationships more easily with others who are similar to us than with those who are different. It's easier to interact with others who look the same as we do, who come from similar backgrounds, and who share our race, ethnicity, and culture because we can take for granted certain shared cultural assumptions and views of the world.

But that doesn't mean that "easy" and "comfortable" translate into "good" or "right." We can learn a great deal more, and grow and be challenged, if we seek out people who are different from us. If you look beyond surface differences and find out what motivates other people, you can become aware of new ways of thinking about family, relationships, earning a living, and the value of education. It can be liberating to realize that others may hold very

Cultural competence
Knowledge and understanding about other races, ethnic groups, cultures, and minority groups

different perspectives from your own and that there are many ways to lead your life.

Letting diversity into your own life also has very practical implications: As we discuss in Career Connections on page 316, learning to accept and work with people who are different from you is a crucial skill that will help you in whatever job you hold.

Prejudice

Evaluations or judgments of members of a group that are based primarily on membership in the group, and not on the particular characteristics of individuals

Stereotypes

Beliefs and expectations about members of a group that are held simply because of their membership in the group

Organize: Exploring Your Own Prejudices and Stereotypes

Arab. Gay. African-American. Hispanic. Female. Disabled. Overweight.

Quick: What comes into your mind when you think about each of these labels? If you're like most people, you don't draw a blank. Instead, a collection of images and feelings comes into your mind, based on what you know, have been told, or assume about the group.

The fact that we don't draw a blank when thinking about each of these terms means that we already have a set of attitudes and beliefs about them and the groups they represent. Acknowledging and then examining these pre-existing assumptions is a first step toward developing cultural competence: We need to explore our own prejudices and stereotypes.

Prejudice refers to evaluations or judgments of members of a group that are based primarily on their membership in the group, rather than on their individual characteristics. For example, the auto mechanic who doesn't expect a woman to understand the repair he is undertaking or the supervisor who finds it unthinkable that a father might want to take leave for child care are engaging in *gender prejudice,* evaluating individuals on the basis of their being a male or female and not on their own specific characteristics or abilities. Similarly, prejudice can be directed toward individuals because of their race, ethnic origin, sexual orientation, age, physical disability, or even physical attractiveness.

Prejudice is maintained by **stereotypes,** beliefs and expectations about members of a group. For example, do you think that women don't drive as well as men? Do you agree that "white men can't jump"? Do you believe that people raised in the jungles of South America are less intelligent than those raised in a Western society? Do you think that people on welfare are lazy? If you answered yes to any of these questions, you hold stereotypes about the group being referred to. It is the degree of generalization involved that makes stereotypes inaccurate. Some white men can't jump. But the fact is, many can—and do—and the stereotypes ignore this diversity.

To develop cultural competence, it's important to identify our prejudices and stereotypes and to fight them. Sometimes they are quite subtle and difficult to detect. For instance, a wealth of data taken from observation of elementary school classrooms shows that teachers are often more responsive to boys than to girls. The teachers don't know they're doing it; it's a subtle, but very real, bias.

PREPARE

Accept diversity as a valued part of your life

ORGANIZE

Explore your own prejudices and stereotypes

WORK

Develop cultural competence

EVALUATE

Check your progress in attaining cultural competence

RETHINK

Understand how your own racial, ethnic, and cultural background affects others

P.O.W.E.R. Plan

Why does this happen? In part it's because we're exposed to stereotypes from a very young age. Parents and relatives teach them to us, sometimes unwittingly, sometimes on purpose. The media illustrate them constantly and often in very subtle ways. For instance, African-Americans and Latinos are often portrayed as unemployed or as criminals, women are less likely than men to be shown as employed, and gay men are frequently depicted as effeminate.

But it's not only stereotypes that lead us to view members of other groups differently from those of our own. For many people, their own membership in a cultural or racial or ethnic group is a source of pride and self-worth. There's nothing wrong with this. However, these feelings can lead to a less desirable outcome: the belief that their own group is superior to others. As a result, people inflate the positive aspects of their own group and belittle groups to which they do not belong. The bottom line is continuing prejudice.

To overcome stereotypes and to develop cultural competence, we must first explore and identify our prejudices. To begin that process, complete Try It 2, "Check Your Stereotype Quotient."

W ork: Developing Cultural Competence

Although it's neither easy nor simple to increase your understanding of and sensitivity to other cultures, it can be done. Several strategies are effective:

- **Study other cultures and customs.** Take an anthropology course, study religion, or learn history. If you understand the purposes behind different cultural customs, attitudes, and beliefs, you will be able to understand the richness and meaning of other people's cultural heritage.

  > "Prejudice is the child of ignorance."
  >
  > William Hazlitt, essayist

  Many colleges offer workshops on diversity and prejudice reduction. These can help too. The important point is that understanding comes from knowledge, and you won't be able to fully appreciate others without learning about their background.

- **Travel.** There is no better way to learn about people from other cultures than to see those cultures firsthand. College vacations offer you the time to travel, and relatively inexpensive charter flights can take you to Europe, Asia, and other places around the globe. Sometimes, in fact, it's cheaper to take a transoceanic flight than to travel to closer locations in the United States.

  If you can't afford airfare, take a car or bus ride to Mexico or Canada. In many parts of Canada, French is spoken and the culture is decidedly different from that in the United States (or the rest of Canada, for that matter). Travel needn't be international, however. If you are from the northern states, head south. If you are from California, consider heading east. No matter where you go, simply finding yourself in a new context can aid your efforts to learn about other cultures.

- **Don't ignore people's backgrounds.** None of us is color blind. Or blind to ethnicity. Or to culture. It's impossible to be completely unaffected by people's racial, ethnic, and cultural backgrounds. So why pretend to be? Cultural heritage is an important part of other people's identity, and to

Career Connections

Diversity in the Workplace

Diversity issues are a part of today's workplace. For example, in one California computer assembly company with 3,200 employees, 40 different languages and dialects are spoken among people representing 30 nationalities.[3] Furthermore, employers must deal with issues ranging from whether time off for religious holidays should count as vacation time to whether the partner of a gay or lesbian worker should be covered by the worker's medical insurance.

The gulf in the workplace between people with different cultural backgrounds may be wide. For instance, an immigrant from Japan might consider it the height of immodesty to outline his or her accomplishments in a job interview. The explanation? In Japan, the general cultural expectation is that people should stress their incompetence; to do otherwise would be considered highly immodest.

The increasing diversity of the workplace means that increasing your cultural competence will serve you well. It will help you perform on work teams that are composed of people of different races and ethnic backgrounds; it will help you supervise people whose native language and customs may be different from yours; and it will help you to work for a boss from another country and cultural background.

Equally important, gaining cultural competence will help you respond to the legal issues that surround diversity. It is illegal for employers to discriminate on the basis of race, ethnic background, age, gender, and physical disability. Cultural competence will help you not only to deal with the letter of the law but also to understand why embracing diversity is so important to getting along with others in the workplace.

pretend that their background doesn't exist and has no impact on them is unrealistic at best, and insulting at worst. It's important, though, to distinguish between accepting the fact that other people's backgrounds affect them and pigeonholing people and expecting them to behave in particular ways.

- **Don't treat people as representatives of the groups to which they belong.** If you're a member of a minority group, you've probably been asked how members of your group think, feel, or behave with respect to a particular issue. Somehow, as a member of the group, you're expected to know how every other member feels about a topic.

  Of course that's impossible; no single individual can speak for an entire group. Furthermore, group members are likely to display little uniformity on most issues and in most behaviors, and so this type of question is ultimately impossible to answer. In short, it makes little sense to treat others as if they were representatives of the racial, ethnic, and cultural group to which they belong.

- **Don't make assumptions about who people are.** Don't assume that someone is heterosexual just because most people are heterosexual. Don't assume that someone with an Italian-sounding last name is Italian. Don't assume that a black person has two black parents. (To get a sense of how our assumptions color our thinking, think about the questions in Try It 3 on page 318.)

- **Accept differences.** Different does not mean better. Different does not mean worse. Different just means not looking, acting, or believing exactly the same as you. We shouldn't attach any kind of value to being different; it's neither better nor worse than being similar.

  In fact, even people who seem obviously different on the surface probably share many similarities with you. Like you, they are students; they have fears and anxieties like yours; and they have aspirations and dreams, just as you do.

  The important point about differences

Check Your Stereotype Quotient

Do you hold stereotypes about other people? How pervasive do you think they are? Respond to the following informal questionnaire to get a sense of your susceptibility to stereotyping.

1. When you see five African-American students sitting together in the cafeteria, do you think that they are exhibiting racism? Do you think the same thing when you see five white students sitting together in the cafeteria?

2. When you are speaking with a person who has a speech-related disorder such as stuttering, are you likely to conclude that the person is less intelligent than a fluent speaker?

3. When an elderly woman can't remember something, do you assume her forgetfulness is because she is old or perhaps has Alzheimer's disease?

4. When an attractive blonde female student states an opinion in class, are you surprised if the opinion is intelligent and well expressed?

5. If a person with a mobility disorder turns down your offer for assistance, would you be offended and resentful?

6. If you found out that a star professional football player is gay, would you be surprised?

What do you think your answers tell you about yourself and your views of others?

Working in a Group: Compare your answers with those of your classmates. What do you think causes the similarities and differences in responses?

To Try It online, go to **www.mhhe.com/power**.

is that we need to accept them. Think about some differences you may have with people who are similar to you. Perhaps you really can't stand classical music, yet one of your childhood friends has taken piano lessons since he was five and loves it. Chances are you both accept that you have different tastes and see this difference as part of who each of you is.

Try It! 3

Contemplate a Questionnaire

Read each of the following questions[4]:

1. What do you think caused your heterosexuality?

2. When and how did you decide you were heterosexual?

3. Is it possible that heterosexuality is just a phase you may grow out of?

4. Is it possible your heterosexuality stems from a neurotic fear of others of the same sex?

5. To whom have you disclosed your heterosexual tendencies?

6. Why do you insist on showing off your heterosexuality?

7. Why do heterosexuals place so much emphasis on sex?

8. There seem to be very few happy heterosexuals. Techniques have been developed that might enable you to change. Have you considered changing?

9. Considering the menace of hunger and overpopulation, can the human race survive if everyone were heterosexual like yourself?

How do you think most heterosexuals would react to such questions? What do your own reactions to the questions tell you about the assumptions you hold about who you are and what others are like? How would your reactions differ if you substituted "homosexual" for each occurrence of "heterosexual" in the questionnaire?

To Try It online, go to **www.mhhe.com/power**.

E valuate: Checking Your Progress in Attaining Cultural Competence

Because cultural groups are constantly changing, developing cultural competence is an ongoing process. To evaluate where you stand, ask yourself the following questions:

Travel provides us with an opportunity to become immersed in very different cultures and to see the world—and ourselves—through different eyes.

- Do I make judgments about others based on external features, such as skin color, ethnic background, cultural customs, gender, weight, or physical appearance?

- Who are my friends? Do they represent diversity or are they generally similar to me?

- Do I openly express positive values relating to diversity? Do I sit back passively when others express stereotypes and prejudices, or do I actively question their remarks?

- Am I educating myself about the history and varying experiences of different racial, ethnic, and cultural groups?

- Do I give special treatment to members of particular groups, or am I evenhanded in my relationships?

- Do I recognize that, despite surface differences, all people have the same basic needs?

- Do I feel so much pride in my own racial, ethnic, and cultural heritage that it leads me to look less favorably upon members of other groups?

- Do I seek to understand events and situations through the perspectives of others and not just my own?

R ethink: Understanding How Your Own Racial, Ethnic, and Cultural Background Affects Others

If you are a member of a minority group, you probably don't need to be told that your race, ethnicity, and cultural background affect the way that others treat you. But even if you are a member of a majority group, the way in which others respond to you is, in part, a result of others' assumptions about the groups of which you are a part.

In short, both how we view others and how we ourselves are viewed are affected by the groups to which we—and others—belong. But keep this in mind: No matter how different other students are from you in terms of their race, ethnicity, and cultural background, they undoubtedly share many of the same concerns you do. Like all of us, they question themselves, wonder whether they will be successful, and fret about what they will do for the rest of their lives. Bridging the surface difference between you and others can result in the development of close, lasting social ties—a topic we consider next.

Building Lasting Relationships

Few of us lead our lives in isolation. There's a reason for this: Relationships with others are a critical aspect of our sense of well-being. The support of friends and relatives helps us feel good about ourselves. In fact, studies have found that our physical and psychological health may suffer without friendships. The social support of others acts as a guard against stress and illness. And if we do get sick, we recover more quickly if we have a supportive network of friends.

> "I have met the most amazing individuals and made the most incredible friends in such a short amount of time."
>
> Wittenberg University student[5]

Our relationships with others also help us understand who we are. To understand our own abilities and achievements, we compare them with those of others who are similar to ourselves. Our attitudes, beliefs, and values are influenced—and shaped—by others. We are who we are largely because of the people with whom we come in contact.

Making Friends

Although some of us naturally make friends with ease, for others making friends is more difficult. But building relationships is not a mystery. Here are several ways to go about it:

- **Invest time in others.** There's no better way to demonstrate that you are interested in being friends than investing time. Relationships need to be nourished by the commitment of time. You can't expect friendships to flourish unless you spend time with people.

- **Reveal yourself.** Good friends understand each other. The best way to make that happen is to let others get to know you. Be open and honest about the things you like and dislike. Talk about where you come from, what your family is like. Find out about the other person. Having a deeper understanding of where someone comes from not only helps build bridges between people of different racial and ethnic backgrounds, but it also helps build friendships. By honestly communicating your beliefs and attitudes, you give others the chance to learn those things you have in common.

- **Let others know you like them.** It may seem scary, but don't be coy and try to pretend you are uninterested in the friendships of others. Take the risk of being rebuffed. You don't have to announce outright that you like someone. Instead, reveal your interest in a friendship by inviting the person to do something with you or simply by engaging in conversation, sharing something about your life. Your actions will speak louder than words.

- **Accept others as they are, not as you would like them to be.** One mark of friendship is acceptance of people the way they are, warts and all, and not the way you would like them to be. Do not impose conditions on accepting others. Keep in mind that no one is perfect and that everyone has both good and bad qualities.

- **Show concern and caring.** This is really the substance of friendship and the basis for the trust that develops between friends. Don't be afraid to show your interest in the fortunes of others and to share the sadness when they suffer some setback or loss.

- **Not everyone makes a good friend.** People who put you down, consistently make you feel bad, or behave in ways that violate your own personal standards are not friends. Choose your friends based on the good feelings you have when you are with them and the concern and caring they show for you. Friendship is a two-way street.

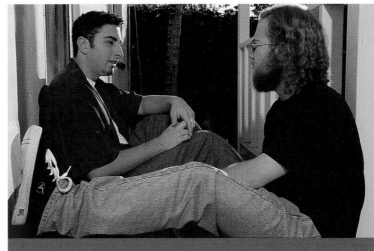

What you *don't* say matters. Close, lasting relationships are often built on good listening skills.

The R-Word: Relationships

Relationships move beyond friendship. They occur when two people feel emotionally attached, fulfill each other's needs, and generally feel interdependent. When a true relationship exists, several components are present:

- **Trust.** Relationships must be built on a foundation of trust. We need to be able to count on others and feel that they will be open with us.

- **Honesty.** No relationship can survive if the partners are not honest with one another. Each partner must share a commitment to the truth. Your life does not have to be a completely open book—it's the rare individual who has no secrets whatsoever—but it is important to be honest about your fundamental beliefs, values, and attitudes. Those in good relationships accept one another, blemishes and all. A relationship based on untruths or even half-truths lacks depth and meaning.

- **Mutual support.** Healthy relationships are characterized by mutual support. A partner's well-being should have an impact on you, and your well-being should affect your partner. In good relationships, the partners seek out what is best for both, and they act as advocates for and defend each other.

- **Loyalty.** The mark of a good relationship is loyalty. Loyalty implies that relationship partners are supportive of each other, even in times of adversity and difficulty.

- **Acceptance.** Your best friend develops a love for the Dave Matthews Band and listens to their CDs seemingly without interruption. You can't stand to listen to them. Do you decide that you can no longer be friends? Of course not.

In good relationships small annoyances don't get in the way of the deeper connection between you and another person. We don't have to like everything others do to maintain relationships with them. We don't even have to appreciate or approve of every aspect of their personality. What is crucial is the willingness to accept others as they are, without constantly yearning for changes. All of us wish to be accepted by others as we are, not as they'd like us to be; we should offer the same approval to those with whom we maintain relationships.

- **Willingness to embrace change.** Change is part of everyone's life. As people grow and develop, they change. So do relationships.

  We need to accept change as a fundamental part of relationships and build upon that change. In fact, we need to welcome change. Although change brings challenges with it, it also helps us to understand ourselves and our own place in the world more accurately.

  It is only natural that some relationships will fade over time. People do outgrow one another. That's inevitable. What's important is not to live in fear that your relationship is so fragile that you have to avoid or ignore changes in who you and a partner are. Instead, both partners in a relationship should do their best to accept transformations in the relationship as a part of life. (To learn more about your views of close relationships, complete Try It 4.)

Communicating in Relationships

Communicating well in personal relationships is a blend of talking and listening. Not only does it help to do both well, but it is also important to know when it's time to listen and when it's time to speak up. Listening is an often overlooked skill in personal relationships. We may be so busy trying to communicate our feelings and interests that we overlook the need of the other person to be heard. As friendships develop into personal relationships, simply talking isn't enough. How you express yourself, especially in moments of difficulty, can be very important to getting your message across.

Being a Good Listener: The Power of Supportive Silence

When it comes to building relationships, how you listen is sometimes more important than what you say. The silence involved in listening is a powerful force, one that can bind us more closely to others.

We've already discussed the art and science of listening as it applies to academic success in Chapter 4. The same principles that promote learning about lecture topics also promote learning about our friends. You can't call yourself a good friend without knowing what others are like and what they are thinking. Good listening is one of the ways to enhance your understanding of others.

When we are heard, we appreciate it because we get the message that our listeners care about us, not just about themselves. Similarly, when we listen, we show that we have respect for those who are speaking, are interested in their ideas and beliefs, and are willing to take the time to pay attention to them.

Try It! 4

Personal Styles: Understand Your Relationship Style

Each of us has a general manner in which we approach close relationships with others. Read the three statements below, and determine which best describes you[6]:

1. I find it relatively easy to get close to others and am comfortable depending on them and having them depend on me. I don't often worry about being abandoned or about someone getting too close to me.

2. I am somewhat uncomfortable being close to others; I find it difficult to trust them completely and to allow myself to depend on them. I am nervous when anyone gets too close, and often love partners want me to be more intimate than I feel comfortable being.

3. I find that others are reluctant to get as close as I would like. I often worry that my partner doesn't really love me or won't want to stay with me. I want to merge completely with another person, and this desire sometimes scares people away.

The choice you make suggests the general style of emotional bonds that you develop with others.

If you thought the first statement described you best, it is probably easy for you to develop close ties with others. Around 55 percent of people describe themselves in this way.

If statement 2 describes you best, you probably have a more difficult time getting close to others, and you may have to work harder to develop close ties with other people. About 25 percent of people place themselves in this category.

Finally, if statement 3 describes you best, you, along with the 20 percent of people who describe themselves in this way, aggressively seek out close relationships. However, they probably present a source of concern to you.

Keep in mind that this is an inexact assessment and presents only a very rough estimate of your general approach to close relationships. But your response can be helpful in answering these questions: Are you generally satisfied with your relationships? Would you like to change them in some way?

To Try It online, go to **www.mhhe.com/power**.

There are several ways you can improve your ability to listen:

1. **Stop talking!** Are you the kind of person who revels in telling stories about what happened to you? Do you wait eagerly for others to finish what they are saying so that you can jump in with a response? Do you accidentally cut other people off or finish their sentences while they are speaking?

   No one likes to be interrupted, even in casual conversation. In more personal relationships, it is a sign of not respecting what the other person has to say and is hurtful.

2. **Demonstrate that you are listening.** Linguists call them "conversational markers"—those nonverbal indications that we're listening. They consist of head nods, uh-huhs, OKs, and other signs that we're keeping up with the conversation. Eye contact is important too. Listening this way shows that we're paying attention and are interested in what the other person is saying.

> "The reason why we have two ears and only one mouth is that we may listen the more and talk the less."
>
> Zeno of Citium

3. **Use reflective feedback.** Carl Rogers, a respected therapist, developed a very useful way to lend support to someone and draw him or her out. In **reflective feedback,** a listener rephrases what a speaker has said, trying to echo the speaker's meaning. For example, a listener might say, "as I understand what you're saying . . . ," or "you seem to feel that . . . ," or "in other words, you believe that. . . ."

   In each case, the summary statement doesn't just "play back" the speaker's statements literally. Instead, it is a rephrasing that captures the essence of the message in different words.

   Reflective feedback has two big benefits. First, it provides speakers with a clear indication that you are listening and taking what they're saying seriously. Second, and equally important, it helps ensure that you have an accurate understanding of what the speaker is saying.

4. **Ask questions.** Asking questions shows that you are paying attention to a speaker's comments. Questions permit you to clarify what the speaker has said, and they can move the conversation forward. Further, people feel valued when others ask them about themselves.

5. **Admit when you're distracted.** We've all had those moments: Something is bothering you and you can't get it out of your mind, or you've simply got to finish something and don't really have time to chat. If at the same time someone wants to engage you in conversation, your distraction will undoubtedly show, making the other person feel you are not interested in her or him.

   The way to deal with this situation is to admit that you're distracted. Simply saying, "I'd love to talk, but I've got to finish reading a chapter" is enough to explain the situation to a classmate who wants to talk about his date.

Loneliness

Loneliness is a subjective state: We can be totally alone and not feel lonely, or we can be in the midst of a crowd and feel lonely. Loneliness occurs when we don't experience the level of connection with others that we desire. There are also different types of loneliness. Some of us feel lonely if we lack a deep emotional attachment to a single person, which can occur even if we have many friends. Others feel loneliness because they believe they don't have enough friends.

The reality is that there is no standard that indicates the "right" number of relationships. There's no standard against which to measure yourself and the number, and kind, of relationships that you have. It's something you need to decide. It is clear, though, that first-year college students almost always report higher degrees of loneliness than students in subsequent years of study.

On the other hand, loneliness is not inevitable. Several strategies for dealing with loneliness follow:

- **Become involved in campus activities.** Join a club. Volunteer to help some social organization. Try out for a play. You'll soon get to know others who have similar interests.

- **Find a study partner.** Ask one of your classmates to study with you. You can review your class notes, work together on a project, or study for tests together. Working together will not only help you to master the class material, but it will also help you make what can become an important social connection.

- **Know that you're not alone in your loneliness.** If you're feeling lonely, you may find yourself looking at your classmates and noticing groups of people engaged in social activities. This can make you feel even more isolated. Don't be fooled by such social illusions into believing that you are the only one experiencing loneliness. Remember that for every person you notice who is socializing, there are others who are not doing so.

Participating in campus activities is a good way to meet people with similar interests, and to avoid the loneliness that is sometimes a part of college life.

- **Take advantage of orientation and first-year student social events.** Even if you don't consider yourself particularly good at socializing, it's important to make the effort. If you're shy—and even if you're not—consider it a social success if you meet just one new person at such an event.

- **Take a job on campus.** Campus jobs provide not only income but social connections as well. Through work you can meet members of the college staff and make connections with other students.

- **Remember that loneliness is a subjective—and typically temporary—state.** If you interpret your feelings of isolation as due to your personal failings ("I'm alone because I'm not a very likable or interesting person"), you'll experience loneliness. On the other hand, if you view your isolation as a consequence of temporary, short-term factors ("Everyone has a lot of work this semester and there are few opportunities to socialize"), you're less likely to feel loneliness. In short, don't blame yourself for your sense of loneliness.

    What if your feelings of loneliness are extreme and you experience a sense of complete isolation and alienation from your classmates? If the feeling persists, it's wise to talk to someone at your college counseling center, a health service provider, or your advisor. Although everyone feels isolated at times, such feelings shouldn't be extreme. Counselors can help you deal with them.

It's Not Just Talk: Avoiding and Handling Conflicts in Relationships

Listening communicates a great deal in personal relationships, but, as discussed previously, it is also important to put yourself forward. Generally, close relationships are built on good communication, so day to day there may be no problem in this regard. But when misunderstandings or conflicts occur—as they definitely will from time to time—communication can fall apart. In these situations your ability to communicate in words is tested, and more sensitive listening and more careful ways of saying what you think and feel are needed.

The Subject Is "I," and Not "You"   Suppose a close friend says something with which you disagree: "All you guys are the same—you expect to get everything your way!" You might respond by directing anger at the other person, directly or indirectly accusing the person of some imperfection. "You're always looking for something to complain about!" Such responses (and, as you will notice, the initial statement) typically include the word *you*. For instance, consider these possible responses to indicate disagreement: *"You* really don't understand"; *"You're* being stubborn"; and "How can *you* say that?"

These types of statements cast blame, make accusations, express criticism, and make assumptions about what's inside the other person's head. And they lead to defensive replies that will probably do little to move the conversation forward: "I am *not!*"; "I do *so* understand"; "I'm not being stubborn"; and "I can say that because that's the way I feel."

A far more reasonable tactic is to use "I" statements. **"I" statements** cast responses in terms of yourself and your individual interpretation. Instead of saying, for example, "You really don't understand," a more appropriate response would be, "I think we're misunderstanding each other." "You're being stubborn" could be rephrased as "I feel like you're not really listening." And "how can you say that" becomes "I don't understand why you're saying that." In each case, "I" statements permit you to state your reaction in terms of your perception or understanding, rather than as a critical judgment about the other person. (Practice using "I" statements in Try It 5.)

"I" statements
Statements that cast responses in terms of oneself and one's individual interpretation

Resolving Conflict: A Win–Win Proposition   Even with careful attention to putting our own feelings forward instead of making accusations, whenever two people share their thoughts, concerns, fears, and honest reactions with each other, the chances are that sooner or later some sort of conflict will arise.

Conflict is not necessarily bad.

Often, people are upset simply by the fact that they are having a conflict. It is as though they believe conflicts don't occur in "good" relationships. In fact, however, conflict is helpful in some very important ways. It can force us to say what is really on our minds. It can allow us to clear up misconceptions and

Working in a Group: Switch "You" to "I"

Working in a group or in pairs, turn the following "you" statements into less aggressive "I" statements.

You Statements

1. You just don't get it, do you?

2. You never listen to what I say.

3. You don't see where I'm coming from.

4. You don't really believe that, do you?

5. You never try to see my point of view.

6. Please stop interrupting me and listen to what I'm saying for a change.

7. Stop changing the subject!

8. You're not making sense.

9. You keep distorting what I say until I don't even know what point I'm trying to make.

10. You use too many "you" statements. Use more "I" statements when you're talking to others.

To Try It online, go to **www.mhhe.com/power**.

miscommunications before they begin to undermine the relationship. It can even give us practice at resolving conflicts with others with whom we might not share such good relations.

Like anything else, though, there are good ways to resolve conflict, and there are bad ways. Good ways move people forward, defining the problem and promoting creative problem solving. Bad ways make the situation worse, driving people apart rather than bringing them together. The following are some fundamental principles of conflict resolution that you can use when conflict occurs in personal and professional relationships:

- **Stop, look, and listen.** In the heat of an argument, all sorts of things that otherwise would go unsaid get said. If you find yourself making rash or hurtful statements, stop, look at yourself, and listen to what you and the other person are saying.

  Stopping works like a circuit breaker that prevents a short circuit from causing a deadly fire. You've probably heard about counting to 10 to cool off when you're angry. Do it. Take a break and count to 10 . . . or 20 . . . or more. Whether you count to 10 or 100, stopping gives you time to think and not react rashly.

- **Defuse the argument.** Anger is not an emotion that encourages rational discourse. When you're angry and annoyed with someone, you're not in the best position to evaluate logically the merits of various arguments others may offer. It may feel exhilarating to get our fury off our chests in the heat of an argument, but you can bet it isn't taking anyone any closer to resolving the problem.

  Don't assume that you are 100 percent right and the other person is 100 percent wrong. Make your goal *solving the problem* rather than winning an argument.

- **Get personal.** Perhaps you've heard others suggest that you shouldn't get personal in an argument. In one sense that's true: Accusing people you're arguing with of having character flaws does nothing to resolve real issues.

  At the same time, you should be willing to admit personal *responsibility* for at least part of the conflict. The conflict would not exist without you, so you need to accept that the argument has two sides and that you are not automatically blameless. This creates some solid ground from which you and the other person can begin to work on the problem.

- **Listen to the real message.** When people argue, what they say is often not the real message. There's typically an underlying communication—a subtext—that is the source of the conflict.

  It's important, then, to dig beneath what you're hearing. If someone accuses you of being selfish, the real meaning hidden in the accusation may be that you don't give anyone else a chance to make decisions. Remember, arguments are usually about behavior, not underlying character and personality. What people *do* is not necessarily synonymous with what they *are.*

  If you rephrase the person's statement in your own mind, it moves from an insult ("You're a bad person") to a request for a change of behavior ("Let me participate in decision making"). You're much more likely to respond reasonably when you don't feel that the essence of your being is under attack.

- **Show that you're listening.** It's not enough only to listen to the underlying message that someone is conveying. You also need to acknowledge the *explicit* message. For example, saying something like "OK. I can tell you are concerned about sharing the burden on our group project, and I think we should talk about it" acknowledges that you see the issue and admit that it is worthy of discussion. This is a far more successful strategy than firing back a counter-charge each time your partner makes a complaint.

- **If you are angry, acknowledge it.** Don't pretend that everything is fine if it isn't. Ultimately, relationships in which the partners bottle up their anger may suffer more than those in which the partners express their true feelings. If you're angry, say so.

- **Ask for clarification.** As you're listening to another person's arguments, check out your understanding of what is being said. Don't assume that you know what's intended. Saying something like "Are you saying . . ." or "Do you mean that . . ." is a way of verifying that what you *think* someone means is really what is meant.

- **Make your requests explicit.** If you're upset that your roommate leaves clothes lying around your apartment or dorm room, remarking that he or she is a "pig" shows more than that you are angry. It also shows that your intent is to hurt rather than to solve the problem.

    It's far better to be explicit in your concerns. Say something like "It would make me feel better if you would pick up your clothes from the floor." Couching your concern in this way changes the focus of the message from your roommate's personality to a specific behavior that can be changed.

- **Always remember that life is not a zero-sum game.** Many of us act as if life were a **zero-sum game**, a situation in which when one person wins, the other person automatically loses. It's what happens when you make a bet: If one person wins the bet, the other person loses.

    Life is not like that. If one person wins an argument, it doesn't mean that others automatically have to lose it. And if someone loses an argument, it doesn't mean that others have automatically won. In fact, all too often conflict escalates so much that the argument turns into a lose–lose situation, where everyone ends up a loser.

    However, life can be a win–win situation. The best resolution of conflict occurs when both parties walk away with something they want. Each may not have achieved *every* goal but will at least have enough to feel satisfied.

Zero-sum game
A situation in which when one person wins, the other person automatically loses

Changing Relationships:
Surviving Endings

Not all relationships last a lifetime. Sometimes they just wind down, as the two people involved slowly lose interest in maintaining their partnership. At other times, they break apart, as disagreements build and there is not a strong enough bond to hold the two parties together. Or there may be an abrupt rupture if some event occurs that destroys one partner's feeling of trust.

Caring for others is rewarding, but risky. When relationships don't work out, their endings can be painful, even devastating, for a time. Even when relationships evolve naturally and change is expected, the transformation in a

Speaking of Success

Name: *Sandra Marotta*
Education: *Metropolitan State University, St. Paul, Minnesota*
Home: *Minneapolis, Minnesota*

The first year of college creates a combination of excitement, uncertainty, and anxiety in almost every student. But when you are a nontraditional student, returning to college some 30 years after finishing high school, the experience can be nearly overwhelming.

It was not surprising, then, that when Sandra Marotta started her first year at Metropolitan State University, she found the experience remarkably challenging, despite her strong motivation to succeed. Many of the students were considerably younger than she was, and she wondered how she would fit into a college environment.

"I had no real direction when I was younger," said Marotta, who had started college just after high school but soon dropped out. However, after raising three children, she was determined to get a college degree.

"The biggest step I had to overcome was the self-doubt I had as to whether I could do it. Even taking that initial step of going to first-year orientation was hard," Marotta explained.

"But through programs at Metropolitan State, my advisors, faculty, and my relationships with other students, I found a lot of

METROPOLITAN STATE UNIVERSITY

support. It's a place that is very adult-oriented with a student population that is very international and diverse," she added. "I received a great deal of guidance from teachers and especially my advisor. She knew the teachers and who would be accessible and helpful."

Marotta also had to learn to be a successful student.

"I recall going into the first year experience program, and they were talking about critical thinking," she recalled. "When I heard that, I was concerned, since I have never had to think critically or analyze anything. So I went to my teachers to find how to do it. I had to learn a whole new way of approaching things."

Hard work, diligence, and support from her children and friends paid off. Although Marotta is carrying a heavy course load, she has maintained an A average—in addition to working a 40-hour week.

"I'm a very self-disciplined person, and I just make the time for school," she explained. "A lot of this motivation comes from the support of a good friend, who has encouraged me and made me believe in myself.

"I have more self-confidence, and am definitely much more comfortable with the whole idea of school and how to approach things," she said. "I have the feeling that the teachers and my fellow classmates respect me for what I'm doing at this point in my life."

relationship may not be easy. Parents die. Children grow up and move away from home. Siblings get new jobs on the other side of the country.

There is one sure cure for the heartache of a lost relationship: time. There are some other things you can do, however, as you wait for time to pass and for the pain to ease:

1. **Do something—anything.** Mow the lawn, clean out the closets, go for a run, see a movie. It won't completely get your mind off your loss, but it beats languishing on your bed, thinking about what you might have done differently or what could have been.

2. **Accept that you feel bad.** If you're not experiencing unhappiness over the end of a relationship, it means that the relationship wasn't terribly meaningful in the first place. Understand that unhappiness normally accompanies the end of a relationship, and allow yourself some satisfaction over the fact that you'd been able to maintain a relationship that, at least at one point, was meaningful.

3. **Talk to a friend or relative.** Talking about your sadness will help you to deal with it better. Other people can help you feel better about yourself, offer different perspectives, and simply support you by listening. Make use of your network of existing relationships to get you through a difficult period.

4. **Write about the relationship.** If you have a journal, writing about the relationship and its aftermath can be therapeutic. You can say whatever you want without fear of being contradicted.

5. **Talk to a professional.** If your sadness over a relationship feels totally overwhelming or continues for what you perceive to be too long a time, talk to a counselor or other professional. He or she can help you gain a better understanding of the situation and perhaps help you understand why you are taking it so hard. And remember that, ultimately, the pain will disappear: Time does heal virtually all wounds.

Looking Back

Why is the increasing racial, ethnic, and cultural diversity of society important to me?

- The diversity of the United States—and of U.S. college campuses—is increasing rapidly, and the world is becoming smaller as television, radio, the Internet, the World Wide Web, and international commerce bring peoples and cultures closer together.

- Being aware of diversity can allow you to accept the challenge and opportunity of living and working with others who are very different.

How can I become more at ease with differences and diversity?

- Cultural competence begins with accepting diversity by seeking out others who are different, as well as exploring your own prejudices and stereotypes.

- You can learn about other cultures by traveling to other countries and geographic areas. It also helps to accept differences simply as differences.

How can I build lasting relationships and deal with conflict?

- Relationships not only provide social support and companionship, but they also help people understand themselves.

- The central components of good relationships are trust, honesty, mutual support, loyalty, acceptance, and a willingness to embrace change.

- Listening is an important skill for relationship building, demonstrating that the listener really cares about the other person.

- Conflict is inevitable in relationships, and sometimes it is useful because it permits us to clear up misconceptions and miscommunications before they escalate.

- Although the end of a relationship can be very painful, the pain does subside over time.

Key Terms and Concepts

Cultural competence (p. 313)
Culture (p. 312)
Ethnicity (p. 311)
"I" statements (p. 326)
Loneliness (p. 324)

Prejudice (p. 314)
Race (p. 311)
Reflective feedback (p. 324)
Stereotypes (p. 314)
Zero-sum game (p. 329)

Resources

On Campus

One of the most frequent sources of difficulties for first-year students involves roommate problems. If you and your roommate are having problems getting along, begin by speaking with your resident advisor or residence hall director. If the problem persists, talk with a member of the residential life office. You can also speak with a counselor at the college counseling office.

Anyone who feels he or she is facing discrimination based on race, gender, ethnic status, or national origin should contact a university official *immediately*. Often there is a specific office that handles such complaints. If you don't know which campus official to contact, speak to your academic advisor or someone in the dean's office and you'll be directed to the appropriate person. The important thing is to act and not to suffer in silence. Discrimination is immoral and it's against the law.

In Print

Beverly Tatum's *Why Are All the Black Kids Sitting Together in the Cafeteria?* (HarperCollins, 1998) explores race, racism, and the everyday impact of prejudice. In *Cultural Diversity in the United States* (Blackwell, 2000), Ida Susser and Thomas Patterson present a series of essays on diversity and how it affects everyday life. Finally, Sybil Evans and Sherry Cohen's *Hot Buttons: How to Re-*

solve Conflict and Cool Everyone Down (Cliff Street Books, 2001) suggests a variety of practical approaches to resolving conflict.

On the Web

The following sites on the World Wide Web provide the opportunity to extend your learning about the material in this chapter. (Although the Web addresses were accurate at the time the book was printed, check the P.O.W.E.R. Learning website [**www.mhhe.com/power**] for any changes that may have occurred.)

- "Diversity Resources Online" (**www.nadm.org/**), a site sponsored by the National Association for Diversity Management (NADM), provides a platform for disseminating information and a comprehensive resource center for all aspects of diversity in education, human resources, the public sector, and the society at large. It also provides opportunities for professional networking, research, and global dialogue.

- "Improving Communication and Conflict Resolution Skills" (**www.shs.utoledo.edu/counseling/communication_cristine.htm**) is an outline posted by Toledo University's Counseling Center that provides basic guidance on improving communication and conflict resolution skills and includes a section on effective listening.

- "Language and Culture" (**www.ncbe.gwu.edu/links/langcult/**), a site from George Washington University's National Clearinghouse for Bilingual Education (NCBE), provides links dealing with culture, diversity, and multiculturalism, connecting to everything from the American Folk Life Center to worldwide ethnology resources.

- Understanding "Race Relations" (**racerelations.about.com/library/weekly/aa122899a.htm**), a comprehensive site on About.com, discusses topics ranging from affirmative action to white privilege. Hundreds of links are provided for more in-depth discussions and background on a variety of subjects including race relations, hate crimes, gay/lesbian issues, and many other topics.

Taking It to the Net

1 Explore cultural differences using the Internet. Go to Yahoo! (**www.yahoo.com**), choose "Society and Culture" and then "Cultures and Groups." Click on "Cultures" and type a topic that you find interesting into the search field. Make sure to limit your search to just this category. How many pages did you find? Read and compare the information from different cultural groups.

2 Use the Internet to help find a volunteer organization that sounds interesting to you. Using either Yahoo! (**www.yahoo.com**) or AltaVista (**www.altavista.com**), enter "volunteer organizations" into the search field. Examine the volunteer organizations listed and write down the ones that sound interesting to you. Consider contacting one or more to explore possibilities of participating in the organization that will mesh with your other responsibilities.

The Case of . . .

Answering for All

Jace Kinkaid stood out in any crowd. With his six-foot-eight height, he towered above most of his classmates. Even when he was seated at a desk, he looked huge. And since he was an African American, his skin color set him apart from his classmates, almost all of whom were white.

Although, by and large, people were polite and nice enough to him, Jace felt isolated from most of his peers and instructors. While he had one or two good friends from high school with whom he kept in touch, he was not close to many people on campus. His isolation came to a head, however, in the most public of places: his English literature class. It happened when his instructor, a white man, was leading a discussion on *The Fire Next Time,* a novel by noted black writer James Baldwin. The instructor turned to Jace and asked him to comment on a passage from the novel.

"Does it ring true to you, Jace, as an African American?" asked his instructor, who then went on to inquire, "What do African Americans think about the perspective that Baldwin is taking?"

Jace was taken aback. What was he supposed to say? He hardly felt like a representative of every black person. He barely knew how he felt, let alone everyone else who was African American. What an absurd situation to be placed in—his instructor asking him to answer for millions of other people. He felt awful—embarrassed, upset, and angry at his instructor for putting him on the spot.

1. Why was the instructor's question so troubling to Jace? If the instructor really wanted Jace's opinion about the passage, what should he have said?

2. Would the question have had a different effect if the instructor had also been African American? Why or why not?

3. What are some cultural assumptions that the instructor is making about Jace? About African Americans? About white people?

4. What response might Jace make in this situation to make his feelings clear without causing excessive conflict?

Money Matters

13

eah Flores's college career depended on the contents of the envelope she held in her hands.

The letter inside from the financial aid office spelled out her school's offer of aid for the upcoming term. As she tore open the envelope, Leah wondered whether it would be enough. She knew that without a substantial amount of support, she would have to drop out. She couldn't stand the thought, particularly because she had been doing so well.

As she looked at the numbers on the form, Leah's heart soared. Not only had she been given a loan, but also most of her aid was in the form of a direct scholarship.

Things would still be tight, but she could manage. Her financial worries were over—at least for one more term.

Looking Ahead

Money problems aren't always solved as happily as they were for Leah Flores. Even under the best of circumstances, our finances present us with many challenges. Money often plays a large role in where we go to college, where we live, and what jobs we take. It is the source of many of our problems and stress, forcing us to find a balance between what we need and what we want.

This chapter will show you how to manage your money. It begins by discussing the process of preparing a budget and identifying your financial goals—the basis for money management. The chapter goes on to examine ways you can keep track of your spending and estimate your financial needs and resources, and discusses ways to control your spending habits and save money.

Education is one of the largest financial expenditures anyone encounters in life. Knowing the best ways to meet the costs of a college education—finding loans, grants, and scholarships—can give your finances a big boost and help you avoid graduating with thousands of dollars of debt. You will also learn what to do if your personal finances get out of control and discover how to stop the downward spiral of unpaid bills, defaulted loans, and unfavorable credit ratings. The chapter ends by suggesting ways to develop a financial philosophy.

In sum, after reading this chapter you'll be able to answer these questions:

- **What purpose does a budget serve and how can I prepare and stick to one?**

- **What help is available to pay for my college education?**

- **What is the value of a college education?**

Managing Your Money

Do you know where your money goes? Do you spend more than you think you should? Do you never have quite enough cash to buy the things you want?

Answering these questions and understanding the role money plays in your life is the first step of wise money management. To begin getting a grip on your finances, answer the questions in the Journal Reflections exercise.

If you have money problems—and there's virtually no one who doesn't have some concerns about finances—the solution is to develop a budget. A **budget** is a formal plan that accounts and plans for expenditures and income. Taking your goals into account, a budget helps determine how much money you should be spending each month, based on your income and your other financial resources. Budgets also help prepare for the unexpected, such as the loss of a job or an illness that would reduce your income, or for sudden, unanticipated expenses, such as a major car repair.

Although all budgets are based on an uncomplicated premise—expenditures should not exceed income—budgeting is not simple, particularly when you are a student. There are several times during the year that require especially large expenditures, such as the start of a semester, when you must pay your tuition and purchase books. Furthermore, your income is usually erratic; it is often lower during the school year and higher during the summer. But a budget will help you deal with the ups and downs in your finances, smoothing the curves and extending your view toward the horizon. Learning budgeting skills also helps prepare you for the world of work, as discussed in this chapter's Career Connections.

Most of all, a budget provides security. It will let you take control of your money, permitting you to spend it as you need to without guilt, because you have planned for the expenditure. It also makes it easier to put money aside because you know that your current financial sacrifice will be rewarded later, when you can make a purchase that you've been planning for.

Journal Reflections

My Sense of Cents

Answer the following questions about your financial sense.

1. How much money do you now have in your pockets and wallet? (Guess first, then look.) How close did you come?

2. Do you know how much money you typically spend in a month, including money spent on food, lodging, and other items?

3. How good a sense of your finances do you think you have? How secure do you feel in your understanding of where your money goes?

4. How important is money to you? Why?

Budget
A formal plan that accounts for expenditures and income

"There was a time when a fool and his money were soon parted, but now it happens to everybody."

Adlai Stevenson

Career Connections

Budgeting on the Job

If you've ever held a job, the salary you received was determined, in part, by your employer's budget.

Although they may not always be accessible to every employee, budgets are part of the world of work. Regardless of who the employer is—be it a small dry cleaning store or the massive federal government—there is a budget outlining anticipated income and expenditures. Managers are expected to keep to the budget, and if their expenditures exceed what is budgeted, they are held accountable.

For this reason, the ability to create and live within a budget is an important skill to acquire. Not only will it help keep your own finances under control, but it will also prepare you to be financially responsible and savvy on the job—qualities that are highly valued by employers.

Budgeting is very personal: what is appropriate for one person doesn't work for another. For a few people, keeping track of their spending comes naturally; they enjoy accounting for every dollar that passes through their hands. For most people, though, developing a budget—and sticking to it—does not come easily.

However, if you follow several basic steps—illustrated in the P.O.W.E.R. Plan—the process of budgeting is straightforward.

repare: Identifying Your Financial Goals

Your first reaction when asked to identify your financial goals may be that the question is a no-brainer: You want to have more money to spend. But it's not that simple. You need to ask yourself *why* you want more money. What would you spend it on? What would bring you the most satisfaction? Purchasing a DVD player? Paying off your debt? Saving money for a vacation? Starting a business? Paying for college rather than taking out loans?

You won't be able to develop a budget that will work for you until you determine your short- and long-term financial goals. To determine them, use Try It 1, "Identify Your Financial Goals."

rganize: Determining Your Expenditures and Income

Do you open your wallet for the $10 that was there yesterday and find only a dollar? Spending money without realizing it is a common affliction.

There's only one way to get a handle on where your money is going: Keep track of it. To get an overview of your expenditures, go through any records you've kept to identify where you've spent money for the last year—old checks, rent and utility receipts, and previous college bills can help you.

In addition, keep track of everything you spend for a week. *Everything.* When you spend 50 cents for a candy bar from a vending machine, write it down. When you buy lunch for $2.97 at a fast-food restaurant, write it down. When you buy a 21-cent postcard, write it down.

Record your expenditures in a small notebook that you carry with you all the time. It may be tedious, but you're doing it for only a week. And it will be

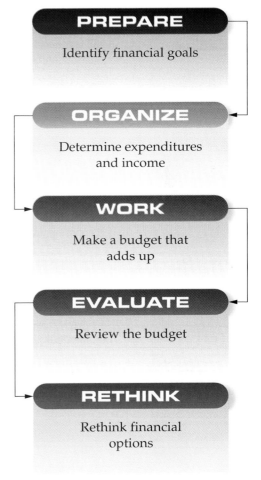

Keeping to a budget is a constant balancing act. For example, even though you know you'll need to purchase books at the start of each semester, you can't predict exactly how much they'll cost.

eye-opening: People are usually surprised at how much they spend on little items without thinking about it.

Finally, make a list of everything you think you'll need to spend over the next year. Some items are easy to think of, such as rent and tuition payments, because they occur regularly and the amount you pay is fixed. Others are harder to budget for because they can vary substantially. For example, the price of gasoline changes frequently. If you have a long commute, the changing price of gasoline can cause substantial variation in what you pay each month. Similarly, the cost of books varies considerably from one term to another. (Use Table 13.1 on page 342 to estimate your expenditures for the coming year.)

Determine Your Income Sources You probably have a pretty good idea of how much money you have each month. But it's as important to list each source of income as it is to account for everything you spend.

Add up what you make from any jobs you hold. Also list any support you receive from family members, including occasional gifts you might get from relatives. Finally, include any financial aid (such as tuition reductions, loan payments, or scholarships) you receive from your college. Use Table 13.2 on page 343 to record this information. When you do, be sure to list the amounts you receive in terms of after-tax income.

W ork: Making a Budget That Adds Up

If you've prepared and organized your budget, actually constructing your budget is as easy as adding 2 + 2. Well, not exactly; the numbers will be larger. But all you need to do is add

PREPARE

Identify financial goals

ORGANIZE

Determine expenditures and income

WORK

Make a budget that adds up

EVALUATE

Review the budget

RETHINK

Rethink financial options

P.O.W.E.R. Plan

👥 **Working in a Group:** Identify Your Financial Goals

Step 1. Use the planning tool below to identify and organize your financial goals.

Short-Term Goals

What would you like to have money for in the short term (over the next 3 months)? Consider these categories:

Personal necessities (such as food, clothes, household supplies, shelter, transportation, loan payments, debts, medical expenses):

Educational necessities (such as tuition, fees, books, school supplies):

Social needs (e.g., getting together with family, friends, and others; charitable contributions; clubs; teams; entertainment):

Lifestyle improvements (optional but desirable personal or educational tools, such as computer hardware and software, living space improvements, transportation improvements, clothing "upgrades"):

Other:

Mid-range Goals

What would you like to have money for soon (3 months from now to a year from now), but not immediately? Use the same categories:

Personal necessities:

Educational necessities:

Social needs:

Lifestyle improvements:

Other:

Long-Range Goals

What would you like to have money for 1 to 3 years from now? Use the same categories:

Personal necessities:

Educational necessities:

Social needs:

Lifestyle improvements:

Other:

Step 2. Now put each of your lists in <u>priority</u> order.

Short-Term Priorities:

Mid-Range Priorities:

Long-Range Priorities:

What does the list tell you about what is important to you? Did you find any surprises? Would you classify yourself as a financial risk-taker or someone who values financial security?

Working in a Group: Consider these questions: Compare your priorities with those of your classmates. What similarities and differences do you find, and what can you learn from others' priorities?

To Try It online, go to **www.mhhe.com/power**.

Table 13.1
Estimated Expenditures, Next 12 Months

Category	Now to 3 Months from Now	3–6 Months from Now	6–9 Months from Now	9–12 Months from Now
Personal Necessities				
Food				
Clothing				
Shelter (rent, utilities, etc.)				
Household supplies				
Transportation (car payments, gas, repairs, bus tickets, etc.)				
Loan and debt payments				
Medical expenses				
Other				
Educational Necessities				
Tuition and fees				
Books				
Tools and hardware				
Computer costs				
Other				
Social Needs				
Relationships				
Clubs and teams				
Charitable contributions				
Other				
Entertainment				
Movies and shows				
Trips				
Recreation and sports				
Other				
Lifestyle Improvements				
Educational				
Living space				
Computer				
Transportation				
Clothing				
Other				
TOTAL				

up your list of expenses, and then add up your sources of income. In a perfect world, the two numbers will be equal.

But most of the time, the world is not perfect: most of us find that expenditures are larger than our income. After all, if we had plenty of excess cash, we probably wouldn't be bothering to make a budget in the first place.

Table 13.2

Estimated Income, Next 12 Months

Category	Now to 3 Months from Now	3–6 Months from Now	6–9 Months from Now	9–12 Months from Now
Wages				
Family Support				
Financial Aid				
Tuition reductions				
Loan income				
Scholarship payments				
Other				
Interest and Dividends				
Gifts				
Other				
TOTAL				

If you find you spend more than you make, there are only two things to do: decrease your spending or increase your income. It's often easiest to decrease expenditures, because your expenses tend to be more under your control. For instance, there are many things you can do to save money, including the following:

- **Control impulse buying.** If you shop for your groceries, always take a list with you, and don't shop when you're hungry.

- **Make and take your own lunch.** Brown-bag lunches can save you a substantial amount of money over purchasing your lunches, even if you go to a fast-food restaurant or snack bar.

- **Read the daily newspaper and magazines at the library.** College libraries subscribe to virtually every daily newspaper and magazine that you could want.

- **Check bills for errors.** Computers make mistakes, and so do the people who enter the data into them. So make sure that your charges on any bill are accurate.

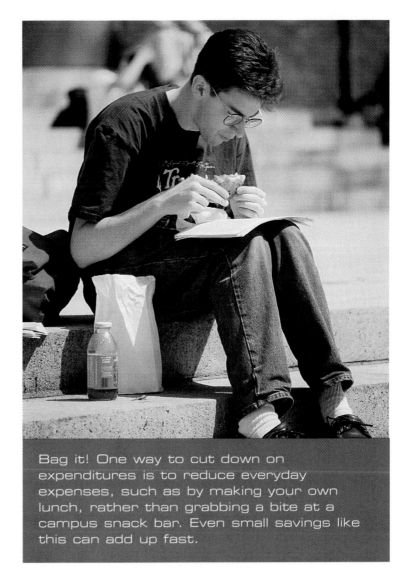

Bag it! One way to cut down on expenditures is to reduce everyday expenses, such as by making your own lunch, rather than grabbing a bite at a campus snack bar. Even small savings like this can add up fast.

- **Cut up your credit cards and pay cash.** Using a credit card is seductive; when you take out your plastic, it's easy to feel as if you're not really spending money. If you use cash for purchases instead, you'll see the money going out.

- **Make major purchases only during sales.** Plan major purchases so they coincide with sales.

- **Share and trade: Pool your resources with friends.** Car pool, share resources such as computers, and trade CDs.

- **Live more simply.** Do you really need a cellular phone or beeper? Is cable TV an absolute necessity? Is it really necessary to eat out once a week? Do you buy clothes because you need them or because you want them?

- **Do well in your classes.** One of the best ways to save money is to get good grades, because you avoid the hidden costs of poor performance. If you are forced to repeat a class because of a low grade, you'll have to take another course in the future as a substitute, and that may be an added expense. Doing well avoids the possibility of additional tuition costs.

There are as many ways to save money as there are people looking to save it. But keep in mind that saving money should not necessarily be an end in itself. Don't spend hours thinking of ways to save a dime, and don't get upset about situations where you are forced to spend money. The goal is to bring your budget into balance, not to become a tightwad who keeps track of every penny and feels that spending money is a personal failure. To help you get started, get a sense of your current style of saving money in Try It 2.

Finally, it's important to remember that budgets may be brought into balance not only by decreasing expenditures, but also by increasing income. The most direct way to increase income is to get a part-time job if you don't already have one.

Many students work during college. Although working adds to the time-management challenges you will face, it does not mean that your grades will necessarily suffer. In fact, many students who work do better in school than those who don't work, because those with jobs need to be more disciplined and focused. In addition, a part-time job in an area related to your future career may prove to be helpful in getting a job after you graduate.

Considering part-time work is often a better strategy for dealing with budget shortfalls than taking out a loan. Because student loans are relatively simple to get, it's easy to use them as a crutch. Loans can be a help in an emergency or if you couldn't afford to attend college without them. If you do take out a loan, remind yourself: one day soon you'll have to pay it back, with interest.

E valuate: Reviewing Your Budget

Budgets are not meant to be set in stone. You should review where you stand financially each month. Only by monitoring how closely actual expenditures and income match your budget projections will you be able to maintain control of your finances.

You don't need to continually keep track of every penny you spend to evaluate your success in budgeting. As you gain more experience with your

Personal Styles: Determine Your Saving Style

Read each of the following statements and rate how well it describes you, using this scale:

1 = That's me

2 = Sometimes

3 = That's not me

	1	2	3
1. I count the change I'm given by cashiers in stores and restaurants.			
2. I always pick up all the change I receive from a transaction in a store, even if it's only a few cents.			
3. I don't buy something right away if I'm pretty sure it will go on sale soon.			
4. I feel a real sense of accomplishment if I buy something on sale.			
5. I always remember how much I paid for something.			
6. If something goes on sale soon after I've bought it, I feel cheated.			
7. I have money in at least one interest-bearing bank account.			
8. I rarely lend people money.			
9. If I lend money to someone repeatedly without getting it back, I stop lending it to that person.			
10. I share resources (e.g., CDs, books, magazines) with other people to save money.			
11. I'm good at putting money away for big items that I really want.			
12. I believe most generic or off-brand items are just as good as name brands.			

Add up your ratings. Interpret your total score according to this informal guide:

12–15: Very aggressive saving style

16–20: Careful saving style

21–27: Fairly loose saving style

28–32: Loose saving style

33–36: Nonexistent saving style

What are the advantages and disadvantages of your saving style? How do you think your saving style would affect your ability to keep to a budget? If you are dissatisfied with your saving style, how might you be able to change it?

To Try It online, go to **www.mhhe.com/power**.

budget, you'll begin to get a better sense of your finances. You'll know when it may be possible to consider splurging on a gift for a friend, and when you need to operate in penny-pinching mode.

The important thing is to keep your expenditures under control. Review, and if necessary revise, your budget to fit any changes in circumstances. Maybe you receive a raise in a part-time job. Maybe the financial aid office gives you more support than you expected. Or maybe you face a reduction in income. Whatever the change in circumstances, evaluate how it affects your budget, and revise the budget accordingly.

R ethink: Reconsidering Your Financial Options

If all goes well, the process of budgeting will put you in control of your financial life. Your expenditures will match your income, and you won't face major money worries.

In the real world, of course, events have a way of inflicting disaster on even the best-laid plans:

- You lose your job and can't afford to pay next semester's tuition.

- Your roommate moves out and leaves you with an $800 phone bill. You don't have $800.

- Your parents, who have promised to pay for your education, run into financial difficulties and say they can't afford to pay your college costs any longer.

- Your car breaks down, and repairing it will cost $1,500. If you don't have a car, you can't get to campus. But if you pay for repairs, you can't afford tuition.

All of us face financial difficulties at one time or another. Sometimes it happens suddenly and without warning. Other times people sink more gradually into financial problems, each month accumulating more debt until they reach a point at which they can't pay their bills.

However it happens, finding yourself with too little money to pay your bills requires action. You need to confront the situation and take steps to solve the problem. The worst thing to do is nothing. Hiding from those to whom you owe money makes the situation worse. Your creditors—the institutions and people to whom you owe money—will assume that you don't care, and they'll be spurred on to take harsher actions.

These are the steps to take if you do find yourself with financial difficulties (also see Table 13.3):

- **Assess the problem.** Make a list of what you owe and to whom. Look at the bottom line and figure out a reasonable amount you can put toward each debt. Work out a specific plan that can lead you out of the situation.

- **Contact each of your creditors.** Start with your bank, credit card companies, and landlord, and continue through each creditor. It's best to visit personally, but a phone call will do.

When you speak with them, explain the situation. If the problem is due to illness or unemployment, let them know. If it's due to overspending, let them know that. Tell them what you plan to do to pay off your debt, and show them

Table 13.3

Steps in Dealing with
Financial Difficulties

Assess the Problem	Make a list of what you owe and to whom.
	Figure out a reasonable amount you can put toward each debt.
	Work out a specific plan.
Contact Each of Your Creditors	Start with your bank, credit card companies, and landlord.
	Explain the situation.
	Show them your plan to pay off debt.
See a Credit Counselor	If you cannot work out a repayment plan on your own, visit a credit counseling service.
Stick to the Plan	Once you have a plan, make a commitment to stick to it.
	Your bank or creditor can help you identify a credit counselor.

your plan. The fact that you have a plan demonstrates not only what you intend to do, but also that you are serious about your situation and capable of financial planning.

If you've had a clean financial record in the past, your creditors may be willing to agree to your plan. Ultimately, it is cheaper for them to accept smaller payments over a longer time than to hire a collection agency.

- **See a credit counselor.** If you can't work out a repayment plan on your own, visit a credit counseling service. These are nonprofit organizations that help people who find themselves in financial trouble. Your bank or a creditor can help you identify one, or you can call the National Foundation for Consumer Credit at 1-800-388-2227 or visit their website at **http://www.nfcc.org**.

- **Stick to the plan.** Once you have a plan to get yourself out of debt, follow it. Unless you diligently make the payments you commit to, you'll find your debt spiraling out of control once again. It's essential, then, to regard your plan as a firm commitment and stick to it.

Credit Cards

"Congratulations! You've been preapproved for a Gold credit card! Just send us your signature on the enclosed authorization form, and we'll rush you your card."

Have you ever gotten such a letter in the mail? If so, you're far from the only one: Millions of people in the United States are regularly enticed to receive credit cards in just such a manner, and college students are especially attractive targets. In many cases, it doesn't even matter if you have income; the mere fact that you're a college student is sufficient to win you approval to receive a card.

Credit cards are not necessarily bad. In fact, used appropriately, they can help get you through brief periods when you must make a purchase—such as replacing a tire for your car—but temporarily don't have

"It is difficult to learn the meaning of fiscal responsibility, especially when you've got a new VISA and there's a great-looking sweater in the shop window. It's even harder when the sweater is on sale."

Lauren Pass, Grossmont Community College[1]

enough money to do so. But there are several questions you should ask when deciding whether to get and use a credit card:

1. Is there an annual fee? Many cards charge an annual fee, ranging from $20 a year to $100 a year. You need to determine whether the advantages of the card are worth the cost of an annual fee.

2. What is the interest rate? Interest rates—the percentage of the unpaid balance you are charged on credit cards—vary substantially. Some interest rates are as low as 12 percent per year, while some are as high as 25 percent per year. If the rate is 25 percent, you will be charged an additional $250 each year if you owe an average of $1,000. Furthermore, although some interest rates are *fixed*, meaning that they don't vary from month to month, others are *variable*, which means they change each month. How much they change is tied to various factors in the overall economy. To get a better sense of how interest rates add up, try "Maintain Your Interest" (Try It 3).

3. **Do I need a credit card?** There are good reasons for getting a credit card, and bad reasons.

The pluses of credit cards

- **Establishing a good credit history.** If you've ever owed money to a bank or your college, a computer file exists describing your payment history. If you have never missed a loan payment and always pay on time, you have a good credit history. If you haven't paid on time or have missed payments, your history will reflect this. Negative information can stay in a file for 7 years, and it can keep you from getting future loans, so it's important to establish and keep a clear credit history. (To get a copy of your credit report, complete Try It 4, "Learn Your Credit History.")

- **Emergency use.** Few of us carry around enough cash to deal with emergencies. A credit card can be a life saver if we're on a trip and the car breaks down and needs emergency repairs.

- **Convenience.** Sometimes it's just easier to make purchases using a credit card. For instance, we can make mail-order purchases from catalogs over the telephone if we have a credit card. Furthermore, credit cards not only provide a record of purchases, but they also give us limited consumer protection should a product prove to be defective.

The minuses of credit cards

On the other hand, there can be significant drawbacks to the use of credit cards. Potential problems include the following:

- **Interest costs can be high.** As you saw above, the interest rate on credit card purchases can be significant. Unless you pay off your entire balance each month, your account will be charged interest, which can add up rapidly.

Maintain Your Interest

Suppose you saw a $275 television set on sale "for a limited time" for $240. The $35 discount tempts you. The trouble is you don't have $240 to spare. But you *do* have a credit card—and you decide to buy the TV with the card and pay it off over time.

The advantages of this strategy are that you get the discount and have immediate use of the television set. The main disadvantage is that you will end up paying more than the $240 figure that you have in mind as the bargain price for the TV. In fact, depending on how high your credit card's interest rate is, how long you take to pay your bill in full, and how large each monthly payment is, you may wipe out most or all of the $35 savings that caused you to make the purchase in the first place. The more slowly you pay off the loan, the more money you pay for the television set.

For example, suppose you use a card with an annual interest rate of 12 percent, compounded monthly, meaning that the interest charge is applied each month, rather than at the end of the year—making the true annual rate 12.68 percent. (Some cards even compound on a *daily* basis, resulting in a real interest rate that is even higher.) At the end of a year, assuming you pay $10 per month toward the $240 purchase, you will have paid $120 and still have $143.61 to pay. At the end of 2 years, you would end up paying $35 in interest on top of the $240 purchase price.

The 12-month calculation is illustrated in the first table below. To see how much of a factor the interest rate is, complete the second table, which shows the same purchase on a credit card with a 20 percent annual (approximately 1.67 percent monthly) interest rate, compounded monthly. (These calculations can also be figured automatically on several websites, including **www.bankrate.com** and **www.quicken.com**.)

Credit Card Payments: 12% Interest, Compounded Monthly (1% per month)

	Month 1	2	3	4	5	6	7	8	9	10	11	12
Unpaid Balance	$240.00	$232.40	$224.72	$216.97	$209.14	$201.23	$193.24	$185.18	$177.03	$168.80	$160.49	$152.09
Plus Interest of	2.40	2.32	2.25	2.17	2.09	2.01	1.93	1.85	1.77	1.69	1.60	1.52
Minus Payment of	10.00	10.00	10.00	10.00	10.00	10.00	10.00	10.00	10.00	10.00	10.00	10.00
Balance Due	$232.40	$224.72	$216.97	$209.14	$201.23	$193.24	$185.18	$177.03	$168.80	$160.49	$152.09	$143.61

Credit Card Payments: 20% Interest, Compounded Monthly (approx. 1.67% per month)

	Month 1	2	3	4	5	6	7	8	9	10	11	12
Unpaid Balance	$240.00	$234.01	$227.92	$221.72	$215.42							
Plus Interest of	4.01	3.91	3.81	3.70								
Minus Payment of	10.00	10.00	10.00	10.00	10.00	10.00	10.00	10.00	10.00	10.00	10.00	10.00
Balance Due	$234.01	$227.92	$221.72	$215.42								

How much would the $240 TV set cost if you bought it with this higher-rate card, paying $10 per month for 12 months and then paying the remaining balance by check? How does this compare with the nondiscounted purchase price of $275?

To Try It online, go to **www.mhhe.com/power**.

Try It! 4

Learn What Your Credit History Shows

Big Brother is alive and well, at least in terms of your credit history. If you've ever had a credit card in your own name, taken out a student loan, or sometimes just received an unsolicited offer for credit in the mail, there's probably a computer file describing who you are, where you live, and your financial history. It shows how high your credit lines are on every credit card you have, if you've ever been late on a payment, and a considerable amount of additional information.

Even worse: many people's credit histories are riddled with errors. That's why it's important to periodically check the record. To get a complimentary copy of your credit report, contact one of the three major credit companies:

- Transunion: **www.tuc.com** or 1-800-888-4213.

- Experian: **www.experian.com** or 1-800-311-4769.

- Equifax: **www.equifax.com** or 1-888-532-0179.

Be prepared: You will be asked for a variety of pieces of information, including your name, address, social security number, your birth date, your prior addresses for the past 5 years and other names (like a maiden name) you may have been known by.

Once you get your credit report, check it carefully. If you find any mistakes, contact the credit bureau and explain the error. They are legally responsible for investigating the report and correcting the file. It's a good idea to check your file at least once a year.

To Try It online, go to **www.mhhe.com/power**.

- **It's too easy to spend money.** Credit cards are so convenient to use that you may not realize how much you're spending in a given period. Furthermore, spending can become addictive. Unless you're careful, you can end up exceeding your budget by a significant amount.

- **If you're late in making your payments or exceed your credit limit, your credit rating will be damaged.** Credit card companies have long memories, and any mistakes you make will be reflected in your credit record for close to a decade. That may prevent you from buying a car or house in the future and jeopardize your ability to take out student loans.

Paying for College

Tuition costs vary greatly from one school to another, but they are substantial everywhere. The average public community college costs $1,627 per year in tuition; the average 4-year public college costs $3,356; and the average private college costs $15,380.[2] If you live on campus, count on another five or six thousand dollars for room and board.

Nothing about college is cheap. It takes enormous expenditures of three often scarce commodities: energy, time, and money. Perhaps surprisingly, many students find money the easiest of them to find. While it's not simple to get financial aid and no one is going to walk up to you and offer you an all-expenses-paid scholarship, you can find many sources of funding for your education if you are persistent.

To find this money, however, you will need to spend ample amounts of the other two scarce commodities: time and energy. The entire process of securing financial aid takes a considerable amount of preparation: you need to identify potential sources of funds and then apply for them. You should assume the process will take somewhere between several weeks and several months, depending on the type of aid you're applying for.

Take the following steps to find funding:

Identify the Different Types of Funding Available

Funding for college comes in three basic categories: loans, grants, and scholarships. Although each supplies you with funds for college, they do so in very different ways.

- **Loans.** When you receive a **loan,** a bank, credit union, or other agency provides funds that must be repaid after a specified period of time. A loan carries a particular interest rate, which is stated as an annual percentage rate. Think of a loan as renting money: As long as you have the use of someone else's money, you have to pay them "rent" for the privilege. Banks and other lending agencies make money through the interest they charge on loans, just as they do with credit cards.

  For example, suppose a bank gives you a $5,000 loan that has an interest rate of 8 percent per year. Not only must you pay back the $5,000 over a specified period, but you must pay the bank interest of 8 percent on the balance that you owe on the loan. Obviously, the higher the interest rate, the more you are paying for the privilege of borrowing the bank's money.

  Three factors must be considered when you receive a loan: the stated amount of the loan (called the **principal**), the interest rate (stated as a percentage), and the length of the loan (referred to as the **term** of the loan). All three factors are important, because they determine how much your payments will be when you pay the loan back.

Loan
Funds provided by a bank, credit union, or other agency that must be repaid after a specified period of time

Principal
The stated amount of a loan

> "Interest works night and day, in fair weather and in foul."
>
> Henry Ward Beecher, author

Term
The length of time for which money is lent

  Many loans for college have an enormous advantage over loans you'll take out for other purchases, such as a car or house, because payments on college loans are *deferred* until you graduate and (presumably!) begin to earn an income—that is, it is often not necessary to start paying back the loan until you graduate. Depending on the type of loan you take out, interest on the loan is either paid for by the government while you are enrolled in college or is deferred until you graduate.

  There are several national loan programs, sponsored by the federal government, that lend money to students. The major ones include the following:

  Stafford loans. Stafford loans are available to any student who is registered at least half time and is a U.S. citizen or permanent resident. They provide from just over $2,600 to $5,500 a year.

  Stafford loans come in two types: subsidized and unsubsidized. *Subsidized Stafford Loans* are awarded through colleges on the basis of student financial need. For subsidized loans, the government pays interest until repayment begins, typically after the student graduates. *Unsubsidized Stafford Loans* do not require demonstration of financial need. Interest is not paid by the government; instead it accumulates while the student is in college. However, the student doesn't have to make any payments until after graduation, when both principal and accumulated interest must be repaid over a specified period, which is up to 10 years.

PLUS loans. If your parents support you and claim you as a deduction on their income tax return, they may take out a PLUS loan. PLUS loans can cover up to the full amount of a student's cost of college attendance and can be paid back over a 10-year period.

Perkins loans. Perkins loans have a low interest rate. They are awarded on the basis of exceptional financial need, as determined by a student's college. The loans are made by a school's financial aid office.

Grant

An award of money that does not have to be repaid

Grants. A **grant** is money that does not have to be repaid. Obviously, it's more advantageous to receive a grant than a loan. And not surprisingly, it's harder to qualify for grants than loans—harder, but not impossible. Several grant programs exist which can help reduce the amount you'll need to pay for college. They include the following:

Pell grants. Based on need, Pell grants are provided to undergraduate students who have earned no previous degrees. They are awarded by college financial aid offices, which follow a formula provided by the federal government. Every student who meets certain need criteria is eligible for a Pell grant, ensuring that the neediest students receive some support.

Federal Supplemental Educational Opportunity Grants (FSEOG). The government supplies a limited number of FSEOGs to every college, which can provide these grants to needy students. Unlike Pell grants, which are guaranteed to every eligible student, FSEOGs are in limited supply. Once a college awards its allotment for a given year, no other awards are possible.

Work-study grants. Work-study grants provide jobs for undergraduates with financial needs. The jobs are typically related to a student's course of study, and the salary is subsidized by the government. Because a work-study position is often part of a student's total package of financial aid, it is generally considered a grant, even though work is required.

Scholarship

An award of money to a student based on need or merit

Scholarships. Scholarships are support awarded by colleges and other organizations. Like a grant, a scholarship is money that does not have to be repaid. Most scholarships are based primarily on a student's financial need, although some are based on merit. For instance, students with exceptional academic or athletic abilities may receive a scholarship even though they wouldn't necessarily qualify under typical need-based measures.

The most frequent source of scholarships is one's own college, which may give money to reduce tuition and fees. But there are literally thousands of organizations that provide scholarships, ranging from companies such as Microsoft to nonprofit groups, such as the Boy Scouts and Girl Scouts.

The federal government also provides some scholarships to students whose family income does not rise above certain levels. These include the following:

Hope scholarship. The Hope scholarship is a tax credit that helps free up funds for college. Students receive a 100 percent tax credit for the first $1,000 of tuition and required fees, and a 50 percent credit on the second $1,000.

Lifetime learning tax credit. This tax credit is targeted to older students who are going back to school, changing careers, or taking courses to upgrade their skills, as well as to juniors and seniors in 4-year colleges. Families can receive a 20 percent tax credit for the first $5,000 of tuition and fees, and the amount will increase in future years.

Research Possible Sources of Financial Aid

As you can see, there are many sources of financial aid. The biggest problem is finding them.

Your first stop on your search for sources of financial aid should be your college's financial aid office. Every college has one, and it tends to be one of the busiest places on campus.

Most student aid offices contain a great deal of information about possible sources of aid. But that's only a starting point. The library and World Wide Web also contain many types of information that can direct you to specific possibilities. One place to get started is the Federal Student Aid Information Center in Washington, which can be reached at 1-800-4-FED-AID (1-800-433-3243) or on the Web at **www.ed.gov/prog_info/SFA/StudentGuide**. The center will send you "The Student Guide," which describes programs that account for almost three-fourths of all financial aid awarded to students.

Keep in mind, however, that where money is involved, there are scams. Do not pay money to someone who offers to identify obscure scholarships that will yield you thousands of dollars. It's unlikely that anyone could find sources that you couldn't find yourself through careful research. Be especially wary of websites that ask for a credit card number to provide you with online information. The results are likely to be disappointing. (The websites we provide at the end of the chapter are completely reputable.)

Whatever the potential source of financial aid, you'll be asked to bare your financial soul. There will also be forms galore. Before actually completing the forms, it will be important to gather the information you will need. Much of it may have to come from your parents, if you are being supported by them, and they will have to complete some of the forms.

Keep track of deadlines! If you miss a deadline for applying for financial aid, you'll be out of luck; no exceptions are made. You'll just have to wait for another aid cycle.

Finally, make sure you know what your needs are. The typical costs of college include not only tuition but also fees, books, and supplies, as well as associated costs, such as transportation, housing, food, and child care.

Apply for Financial Aid

It may seem that for every dollar in aid you get, there is a different line to complete on a complicated form. Prepare yourself for a blizzard of paperwork.

Following are the steps in applying for financial aid:

"Good day, Madam. I'm working my son's way through college."

- **Speak with a financial aid counselor at your school.** Because the best source of financial aid is your own college, make an appointment to discuss your needs with a campus financial aid counselor or officer. In addition to giving you the most up-to-date information about possible sources of aid, the college financial aid officer can provide you with the forms you need to fill out and a list of the deadlines you need to meet.

- **Decide how much aid you need.** It's important to ask for just the right amount of aid, neither too little nor too much. If you ask for too little aid, you may be strapped for funds during the school term. It's much more difficult to get aid in the middle of a term than during the normal application period.

  At the same time, don't apply for more financial aid than you actually need. First there is an issue of equity: What you get in aid may reduce the pool for others, and if you receive surplus aid you may be preventing other students from getting their fair share. Further, you don't want to load yourself up with unnecessary debt. Most graduates pay from $150 to $175 a month to pay off their student loans; you don't want to end up with so much debt that your loan payments are even higher than this.

- **Fill out your college's application for financial aid.** Colleges have their own forms to apply for financial aid. Carefully fill the form out, making sure you file it before the required deadline. In fact, the earlier you get the form in, the better: Most schools have a limited pool of funds, and the earlier you get your application in, the higher your chances of getting an appropriate share of the financial aid pie.

- **Write a personal letter to accompany your application.** If you think there are factors that affect your ability to pay for college which are not adequately reflected in the application, write a letter to the financial aid officer describing them.

- **Complete a Free Application for Federal Student Aid (FAFSA) and Financial Aid PROFILE.** The FAFSA and PROFILE are standard forms used to assess a student's financial capabilities and determine how much the student and family can be expected to contribute toward college expenses. One or both of the forms are used by almost every college. They require a great deal of information, including past, present, and expected income from all sources. Copies of several tax returns from prior years are also required.

  Be scrupulously honest when you complete the forms. If you fail to include a source of income that is later discovered by a financial aid provider, you may be required to repay immediately any aid that you have received. In addition, you may face disciplinary measures that put your education in jeopardy; in the worst case, you may even face legal charges.

- **Wait.** It takes time for loan applications to be processed and financial aid decisions to be made. Be prepared to wait, and consider contingency plans for various possibilities.

Evaluate Your Financial Aid Package

Sometime later, when the college has had time to consider your application for aid, you will receive an official response. This is most likely to be in the form of a "package"—a combination of loans, grants, scholarships, and, perhaps, an offer of an on-campus job. This is the time for a thorough evaluation of the offer. Consider the various elements of the package carefully to determine whether, taken together, they will fully meet your financial needs.

Keep in mind that you may not have to accept every element of the package that is offered to you. For instance, you may decide to accept a scholarship but turn down a loan. That decision may mean that you'll have less debt after you graduate, but that you'll have to work more hours at a part-time job—a trade-off that you may or may not wish to make.

What if the package doesn't seem sufficient? The most important thing is not to give up. A polite call or visit to the financial aid office is in order.

When you speak to someone from financial aid, lay out your difficulty with the package. If the aid is so low that you won't be able to attend college, let the financial aid office know. If you had noted special circumstances in a letter, ask if they were taken into account. (Sometimes letters and other vital pieces of information get overlooked.) Ask if there is a formal appeal process and, if there is, ask how to begin it.

Your main goal is to get the financial aid office to take a second look at your application. By being polite and to-the-point in your dealings with the office staff, you stand a better chance of having them reevaluate your application.

Having good grades will help your chances of getting the financial aid office to take a second look, and poor grades will hurt: If you are not doing well in your classes, you have less bargaining power.

What if the school is unable to come up with a greater level of support? The first step is to ask the staff of the financial aid office for advice. They may be able to suggest an approach that you initially overlooked. The second step is to redouble your research efforts. You may be able to take out a loan to make up the deficit. Finally, consider alternatives to full-time college attendance. It may be preferable to attend school part time while working than to give up college altogether or to get so much into debt that it will be hard to pay off your loans.

Above all, don't give up! If it's important enough to you, you will be able to find some way to afford an education.

Show Me the Money: Building a Financial Philosophy

It's hard to forget the famous line from *Jerry McGuire*, the movie in which Tom Cruise plays a sports agent: "Show me the money." That blunt statement might be used to illustrate one financial philosophy—that life revolves around money.

Try It! 5

Discover Your Personal Financial Philosophy

Begin to create a personal financial philosophy by completing this exercise.

Attitudes toward Money

	Strongly Disagree	Disagree	Neutral	Agree	Strongly Agree
1. Money is essential for happiness.					
2. Having money guarantees happiness.					
3. Money makes no difference to one's happiness.					
4. More money equals more happiness.					
5. Beyond having enough to live modestly on, money doesn't make much of a difference.					
6. I frequently worry about money.					
7. I frequently daydream about having a lot of money.					
8. If I suddenly had to live on very little money, I could adjust easily.					
9. If I suddenly won a lot of money, I would go on a spending spree.					
10. If I suddenly won a lot of money, I would share it with my relatives.					
11. If I suddenly won a lot of money, I would give a large percentage to charity.					
12. If I found a substantial amount of cash in a bag, I would try hard to find its rightful owner.					
13. If I could carry only a briefcase full of $100 bills out of a burning building or my pet dog, I would take the dog.					
14. I plan to make a lot of money in my career.					
15. I plan to make only enough money to live in reasonable comfort.					
16. It's great to have money.					
17. Money is a necessary evil.					
18. Money is the root of all evil.					

Many would disagree. For instance, authors Vicki Robin and Joe Dominguez argue in their book *Your Money or Your Life*[3] that most people find that money is a controlling force in their lives and, consequently, their major source of stress. Acquiring and spending money becomes an obsession, and the simple pleasures of life are lost. They outline an alternative approach in which we reprioritize our values, live frugally, and ultimately achieve financial independence.

Sources of Satisfaction

1. Which activities that you engaged in over the last 5 years have given you the greatest satisfaction?

2. How much money did those activities cost?

3. How would you spend your time if you could do anything you chose?

4. How much money would this cost each year?

Personal Financial Philosophy

Consider your attitudes toward money and the sources of your satisfaction. Sum up your personal financial philosophy here:

To Try It online, go to **www.mhhe.com/power**.

Whether you choose to follow the path of Jerry McGuire or that of Vicki Robin and Joe Dominguez, the important thing is to develop your own personal financial philosophy. Consider the role that money plays in your life. How much does money motivate what you do? Are you interested in becoming rich, or do you tend to think more in terms of simply having enough to have a comfortable life, without lots of luxuries? What activities bring you the

Speaking of Success

Name: *Jerry Yang*
Education: *Stanford University*
Home: *Sunnyvale, California*

I f you've ever used Yahoo!, one of the most popular search engines on the World Wide Web, you've relied on the handiwork of Jerry Yang. Yang, along with his partner David Filo, developed the Yahoo! navigational guide in the mid-1990s.

Yang was born in Taiwan, and his father died 2 years later. Seeking a better life, his mother immigrated to the United States. Legend has it that "shoe" was the only English word Yang knew when he started school in San Jose, California, at the age of 10.

After graduating from high school, Yang enrolled in a college electrical engineering program. While still a student, Yang and his friend David

Filo began, as a hobby, to catalog their favorite websites. The list of sites was initially called "Jerry's Guide to the World Wide Web." As the popularity of their list began to increase, Yang and Filo were forced

to refine the listing into categories, and then subcategories. They also renamed their list "Yahoo!" standing for "Yet Another Hierarchical Officious Oracle."

In only a few years, what had started as a hobby had grown into a

huge business. Today, with Yang and Filo as "Chief Yahoo!s," the search engine is used by 200 million people each month.

Despite his extraordinary success, Yang feels the future holds even more promise. "It'll probably be strange for me to say this, but I don't consider myself successful yet," Yang says. "So much that I want to do remains to be done . . . It's important to continue to be modest and paranoid."[4]

But he adds, "It's not often that we get time to reflect on what we've done. But in the rare moments that I do, I look at the people that I work with at Yahoo!, and feel pride and satisfaction."[5]

greatest satisfaction in life? Do those activities require a certain level of income? Explore these questions further in Try it 5.

College is one of the biggest investments that you'll ever make. If you only think of it in terms of its eventual financial payoff—getting a better job and leading a more affluent life—you'll be missing some central aspects of the process of educating yourself.

Keeping in Mind the Value of a College Education

Our present focus on paying for college has led us, of necessity, to focus on the dollars-and-cents of education. Without a doubt, college is expensive. On the other side of the equation, there's no question that having a college education has vast financial value: People who are college graduates earn nearly twice as much money each year as those with only a high school degree.

But the money we spend on education buys us far more than a better salary. It gives us a better understanding of the world and its people, insight into who we are, better job opportunities, and a chance to befriend people who share the common goal of becoming well-educated citizens of a global society.

It would be terribly shortsighted to put a price tag on education, deciding, in effect, that if you must pay a lot you won't bother with an education. You may need to choose your school according to the tuition it charges and the financial aid package it offers you, but that's not the same as choosing to skip college altogether because it is going to be financially stressful. An experience that will permit us to reach our potential is worth *everything*.

Looking Back

What purpose does a budget serve and how can I prepare and stick to one?

- Concerns about money can be significantly reduced through the creation of a budget by which spending and income can be planned, accounted for, and aligned with your goals.

- Budgets provide security by helping you control your finances and avoid surprises.

- The process of budgeting involves identifying your financial goals, keeping track of current expenses and estimating future expenses, and making the necessary adjustments to keep income and spending in balance.

- If financial difficulties arise, contact your creditors and arrange a plan for paying off the debt. If you need help in designing a repayment plan, nonprofit credit counselors can help.

What help is available to pay for my college education?

- Loans for education are available with reasonable interest rates and conditions, especially the ability to defer paying the loans back until after graduation. Several federal programs offer loan guarantees, interest subsidies, and lower interest rates.

- Grants offer money without requiring repayment. They are harder to receive than loans because they are typically reserved for people with exceptional financial need.

- Scholarships are usually awarded by colleges and other institutions based on either financial need or academic, athletic, or other abilities.

What is the value of a college education?

- A college degree not only leads to a higher salary (college graduates earn nearly twice as much as those with only a high school degree) but also provides a better understanding of the world, insight into ourselves, better job opportunities, and a chance to befriend people in a global society.

Key Terms and Concepts

Budget (p. 337)   Principal (p. 351)
Grant (p. 352)   Scholarship (p. 352)
Loan (p. 351)   Term (p. 351)

Resources

On Campus

The bursar's or treasurer's office handles money affairs. Not only does it collect money owed for tuition but may perform other services such as cashing checks.

If you are receiving financial aid, there is usually a particular office devoted to the complexities of scholarships, loan processing, and other forms of aid. The personnel in the office can be very helpful in maximizing your financial aid package as well as in solving financial problems related to your schooling. If you have a problem with your finances, see them sooner rather than later.

In Print

Marshall Loeb's *52 Weeks to Financial Fitness* (Crown, 2001) offers a clear path to getting all your finances under control. *Paying for College* (Time Life, 1997), by Marc Robinson, includes many practical tips for finding ways to finance a college education. Finally, *The Student Guide* (U.S. Department of Education, 2002) is the most complete resource on student financial aid, providing up-to-date and thorough explanations of financial aid programs. You can get a free copy by calling 1-800-4-FED-AID.

On the Web

The following websites provide additional information about money matters. (Although the Web addresses were accurate at the time the book was printed, check the P.O.W.E.R. Learning website [**www.mhhe.com/power**] for any changes that may have occurred.)

- The home page for College Aid Sources for Higher Education (CASHE) (**www.cashe.com/**) is a valuable, time-saving tool for students and their parents who are trying to identify sources of funds to pay for college. Through this service you can receive information about scholarships, fellowships, grants, work study, loan programs, tuition waivers, internships, competitions, and work co-operative programs.

- "FinAid: The SmartStudent Guide to College Financial Aid" (**www. finaid.org/finaid.html**) provides a free, comprehensive, independent, and objective guide to student financial aid. It was created by Mark Kantrowitz, author of *The Prentice Hall Guide to Scholarships and Fellowships for Math and Science Students.* The site's "calculators" page (**www. finaid.org/finaid/calculators/finaid_calc.html**) offers loads of online calculators including: College Cost Projector, Savings Plan Designer, Financial Aid Estimation Form, Loan Payment Calculator, and Student Loan Advisor (undergraduate).

- "Managing Your Money" (**www.nd.edu/~finaid/managing_your_ money.htm**), sponsored by the Office of Financial Aid at Notre Dame University, offers eight links covering everything from responsible borrowing to tips on developing credit card smarts.

Taking It to the Net

1 Find four sources of financial aid. One possible strategy: Go to Yahoo! (**www.yahoo.com**) and choose "education," "financial aid," then "grants" or "scholarship programs." What is available? What are the differences between scholarships and grants?

2 Discover three new ways to save money. Possible strategy: Using the search engine of your choice, enter the phrase "saving money." Examine the sites for tips and tricks to help you hold on to what you earn.

The Case of . . .

Overdrawn, Overwrought, and Over Her Head

Her life was a house of cards, and someone had just pulled one out from the bottom.

At least that's what it felt like to Tara Kenko. The month had started out badly when Tara found that she had made a mistake in her checking account balance and had only $439, instead of the $939 she thought she had. After paying her share of the rent—$210—she didn't have enough money left to make her car payment. So she just put the bill aside, figuring that she'd take care of it later in the month when she got paid.

Things went from bad to worse 2 days later when her car refused to start. She had to have it towed to a mechanic, who told her that it would cost about $350 to get it fixed. She didn't have that, either, but she figured she could put it on her credit card. But later, when she went to pick up her car and pay for the repair, which turned out to be closer to $400 than $350, her card was rejected. She called the credit card company from the repair shop and was told that she had exceeded her authorized credit limit. The mechanic wouldn't let her take her car until she paid for the repairs, so she was forced to leave it and catch a bus to campus.

The final straw came in her chemistry class. The instructor announced that students in the class would have to buy yet another textbook to help them with a particular set of experiments. Having already spent $150 for books in that class alone, Tara was both angry and dismayed. She had no idea how she was going to find the money to pay for the book, let alone her regular car payment and the car repairs. She was in deep financial trouble, and she didn't know what to do.

1. What should Tara do now to start addressing her problem? What steps should she take immediately?

2. Can you suggest some approaches Tara can take to deal with the problem of the new book for her chemistry class?

3. How do you think the mistake may have occurred in Tara's checking account? What advice would you give her to avoid a similar mistake in the future?

4. Given that Tara does not have a lot of leeway in her finances for multiple disasters such as the ones that befell her this month, what general course would you advise her to take as a way to plan her expenditures more effectively?

5. What steps might Tara take to decrease her expenses? What might she do to increase her income?

Stress, Health, and Wellness

14

Louisa Denby's day began badly: She slept through her alarm and had to skip breakfast to catch the bus to campus. Then, when she went to the library to catch up on the reading she had to do before taking a test the next day, the one article she needed was missing. The librarian told her that replacing it would take 24 hours. Feeling frustrated, she walked to the computer lab to print out the paper she had completed at home the night before.

The computer wouldn't read her disk. She searched for someone to help her, but she was unable to find anyone who knew any more about computers than she did.

It was only 9:42 A.M., and Louisa had a wracking headache. Apart from that pain, she was conscious of only one feeling: stress.

Looking Ahead

Have you had days like Louisa's? Are *most* of your days like hers? Then you're no stranger to stress. It's something that all college students experience to varying degrees throughout their college careers. In fact, almost a third of first-year college students report feeling frequently overwhelmed with all they need to do.[1]

Coping with stress is one of the challenges that college students face. The many demands on your time can make you feel that you'll never finish what needs to get done. This pressure produces wear-and-tear on your body and mind, and it's easy to fall prey to ill health as a result.

However, stress and poor health are not inevitable outcomes of college. In fact, by following simple guidelines and deciding to make health a conscious priority, you can maintain good physical and mental health.

This chapter covers the ways you can keep fit and healthy during—and beyond—college. It offers suggestions on how you can cope with stress, improve your diet, get enough exercise, and sleep better. It also will help you consider particular threats to mental and physical health that you're likely to face while you are in college, including alcohol and drugs, pregnancy, sexually transmitted diseases, and rape.

In sum, after reading this chapter you'll be able to answer these questions:

- **What is stress and how can I control it?**

- **What is involved in keeping fit and healthy, and why is it important for me to do so?**

- **What are the main threats to my health and well-being?**

- **What are the components of sexual health?**

Living with Stress

Stressed out? Tests, papers, reading assignments, job demands, roommate problems, volunteer activities, committee work. . . . It's no surprise that these can produce stress. But it may be a surprise to know that so can graduating from high school, starting your dream job, falling in love, getting married, and even winning the lottery.

Virtually *anything*—good or bad—is capable of producing stress if it presents us with a challenge. **Stress** is the physical and emotional response we have to events that threaten or challenge us. It is rooted in the primitive "fight or flight" response wired into all animals—human and nonhuman. You see it in cats, for instance, when confronted by a dog or other threat: Their backs go up, their hair stands on end, their eyes widen, and, ultimately, they either take off or attack. The challenge stimulating this revved-up response is called a *stressor*. For humans, stressors can range from a first date to losing our chemistry notes to facing a flash flood.

Because our everyday lives are filled with events that can be interpreted as threatening or challenging, stress is commonplace in most people's lives. There are three main types of stressors:

1. **Cataclysmic events** are events that occur suddenly and affect many people simultaneously. Tornadoes, hurricanes, and plane crashes are examples of cataclysmic events. Although they may produce powerful immediate consequences, ironically they produce less stress than other types of stressors. The reason? Cataclysmic events have a clear endpoint, which can make them more manageable. Furthermore, because they affect many people simultaneously, their consequences are shared with others, and no individual feels singled out.

2. **Personal stressors** are major life events that produce a negative physical and psychological reaction. Failing a course, losing a job, and ending a relationship are all examples of personal stressors. Sometimes positive events—such as getting married or starting a new job—can act as personal stressors. Although the short-term impact of a personal stressor can be difficult, the long-term consequences may decline as people learn to adapt to the situation.

3. **Daily hassles** are the minor irritants of life that, singly, produce relatively little stress. Waiting in a traffic jam, receiving a tuition bill riddled with mistakes, and being interrupted by noises of major construction while trying to study are examples of such minor irritants. However, daily hassles add up, and cumulatively they can produce even more stress than a single larger-scale event. (Figure 14.1 indicates the most common daily hassles in people's lives.[2])

What Is Happening When We Are Stressed Out

Stress does more than make us feel anxious, upset, and fearful. Beneath those responses, we are experiencing many different physical reactions, each placing a high demand on our body's resources. Our hearts beat faster, our breath-

Stress
The response to events that threaten or challenge us

Cataclysmic events
Sudden, powerful events that occur quickly and affect many people simultaneously

Personal stressors
Major life events that produce stress

Daily hassles
The minor irritants of life that, by themselves, produce little stress, but which can add up and produce more stress than a single larger-scale event

Figure 14.1

Daily Hassles

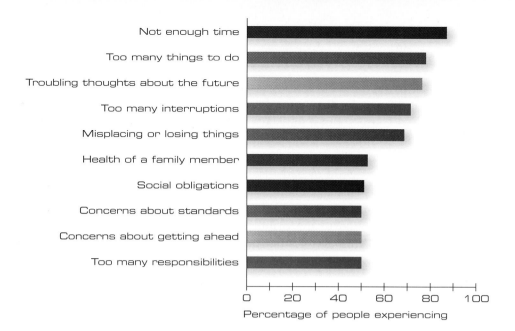

Percentage of people experiencing

ing becomes more rapid and shallow, and we produce more sweat. Our internal organs churn out a variety of hormones. In the long run, these physical responses wear down our immune system, our body's defense against disease. We become more susceptible to a variety of diseases, ranging from the common cold and headaches to strokes and heart disease. In fact, surveys have found that the greater the number of stressful events a person experiences over the course of a year, the more likely it is that he or she will have a major illness (see Try It 1, "Assess Your Susceptibility to Stress-Related Illness").

Handling Stress

Stress is an inevitable part of life. In fact, a life with no stress at all would be so boring, so uneventful, that you'd quickly miss the stress that had been removed.

That doesn't mean, though, that we have to sit back and accept stress when it does arise. **Coping** is the effort to control, reduce, or tolerate the threats that lead to stress. Using the P.O.W.E.R. principles can help you ward off stress and actively deal with it.

Coping
The effort to control, reduce, or learn to tolerate the threats that lead to stress

Prepare: Readying Yourself Physically

Being in good physical condition is the primary way to prepare for future stress. Stress takes its toll on your body, so it makes sense that the stronger and fitter you are, the less negative impact stress will have on you. For example, a regular exercise program reduces heart rate, respiration rate, and blood pressure at times when the body is at rest—making us better able to withstand the negative consequences of stress. Furthermore, vigorous exercise produces endorphins, natural painkilling chemicals in the brain. Endorphins produce feelings of happiness—even euphoria—and may be responsible for the "runner's high," the positive feelings often reported by long-distance runners following long runs. Through the production of endorphins, then, exercise can help our bodies produce a natural coping response to stress.

If you now drink a lot of coffee or soda, a change in your diet may be enough to bring about a reduction in stress. Coffee, soda, chocolate, and a surprising number of other foods contain caffeine, which can make you feel jittery and anxious even without stress; add a stressor, and the reaction can be very intense and unpleasant.

Eating right can alleviate another problem: obesity. Around one-third of people in the United States are *obese,* defined as having body weight more than 20 percent above the average weight for a person of a given height. Obesity can bring on stress for several reasons. For one thing, being overweight drags down the functioning of the body, leading to fatigue and a reduced ability to bounce back when we encounter challenges to our well-being. In addition, feeling heavy in a society that acclaims the virtues of slimness can be stressful in and of itself.

O rganize: Identifying What Is Causing You Stress

You can't cope effectively with stress until you know what's causing it. In some cases, it's obvious—a series of bad test grades in a course, a roommate problem that keeps getting worse, a job supervisor who seems to delight in making things difficult. In other cases, however, the causes of stress may be more subtle. Perhaps your relationship with your boyfriend or girlfriend is rocky, and you have a nagging feeling that something is wrong.

Whatever the source of stress, you can't deal with it unless you know what it is. To organize your assault on stress, then, take a piece of paper and list the major circumstances that are causing you stress. Just listing them will help put you in control, and you'll be better able to figure out strategies for coping with them.

> ## Sources of Stress
> 1. Government professor talks so fast that notetaking is nearly impossible
> 2. Difficulty paying rent this month.
> 3. Not enough time to study for Tuesday's psych test

W ork: Developing Effective Coping Strategies

A wide variety of tactics can help you deal with stress. Among the most effective approaches to coping are these:

- **Take charge of the situation.** Stress is most apt to arise when we are faced with situations over which we have little or no control. If you take

Try It! 1

Assess Your Susceptibility to Stress-Related Illness

Are you susceptible to a stress-related illness? The more stress in your life, the more likely it is that you will experience a major illness.

To determine the stress in your life, take the stressor value given beside each event you have experienced and multiply it by the number of occurrences over the past year (up to a maximum of four), and then add up these scores.[3]

87	Experienced the death of a spouse
77	Got married
77	Experienced the death of a close family member
76	Were divorced
74	Experienced a marital separation
68	Experienced the death of a close friend
68	Experienced pregnancy or fathered a pregnancy
65	Had a major personal injury or illness
62	Were fired from work
60	Ended a marital engagement or a steady relationship
58	Had sexual difficulties
58	Experienced a marital reconciliation
57	Had a major change in self-concept or self-awareness
56	Experienced a major change in the health or behavior of a family member
54	Became engaged to be married
53	Had a major change in financial status
52	Took on a mortgage or loan of more than $10,000
52	Had a major change in use of drugs
50	Had a major conflict or change in values
50	Had a major change in the number of arguments with your spouse
50	Gained a new family member
50	Entered college
50	Changed to a new school
50	Changed to a different line of work

charge of the situation, you'll reduce the experience of stress. For example, if several assignments are all due on the same day, you might try negotiating with one of your instructors for a later due date.

49	Had a major change in amount of independence and responsibility
47	Had a major change in responsibilities at work
46	Experienced a major change in use of alcohol
45	Revised personal habits
44	Had trouble with school administration
43	Held a job while attending school
43	Had a major change in social activities
42	Had trouble with in-laws
42	Had a major change in working hours or conditions
42	Changed residence or living conditions
41	Had your spouse begin or cease work outside the home
41	Changed your choice of major field of study
41	Changed dating habits
40	Had an outstanding personal achievement
38	Had trouble with your boss
38	Had a major change in amount of participation in school activities
37	Had a major change in type and/or amount of recreation
36	Had a major change in religious activities
34	Had a major change of sleeping habits
33	Took a trip or vacation
30	Had a major change in eating habits
26	Had a major change in the number of family get-togethers
22	Were found guilty of minor violations of the law

Scoring: If your total score is above 1,435, you are in a high-stress category and therefore more at risk for experiencing a stress-related illness. A high score does *not* mean that you are sure to get sick. Many other factors determine ill health, and high stress is only one cause. Other positive factors in your life, such as getting enough sleep and exercise, may prevent illness. Still, having an unusually high amount of stress in your life is a cause for concern, and you may want to take steps to reduce it.

To Try It online, go to **www.mhhe.com/power**.

- **Don't waste energy trying to change the unchangeable.** There are some situations that you simply can't control. You can't change the fact that you have come down with a case of mono, and you can't change your performance on a test you took last week. Don't hit your head against a brick wall and try to modify things that can't be changed. Use your energy to improve the situation, not to rewrite history.

- **Look for the silver lining.** Stress arises when we perceive a situation as threatening. If we can change how we perceive that situation, we can change our reactions to it. For instance, if your computer science instructor requires you to learn a difficult spreadsheet program in a very short time, the saving grace is that you may be able to use the skill to your advantage in getting a high-paying temporary job during school vacation. (You can practice finding the silver lining in Try It 2.)

> "A smooth sea never made a skillful mariner."
>
> English proverb

Social support
Assistance and comfort supplied by others in times of stress

- **Talk to your friends. Social support,** assistance and comfort supplied by others, can help us through stressful periods. Turning to our friends and family and simply talking about the stress we're under can help us tolerate it more effectively. Even anonymous telephone hotlines can provide us with social support. (The U.S. Public Health Service maintains a master toll-free number that can provide telephone numbers and addresses of many national helplines and support groups. You can reach it by calling 800-336-4794.)

- **Relax.** Because stress produces constant wear and tear on the body, it seems possible that practices that lead to the relaxation of the body might lead to a reduction in stress. And that's just what happens. Using any one of several techniques for producing physical relaxation can prevent stress. Among the best relaxation techniques:

  Meditation. Though often associated with its roots in the ancient Eastern religion of Zen Buddhism, meditation, a technique for refocusing attention and producing bodily relaxation, is practiced in some form by members of virtually every major religion. Meditation reduces blood pressure, slows respiration, and in general reduces bodily tension.

  How do you meditate? The process is actually rather simple. As summarized in Table 14.1, it includes sitting in a quiet room with eyes

Table 14.1
Methods of Meditation

Step 1. Pick a focus word or short phrase that's firmly rooted in your personal belief system. For example, a nonreligious individual might choose a neutral word like *one* or *peace* or *love*. A Christian person desiring to use a prayer could pick the opening words of Psalm 23. *The Lord is my shepherd;* a Jewish person could choose *Shalom.*

Step 2. Sit quietly in a comfortable position.

Step 3. Close your eyes.

Step 4. Relax your muscles.

Step 5. Breathe slowly and naturally, repeating your focus word or phrase silently as you exhale.

Step 6. Throughout, assume a passive attitude. Don't worry about how well you're doing. When other thoughts come to mind, simply say to yourself, "Oh, well," and gently return to the repetition.

Step 7. Continue for 10 to 20 minutes. You may open your eyes to check the time, but do not use an alarm. When you finish, sit quietly for a minute or so, at first with your eyes closed and later with your eyes open. Then do not stand for 1 or 2 minutes.

Step 8. Practice the technique once or twice a day.

Look for the Silver Lining

Consider the following list of potentially stressful situations. Try to find something positive—a silver lining—in each of them. The first two are completed to get you started.

Situation	Silver Lining
1. Your car just broke down and repairing it is more than you can afford right now.	1. This is the perfect time to begin exercising by walking and using your bicycle.
2. Your boss just yelled at you and threatened to fire you.	2. Either this is a good time to open an honest discussion with your boss about your job situation, OR this is a good time to get a more interesting job.
3. You have two papers due on Monday and there's a great concert you wanted to go to on Saturday night.	3.
4. You just failed an important test.	4.
5. You're flat broke, you have a date on Saturday, and you wanted to buy some things beforehand.	5.
6. Your last date went poorly and you think your girlfriend/boyfriend was hinting that it was time to break up.	6.
7. Your parents just told you that they can't afford to pay your tuition next semester.	7.
8. You just got cut from a sports team or club activity you loved.	8.
9. Your best friend is starting to turn weird and seems not to enjoy being with you as much as before.	9.
10. You just realized you don't really like your academic major, and you're not even sure you like your college much anymore.	10.

Working in a Group: After you have considered each of these situations individually, discuss each of them in a group. What similarities and differences in others' responses did you find? Evaluate the different responses, and consider whether—and why—some ways of reframing the situations were better than others.

To Try It online, go to **www.mhhe.com/power**.

closed or focused on a point about 6 feet away from you and paying attention to your breathing. Though the specifics of what you do may vary, meditation works by helping you concentrate on breathing deeply and rhythmically, sometimes murmuring a word or sound repeatedly.

Career Connections

Anticipating Job Stress

Students are not the only ones who have to cope with stress. It's also one of the prime hazards of the world of work. Illnesses related to job stress result in costs of $150 billion each year.

Consequently, taking potential stress into account should be an important consideration when choosing a profession. Asking yourself the following questions can help you identify the factors that may induce stress on the job:

- How much control over working conditions will I have? (The more control an employee has in day-to-day decision making, the lower the level of stress.)

- What are the demands of the job? Will I face constant demands to do more work and to work more quickly? (Higher work demands create a more stressful work environment.)

- What is the tolerance for error? (Some occupations, such as air traffic controller, have no margin for error, while others, such as many white-collar professions, give workers a second chance if they make a mistake.)

- How closely do my abilities and strengths match the requirements of the job? (A good match between one's abilities and the demands of a job is the best insurance against an unduly stressful work environment.)

- How well do I cope with stress?

If your coping skills are good, you may be suited for entering a high-stress occupation. But if you have difficulty dealing with stress, choosing a career in a field that produces less stress makes more sense.

Progressive relaxation. Progressive relaxation does some of the same things that meditation does, but in a more direct way. To use progressive relaxation, you systematically tense and then relax different groups of muscles. For example, you might start with your lower arm, tensing it for 5 seconds and then relaxing it for a similar amount of time. By doing the same thing throughout the parts of your body, you'll be able to learn the "feel" of bodily relaxation. You can use the technique when you feel that stress is getting the better of you. (Use Try It 3 to experience progressive relaxation for yourself.)

- **Remember that wimping out doesn't work—so keep your commitments.** Suppose you've promised a friend that you'll help him move, and you've promised yourself that you'll spend more time with your children. You've also been elected to the student body governing board, and you've made a commitment to bring more speakers to campus. Now you are facing all the demands connected to these commitments and feeling stressed.

  You may be tempted to cope with the feeling by breaking some or all of your commitments, thinking, "I just need to sit at home and relax in front of the television!" This is not coping. It is escaping, and it doesn't reduce stress. Ducking out of commitments, whether to yourself or to others, will make you feel guilty and anxious, and will be another source of stress—one without the satisfaction of having accomplished what you set out to do. Keep your promises.

ry It!
3

Try Progressive Relaxation

You can undertake progressive relaxation almost anywhere, including the library, a sports field, or a classroom, since tensing and relaxing muscles is quiet and unobtrusive. Although the following exercise suggests you lie down, you can use parts of it no matter where you are.

1. Lie flat on your back, get comfortable, and focus on your toes.

2. Become aware of your left toes. Bunch them up into a tight ball, then let them go. Then let them relax even further.

3. Now work on your left foot, from the toes to the heel. Without tensing your toes, tighten up the rest of your foot and then let it relax. Then relax it more.

4. Work your way up your left leg, first tensing and then relaxing each part. You may move up as slowly or as quickly as you wish, using big leaps (e.g., the entire lower leg) or small steps (e.g., the ankle, the calf, the front of the lower leg, the knee, etc.).

5. Repeat the process for the right leg.

6. Now tense and relax progressively your groin, buttocks, abdomen, lower back, ribs, upper back, and shoulders.

7. Work your way down each arm, one at a time, until you reach the fingers.

8. Return to the neck, then the jaw, cheeks, nose, eyes, ears, forehead, and skull.

By now you should be completely relaxed. In fact, you may even be asleep—this technique works well as a sleep-induction strategy.

To vary the routine, play with it. Try going from top to bottom, or from your extremities in and ending with your groin. Or target any other part of your body to end up at, and take the most circuitous route you can think of.

To Try It online, go to **www.mhhe.com/power**.

 valuate: Asking If Your Strategies for Dealing with Stress Are Effective

Just as the experience of stress depends on how we interpret circumstances, the strategies for dealing with stress also vary in effectiveness depending on who we are. So if your efforts at coping aren't working, it's time to reconsider your approach. If talking to friends hasn't helped ease your stress response, maybe you need a different approach. Maybe you need to see the silver lining or cut back on some of your commitments.

If one coping strategy doesn't work for you, try another. What's critical is that you not become paralyzed, unable to deal with a situation. Instead, try something different until you find the right combination of strategies to improve the situation.

PREPARE
Ready yourself physically

ORGANIZE
Identify what is causing you stress

WORK
Develop effective coping strategies

EVALUATE
Ask yourself if your strategies for dealing with stress are effective

RETHINK
Place stress in perspective

P.O.W.E.R. Plan

R ethink: Placing Stress in Perspective

It's easy to think of stress as an enemy. In fact, the coping steps outlined in the P.O.W.E.R. Plan are geared to overcoming its negative consequences. But consider the following two principles, which in the end may help you more than any others in dealing with stress:

- **Don't sweat the small stuff . . . and it's all small stuff.** Stress expert Richard Carlson[4] emphasizes the importance of putting the circumstances we encounter into the proper perspective. He argues that we frequently let ourselves get upset about situations that are actually minor. So what if someone cuts us off in traffic, or does less than his or her share on a group project, or unfairly criticizes us? It's hardly the end of the world, and the behavior of the other people involved in such situations reflects negatively on them, not us. One of the best ways to reduce stress, consequently, is to maintain an appropriate perspective on the events of your life.

- **Make peace with stress.** Think of what it would be like to have no stress—none at all—in your life. Would you really be happier, better adjusted, and more successful? The answer is "probably not." A life that presented no challenges would probably be, in a word, boring. So think about stress as an exciting, although admittedly sometimes difficult, friend. Welcome it, because its presence indicates that your life is stimulating, challenging, and exciting—and who would want it any other way?

Keeping Well

Eat right. Exercise. Get plenty of sleep.

Pretty simple, isn't it? We learn the fundamentals of fitness and health in the first years of elementary school.

Yet for millions of us, wellness is an elusive goal. We eat on the fly, stopping for a bite at the drive-in window of a fast-food restaurant. Most of us don't exercise enough, either because we feel we don't have enough time or because it's not much fun for us. And as for sleep, we're a nation in which getting by with as little sleep as possible is seen as a badge of honor.

> "The first wealth is health."
>
> Ralph Waldo Emerson

You can buck the trends, however; you can begin to eat more properly, exercise effectively, and sleep better by following several basic rules. They include the following:

Eating Right

- **Eat a variety of "whole" foods, including fruits, vegetables, and grain products.** Strive to eat a range of different foods. If you make variety your goal, you will end up eating the right foods. Also, the less processed the foods are, the better. Make an effort to choose "whole" foods, or foods in a state as close as possible to their natural state: brown rice is better than white rice, and both are better than a preservative-filled, packaged "rice casserole" mix.

- **Avoid foods that are high in sugar and salt content.** Read labels on product packages carefully and beware of hidden sugars and salts. Many ingredients that end in *-ose* (such as dextrose, sucrose, maltose, and fructose) are actually sugars; salt can lurk within any number of compounds beginning with the word *sodium.*

- **Seek a diet low in fat and cholesterol.** The fat that is to be especially avoided is saturated fat— the most difficult for your body to rid itself of.

- **Remember: Less is more.** You don't need to walk away stuffed from every meal. Moderation is the key. To be sure you don't eat more than your body is telling you to eat, pay attention to internal hunger cues.

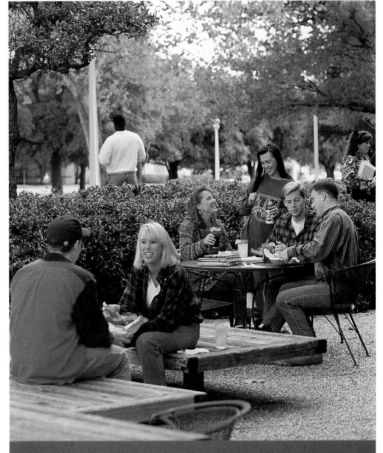

The lure of fast foods is difficult to resist, and eating a balanced, nutritious diet is a challenge for most college students.

- **Schedule three regular meals a day.** Eating should be a priority—a definite part of your daily schedule. Avoid skipping any meals. Breakfast is particularly important; get up early enough to eat a full meal.

- **Be sensitive to the hidden contents of various foods.** Soda and chocolate can contain substantial quantities of caffeine, which can disrupt your sleep and, along with coffee, become addictive. Many cereals—even those labeled "low fat"—contain a considerable amount of sugar or salt. Pay attention to labels.

- **Beware of eating disorders.** Between 1 and 4 percent of college-age women, and a smaller percentage of men, suffer from an eating disorder. Those with *anorexia nervosa* may refuse to eat, while denying that there is anything unusual in their behavior and appearance—which can become skeletal. Some 15 to 20 percent of those with anorexia literally starve themselves to

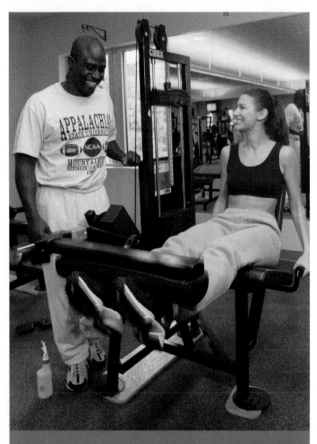

In order to maintain the habit of exercising, you need to choose an activity you enjoy doing. In addition, working out with others, as these students at Appalachian State University's fitness center are doing, turns exercise into a social activity and gives you social support, increasing the chances you'll stick with an exercise regimen.

death. *Bulimia* is a disorder in which individuals binge on incredibly large quantities of food, such as a gallon of ice cream and a whole pie, but later feel so much guilt and depression that they induce vomiting or take laxatives to rid themselves of the food. Eating disorders represent serious threats to health and require aggressive medical intervention.

Making Exercise a Part of Your Life

Exercise produces a variety of benefits. Your body will run more efficiently, you'll have more energy, your heart and circulatory system will run more smoothly, and you'll be able to bounce back from stress and illness more quickly.

- **Choose a type of exercise that you like.** Exercising will be a chore you end up avoiding if you don't enjoy what you're doing.

- **Incorporate exercise into your life.** Take the stairs instead of elevators. Leave your car at home and walk to campus or work. When you're on campus, take the longer way to reach your destination.

- **Make exercise a group activity.** Exercising with others brings you social support and turns exercise into a social activity. You'll be more likely to stick to a program if you have a regular "exercise date" with a friend.

- **Vary your routine.** You don't need to do the same kind of exercise day after day. Choose different sorts of activities that will involve different parts of your body and keep you from getting bored.

One note of caution: Before you begin an exercise program, it is a good idea to have a physical checkup, even if you feel you're in the peak of health. This is especially true if you're starting an exercise program after years of inactivity. You also might consult a trainer at the gym to set up a program that gradually builds you up to more vigorous exercise.

Getting a Good Night's Sleep

Do you feel as if you don't get enough sleep? You probably don't. Most college students are sleep-deprived, a condition that causes them to feel fatigued, short-tempered, and tense. Insufficient sleep also leads to declines in academic and physical performance. You can't do your best at anything if you're exhausted—or even tired.

Often the solution to the problem is simply to allow yourself more time to sleep. Most people need around 8 hours of sleep each night, although there are wide individual differences. In addition to sleeping more, there are also some relatively simple changes you can make in your behavior that will help you to sleep better. They include the following:

- **Exercise more.** Regular exercise will help you sleep more soundly at night, as well as help you cope with stress that might otherwise keep you awake.

- **Have a regular bedtime.** By going to bed at pretty much the same time each night, you give your body a regular rhythm and make sleep a habit.

- **Use your bed for sleeping and not as an all-purpose area.** Don't use your bed as a place to study, read, eat, or watch TV. Let your bed be a trigger for sleep.

- **Avoid caffeine after lunch.** The stimulant effects of caffeine (found in coffee, tea, and some soft drinks) may last as long as 8 to 12 hours after it's consumed.

- **Drink a glass of milk at bedtime.** Your mom was right: Drinking a glass of milk before you go to bed will help you get to sleep. The reason: Milk contains a natural chemical that makes you drowsy.

- **Avoid sleeping pills.** Steer clear of sleeping pills. Although they may be temporarily effective, in the long run they impair your ability to sleep because they disrupt your natural sleep cycles.

- **Don't try to force sleep on yourself.** Although this advice sounds odd, it turns out that one of the reasons that we have trouble sleeping is that we try too hard. Consequently, when you go to bed, just relax, and don't even attempt to go to sleep. If you're awake after 10 minutes or so, get up and do something else. Only go back to bed when you feel tired. Do this as often as necessary. If you follow this regimen for several weeks— and don't take naps or rest during the day—eventually getting into your bed will trigger sleep.

Drug Abuse

For better or worse, drugs are part of all of our lives. It's virtually impossible to be unaware of the extent of the U.S. and international problem of illegal drug use, which involves millions of individuals who have used illegal substances at least once. Patterns of drug use or avoidance are often established in college. These patterns can have a big impact on your college career and your life, so it is a good idea to learn what you can now, before negative patterns of abuse, and in some cases, addiction, take hold.

Alcohol and Its Allure

The drug most likely to be found on college campuses is alcohol. It may surprise you to know that though it initially seems to raise your spirits, alcohol is actually a depressant. As the amount of alcohol one consumes increases, its depressive effects become more obvious. You've probably seen its other negative effects: Drinkers show poor judgment, their memory is impaired, and

Journal Reflections

College Drinking Experiences

Examine your own feelings about alcohol use by answering these questions.

1. Why do you think people use alcohol?

2. What do you think the minimum age to legally drink alcohol should be, and why?

3. Do you know people who drink only to get drunk?

4. Have you ever suspected any of your friends or acquaintances of being alcoholics? Why?

5. Have you ever witnessed a scene in which drunkenness played a part in violence? Obnoxious behavior? Abuse of women?

Binge drinking
Having at least four (for females) or five (for males) drinks in a single sitting

Alcoholics
Individuals with serious alcohol-abuse problems who become dependent on alcohol and continue to drink despite serious consequences

their speech becomes slurred and eventually incoherent. If you drink enough, you'll pass out. And as some of the more dramatic cases in the news illustrate, if you consume enough alcohol in a short period, you can die. It's that simple.

The potential negative consequences of drinking have done little to prevent the use of alcohol on college campuses. More than 75 percent of college students say they've had a drink within the last 30 days, and the average person over the age of 14 drinks 2½ gallons of pure alcohol over the course of a year—some 200 drinks, on average, per person.

Some students drink even more, and the extent of alcohol consumption can reach astonishing levels. Half of all male college students and 40 percent of all female college students have engaged in **binge drinking,** defined as having at least four (for females) or five (for males) drinks in a single sitting. Such heavy drinking doesn't just affect the drinker. Most college students report having had their studying or sleep disturbed by drunk students. Further, around a third of students have been insulted or humiliated by a drunk student, and 25 percent of women have been the target of an unwanted sexual advance by a drunk classmate.

Close to 20 million people in the United States are alcoholics, and college students make up their fair share of the total. **Alcoholics,** individuals with serious alcohol-abuse problems, become dependent on alcohol, experiencing a physical craving for it. They continue to drink despite serious consequences. Furthermore, they develop a tolerance for alcohol and must drink increasing amounts to experience the initially positive effects that alcohol brings about.

The long-term consequences of high levels of alcohol consumption are severe. Heavy drinking damages the liver and digestive system, and can even affect brain cells. In fact, virtually every part of the body is eventually affected by heavy alcohol use.

To examine your own use of alcohol, complete Try It 4.

Nicotine

Despite the recent multi-billion-dollar tobacco settlements between all 50 state governments and the manufacturers of cigarettes, smoking remains a signifi-

Personal Styles: Consider Your Drinking Style

If you drink alcohol, do you have a style of use that is safe and responsible? Read the statements below and rate the extent to which you agree with them, using the following scale:

1 = Strongly disagree

2 = Disagree

3 = Neutral

4 = Agree

5 = Strongly agree

	1	2	3	4	5
1. I usually drink alcohol a few times a week.					
2. I sometimes go to class after I've been drinking alcohol.					
3. I frequently drink when I'm alone.					
4. I have driven while under the influence of alcohol.					
5. I've used a fake ID card to purchase alcohol.					
6. I'm a totally different person when I'm drinking alcohol.					
7. I often drink so much that I feel drunk.					
8. I wouldn't want to go to party where alcohol wasn't being served.					
9. I avoid people who don't like to drink alcohol.					
10. I sometimes urge others to drink more alcohol.					

The lower your score (i.e., the more 1s and 2s), the better able you are to control your alcohol consumption and the more likely it is that your alcohol use is responsible. The higher your score (i.e., the more 4s and 5s), the greater is your use and reliance on alcohol, and the more likely it is that your alcohol consumption may be reckless. If your score is over 40, you may have an alcohol problem and should seek professional help to control your alcohol usage.

To Try It online, go to **www.mhhe.com/power**.

cant health problem. Smoking causes lung damage and increases the risks of developing cancer, emphysema, and a host of other diseases.

Why do people smoke, when the evidence is so clear about its risks? They start to smoke for a variety of reasons. Smoking is sometimes viewed as a kind of initiation into adulthood, a sign of growing up. In other cases, teenagers see smoking as "cool," a view promoted by movies and television.

> "I set some limits for myself, and my transcript thanked me for it from then on."
>
> Betty Baugh Harrison, University of North Carolina[5]

The problem is that, no matter what reason persuades a person to try out a few cigarettes, smoking can quickly become a habit, because a major ingredient of tobacco—nicotine—is an addictive drug. An *addictive drug* produces a biological or psychological dependence. The absence of the drug leads to a craving for it that may be nearly irresistible.

Smoking is one of the hardest addictions to break. Among the suggestions for quitting are the following:

- **Remain smoke-free one day at a time.** Don't think about not smoking tomorrow, or next week, or for the rest of your life. Instead, think of not smoking for the rest of the day. You can worry about tomorrow . . . tomorrow.

- **Visualize the consequences of smoking.** Visualize blackened, rotting lungs filled with smoke. Then think about the fresh, pink lungs that you'll have after you've stopped smoking.

- **Exercise.** The all-purpose antidote, exercise, will make you feel better physically and take your mind off smoking.

- **Use nicotine patches or nicotine gum.** "The Patch" and nicotine gum can provide enough nicotine to satisfy your craving for the drug, while permitting you to stop smoking. Physicians can also sometimes prescribe drugs that help reduce the craving for nicotine.

- **Avoid people when they're smoking.** It's nearly impossible to avoid the urge to smoke when others are lighting up. If you're trying to quit, stay away from people who are smoking.

- **Enlist the social support of family and friends.** Tell others that you're trying to quit, and accept their encouragement and praise.

- **Reward yourself.** Every few days, give yourself some kind of reinforcement for spending a period of time smoke-free. Go to a movie; buy a CD. Think about how you can afford these more easily since you aren't buying cigarettes anymore.

- **Join a quit-smoking program.** Many college health services hold periodic programs to help students who want to stop smoking. By enrolling in one, you'll receive the support of others who are in the same boat as you are.

- **Keep trying.** If after quitting you start smoking again, just consider that lapse as part of the process of quitting. Many people quit several times before they manage to quit for good.

Illegal Drugs

"Just say 'no.'"

If it were only so easy. Decisions about drugs are quite a bit more complicated than simplistic antidrug slogans would have you believe. Using or not using drugs involves, at a minimum, peer pressure, your values, and the effects they have on your body, your behavior, and your self-image.

Several things are clear, however. Despite the prevalence of illicit drug use among college students—surveys show that around a third of college students report having used an illegal drug at least once in the previous year—the benefits of drug use are difficult to enumerate. Apart from a temporary high, the advantages of using drugs are nil, and the use of illegal drugs is among the riskiest activities in which people can engage. Not only does drug use make you vulnerable to arrest, but it also poses short- and long-term health risks. The escape from one's responsibilities that drugs provide is likely to make it even harder to later deal with those responsibilities—which aren't going to go away.

Not all illegal drugs are the same, and they produce widely varying effects and consequences (see Table 14.2). But they all share a common result: a reduction in awareness of and engagement with what is happening around you.

People often fall into drug use without much thought. But doing so is still a choice. Preaching and slogans are not going to help you to make a sensible

Table 14.2
Illegal Drugs

Drug	Street Name	Effects	Withdrawal Symptoms
Stimulants			
Cocaine	Coke, blow, snow, lady, crack	Increased confidence, mood elevation, sense of energy and alertness, decreased appetite, anxiety, irritability, insomnia, transient drowsiness, delayed orgasm	Apathy, general fatigue, prolonged sleep, depression, disorientation, suicidal thoughts, agitated motor activity, irritability, bizarre dreams
Amphetamines			
Benzedrine	Speed		
Dexedrine	Speed		
Depressants			
Alcohol	Booze	Anxiety reduction, impulsiveness, dramatic mood swings, bizarre thoughts, suicidal behavior, slurred speech, disorientation, slowed mental and physical functioning, limited attention span	Weakness, restlessness, nausea and vomiting, headaches, nightmares, irritability, depression, acute anxiety, hallucinations, seizures, possible death
Barbiturates			
Nembutal	Yellowjackets, yellows		
Seconal	Reds		
Phenobarbital			
Rohypnol	Roofies, rope, "date-rape drug"	Muscle relaxation, amnesia, sleep	Seizures
Narcotics			
Heroin	H, hombre, junk, smack, dope, crap, horse	Anxiety and pain reduction, apathy, difficulty in concentration, slowed speech, decreased physical activity, drooling, itching, euphoria, nausea	Anxiety, vomiting, sneezing, diarrhea, lower back pain, watery eyes, runny nose, yawning, irritability, tremors, panic, chills and sweating, cramps
Morphine	Drugstore dope, cube, first line, mud		
Hallucinogens			
Cannabis			
Marijuana	Bhang, kif, ganja, dope, grass, pot, smoke, hemp, joint, weed, bone, Mary Jane, herb, tea	Euphoria, relaxed inhibitions, increased appetite, disoriented behavior	Hyperactivity, insomnia, decreased appetite, anxiety
Hashish			
Hash oil			
MDMA	Ecstasy	Heightened sense of oneself and insight, feelings of peace, empathy, energy	Not reported
LSD	Acid, quasey, microdot, white lightning	Heightened aesthetic responses; vision and depth distortion; heightened sensitivity to faces and gestures; magnified feelings; paranoia; panic; euphoria	Not reported

decision. You need to employ every critical thinking skill you can to determine exactly what you wish—and don't wish—to introduce into your body. Give some thought to why escape is attractive and consider seeking counseling instead. Allow yourself to consider the long- and short-term effects of drug use—both the physical effects as well as the potential effects on your own aspirations and dreams. Think about the legal consequences of drug use: A drug conviction can lead to expulsion from college and refusal by many employers to hire you. Furthermore, random drug tests are increasingly a part of corporate life, and your ability to keep a job may be placed at risk if you use drugs—even only occasionally.

Drugs that produce addiction, such as cocaine and heroin, present a further set of problems. The lives of people with drug addictions become centered on the drug. They enter into a pattern of alternating highs—when on the drug—and lows. During their lows, much of their thinking is centered on obtaining the drug and looking forward to their next high.

Addiction's Warning Signs Addictions to drugs—including alcohol—can begin subtly, and you may not be aware of the extent of the problem. Here are some signs that indicate when use becomes abuse:

- Feeling you need to be high to have a good time.
- Being high more often than not.
- Getting high to "get yourself going."
- Going to class or work high.
- Missing class or work because you are high.
- Being unprepared for class because you were high.
- Feeling regret over something you did while you were high.
- Driving while high.
- Having a legal problem due to being high.
- Behaving, while high, in a way you wouldn't otherwise.
- Being high in nonsocial, solitary situations.
- Thinking about drugs or alcohol much of the time.
- Avoiding family or friends while using liquor or drugs.
- Hiding drug or alcohol use from others.

Any one of these symptoms indicates that you have a drug or alcohol problem. If you do have a problem, seek professional help. Addictions to illegal drugs or alcohol are extremely difficult to deal with on your own. No matter how good your intentions, almost no one can overcome the cravings brought about by an addiction to a particular substance without help.

Here are some places to which you can turn:

1. **College health services, counseling centers, and mental health centers.** Most colleges provide services to help you overcome an addiction. They can evaluate the extent of the problem and refer you to the proper place for further help. (To learn about your own campus resources, complete Try It 5.)

ry It!

5

Tap Campus Resources

Complete the following chart to identify the campus office locations and their services that deal with alcohol and drug problems.

Campus Resource	Where Is It?	What Service Does It Provide?	How Do You Get in Touch?
Health Center			
Mental Health Center			
Campus Chaplain			
Drug and Alcohol Education Center(s)			
Counseling Center			
Residential Life Office			
Ombudsman			
Campus Security Services			
(add other offices here)			
(add other offices here)			
(add other offices here)			
(add other offices here)			

To try it online, go to **www.mhhe.com/power**.

2. **Drug treatment centers and clinics.** Sometimes located in hospitals and sometimes independently run, drug treatment centers or clinics can provide help. You can also check your telephone book for a local listing of Alcoholics Anonymous or Narcotics Anonymous.

3. **Government hotlines.** The federal government provides extensive information about drug and alcohol use. For starters, call The National Clearinghouse on Alcohol and Drug Information at 1-800-729-6686. For alcohol difficulties in particular, call the National Council on Alcoholism at (800) 622-2255. For drug problems, you can call the National Institute on Drug Abuse at (800) 662-4357. Finally, you can write to the National Council on Alcoholism and Drug Dependence, 12 West 21 Street, New York, NY 10010, for help with alcohol and drug problems.

Sexual Health and Decision Making

Relationships. Contraception. AIDS. Rape.

Sexual health includes a host of issues, involving not just your body but your heart and mind as well. In fact, it is often said that our most important sexual organ is our brain. It determines what we view as sexually arousing, and it's what we use to make decisions and choices about our sexuality.

Although the focus of the brief discussion of sexual health here is on strategies for protecting yourself (from pregnancy, sexually transmitted diseases, and rape), sexual decisions are also a reflection of your basic values. You can't make responsible decisions about sex without knowing what is important to you and how you view yourself. So you don't want to wait until a sexual encounter begins before thinking through your views of sexuality and what is and is not right for you.

Preventing Unwanted Pregnancy

Abstinence

The avoidance of sexual contact

There is one and only one totally effective means of preventing pregnancy: Not having sexual intercourse. **Abstinence**, refraining from intercourse, only works, however, if you practice it with absolute consistency—something that many people find difficult. But it certainly is possible. Despite the folklore that insists "everybody's doing it," they're not. In fact, if you think critically about what others say about their sexual activity, you'll probably conclude that what they say is more boasting (and outright lying) than straight talk.

Those who do want to have a sexual relationship can still avoid pregnancy. Methods of contraception include the following:

- **Birth control pills.** Composed of artificial hormones, birth control pills are among the most effective ways of preventing pregnancy—as long as they are taken as prescribed. Except for women with particular medical conditions, the side effects are minimal.

- **Implants.** One of the newest forms of birth control, implants work through a simple surgical procedure in which a small capsule is inserted into a woman's arm. Implants last for 5 years, preventing pregnancy for the entire period. With few side effects, implants are highly effective, but they are only practical for women who wish to avoid pregnancy for extended periods.

- **Intrauterine device, or IUD.** IUDs are small pieces of plastic inserted by a medical practitioner into a woman's uterus. Although highly effective, some have been found to produce unacceptable side effects, including infections and scarring that can make it impossible for a woman to get pregnant when she wants to.

- **Diaphragms and cervical caps.** Diaphragms and cervical caps are circular, dome-shaped pieces of thin rubber that a woman inserts into her vagina to cover the cervix. A sperm-killing cream or jelly must be used simultaneously, and the diaphragm or cervical cap must be removed after sexual intercourse. Although side effects are few, the risk of pregnancy is somewhat higher than with the other forms of birth control we've discussed; some 18 percent of women using them become pregnant.

- **Condoms.** Condoms are thin sheaths that fit over the penis. By preventing sperm from entering the vagina, they are highly effective in preventing pregnancy when used properly and consistently. When used with a contraceptive jelly that kills sperm and positioned properly, condoms are highly effective.

- **Contraceptive sponge.** The sponge, shaped like a large mushroom cap, is inserted into the vagina. It can be left in place for 24 hours, during which time it can be used for multiple acts of intercourse. Although it has few side effects, it has a failure rate of between 17 and 25 percent.

- **Periodic abstinence.** The only form of birth control that involves no chemical or mechanical intervention, periodic abstinence consists of refraining from intercourse during times in a woman's menstrual cycle when pregnancy is possible. With a failure rate of 20 percent, periodic abstinence requires close scrutiny of calendars, body temperature, and cervical mucus—all of which can be indicators of the time of the month to avoid intercourse.

- **Sterilization.** Sterilization is a surgical procedure that causes a person (either a man or a woman) to become permanently incapable of having children.

- **Emergency contraception.** Several forms of birth control can prevent pregnancy after unprotected intercourse. These involve using increased doses of certain oral contraceptive pills within 72 hours or insertion of a copper intrauterine device (IUD) within 5 to 7 days following unprotected sex.

- **Withdrawal and douching (*ineffective* birth control).** Withdrawal, in which a man removes his penis from a woman's vagina before ejaculating, and douching, flushing the vagina with a liquid *after* the man has ejaculated, just don't work. *They should not be used for birth control* because they are so ineffective.

Relationships and sexuality raise substantial issues, involving your attitudes, beliefs, values, and emotions, as well as your body, in a complex intermix. Making responsible decisions requires that you know who you are and what's important to you.

What You Can Do to Avoid Sexually Transmitted Diseases

Right now, one out of five people in the United States is infected with one of the many types of **sexually transmitted diseases (STDs)**—medical conditions acquired through sexual contact. At least one out of four will eventually contract an STD at some point in life.

There are many varieties of STDs, although all share a similar origin: sexual contact. Depending on the type of disease, symptoms may include warts in the genital area, pelvic infection, painful urination, infertility, blindness, and even death.

The STD that has had the greatest impact in the last decade is **acquired immune deficiency syndrome (AIDS).** Although in the U.S. it initially most often affected homosexuals, AIDS quickly spread among heterosexuals. Some populations are particularly affected, such as intravenous drug users.

Sexually transmitted diseases (STDs)
Medical conditions acquired through sexual contact

Acquired immune deficiency syndrome (AIDS)
A lethal, sexually transmitted disease that causes the destruction of the body's immune system

Worldwide, more than 16 million people have already died from the disease. Some estimates suggest that 40 million people now carry the AIDS virus. Despite new treatments, AIDS remains incurable. In the U.S., AIDS is the leading cause of death among men 25 to 44 years of age and the third leading cause of death among women in that age range.

Although AIDS is the best-known STD, the most common is *chlamydia*, a disease that if left untreated can cause sterility in some sufferers. *Genital herpes* is a virus that appears as small blisters or sores around the genitals. Although the sores heal after several weeks, the disease can remain dormant and reappear periodically. Other STDs, although somewhat less common, afflict millions of people. (See Table 14.3 for a summary of the common STDs.)

The only completely effective way to avoid sexual transmission of these diseases is through abstinence. However, many people are unwilling to make such a choice. Several alternative approaches, called "smart sex" or "safe sex" practices, reduce the risk of contracting STDs. They include the following:

- **Know your sexual partner—well.** You should not have sexual contact with a person who is only a casual acquaintance. You want to know the person well enough to have a discussion with him or her in which you both talk about your sexual histories.

- **Prevent the exchange of bodily fluids during all sex acts.** Avoid unprotected intercourse (vaginal or anal) and oral sex.

- **Use condoms.** Condoms not only prevent the spread of AIDS and other STDs, but they also prevent pregnancy.

- **Be faithful to a single partner.** People in long-term relationships with only one other individual are less likely to contract AIDS and other STDs than those with multiple sexual partners.

Date Rape

We usually think of rape as a rare crime, committed by strangers. Unfortunately, rape is surprisingly common and rapists usually know their victims. In a national survey conducted on college campuses, one out of eight women reported having been raped. In about half the reported cases, the rapists were first dates, casual dates, or romantic acquaintances—situations categorized as **date rape.** Overall, women are far more likely to be raped by someone they know than by a stranger. There is a 14 to 25 percent chance that a woman will be the victim of rape during her lifetime. Although date rape is the more common type on campus, it is only different from any other form of rape in that the victim is acquainted with the rapist.

What leads to rape? Most often, rape has less to do with sex than with power and anger. Rapists use forced sex to demonstrate their power and control over the victim. The rapist's pleasure comes not so much from sex as from forcing someone to submit. Sometimes sexual behavior is a demonstration of the rapist's rage at women in general.

In addition, rapes sometimes are brought about by the common—but untrue—belief that when women offer resistance to sex, they don't really mean it. If a man holds the view that when a woman says no to sex, she really means yes, he is likely to ignore the woman's protests, and the encounter may end in rape. Some men may even believe that it is unmasculine to accept no for an answer.

Date rape

Forced sex in which the rapist is a date or romantic acquaintance

Table 14.3
Common Sexually Transmitted Diseases (STDs)

	Cause	Transmission	Symptoms

AIDS—HIV	Human immuno-deficiency virus (HIV)	Coming in direct contact with infected blood, semen, or vaginal secretions.
		
		Anal or vaginal intercourse, being born to an infected female, receiving infected blood or blood products, or sharing needles and syringes with someone infected with the HIV virus.
			In early stages of infection with HIV there typically are no symptoms. As the disease progresses the following are usual symptoms:
			  Chronic or swollen glands.
			  Weight loss of more than 10 pounds.
			  Flu-like symptoms that persist.
			  Purple spots on the skin and inside the mouth, nose, or rectum.
			  Unusual susceptibility to parasitic, fungal, bacterial, and viral infections or certain cancers.

Chlamydia	Bacteria	Vaginal or anal intercourse or oral sex with someone who is infected.	Many infected people have no symptoms, but when present the most common are the following:
			  Pain, burning or "itching" sensations with urination.
			  Vaginal infections may be associated with abnormal discharge.
			  Oral infections may be exhibited by a sore throat but usually have no symptoms.
			  Penile infections may be associated with a yellowish discharge.

Gonorrhea	Bacteria	Vaginal or anal intercourse or oral sex with someone who is infected.	Many infected people have no symptoms but are still contagious. Most common symptoms are the following:
			  Pain, burning or "itching" sensations with urination.
			  Vaginal infections may be associated with abnormal discharge.
			  Oral infections may be exhibited by a sore throat but usually have no symptoms.
			  Penile infections may be associated with a yellowish discharge.

Hepatitis A	Virus	Spread through contaminated feces and anal–oral contact during sexual activity.	Symptoms for hepatitis A and B will be similar: nausea, vomiting, diarrhea, fatigue, lack of appetite, dark urine, light stools, and/or abdominal tenderness.
Hepatitis B	Virus	Spread via blood by sexual contact or via an injection with a contaminated needle.	Symptoms for hepatitis A and B will be similar: nausea, vomiting, diarrhea, fatigue, lack of appetite, dark urine, light stools, and/or abdominal tenderness.
Genital Herpes	Herpes simplex virus (HSV)	Contact with virus in infected blisters or within virus being shed from the site of previous infections that may have no symptoms.	Cluster of tender, painful blisters, ulcers, or sores typically on or around the lips, mouth, genitals, or anus. Symptoms may be very mild or not present at all, but people are still infected and contagious. Blisters, ulcers, and sores last one to three weeks during initial outbreaks. Lesions heal, but person still has herpes. Lesions commonly recur without being re-exposed to the disease.
Genital Warts	Human papilloma virus (HPV)	Vaginal or anal intercourse or oral sex with someone who has the virus.	Small bumpy "cauliflower" looking warts that are usually painless and appear on or around the genitals or anus. Itching and burning around the lesions may occur, but such symptoms are rare. Infections without symptoms are common.

Speaking of Success

Name: *Justin McCarthy*
Education: *Washington College, Chestertown, Maryland; senior majoring in political science*
Home: *Ardmore, Pennsylvania*

Justin McCarthy was an all-around athlete in high school—he wrestled and played football, soccer, and lacrosse. He was a good student, too. But things changed when he became a freshman at Washington College.

"Sports always played a huge role in my life," McCarthy says. "In high school I could play sports and do my work, but in college I found both to be much more demanding. I had almost convinced myself that studying and sports were no different in college, but soon I was struggling at both."

McCarthy attributes his problems to his living situation in college. He shared a residence with an all-male, all-athlete group, and it proved to be the wrong setting for him.

"We all just hung out and procrastinated. Wasting time was our biggest problem," he says. "We were all so happy to be in college, but we didn't understand that to stay there we had to commit ourselves and discipline ourselves to the work."

At the end of his freshman year McCarthy had a dismal 1.75 grade point average, and it became clear that something had to give.

"My mother would tell me that if I put half the effort into my studies

that I put into sports, I would be fine," McCarthy recalls. "I heard her, but I never listened. But that summer I realized I had to make some changes and reevaluate my priorities."

McCarthy made two major changes when he returned to campus as a sophomore. First, he changed his living situation, and second, he got organized.

"I went from living with all these guys who weren't sure what they wanted to do, to a more controlled environment. I moved in with some of my best friends who were organized and motivated," he says. "I started to take notes, to highlight reading assignments. I noted when tests and papers were due, established a rapport with my teachers, and, instead of sitting in the back of the class, I started to sit up front.

"I've completely evolved into this person who is constantly organized and dedicated to his goals. Now I'm willing to sacrifice and study that extra hour. I didn't know what success was like before."

At the end of his sophomore year McCarthy's grade point average jumped to 3.1.

"My whole outlook and perspective have come full circle since my freshman year," he notes. "I know if I try a little harder I can attain the goals that I set for myself."

Some rapists employ the illegal drug rohypnol, which has come to be known as the "date rape drug." When it is mixed with alcohol, it can prevent victims from resisting sexual assault. Sometimes people who are unknowingly given the drug don't even remember the rape.

Whatever the causes, rape is devastating to the victim. Victims experience extreme anxiety, disbelief, fear, and shock. These reactions may linger for years, and rape victims may experience a long-lasting fear of entering into relationships.

Both men and women must be sensitive to the issue of date rape. Among the suggestions for reducing its incidence are the following:

- **Set limits.** Women have the right to set firm limits, and these should be communicated clearly, firmly, and early on.

- **No means no.** When a partner says no, it means no—nothing else.

- **Be assertive.** You should never passively accept being pressured into an activity in which you don't want to engage. Remember that passivity may be interpreted as consent.

- **Communicate.** Women and men should talk about their views of sexual behavior and what is and is not permissible.

- **Keep in mind that alcohol and drugs cloud judgment.** Nothing hinders communication more than alcohol and drugs.

Looking Back

What is stress and how can I control it?

- Stress is a common experience, appearing in three main forms: cataclysmic events, personal stressors, and daily hassles. Excessive stress is not only unpleasant and upsetting, but it also has negative effects on the body and mind.

- Coping with stress involves becoming prepared for future stress through proper diet and exercise, identifying the causes of stress in one's life, taking control of stress, seeking social support, practicing relaxation techniques, training oneself to redefine and reinterpret stressful situations, and keeping one's promises.

What is involved in keeping fit and healthy, and why is it important for me to do so?

- For all people, keeping fit and healthy is both essential and challenging. It is vital to learn to eat properly, especially by eating a variety of foods on a regular schedule and by restricting your intake of fat, cholesterol, and salt.

- Exercise is valuable because it improves health and well-being. Choosing exercises that we like, making everyday activities a part of exercise, and exercising with others can help form the habit of exercise.

- The third key element of good health is sleeping properly. Good exercise and eating habits can contribute to sound sleep, as can the development of regular sleeping habits and the use of sleep-assisting practices.

What are the main threats to my health and well-being?

- One of the major threats that college students (and others) face is the improper use of drugs. The most commonly abused drug is alcohol, which is a depressant (despite an initial reduction of inhibitions and feeling of euphoria) and can lead to a physical or psychological dependence. Nicotine is the second most commonly abused drug.

- The use of illegal drugs presents not only potential dangers related to law-breaking and prosecution, but short- and long-term health risks as well. Drugs cause a reduction in awareness and involvement in life, and some drugs can be dangerously addictive.

What are the components of sexual health?

- Sexual health is as important as other forms of health. People must make their own individual decisions about their sexuality and how they will express it.

- Many forms of contraception are available, ranging from abstinence to surgical implants. Each form has different procedures, risks, and effectiveness.

- The incidence of sexually transmitted diseases (STDs) is high in the United States, with about 25 percent of the population experiencing an STD at some point in life.

- Rape is a surprisingly common crime, with most victims knowing the rapist—often in a circumstance known as date rape.

Key Terms and Concepts

Abstinence (p. 384)
Acquired immune deficiency
  syndrome (AIDS) (p. 385)
Alcoholics (p. 378)
Binge drinking (p. 378)
Cataclysmic events (p. 365)
Coping (p. 366)

Daily hassles (p. 365)
Date rape (p. 386)
Personal stressors (p. 365)
Sexually transmitted diseases
  (STDs) (p. 385)
Social support (p. 370)
Stress (p. 365)

Resources

On Campus

Your college health service/medical provider is the first line of defense if you become ill. The staff can provide you with advice and often medical care and can give help if you are the victim of rape or in other emergencies. Furthermore, colleges often have health education offices that help educate students on safer sex practices, on how to eat in healthier ways, and generally on how to increase wellness. Finally, colleges sometimes offer stress reduction workshops to help students cope more effectively.

In Print

The title says it all: *The Everything Stress Management Book: Practical Ways to Relax, Be Healthy, and Maintain Your Sanity* (Adams Media, 2002), by Eve Adamson, offers a guide to both the reasons we experience stress and ways of coping with it. *The New York Times Book of Health: How to Feel Fitter, Eat Better, and Live Longer* (Times Books, 1998), by Jane Brody, provides an up-to-date, commonsense guide to living well. Deborah Schoeberlein's *EveryBody: Preventing HIV and Other Sexually Transmitted Diseases, Revised Edition* (RAD, 2001) offers clearheaded and accurate advice on decisions relating to sexual behavior.

On the Web

The following sites on the World Wide Web provide the opportunity to extend your learning about stress, health, and wellness. (Although the Web addresses were accurate at the time the book was printed, check the P.O.W.E.R. Learning website [www.mhhe.com/power] for any changes that may have occurred.)

- "Guidelines for a Healthy Diet" (**www.amwa-doc.org/publications/ WCHealthbook/dietamwa-ch03.html**), from the American Medical Women's Association website, offers suggestions on healthy eating and dieting. Sections include choosing and preparing foods, the health risks of obesity, and dietary myths.

- "Stress Management" (**stress.about.com/cs/copingskills/**), on About.com, offers in-depth and comprehensive information on coping with stress. Dozens of links cover teens through the elderly, self-assessment, psychotherapy and relaxation techniques.

- "Eating Disorders: Mirror, Mirror" (**www.mirror-mirror.org/eatdis.htm**) is a guide to eating disorders offering definitions, coping strategies, links to related organizations, and personal messages from survivors.

- "Healthy Women" (**www.healthywomen.org/content.cfm?L1=3**), from the National Women's Health Resource Center, offers a number of good articles on health issues, including a concise presentation and discussion of various methods of contraception.

- The Massachusetts Department of Public Health (**www.state.ma.us/ dph/cdc/bcdc.htm**) offers information on the prevention and control of sexually transmitted diseases, including links to fact sheets and publications containing further information. Also discussed are tuberculosis and the West Nile virus.

Taking It to the Net

1 Find two stress reduction techniques. One possible strategy: Go to AltaVista (**www.altavista.com**) and enter the phrase "stress reduction techniques" into the search field. Examine the sites located until you find two stress reduction techniques. Try each of the techniques. Do you feel less stressed and more relaxed? Which of the techniques works best for you?

2 Locate the most-recent statistics on drug use by U.S. students. One possible approach: Go to Yahoo! (**www.yahoo.com**) and enter the phrase "drug statistics government." Examine the results and consider how they compare to your own perceptions of the extent of drug use.

The Case of . . .

The Opposing Perspectives

It started out innocently, as a date to study for an exam. And then it turned wrong. Here's what Bob had to say:

Patty and I were in the same statistics class. She usually sat near me and was always very friendly. I liked her and thought maybe she liked me, too.

Last Thursday after class I suggested that she come to my place so we could study for midterms together. She agreed immediately.

That night everything seemed to go perfectly. We studied for a while and then took a break. I could tell that she liked me, and I was attracted to her. I started kissing her. I could tell that she really liked it.

We started touching each other and it felt really good. All of a sudden she pulled away and said "stop." I figured she didn't want me to think that she was "easy" or "loose". . . .

I just ignored her protests and eventually she stopped struggling. I think she liked it but afterwards she acted bummed out and cold.

Patty, on the other hand, had a very different view of their encounter:

I knew Bob from my statistics class. He's cute and we are both good at statistics, so when a tough midterm was scheduled, I was glad that he suggested we study together. It never occurred to me that it was anything except a study date.

That night everything went fine at first. We got a lot of studying done in a short amount of time, so when he suggested we take a break, I thought we deserved it.

Well, all of a sudden he started acting really romantic and started kissing me. I liked the kissing, but then he started touching me below the waist. I pulled away and tried to stop him but he didn't listen. After a while I stopped struggling; he was hurting me and I was scared. He was so much bigger and stronger than me. I couldn't believe it was happening to me. I didn't know what to do.

He actually forced me to have sex with him. I guess looking back on it I should have screamed or done something besides trying to reason with him, but it was so unexpected. I couldn't believe it was happening.[6]

1. Was Bob being dishonest in setting up the study date? Was he dishonest during the sexual encounter?

2. What could Patty have done when Bob began acting "romantic"?

3. Was Bob right to interpret Patty's initial responsiveness to his advances as acceptance of a sexual relationship? Was Patty "leading him on"?

4. Did Patty's initial responsiveness justify Bob's pursuing sex beyond the point at which she said "stop"?

A Final Word

Throughout this book you've seen how the principles of P.O.W.E.R. Learning can be applied to a variety of situations, ranging from reading and writing to coping with stress. You can use the framework in any situation where you need to organize your thinking and behavior in a systematic way. It's a tool you can call on throughout life.

College is the beginning of a journey through adulthood. This book has been designed to help you with the immediate demands and challenges of college, but at the same time to prepare you for life after school. It has tried to show you that it is *you* who must make things happen to fulfill your goals and aspirations.

Ultimately, however, there are some key ingredients to success that no book can teach you and that only you can provide: integrity and honesty, intellectual curiosity, and love. I hope this book will help you as you consider what your contribution to the world will be and as you work to make that contribution.

Glossary

ABBCC structure: The structure of the typical research paper, consisting of *a*rgument, *b*ackground, *b*ody, *c*ounterarguments, and *c*onclusion.

Abstinence: The avoidance of sexual contact.

Abstract: A short summary of the contents of a journal article.

Academic honesty: Completing and turning in only one's own work under one's own name.

Acquired immune deficiency syndrome (AIDS): A lethal, sexually transmitted disease that causes the destruction of the body's immune system.

Acronym: A word or phrase formed by the first letters of a series of terms.

Acrostic: A sentence in which the first letters of the words correspond to material that is to be remembered.

Active listening: The voluntary act of focusing on what is being said, making sense of it, and thinking about it in a way that permits it to be recalled accurately.

Advance organizers: Broad, general ideas related to material that is to be read or heard, which pave the way for subsequent learning.

Alcoholics: Individuals with serious alcohol-abuse problems who become dependent on alcohol and continue to drink despite serious consequences.

Analogy: A comparison between concepts or objects that are alike in some respects, but dissimilar in most others.

Analytic learning style: A style that starts with small pieces of information and uses them to build the big picture.

Attention span: The length of time that attention is typically sustained.

Auditory/verbal learning style: A style that favors listening as the best approach to learning.

Binge drinking: Having at least four (for females) or five (for males) drinks in a single sitting.

Brainstorming: A technique for generating ideas by saying out loud as many ideas as can be thought of in a fixed period of time.

Browser: A program that provides a way of navigating around the information on the World Wide Web.

Budget: A formal plan that accounts for expenditures and income.

Call number: A unique classification number assigned to every book (or other resource) in a library. Call numbers are used for ease of location.

Cataclysmic events: Sudden, powerful events that occur quickly and affect many people simultaneously.

Civic engagement: Broadly, making contributions to the society and community in which you live.

Civility: Respectful, courteous behavior.

College advisor: An individual who provides students with advice about their academic careers.

Concept mapping: A method of structuring written material by graphically grouping and connecting key ideas and themes.

Coping: The effort to control, reduce, or learn to tolerate the threats that lead to stress.

Cramming: Hurried, last-minute studying.

Critical thinking: A process involving reanalysis, questioning, and challenge of underlying assumptions.

Cultural competence: Knowledge and understanding about other races, ethnic groups, cultures, and minority groups.

Culture: The learned behaviors, beliefs, and attitudes that are characteristic of an individual society or population, and the products that people create.

Daily hassles: The minor irritants of life that, by themselves, produce little stress, but which can add up and produce more stress than a single larger-scale event.

Daily to-do list: A schedule showing the tasks, activities, and appointments due to occur during that day.

Date rape: Forced sex in which the rapist is a date or romantic acquaintance.

Decision making: The process of deciding among various alternatives.

Distance learning: The teaching of courses at another institution, with student participation via video technology or the World Wide Web.

Double-major: A course of study that fulfills all the requirements for two majors.

E-mail: Electronic mail, a system of communication that permits users to send and receive messages via the Internet.

Educated guessing: The practice of eliminating obviously false multiple-choice answers and selecting the most likely answer from the remaining choices.

Electives: Courses that are not required.

Emoticons (or smileys): Abbreviations used in e-mail messages that provide information on the emotion that the writer is trying to convey. Emoticons usually look like faces on their side, with facial expressions related to the intended emotion or tone.

Ethnicity: Shared national origins or cultural patterns.

Evaluation: An assessment of the match between a product or activity and the goals it was intended to meet.

Exam: The most substantial kind of assessment. In many classes, just one exam is given—a *final exam* at the end of the term.

Extemporaneous talk: An unprepared, off-the-cuff oral presentation.

Flash cards: Note cards that contain key pieces of information to be remembered.

Freewriting: A technique involving continuous, nonstop writing, without self-criticism, for a fixed period of time.

Frontmatter: The preface, introduction, and table of contents of a book.

Grade point average (GPA: also known as *quality point average*): A numeric average in which letter grades are transformed into numbers.

Grant: An award of money that does not have to be repaid.

Hardware: The physical part of a computer—the metal, glass, plastic, and other substances—that can be touched and seen, such as the display, keyboard, and mouse.

Hearing: The involuntary act of sensing sounds.

"I" statements: Statements that cast responses in terms of oneself and one's individual interpretation.

Interlibrary loan: A system by which libraries share resources, making them available to patrons of different libraries.

Internet: A vast network of interconnected computers that share information around the world.

Learning disabilities: Difficulties in processing information when listening, speaking, reading, or writing, characterized by a discrepancy between learning potential and actual academic achievement.

Learning style: One's preferred manner of acquiring, using, and thinking about knowledge.

Left-brain processing: Information processing primarily performed by the left hemisphere of the brain, focusing on tasks requiring verbal competence, such as speaking, reading, thinking, and reasoning; information is processed sequentially, one bit at a time.

Link: A means of "jumping" automatically from one Web page to another.

Listserv: A subscription service through which members can post and receive messages via e-mail on general topics of shared interest.

Loan: Funds provided by a bank, credit union, or other agency that must be repaid after a specified period of time.

Loneliness: A subjective state in which people do not experience the level of connection with others that they desire.

Long-term goals: Aims relating to major accomplishments that take some time to achieve.

Major: A specialization in a particular subject area, requiring a set course of study.

Master calendar: A schedule showing the weeks of a longer time period, such as a college term, with all assignments and important activities noted on it.

Memory consolidation: The process by which the physical links between brain cells that represent memory become fixed and stable over time.

Meta-message: The underlying main ideas that a speaker is seeking to convey; the meaning behind the overt message.

Method of loci: A memory technique by which the elements in a list are visualized as occupying the parts of a familiar place.

Microform: A means of storing greatly reduced photographs of printed pages, which can be read by using special microform readers; the two main types of microform are microfiche and microfilm.

Minor: A secondary specialization in a discipline different from one's major.

Mnemonics: Formal techniques used to make material more readily remembered.

Motivation: The inner power and psychological energy that directs and fuels behavior.

Newsgroup: An electronic Internet area in which users may post and read messages relevant to a particular topic of the group's choosing.

Overlearning: Studying and rehearsing material past the point of initial mastery to the point at which recall becomes automatic.

P.O.W.E.R. Learning: A system designed to help people achieve their goals, based on five steps: *P*repare, *O*rganize, *W*ork, *E*valuate, and *R*ethink.

Paraphrase: A restatement of a passage using different words.

Peg method: A memory technique by which a series of memorized words is linked by images to a list of items to be remembered.

Personal stressors: Major life events that produce stress.

Plagiarism: Taking credit for someone else's words, thoughts, or ideas.

Prejudice: Evaluations or judgments of members of a group that are based primarily on membership in the group and not on the particular characteristics of individuals.

Prerequisites: Requirements that must be fulfilled before a student may enroll in a course or discipline.

Presentation programs: Computer application software that helps you create impressive, professional-looking visual materials that include words, charts, maps, and other graphical elements.

Principal: The stated amount of a loan.

Priorities: The tasks and activities that one needs and wants to do, rank-ordered from most important to least important.

Problem solving: The process of generating alternatives to work on.

Procrastination: The habit of putting off and delaying tasks that are to be accomplished.

Quiz: A brief assessment, usually covering a relatively small amount of material.

Race: Traditionally, biologically determined physical characteristics that set one group apart from others.

Recall: A way to request library materials from another user who has them.

Receptive learning style: The way in which we initially receive information.

Reflective feedback: A technique of verbal listening in which a listener rephrases what a speaker has said, trying to echo the speaker's meaning.

Register: To enroll formally in courses.

Registrar: The college official designated to oversee the scheduling of courses, the maintenance of grades and transcripts, and the creation and retention of other official documents.

Rehearsal: The process of practicing and learning material to transfer it into memory.

Relational learning style: A style that starts with the big picture and breaks it down into its individual components.

Retrieval: The process of finding information stored in memory and returning it to consciousness for further use.

Right-brain processing: Information processing primarily performed by the right hemisphere of the brain, focusing on information in nonverbal domains, such as the understanding of spatial relationships, recognition of patterns and drawings, music, and emotional expression.

Scholarship: An award of money to a student based on need or merit.

Search engine: A computerized index to information on the World Wide Web.

Self-concept: People's view of themselves that forms over time, comprising three components: the physical self, the social self, and the personal self.

Self-actualization: A state of self-fulfillment in which people realize their highest potential in their own unique way.

Self-efficacy: The expectation that one is capable of achieving one's goals in many different kinds of situations.

Self-esteem: The overall evaluation we give ourselves as individuals.

Self-fulfilling prophecy: A phenomenon that occurs when we hold a belief or expectation that affects our behavior, thereby increasing the likelihood that our beliefs or expectations *will* come true.

Sexually transmitted diseases (STDs): Medical conditions acquired through sexual contact.

Short-term goals: Relatively limited steps toward the accomplishment of long-term goals.

Social support: Assistance and comfort supplied by others in times of stress.

Software: Programs that inform the computer about what it should do, telling it what operations it needs to carry out. *Windows, Mac Os* for Apple computers, and *Linux* are some examples.

Spreadsheet programs: Computer application software that helps with budgeting and financial projections and is necessary for accounting and engineering courses.

Stacks: The shelves on which books and other materials are stored in a library.

Stereotypes: Beliefs and expectations about members of a group that are held simply because of their membership in the group.

Stress: The response to events that threaten or challenge us.

Study groups: Small, informal groups of students whose purpose is to help members work together and study for a test.

Study notes: Notes taken for the purpose of reviewing material.

Tactile/kinesthetic learning style: A style that involves learning by touching, manipulating objects, and doing things.

Telnet: A dial-up communication system that permits users at remote locations to use computer databases and other resources housed on distant computers.

Term: The length of time for which money is lent.

Test: A more extensive, more heavily weighted assessment than a quiz, covering more material.

Test anxiety: A temporary condition characterized by fears and concerns about test taking.

Thesis: The main point of a paper, typically stating the writer's opinion about the topic of the paper.

Time log: A record of how one spends one's time.

Transcript: A college's official record of courses taken and grades received by students.

Transferring: Changing colleges.

Visual/nonverbal learning style: A style that favors material presented visually in a diagram or picture.

Visual/verbal learning style: A style that involves a preference for written material, favoring reading over hearing and touching.

Visualization: A memory technique by which images are formed to help recall material.

Voice: The unique style of a writer, expressing the writer's outlook on life and past writing experiences.

Web page: A location (or site) on the World Wide Web housing information from a single source and (typically) links to other pages.

Weekly timetable: A schedule showing all regular, prescheduled activities due to occur in the week, together with one-time events and commitments.

Word-processing programs: Application software that turns a computer into a very smart typewriter.

Working backward: The strategy of starting at the desired solution or goal and working toward the starting point of the problem.

World Wide Web: A highly graphical interface between users and the Internet that permits users to transmit and receive not only text but also pictorial, video, and audio information.

Zero-sum game: A situation in which when one person wins, the other person automatically loses.

Endnotes

Chapter 1

1. The American Freshman: National Norms for Fall 2000," Published by American Council on Education and University of California at Lost Angeles Higher Education Research Institiue.

2. Adapted from "Do you control what happens to you," in Nathenson, M. (1985). *The book of tests.* NY: Penguin.

3. Gottesman, G. (1994). *College survival.* New York: Macmillan. p. 70.

4. Adapted from "How Is College Different from High School?" Website at Southern Methodist University Altshuler Learning Enhancement Center, **http://www.smu.edu/~alec/whyhighschool.html.**

5. Adapted from **http://www.smu.edu/~alec/whyhighschool.html.**

6. Adapted from "How Is College Different from High School?" Web pages at Southern Methodist University Altshuler Learning Enhancement Center, **http://www.smu.edu/~alec/whyhighschool.htm**l.

Chapter 2

1. Adapted from Ferner, J. D. (1980). *Successful time management.* New York: Wiley. p. 33.

2. Ibid.

3. Gottesman, G. (1994). *College survival.* New York: Macmillan. p. 61.

Chapter 3

1. Adapted from Lazear, D. (1999). *The Intelligent Curriculum: Using MI to Develop Your Students' Full Potential.* Tucson, AZ: Zephyr Press.

2. Rosenberg, M. (1979). *Conceiving the self.* New York: Basic Books.

3. Maslow. A. H. (1987). *Motivation and personality* (3rd ed.). New York: Harper & Row.

4. http://www.benjerry.com

5. Waldron, C. (1988, ausut, 29). How college education enriched lives of stars. *Jet*, 16–18.

6. Herbert, S. J., & Hill, G. H. (1990). *Bill Cosby.* Danbury, CT: Grolier, p. 38.

7. Ibid., p. 40.

Chapter 4

1. Pauk, W. (1974). *How to Study in College.* Boston: Houghton Mifflin.

2. Tyler, S. (1997). *Been there, should've done that.* Haslett, MI: Front Porch Press, p. 117.

3. Based on McPherson, J. M. (1988). *Battle Cry of Freedom: The Civil War Era.* New York: Ballantine Books, pp. 504–510.

4. Tyler, S. (1997). *Been there, should've done that.* Haslett, MI: Front Porch Press, p. 117.

5. Lobo, R. A., & Lobo, R. (1996). *The home team: Of mothers, daughters & American champions.* New York: Kodansha International.

6. Ibid.

7. Ibid.

8. Ibid.

9. Ibid.

Chapter 5

1. Tyler, S. (1997). *Been there should've done that!* Haslett, MI: Front Porch Press. p. 126.

2. Tobias, S. (1995). *Overcoming math anxiety.* NY: W. W. Norton & Company.

3. Tyler, S. (1997). op. cit., p. 128.

Chapter 6

1. Bransford, J. D., & Johnson, M. K. (1972). Contextual prerequisites for understanding: Some investigations of comprehension and recall. *Journal of Verbal Learning and Verbal Behavior*, 11. p. 722.

2. Quotes from Irving, J. (December 11, 1995). Slipped away: At fifty-three, the novelist remembers his first love: wrestling. *The New Yorker*, pp. 70–77; and Gussow, M. (April 28, 1998). *John Irving: A novelist builds out from fact to reach the truth.* **http://www.nytimes.com/library/books/042898irving-novel.html.**

Chapter 7

1. Elbow, Peter. (2001). *A community of writers.* NY: McGraw-Hill.

2. Gregory, H. (1999). *Public speaking for college and career.* New York: McGraw-Hill.

3. Davidson, J. W., Gienapp, W. E., Heyrman, C. L., Lytle, M. H., & Stoff, M. B. (1996). *Nation of nations. A concise narrative of the American republic.* New York: McGraw-Hill, p. 540.

4. Scale items are adapted from A. Fenigstein, A. Scheier, and A. Buss (1975). Public and private self-consciousness, assessment and theory. *Journal of Consulting and Clinical Psychology, 43*, Table 1, p. 324.

5. Wydro, K. (1985). *Thinking on your feet: The art of thinking and speaking under pressure.* Englewood Cliffs, NJ: Prentice Hall.

Chapter 8

1. Halpern, D. F. (1996). *Thought and knowledge: An introduction to critical thinking.* Mahwah, NJ: Erlbaum, p. 48.

2. Gottesman, G. (1994). *College survival.* NY: Macmillan, p. 59.

3. Greenberg, J., & Baron, R. A. *Behavior in organizations* (6th ed.) Upper Saddle River, NJ: Prentice Hall.

4. Abel, T., Alberini, C., Ghiradi, M., Huang, Y. Y., Nguyen, P., & Kandel, E. R. (1995). Steps toward a molecular definition of memory consolidation. In D. L. Schacter (Ed.), *Memory distortions: How minds, brains, and societies reconstruct the past.* Cambridge, MA: Harvard University Press.

Chapter 9

1. Tyler, S. (1997). *Been there, should've done that!* Haslett, MI: Front Porch Press.

2. Ibid.

Chapter 10

1. Zetter, K., & McCracken, H. (September 2000). How to stop search and start finding. *PC World.* p. 131.

2. Liebovich, L. (2000, August 10). Choosing quick hits over the card catalog. *The New York Times.* pp. 1, 6. Based on material from Eliot Soloway, University of Michigan School of Education.

3. Harden, B. (2001, May 27). Out of Africa, ready for anything. *The New York Times.* p. 20.

Chapter 11

1. Adapted from Halpern, D. F. (1996). *Thought and knowledge: An introduction to critical thinking* (3rd ed.). Mahwah, NJ: Erlbaum; and Bransford, J. D. & Stein, B. S. (1993). *The Ideal Problem Solver* (2nd ed.) New York: W. H. Freeman.

2. Table 1, "The scale of tolerance-intolerance of ambiguity," p. 34, in Budner, Stanley. "Intolerance of ambiguity as a personality variable." *Journal of Personality,* Vol. 30, No. 7, pp. 29–50. Copyright Duke University Press, 1962.

3. Forer, B. (1949). The fallacy of personal validation: A classroom demonstration of gullibility. *Journal of Abnormal and Social Psychology, 44,* 118–123.

4. Byrne, D., & Kelley, L. (1981). *An introduction to personality* (3rd ed.). Englewood Cliffs, NJ: Prentice-Hall. p. 304.

6. *21st century lives: Neurosurgeon Ben Carson.* (September 8, 2000). **http://www.abcnews.go.com/onair/WorldNews Tonight/wnt000908_21st_carson_feature.html**. ABC News.

7. Ibid.

Chapter 12

1. Nolan, M. F. (1997 April 26). Tiger's racial multiplicity. *Boston Globe,* p. A11.

2. Tatum, B. D. (1997). *"Why are all the black kids sitting together in the cafeteria?" And other conversations about race.* New York: Basic Books.

3. Malone, M. S. (1993 July 18). Translating diversity into high-tech gains. *The New York Times,* B2.

4. Adapted from *Working it out: The newsletter for gay and lesbian employment issues,* 1992.

5. Sponholz, M., & Sponholz, J. (1996). *The Princeton Review college companion.* NY: Random House. p. 24.

6. Adapted from Hazan, C., & Shaver, P. (1987). Romantic love conceptualized as an attachment process. *Journal of Personality and Social Psychology, 52,* 511–524.

Chapter 13

1. Gottesman, G. (1994). *College survival.* NY: Macmillan. p. 206.

2. The College Board. (2000). *Trends in college pricing 1999.* New York: The College Board.

3. Dominguez, J., & Robin, V. (1993). *Your money or your life: Transforming your relationship with money and achieving financial independence.* NY: Penguin USA.

4. Schibsted, E. (June 1999). The legends: Jerry Yang and David Filo. *Business,* 20 June 1999.

5. Ibid.

Chapter 14

1. Sax, L. J., Astin, A. W., Korn, W. S., & Mahoney, K. (1999). *The American freshman: National norms for fall 1999.* Los Angeles: Higher Education Research Institute, UCLA.

2. Chamberlain, K., & Zika, S. (1990). The minor events approach to stress: Support for use of daily hassles. *British Journal of Psychology, 81,* 469–481.

3. Source of table: Marx, M. B., Garrity, T. F., & Bowers, F. R. (1975). The influence of recent life experience on the health of college freshman. *Journal of Psychosomatic Research, 19,* 87–98.

4. Carlson, R. (1997). *Don't sweat the small stuff . . . and it's all small stuff.* New York: Hyperion.

5. Gottesman, G. (1994). *College survival.* NY: Macmillan. p. 160.

6. Adapted from Hughes, J. O., & Sandler, B. R. (1987). *"Friends" raping friends: Could it happen to you?* Washington, DC: Association of American Colleges.

Acknowledgments

Page 3, Figure 1-1 "The American Freshman: National Norms for Fall 2000," UCLA Higher Education Research Institute and American Council on Education. Used by permission of HERI, UCLA.

Page 13, "Try It! #4" "Who's In Charge?" Adapted from Nathenson, M. (1985). *The book of tests.* Used by permission of Creative Media International.

Page 20, "Try It! #6" "What's Different About College?" Adapted from **http://www2.smu.edu/ alec/whyhighschool.html**. Used by permission of Altshuler Learning Enhancement Center at Southern Methodist University in Dallas, Texas.

Page 21, Logo of the University of Massachusetts. Reprinted by permission of the University of Massachusetts.

Page 31, Cartoon: "Procrastination!" © 2001 Michael Maslin from cartoonbank.com. All rights reserved.

Page 49, Logo of the University of Hartford. Used with the permission of the University of Hartford.

Page 64, Table 3-1 "Learning, Personality, and Processing Styles." See also D. Lazear, *The Intelligent Curriculum: Using MI to Develop Your Students' Full Potential* (Tucson: Zephyr Press).

Page 67, Cartoon: "Know Thyself." © The New Yorker Collection 1991 William Steig from cartoonbank.com. All rights reserved.

Page 71, Cartoon: ". . . doing homework?" CALVIN AND HOBBES © 1992 Watterson. Reprinted by permission of the Universal Press Syndicate. All rights reserved.

Page 82, Logo of Temple University. Reprinted by permission of the Collegiate Licensing Company and Temple University.

Page 106, Quote (Junior, Duke University) from Suzette Tyler (1997). *Been there, should've done that!* © 1997 by Suzette Tyler. Reprinted by permission of Front Porch Press.

Page 111, Quote from Rebecca Lobo & R. Lobo (1996). *The home team: Of mothers, daughters, and American champions.* Reprinted by permission of Kodansha International Publishing.

Page 111, Logo of the University of Connecticut. Reprinted by permission of the University of Connecticut.

Page 130, Quote (Graduate, Physiology, Michigan State University) from Suzette Tyler (1997). *Been there, should've done that!* © 1997 by Suzette Tyler. Reprinted by permission of Front Porch Press.

Page 133, Cartoon: ". . . is life a multiple choice test?" PEANUTS by Charles Schulz. Reprinted by permission of the United Feature Syndicate, Inc.

Page 140, Logo of Austin Community College. Reprinted by permission of Austin Community College.

Page 150, Cartoon: " . . . about this book . . ." PEANUTS by Charles Schulz. Reprinted by permission of the United Feature Syndicate, Inc.

Page 165, Logo of University of New Hampshire. Reprinted by permission of the University of New Hampshire.

Page 188, Quote from Stephen Jay Gould (1991), "The Streak of Streaks" in *Bully for Brontosaurus,* 466–67. Used by permission of W. W. Norton & Company.

Page 194, Cartoon: ". . . fear of public speaking." © 2001 Leo Cullum from cartoonbank.com. All rights reserved.

Page 196, Logo of Mount Holyoke College. Reprinted by permission of Mount Holyoke College.

Page 218, Logo of Virginia Commonwealth University. Reprinted by permission of Virginia Commonwealth University.

Page 227, Quote (Junior, University of Colorado) from Suzette Tyler (1997). *Been there, should've done that!* © 1997 by Suzette Tyler. Reprinted by permission of Front Porch Press.

Page 240, Quote (Senior, University of Connecticut) from Suzette Tyler (1997). *Been there, should've done that!* © 1997 by Suzette Tyler. Reprinted by permission of Front Porch Press.

Page 243, Cartoon: ". . . what I'm going to be when I grow up . . ." © The New Yorker Collection 1999 Barbara Smaller.

Page 244, Logo of California State University, San Marcos. Reprinted by permission of California State University, San Marcos.

Page 254, Screen image: PowerPoint—Technology in the Classroom. "Number of Post-Secondary Students who own PCs . . ." PowerPoint is a fully protected product of Microsoft Corporation.

Page 256, Screen image: Excel—Expense Report Jan 1 02.xls. Excel is a fully protected product of Microsoft Corporation.

Page 257, Screen image: Hotmail Compose—Microsoft Internet Explorer. Microsoft Internet Explorer is a fully protected product of Microsoft Corporation.

Page 268, Screen image: LibraryWeb homepage, searching for *Conversations with Ernest Hemingway.* Columbia University Library Web, used by permission.

Page 270, Screen image: Netscape.com Welcome page from Thurs 11/15/01. Netscape is a fully protected product of Netscape Communications. Photos © AP / Wide World.

Page 271, Cartoon: ". . . ask your search engine." © The New Yorker Collection 2000 John Caldwell from cartoonbank.com. All rights reserved.

Page 272, Screen image: Yahoo! Directory: Animal Rights. Reproduced with permission of Yahoo! Inc. © 2000 by Yahoo! Inc. YAHOO! and the Yahoo! logo are trademarks of Yahoo! Inc.

Page 275, Screen image: Google Search: + "Animal Rights" + experimentation. Used by permission of Google, Inc.

Page 275, Cartoon: "First they do an on-line search." © The New Yorker Collection 1998 Arnie Levin from cartoonbank.com. All rights reserved.

Page 278, Logo of Carthage College. Used by permission of Carthage College.

Page 296, "Try It! #2" adapted in part from Halpern, D. F. (1996). *Thought and Knowledge: An Introduction to Critical Thinking,* 3rd ed. Used by permission of Lawrence Erlbaum Associates and Diane Halpern. And adapted in part from Bransford, J. D. & Stein, B. S. (1993). *The Ideal Problem Solver,* 2nd ed. © 1984, 1993 by W. H. Freeman & Co. Used with the permission of Worth Publishers.

Page 291, "The scale of tolerance-intolerance of ambiguity," Table 1 p. 34, in Budner, Stanley (1962). "Intolerance of ambiguity as a personal variable." *Journal of Personality,* Vol. 30, No. 7, pp. 29–50. Reprinted by permission of Blackwell Publishing, U.K.

Quote from Forer, B. (1949). The fallacy of personal validation: A classroom demonstration of gullibility. *Journal of Abnormal and Social Psychology,* 44, 118–123. Reprinted by permission of the American Psychological Association.

Page 304, Logo of Yale University. Reprinted by permission of Yale University.

Page 323, "Try It! #4" adapted from Hazan, C., & Shaver, P. (1987). Romantic love conceptualized as an attachment process. *Journal of Personality and Social Psychology, 52,* 511–524. © 1987 by the American Psychological Association. Adapted with permission of the publisher and authors.

Page 330, Logo of Metropolitan State University. Reprinted by permission of Metropolitan State University.

Page 352, Cartoon: "Tradition. Competition. Tuition." © 2001 Michael Maslin from cartoonbank.com. All rights reserved.

Page 354, Cartoon: ". . . working my son's way through college." © The New Yorker Collection 1974 J. B. Handelsman from cartoonbank.com. All rights reserved.

Page 368, "Try It! #1" from Marx, M. B., Garrity, T. F., & Bowers, F. R. (1975). "Assessing Your Susceptibility to Stress-Related Illness" in The influence of recent life experience on the health of college freshmen. *Journal of Psychosomatic Research,* 19, 87–98. Reprinted with permission from Elsevier Science.

Page 388, Logo of Washington College. Reprinted by permission of Washington College.

Photo Credits

Page 261, Alden Pellet/AP Photo

Page 265, PhotoDisc

Page 267, PhotoDisc

Page 269 (top),Index Stock

Page 269 (bottom), Bob Daemmrich/Stock Boston

Page 277, Oscar Chavez/Courtesy Pasadena City College

Page 278, Todd Buchanan

Page 283, PhotoDisc

Page 284, PhotoDisc

Page 286, Spencer Platt/Getty Images News Services

Page 288, Superstock

Page 300, Myrleen Ferguson/PhotoEdit

Page 302, PhotoDisc

Page 304, Courtesy of Carson Scholars Fund, Inc.

Page 309, Gaye Hilsenrath/Index Stock

Page 310, PhotoDisc

Page 311, Henley/Corbis Stock Market

Page 319, Sonda Dawes/Image Works

Page 321, Bill Aron/PhotoEdit

Page 322, Eyewire/Gettyone

Page 324, PhotoDisc

Page 325, Richard Pasley/Stock Boston

Page 326, PhotoDisc

Page 329, PhotoDisc

Page 335, Chuck Savage/Corbis Stock Market

Page 336, Corbis Stock Market

Page 339, Tom Stewart/Corbis Stock Market

Page 343, Margot Granitsas/Image Works

Page 344, PhotoDisc

Page 346, PhotoDisc

Page 348, Pat O'Leary/PhotoEdit

Page 353, PhotoDisc

Page 358, Robyn Beck/AFP/Corbis

Page 363, Gregg Adams/Stone

Page 364, Corbis

Page 365, PhotoDisc

Page 375 (top) Jeff Zaruba/Corbis Stock Market

Page 376, Mike Rominger/Courtesy Appalachian State University

Page 382, PhotoDisc

Page 385, David Hanover/Stone

Index

The P.O.W.E.R. Plan for Test Preparation

PREPARE

Review your work on a regular basis

ORGANIZE

Bring the right tools to the test; follow directions carefully

WORK

Tackle the test

EVALUATE

Save time to check your work; know when to stop

RETHINK

Reflect on what you've learned when you get a test back

Dealing with Test Anxiety

1. *Prepare thoroughly.* The more you prepare, the less test anxiety you'll feel.

2. *Take a realistic view of the test.* Remember that your future success does not hinge on your performance on any single exam. Think of the big picture.

3. *Learn relaxation techniques.* You can learn to reduce or even eliminate the jittery physical symptoms of test anxiety by using relaxation techniques.

4. *Visualize success.*

Note-Taking Abbreviations

and	& *or* +	and so forth	*etc.*
with	*w/*	no good	*n.g*
without	*w/o*	question	?
care of	*c/o*	compared with	*c/w*
leads to; resulting in	→	page	*p.*
as a result of	←	important!	*!!*
percent	%	less than	‹
change	Δ	more than	›
number	#	equals, same as	=
that is	*i.e.*	versus	*vs.*
for example	*e.g.*		

Use This Test Preparation Checklist before Taking Your Next Test

- I checked whether it's a quiz, test, or exam.
- I began preparation long before the test (e.g., by taking notes in class).
- I understand what material will be covered.
- I know how many questions will be on the test.
- I know how long it will take.
- I know what kinds of questions will be on the test.
- I obtained sample questions and/or previous tests, if available.

- I know how it will be graded.
- I formed or participated in a study group.
- I used different and appropriate preparation strategies for different types of questions.
- I read my class notes.
- I composed some essay questions.
- I answered essay questions aloud.
- I actively memorized facts and details.
- I made and used note cards.
- I created and used a test like the real test.

Quick Math Facts and Conversions

Fractions, Decimals, Percentages

$\dfrac{3}{5}$ numerator
denominator

To **add** or **subtract** different fractions, first obtain a common denominator:

$$\frac{1}{3} + \frac{2}{5} = \frac{5}{15} + \frac{6}{15} = \frac{11}{15}$$

To **multiply:**

$$\frac{1}{3} \times \frac{2}{5} = \frac{1 \times 2}{3 \times 5} = \frac{2}{15}$$

To **divide,** multiply the first with the reciprocal of the second fraction:

$$\frac{2}{3} \div \frac{1}{6} = \frac{2}{3} \times \frac{6}{1} = 4$$

1	= 1.0	= 100%
1/2	= 0.5	= 50%
1/3	= $0.\bar{3}$	= $33.\bar{3}\%$
1/4	= 0.25	= 25%
1/5	= 0.2	= 20%
1/6	= $0.1\bar{6}$	= $16.\bar{6}\%$
1/8	= 0.125	= 12.5%
1/9	= $0.\bar{1}$	= $11.\bar{1}\%$
1/10	= 0.1	= 10%
1/12	= $0.08\bar{3}$	= $8.\bar{3}\%$
2/3	= $0.\bar{6}$	= $66.\bar{6}\%$
3/4	= 0.75	= 75%

Factoring:

$a^2 - b^2 = (a + b)(a - b)$	$a^3b - ab = ab(s + 1)(a - 1)$
$a^2 + 2ab + b^2 (a + b)^2$	$a^2 - 2ab + b^2 (a - b)^2$
$a^3 + b^3 = (a + b)(a^2 - ab + b^2)$	$a^3 - b^3 = (a - b)(a^2 + ab + b^2)$

Expanding:

$a(b + c) = ab + ac$	$(a + b)(c + d) = ac + ad + bc + bd$
$(a + b)^2 = a^2 + 2ab + b^2$	$(a + b)^3 = a^3 + 3a^2b + 3ab^2 + b^3$
$(a - b)^2 = a^2 - 2ab + b^2$	$(a - b)^3 = a^3 - 3a^2b + 3ab^2 - b^3$

ENGLISH / METRIC EQUIVALENT

Length

ENGLISH		METRIC EQUIVALENT
	1 inch	= 2.54 centimeters
1 foot	= 12 inches	= 30.48 centimeters
1 yard	= 3 feet	= .914 meter
1 mile	= 1,760 yards	= 1.609 kilometers

Area

	1 square inch	= 6.452 square centimeters
1 square foot	= 144 square inches	= 929.03 square centimeters
1 acre	= 160 square rods	= .405 hectare
1 square mile	= 649 acres	= 2.59 square kilometers

Weight

	1 ounce	= 28.35 grams
1 pound	= 16 ounces	= .4536 kilogram
1 ton	= 2,000 pounds	= .907 metric ton

Volume

	1 fluid ounce	= 29.574 milliliters
1 liquid pint	= 16 fluid ounces	= .473 liter
1 liquid quart	= 2 liquid pints	= .946 liter
1 gallon	= 4 liquid quarts	= 3.785 liters

1,000	100	10	1	.1	.01	.001
kilo	hecto	deca		deci	centi	milli
km	hm	dam	m	dm	cm	mm
kg	hg	dag	g	dg	cg	mg
kl	hl	dal	l	dl	cl	ml

Key Websites